THE

# IMMORTALITY OF THE SOUL

AND THE

# FINAL CONDITION OF THE WICKED

CAREFULLY CONSIDERED.

By ROBERT W. LANDIS.

*Ἀθάνατοι πᾶσαι αἱ ψυχαὶ, καὶ τῶν ἀσεβῶν· αἷς ἄμεινον ἦν μὴ ἀφθάρτους εἶναι. κολαζόμεναι γὰρ ὑπὸ τοῦ ἀσβέστου πυρὸς ἀπεράντῳ τιμωρίᾳ, καὶ μὴ θνήσκουσι ἐπὶ κακῷ τῷ ἑαυτῶν τέλος λαβεῖν ὀυκ ἔχουσι.*
Sequutus sum arguentes *κατὰ πόδας*. Nihil, sciens, omisi.

SECOND THOUSAND.

New York:
PUBLISHED BY CARLTON & PORTER,
200 MULBERRY-STREET.
1859.

TO

The Memory of

THE LATE

EMMA CAROLINE BEARDSLEE,

MY BELOVED WIFE,

THIS, MY FIRST LITERARY PRODUCTION IN THE FIELD OF LABOR WHICH WE HAD SELECTED FOR THE PURPOSE OF AIDING TO ESTABLISH THE INSTITUTIONS OF THE PRECIOUS GOSPEL OF CHRIST IN THE GREAT WEST,

Is most affectionately Dedicated.

R. W. L.

# PREFACE.

The subject of the tractate here submitted to the public has been, for several years past, specifically before the mind of the author. While in the discharge of his pastoral duties in the city of Paterson, New Jersey, he delivered a course of sermons on the last judgment, and when treating upon the *issues* of that event, he received a request from a number of respectable gentlemen (to whom the Rev. George Storrs was statedly preaching) to discourse upon the immortality of the soul. He complied with the request, and, as one of the results, the contemplated enterprise of building a church for Mr. Storrs was abandoned. The author was then solicited to publish the three discourses delivered by him on the subject; but concluding that it would be better to present a more extended discussion of the theme, he procured from the Annihilationists the works mentioned in the subjoined catalogue, with the mutual and distinct understanding that they should be considered as truly representing the theory in question; and every work which they recommended for this purpose he was careful to procure. These works he read and analyzed, and then carefully synthesized, studiously arranging, under every distinct feature of the system, all that was therein alleged in its support; and thus having concentrated their whole force, he commenced the subjoined reply.

After writing about one hundred and fifty pages, however, his health failed, and he was obliged to desist utterly from the undertaking; and on removing subsequently to the West, the duties devolving upon him in his new field of labor seemed to require that he should relinquish all thought of any further prosecution of the design. But at the meeting of the General Assembly in Chicago, in May last, a large number of valued brethren urged him with so much earnestness to finish the work, that he concluded to resume it, and did so with as little delay as possible. The whole subject and plan of the work were in his mind and thoroughly digested, and, bating the prostrating effects of a long and severe illness from typhoid fever, from which he was just recovering, he had only to overcome a natural aversion to writing. Should the style of the work, therefore, exhibit traces of rapid composition, he hopes the reader will, at the same time, remember that the thoughts presented are the result of long-continued and matured reflection.

It was remarked by the learned editor of the Presbyterian, (the Rev. Dr. Engles,) in his notice of my work on the Resurrection, that perhaps it was a defect that the author, in treating the subject, was too anxious to demolish every part of the theory of Professor Bush. This may have been so. But though the judicious suggestion has been constantly in mind during the preparation of the present tractate, the appearance of being too particular in meeting the recent assaults on the doctrine of immortality could not well be avoided. The theme, in its far-reaching relations to theology, philosophy, tradition, and Scripture exegesis, is most extensive. The writers to whom I reply, moreover, are very numerous, and taken collectively have, in one way or another, traversed the whole field of argument, pressing their assaults with great zeal and earnestness, and their writings are widely disseminated both in this country and Great Britain, and have made a deep impression on multitudes of minds.

I have reduced their speculations into systematic order, and have, so to speak, retraversed in their company the whole field, and in doing so have felt it to be necessary to bestow specific attention upon those branches of their argument which have most perplexed their readers, and I may add that in no instance whatever have I attempted to conceal the full strength of any of their positions. So far from this are the facts, that if the reader will take the trouble to examine, I am assured he will discover many instances in which I have expressed, much more strongly than they have done, the arguments they offer. For I hold that there is not a more pitiable object on earth than the writer who, while pretending to give a full and fair presentation of an important subject, purposely misstates or conceals the truth respecting it. Still, in a work such as this purports to be, although it is needless to refute formally every opposing statement, it yet is necessary to notice, and refute specifically, many which might appear unimportant to persons who are not fully aware of the real state of the question. I design the work, moreover, as a handbook on the topic of which it treats, presenting fairly, and with all the fullness which the prescribed limits would allow, the merits and literature of the subject in the entire range of the argument as pursued by our antagonists; and hence I have adduced, likewise, the statements and arguments of the older schools of Materialists, for example, those of the Polish Socinians, and of Messrs. Hobbes, Blackburne, Priestley, Belsham, Kneeland, as well as those of modern Universalists.

Most of the writers whose works have been furnished me as containing a fair and proper *exposé* of the system of the Annihilationists are Materialists, but some are not; the former holding that the soul is a result of corporeal organization, and the latter admitting its separability from the body; the one asserting its utter extinction at death, and the other its inactive, unconscious repose. Our antagonists, it seems, would be fully satisfied, provided they can only get rid of the conscious existence of the soul after death, and hence, with a spirit of *liberality* in such matters, of which, heretofore, only atheists have ventured to furnish an example, they zealously disseminate works which inculcate both ideas. Even Paul, with his enlarged charity and magnanimous spirit, never attained to a *liberality* like this, nor does the Bible anywhere (except in such historical statements as 1 Kings xii, 26–33; 2 Kings xvii, 28–41; 2 Chron. xxxiii, 3–10) even approximate it. In meeting these conflicting views, however, I have not deemed it necessary to separate the arguments into classes, but have arranged them all under one general head.

As to the employment of such terms as "antagonists" and "opponents," they are used only to avoid circumlocution, for, as men, I do not consider the authors quoted and referred to as personally my enemies; and though I have been obliged to speak of many of their statements with point and severity, and to expose the pretensions of some of them to literature, I have not in the whole work uttered a word or sentiment, however expressed, which may, on such account, inflict pain on any of those gentlemen, without feelings of real regret, and which, could I have done so, the whole circumstances being considered, I would not gladly have spared. I do not, therefore, agree with Dr. Johnson, that an antagonist in any important question of morals or of faith should be, if possible, personally crippled or crushed, except so far as this must result from a deserved exposure of unfairness, ignorance of the subject, and the like. Nor can I, in this connection, omit noticing a matter which has given me continued pain throughout the preparation of the volume. I refer to the necessity, which in now treating upon the subject is absolutely imperative, of calling frequent and special attention to the position assumed by Archbishop Whately. In connection with many, I have long entertained a high regard for that distinguished prelate. But his course in relation to the matter in hand is so inexplicable and extraordinary, that it cannot be passed over in silence. The use which our antagonists have made and are making of his dogmatical but most unfounded utterances on the subject, is such as requires that primary regard be had to the *principles* mainly involved in the discussion itself, whatever may become of the man. And Dr. Whately must be content to sustain the responsibilities of the position which he has thus incautiously assumed, until he is willing to abandon it, or shows that he has discovered new facts, and developed new processes of reasoning on the subject, which entitle him to regard the results of all previous investigation as entirely superseded. Gladly would I have omitted all reference to this topic. But such a procedure is, I repeat it, irreconcilable with any honest or serious attempt to do justice to the merits of the theme under discussion; and I cannot doubt that Dr. Whately will frankly admit the accuracy of this representation.

The prominence given to the question (section 24) as to the views of Socrates and Aristotle could not be avoided. But I have stated the facts in the case as briefly as justice to the subject would permit. From the representation made of the views of those philosophers by Dr. Whately, and on his authority, by the Annihilationists, and from the conclusions attempted to be drawn therefrom, it became necessary to go thoroughly into the matter. It is, however, at best but a side-issue, which Dr. Whately had no just reason for dragging into the discussion.

In order to do justice to the *Argument from Reason and Tradition*, (presented in Part I,) I considered it my duty to review what has been written on the subject by the English deists and German Rationalists, for example, Hobbes, Tindal, Wegscheider, *et id genus omne*, and the discussions also of Cudworth, Dr. Henry More, Grotius, Leland, Warburton, Blackburne, and others; and on the *Scripture Argument*, in Part II, to consult the best authorities of our antagonists, such as the Fratres Poloniæ, Dr. Priestley, etc.; and having, as above stated, designed the work as a plain and useful handbook, both for the scholar and the unlearned inquirer after truth, I have presented throughout a compendium of the literature of the whole question. And in order that any one may know where to find a given topic more fully treated, and sometimes also to render a longer discussion unnecessary on my part, I have made copious references to works wherein a specific point is treated more extensively. I have endeavored to be very careful in this, so that the reader may be able to pursue his inquiries further, should he deem it desirable.

The connection of the grand theme of immortality with eschatology is brought forward in all the writings of the Annihilationists, and hence I have devoted Part III entirely to that subject. The connection, moreover, is not only very obvious, but it is that which imparts to the whole question of immortality its intense and absorbing interest. To treat the subject as it should be treated at the present time, when every shallow aspirant after notoriety sets up to be a "philosopher," it was requisite to proceed to the first principles which underlie the whole question, and I have done so. It was necessary, moreover, to notice the exceptions made to the evangelical view, not only by the Annihilationists, but by the Restorationists, Universalists, and such superficial *philosophers* as "Thorndale." This gives the appearance of reiteration to some parts of the discussion, though, as the careful reader will perceive, they are not reiterative. For instance, it was necessary to consider the subject of endless punishment, not only as presented from the stand-point assumed by the Annihilationists, but also from that of the Restorationists. But I believe that nothing of importance is left unnoticed which is urged by either class in support of their views, or which can operate as an opiate to the consciences of the impenitent and ungodly.

There has been but little, comparatively, written—at least since the Reformation—directly on the subject of immortality, aside from the treatment of the question in systematic theology. Calvin's *Psychopannychia* I have not been able to obtain. Knapp has treated the question, but not very profoundly, in his *Scripta Varii Argumenti.* The work of the excellent Dr. Henry More will not repay perusal. In our own day the Rev. T. M. Post, D.D., has published several essays of much excellence; and President Campbell, of Bethany College, Va., has issued a little manual in which his powerful intellect has elaborated an argument of great force, and which (judging from the dissatisfaction which it has aroused among the Annihilationists) has done a good work in our Western and Southern states. I regret that this tractate, and the last two essays of Dr. Post, did not come to hand till after I had completed the present treatise. The Rev. N. D. George and Rev. Luther Lee have likewise written well on the subject. In England the Rev. Mr. Hinton and Geo. Moore, M.D., (not to mention Isaac Taylor,) have ably vindicated the truth against the Materialists; but in no instance has the whole theme been taken up and considered throughout, as is done in the present volume.

If in dedicating the work to the memory of one of the loveliest and best of women, and so associating it with a private and personal interest, the author has erred, he hopes the error may not be deemed unpardonable. Feeling that the problem of our beloved country must be ultimately solved in the West, my wife and I left our endeared Eastern associations, and came hither to do what we could to preoccupy a portion of the great field for Christ. But though she and our offspring were soon taken home to their rest, she came not hither in vain. The hallowed influence of her life, and example, and self-sacrifices, is still living and operative, and long will continue to be so. And with this, my first publication in the West, I have fondly desired to associate the name so truly precious to my heart.

R. W. L.

IONIA, MICHIGAN,
*August* 27, 1858.

# NOTE TO THE READER.

As I have had occasion in the ensuing work to refer very frequently to the recent publications of the Annihilationists, the reader will please observe that, to save room, I have abridged the references to them, according to the subjoined schedule. In my references throughout this volume the letter which here stands opposite to the work will stand for the work itself, and the figures for the pages. For example, "A. 23," refers to "The Unity of Man, by Anthropos," page 23, and so of the others.

A. The Unity of Man, by Anthropos, in reply to Rev. L. Lee.

B. Death not Life, or the Theological Hell and Endless Misery disproved, etc., by Jacob Blain.

C. The Age of Gospel Light, etc., by Z. Campbell.

D. The Scripture Doctrine of Future Punishment, by H. H. Dobney. Third American Edition.

E. The Bible *versus* Tradition, by Ellis and Read. Second Edition.

F. Dialogue on the Separate Existence of the Soul, by a Friend of Truth.

C. F. A Debate on the State of the Dead. Louisville, Ky., 1854.

G. The Intermediate State, by Henry Grew.

H. 1. Life and Death, by J. P. Ham.

H. 2. The Generations Gathered and Gathering. Ibid. The pages of these works herein referred to are those of Storrs's American Editions.

Has. Pauline Theology, by H. L. Hastings.

Hud. Debt and Grace, as related to the Doctrine of a Future Life, by C. F. Hudson. Boston, 1857.

J. Christ our Life; or, the Scripture Testimony concerning Immortality. Anonymous. Dublin, 1835.

J. T. Is Man Immortal? A Discussion. Hartford, 1850.

M. Dialogues on Future Punishment, by W. G. Moncrieff, Scotland. American edition.

R. The Immateriality of the Soul; or, Man dependent on his Organization for all his Mental and Moral Powers, by Thomas Reed.

S. An Inquiry: Are the Wicked Immortal? in six Sermons. Also, Have the Dead Knowledge? By Geo. Storrs. Twenty-first edition. There is an Appendix, also, to which we refer thus: S. App.

W. A View of the Scripture Revelations concerning a Future State, by Richard Whately, D.D., late Archbishop of Dublin. Philadelphia, 1855.

These works, with the exceptions of Hud., J., and W., have been, as already stated, furnished me by the Annihilationists themselves, as containing a correct exhibition of their doctrines, and with the distinct understanding that my reply should regard them as truly representing the system.

# CONTENTS.

## PART I.

IN WHICH IS CONSIDERED THE ARGUMENT FROM REASON AND ANCIENT TESTIMONY.

---

# PART II.

IN WHICH THE ARGUMENT FROM THE SCRIPTURES IS CONSIDERED, AND ALSO THE VIEWS ENTERTAINED ON THE SUBJECT BY THE ANCIENT JEWS AND CHRISTIANS.

# PART III.

## ON DEATH AND PENALTY, CONSIDERED IN THEIR RELATIONS TO THE ARGUMENT.

# DOCTRINE

OF THE

# IMMORTALITY OF THE SOUL.

## PART I.

IN WHICH IS CONSIDERED THE ARGUMENT FROM REASON AND ANCIENT TESTIMONY.

## CHAPTER I.

### PRELIMINARY REMARKS.

§ 1. *Materialism and Spiritualism.*

After I had, as stated in the preface, resolved to undertake the preparation of a treatise on the doctrine of man's immortality, I was somewhat at a loss to determine upon the form which the discussion should assume. Two plans suggested themselves. The *first* was to present it in a purely philosophical method; and the *second*, to give it the form in which it is here brought before the public. As the material philosophy has found some able advocates in our time, and as the theory they adopt is the very basis of most of those theological errors which it is important now to expose and refute, the question occurred, whether it would not be more advisable to take up the subject metaphysically, and demonstrate the futility and untenableness of that theory itself, (for I am well assured that the whole scheme can be metaphysically shoved out of existence,) than to descend to the literary drudgery of historical detail and philological investigation. My own inclination and taste would have preferred the former method; but the conviction that greater practical utility would be secured by following the latter, has induced me to adopt it. For on this plan alone can that mass of works now before the public, and claiming to establish the Materialist theory as a part of the teachings of revelation, be met and refuted, and their evil tendency successfully counteracted. The question whether man is immortal may well command our most serious consideration, for if our existence is not to be interrupted by death, nothing is more important to us than the knowledge which relates to our future state; and as we have the means for prosecuting the inquiry to a successful issue, all indifference to the subject cannot but be regarded as irrational and criminal.

In the last age philosophy united her testimony to that of revelation on this subject, and even uttered as oracular the decision that the existence of mind or spirit is at *least* as demonstrably certain as the existence of matter. But a reaction has commenced in her schools; and M. Comte, who, in the present age, assumes to be her oracle, has, with his numerous disciples, undertaken to reverse those decisions, while many who profess to have adopted his philosophy are endeavoring to prove that its enunciations in respect to man are not contrary to those of the sacred Scriptures; in other words, that revelation does not assert that man is endowed with a spiritual nature. The result may be easily imagined. Doubt on the subject has taken possession of the minds of multitudes; and in proportion as such doubts are entertained, and favored by authoritative announcements,* indifference is felt in respect to a future life, and the retributions of the world to come lose their motive power; and as was the case when the Epicurean philosophy took possession of the Roman republic, the pursuit of pleasure claimed precedence of everything else; so

* The deplorable effects of the writings of Archbishop Whately on the subject will be considered in the sequel.

now, wherever the principles of the material philosophy are received, the maxim is practically revived, "Let us eat and drink, for to-morrow we die."

The principles of Materialism, therefore, have not only taken possession of some of the schools of philosophy, but the most strenuous efforts have been made to adapt them to the popular mind, not even sparing the unrefined and illiterate. And as no speculations on the subject are offered with so much assurance and dogmatism as those of the Annihilationists, (who spare neither effort nor expense to propagate their views,) no writer in treating the subject now can possibly meet the existing desire of the community thereon, who does not thoroughly consider the arguments and statements which are set forth in their multifarious publications. The intelligent reader of their works cannot fail to be struck by the anxiety which the authors evince to make the impression, irrespective of all reason and argument, that the current views on the subject of immortality are wrong; and also with their endeavors to supply their deficiency of argumentative resources by means of epithet, denunciation, and misrepresentation, as well as by the most solemn obtestations respecting the purity of their motives in these assaults—asseverations, however, which are by no means evidential of such purity when employed to supply the place of argument.* And yet, as those works have done, and are doing, incalculable injury, it would be highly improper in a discussion of the subject to treat them as unworthy of notice; still, however, I have by no means confined myself to a consideration of *their* arguments and objections, but have endeavored to present a fair and full view of the whole question in all its various bearings; and to meet the exceptions to the doctrine of man's uninterrupted immortality from whatever source they have emanated. But as one *immediate* object of this work is to consider the

* They may be found, *ad nauseam*, in such writers as Tindal and Paine. See likewise, S. 82; A. 44, 45, 83; E. 3, 10, 134, 230; H. 1, pp. 118,133, and 136; H. 2, pp. 83, 85, etc.; C. 22, 23; B. 2.

numerous and recent assaults upon the doctrine by the Annihilationists, it is only fair and proper that, in delineating their *system*, no works should be employed but those which they themselves put in circulation for the avowed purpose of disseminating their views, and accordingly I have followed this rule.*

### § 2. *Theories of Professor Bush, of Dr. E. Beecher, and of the Annihilationists.*

It is both interesting and profitable to consider how the truth which was once delivered to the saints (though it has been and yet is on all sides assailed) still holds on its way steadily and unharmed, and, through the power of the blessed Spirit, continues its work of renewing, sanctifying, and leading home to glory the redeemed of Christ. On the one side the theory of the mighty Swedish seer, through its fearless and most accomplished champion, Professor Bush, is arrayed against it, and man is substantially declared to be *only spirit*, for the material body is to be laid forever aside at death. On the other hand, the plausible Storrs and Ham, with their coadjutors in England and in this country, fiercely assail it, and maintain that man is essentially corporeal, and that what is called the soul or spirit is laid aside at death, perhaps to be resumed no more; while Archbishop Whately comes forth to moderate the dispute, and by his decision "more embroils the fray," and seeks to cast doubt and uncertainty over the whole subject in question. Then, from the putrid charnel-house in which it had long lain entombed, comes forth into galvanic reviviscence the old incarnate-devil theory, with its renewed assault, both in this land and in Germany, maintaining that man when first created had no material organism, but was a pure spirit, which, having sinned, was subsequently embodied in flesh in

* Through the polite attention of Rev. Thomas Reed, himself a writer of considerable prominence among the Annihilationists, I have been furnished with the preceding catalogue of works, for which I would here repeat to him my obligations.

order to be admitted to a second probation.* What other conception may yet seek to engraft itself upon the Gospel of Christ remains to be seen. It will probably be a resurrection of the doctrine of Hume—that man has neither body, soul, nor spirit, but is merely an *impression* or *idea.*

## § 3. *Modern Spiritism.*

The so-called "*Harmonial Philosophy*," or *Spiritism*, (incorrectly named "Spiritualism,") has come forward in the present age with high-sounding pretensions to the claim of having forever settled the question of man's uninterrupted immortality. But from the proffered conditions of settlement the Christian community has been compelled to say:

* It is difficult to imagine how a man of Dr. Beecher's confessed ability, after spending twenty years in the investigation of his theme, should fail to see that he has so completely laid himself open therein that a shrewd antagonist can sweep the theory utterly away, root and branch, and leave its advocate without even the power of defense, except on grounds which are wholly subversive of the revealed will of God. It would seem, however, at all events, that Dr. B. has been somewhat partial in stating the problem which, according to his representations, requires solution. In his statement he refers merely *to the human race*, and its "new probation" in this world; (though multitudes evidently pass out of this world before they personally enjoy any probation whatever;) but the real difficulty does not relate to man alone. For *why should brutes be subject to so much suffering and misery as they are required to endure?* Have they, too, a state of probation? A sort of innocency is attributed to them along with infants, (Jonah iv, 11,) and a sort of responsibility, (Ex. xxi, 28,) and some have regarded them as rational creatures. See § 17, *infra.* Ought they not, therefore, to be taken into the account? The following passage, also, might answer as a starting point: "*What if we should suppose that the souls of brutes are spirits who have misbehaved themselves in a former state, and are imprisoned in bodies by way of punishment?* You will say, perhaps, that punishment ought to be attended with a consciousness in the intelligent agent that he suffers for past transgressions. But how do you know that they have not this knowledge? And supposing that they have it not at present, yet they may in another removal to another state retrieve their consciousness and reminiscence." *Sermons by Dr. Jortin*, vol. 1, ser. 9, page 185. This is certainly as plausible as anything urged by Dr. Beecher.

"Non tali auxilio, nec defensoribus istis
Tempus eget."

But not to dwell upon these conditions, the whole subject, in its asserted connection with the theme before us, may be disposed of in a few remarks:

1. And first, the claim to novelty which is set up for the demonstrations on which this pretentious "philosophy" is based, is simply absurd; for in regard to their nature, and even extent, there is nothing new belonging to them. The "*new* philosophy," therefore, is new, only in the sense that the doctrine of the metempsychosis is new; and that it existed in the time of Moses can be successfully disputed by no one who will examine the import in the original of the words in which it is described in Deut. xviii, 9–14. Its practices were expressly prohibited to the Jews; and God declares that it was because of them that he expelled the nations of Canaan, and gave them over to destruction. Its continued existence may be inferred from many passages, such, for example, as 1 Sam. xxviii, and 2 Chron. xxxiii, 6; and no one acquainted with the New Testament can fail to perceive therein that in our Saviour's time there was a pretty extensive "spirit manifestation." As to its prevalence in later times, the few following facts and statements may be taken as representative. And as it is impossible here to go into a thorough discussion of the topic, I would merely say that it will hardly be prudent for any man of literary reputation to question the accuracy of the subjoined statements.

In exact accordance with the *new* revelations of this philosophy, old Porphyry asserts that those spirits which were in his day consulted by men were a deceiving race; now feigning to be gods, then demons, and then the souls of the dead. Albertus, who was born about A.D. 1193, anticipated our own Dr. Hare, of Philadelphia, in the construction of a machine for receiving communications from the spirits. The same substantially is reported also of his cotemporary, Roger Bacon. In fact, in the twelfth and thirteenth centuries especially, (not to mention previous ages,) it was a very general doctrine that spirits teach the liberal arts, and produce great wonders in nature; and multitudes of instances of each are specified. Petrus Aponus, a celebrated Italian physician, and a Materialist, is mentioned as having become convinced thereby of the existence of spirits and of the immortality of the soul, and as having become most prominent as a consulter of the dead. Spirit-rapping was universally known, and the spirits purported to clothe themselves with flesh, in the manner that our "*new*" philosophers affirm is now done at Koon's Station, in Ohio, and other places. It was moreover in ancient times a custom to consult them by writing the questions, as is common now. Dr. Hare in his book declares that he had "a familiar spirit." So did old Hildebrand and others; and Pomponatius avers that the spirits were consulted in respect to curing diseases, and that often a cure was effected by means of them. They were said to carry material objects through the air, to assume the shapes of men and beasts, and to make themselves visible. They purported then, as now, to speak all languages, (though Balzac charges them with being grossly ignorant.) They were subject to the call of men then as now. In the latter part of the fifteenth century there was a great spiritual demonstration in Italy, an account of which was published in four dissertations by a celebrated author of that age. And still later, the famous Antoinette Bourignan, with any number of others, abandoned the revelation of God to follow the teachings of the spirits. The communication of men with spirits was asserted to be good and useful to man; and Rev. Mr. Beeker, of Amsterdam, who derided the idea of holding such intercourse, was on that account, in a still later age, deposed from the ministry, so universal was the "*new* Harmonial Philosophy" in all past ages.

2. As to any demonstrable proof of the immortality of the human soul, derivable from this source, it is all mere moonshine. A single fact will make this apparent. All the advocates of this "philosophy" are compelled to admit that among the spirits there are numbers who delight in deceiv-

ing man, and who are perpetually practising such deception. They personate men who have lived on earth, pretend to come from superior spheres, etc. Now the simple fact that man has no certain or available test by which to detect and expose such attempted deception, involves the whole subject of their communications, through "mediums," or any other means, in uncertainty. How are we to know that a communication in any given case, even admitting its reality, does not come from some mighty malignant spirit, who, in order to deceive and lead us to ruin and death, personates the soul we wish to consult? They are confessedly able thus to deceive, and how know we that they do not? The fact that they may utter some truth, and speak kindly of man, and in some things seek to do him good, is not inconsistent with such a procedure, but is just what might be expected in the circumstances. The argument for man's immortality, therefore, from such a source, is worthless.

### § 4. *The Issue stated.*

The issue between the annihilationists and those who maintain the current doctrine of immortality is thus stated by the former:

"The question is not whether the soul *can* be immortal, nor whether the souls of the righteous *will* be immortal, but will the wicked who live and die in their sins *continue* eternally, or *without end*, in a state of conscious being? Or, once more, is the punishment God has threatened to sinners an *eternal state of conscious being in misery?* This involves the question of the immortality of the soul. *For if all men can be proved to be immortal, I conceive it follows from the Bible that the finally impenitent will be punished with eternal conscious being in misery.*" See S, pp. 4, 5. A careful analysis of this phraseology would not be very flattering to the exorbitant literary pretensions of its author, but still the ideas which he sought to communicate obviously lie upon the surface and cannot well be misunderstood. In like manner speaks Mr. Dobney, pp. 82, 83, and 111. See also pp. 177, 182, 185 of "Whately's Future State" for language similar.

## § 5. *The Fundamental Principles of the Annihilationists.*

We shall now present an outline of the system in their own words. But where their views, as they sometimes do, conflict with each other on the points presented, we shall of course not attempt to decide which is the fair exponent of the system, but shall merely present the fact as it is, and leave it with the reader.

1. In respect to the SOUL itself, they teach that "there *is* such a thing as a *living* soul, hence there must be such a thing as a *dead* soul." "If the soul is a part of the man, it also is of the dust of the ground; and if it is not a part of him, it is not liable to sin or punishment, *and it is of no consequence to the man what becomes of it.*" "No Scripture or philosophy has ever yet been shown to prove the mind anything more than an attribute of the living, organized dust, and if so, it must cease with the life of the body." "Christ's soul was not left in the grave; then it must have been in the grave, and *dead.* It did not die a spiritual death, for that would be dead in sin. It follows, then, that it died a literal death." "Spiritual rapping and immortal soulism are destined to run parallel to each other." "Immortal soulism can be no longer sustained but at the expense of rejecting the word of God." (C., 14, 16, 20, 23.)

"A soul, in Scripture phraseology, means an animal, or creature, or life." "It is absurd and wicked to infer that it is immaterial and immortal, to favor a pagan fable." "Souls can be killed or murdered." "The soul of man can die, and does die." "It can be cut off and destroyed." "Man has no soul nor spirit that can exist, as a living thing, apart from his body; his whole nature is mortal." "The soul has not and cannot have a conscious existence independently of the organized being animated." "All the dead are unconscious in their graves; if there be no resurrection they have perished like brutes; *they have been* *already blotted out of existence.*" (E. 31, 41, 42, 43, 49, 233.) "Man has no immaterial principle, or thing, or substance, or essence, or naturally immortal soul." "Man is entirely dependent upon his organization for all his thoughts, feelings, sensations, and for all the developments of his soul or life, and consequently, if the dead rise not, they have perished." "Man resembles the animals in these particulars; both are material, both are mortal; both having souls, both have spirits; and both alike are entirely dependent upon their organization for all their mental phenomena."* "For the production of any mental or moral action, there is required a body, brains, nerve-fibre, and bright-red arterial blood;" (*as in the case of angels*, I presume.) "The whole man, save the breath, proceeds from the parents." (R. 4, 5, 12, 13, 14; and M. 24, 25.)

Thus man is body and soul created from matter, and is dependent upon his bodily organization for his mental and moral powers. The soul is merely the result of organization, and is so wholly inseparable from the body as to be incapable of separate existence. The same doctrine was taught by Epicurus, Lucretius, and many other ancient atheistic philosophers; and also by Spinosa, Hobbes, Toland, Voltaire, Volney, etc. A parentage worthy of its offspring.

2. *Their Ideas concerning Death.* They are sadly confused on the subject whether the soul sleeps at death or is utterly blotted out of being, and some of them, like S., endeavor to blend both ideas in their theory. Their generally avowed belief is, however, that as the

* Water, for example, is a constituent body, (our Materialist friends, whose philosophy we quote above, must admit this,) and in winter it assumes something of an organized form. May it not then possess *a sort of intelligence?* And may not that statement of an old philosopher be, after all, true, who said, "*The waters of this world are mad, which makes them rave and run up and down so, as they do in the channels of the earth.*" If physical constituency may impart intellectuality, (and this is the principle which underlies this Materialism,) can our antagonists give any reason for thinking that this old philosopher's notion is not the profoundest philosophy? I know not who he was, but have taken the quotation from Dr. Henry More.

soul cannot exist separate from the body, it is annihilated at death. Thus D. says: "The death threatened to Adam was the death of the entire man;" "the extinction of being;" pp. 135, 148, 152. "The existence of man from that hour [the fall] became one of pain, sorrow, misery, and is hastening *to its wind up*, and will result in the utter extermination of his being, unless counteracted by eating that bread that came down from heaven." (S. 61.) "*The Bible teaches that man*, THE SOUL *as well as the body*, *dies*," "and that man is dependent on his resurrection from the grave for all future existence." (G. 7, 9.) "Death is that state of being in which there is a total and permanent cessation of all the vital actions, when the organs have not only ceased to act, but have lost the susceptibility of renewed action." "Nothing can more clearly indicate the utter dissolution of the finally impenitent than this oft-repeated declaration, they *shall die*." (Has. 14, 19.) "I think I am fairly permitted to affirm, that what has already been advanced under the preceding sections, is sufficiently definite and unmistakable to justify the conclusion that both our Lord and his apostles taught no such doctrines as that the disembodied soul is the human personality, and that the soul or spirit exists after death in a state of consciousness; but that, on the contrary, they taught the state of death to be a complete decease of the conscious being, and that the life will not be rekindled until the period of the resurrection." (H. 2, p. 85.)

In respect to this matter, also, Voltaire and the other French atheists, and the Robert Owen school of infidels, all agree perfectly with our Annihilation friends. Their philosophy is the same. The former, however, oppose these views to the Bible, while the latter attempt to reconcile them with it. The former also aver that death is perpetual to ALL our race, while the latter hold that the righteous will live again. We need not here adduce extracts to prove the truth of these statements, for in another chapter we shall have occasion to refer more particularly to the ancient and modern advocates of the material philosophy.

3. *Their Idea of the Penalty of the Law.*—This idea is so fully developed in the above extracts as to render further quotation on the subject scarcely necessary. They make annihilation to be a positive infliction of punishment by God *on account of sin*, and of course, therefore, it is the penalty of the law. A single passage may be given in illustration: "Any torment or punishment that comes short of terminating the very being of the sufferer, is not death, and therefore is not the penalty of the law." (E. 235.) They equivocate greatly, however, on the word *annihilate*, pretending that we employ it in a sense altogether different from that which they attach to the term. But this is puerile, and they may here define it themselves. They say: "*The wicked shall be destroyed.* To destroy means to demolish, to ruin, to annihilate." "The Hebrew word *tsomath*, rendered *destroy*, means to *annihilate*." On the same page annihilation is defined to be "*the deprivation of life and being.*" "The souls that reject Christ shall be utterly exterminated. If these exceedingly emphatic expressions do not teach the utter annihilation of the being of the wicked, we ask how can any language possibly teach it?" (E. 239, 241; and also pp. 243–257. See also D. 167; A. 96, 115; H. 1, pp. 120, 142; S. 39; Has. 7–14 and 29–34. See also infra. §§ 49–64.)

4. As to *the punishment of sin*, they all most emphatically deny that it is a mere *natural* result, and maintain that it is a positive penal infliction. On this point *some* of our own theologians may study their works with advantage. (See § 56, infra.)

5. They all insist on a distinction between *future life and immortality*, and define immortality to be *uninterrupted and unending life;* while future life, being simply life in a future state, is consistent with the interruption of life between death and the resurrection.

6. *The wicked, as well as the righteous, are raised from the state of non-existence into which they pass at death.* (C. 21, 22; Has. 25, 38; S. 14, 64; D. 111, 164, 165, 185,

H. 2. p. 93.) Some, however, appear to regard the resurrection of the wicked as rather doubtful. (E. 234.)

7. At the resurrection the same soul or animating principle is not restored to the body. "Eccles. xii, 7, says the *ruah* goes to the God who gave it. Now if God intends to restore this *ruah* to the man so that he may *live again*, where does God bring this *ruah* from? We shall see that it is not the SAME RUAH, but *ruah* of the *same kind*, though perhaps less diluted with atmospheric air." And after quoting Ezek. xxxvii, he adds: "Thus we see that the *ruah* in Eccles. xii, 7, went to the *four winds*, and at the resurrection comes again from the *four winds*. Thus we see that it is God's *ruah*, one universal principle pervading the atmosphere, and not many distinct *ruah*, as theologians teach, and is not a living thing, though the cause of life, but which our *honest* translators have translated wind, breath, spirit, and Spirit of God, so as best to favor the pagan fable of the separate conscious existence of a spirit belonging to man!!" (E. 89, 90.)

This idea is substantially a reiteration of the notion of Dicæarchus and Epicurus, who, in like manner, maintained that the soul was divisible into parts. It is pagan and atheistic in its origin and tendency. It was also advanced in the time of Leo X., who issued a bull against it. In that century the Anabaptist, Sebastian Francus, endeavored to revive it, and subsequently Spinosa. It is therefore peculiarly becoming in the advocates of this fable to stigmatize as a "pagan notion" the doctrine of uninterrupted immortality.

8. *After their resurrection* the wicked are annihilated over again, or blotted out of existence a second time. See D. 167, and their writers *passim*. This they denominate "the second death." (C. 21, 22; S. 34; D. 166; E. 228; Has. 19.)

9. *There is no hell now in existence.* "Paul does not once speak of there being a hell of fire in existence at the present hour." (Has. 39.) "We have now examined all those words which are translated *hell*, and all others that bear

any relation to the word hell, and the result is the Bible does not teach that there is any place now in existence where the wicked dead are in torments." (E. 170, 171, 231.) "It is too commonly taken for granted that *place and elements of torment are actually in existence*, and that the wicked, the moment of their decease, are transferred thither." "The agent of the future punishment *is literal fire*. The fire of hell is not yet kindled, and will not be until after the wicked are raised from the dead, and the processes of the great judgment are completed. The future punishment will not be an endless preservation in misery, but a total destruction or annihilation." (H. 1, pp. 142, 143.) Of course, therefore, those of this sect who deny the resurrection of the wicked, deny also that there ever has been or ever will be a hell.

10. *Angels and demons truly exist*, (see E. 85, 136; S. 53; D. 72, 73,) though A. 108 regards it as doubtful, and seems in a great quandary to know what to believe on the subject.

11. *The devil and demons are, however, to be annihilated.* (Has. 26; S. 33, 34; H. 1, p. 144.)

12. *They claim the Bible to be the ultimate ground of appeal*, and regard it as written by inspiration of God. (D. 89, and all other writers *passim*.) Some of them, however, are clandestinely endeavoring to undermine its authority. (E. 10.)

Such are the outlines of this theory. I do not say that each one of their writers entertains every feature of the system; but only that the books which they have placed in my hands with a view to this discussion, maintain the doctrines here presented; and that the authors of those works regard them as essential to the integrity of the system.*

* It is truly painful to find Dr. Whately attempting to sustain, by a metaphysical speculation, the philosophy upon which are based the foregoing representations. In his "Future State," p. 59, for example, he says: "Whatever is actually *seen* or presented *to any of the senses* whether naturally or supernaturally, *must of course be material*; but a like *effect* may be produced on the *mind* (as we experience in the case of imagination and

§ 6. *This System is properly named Materialism.*

That it is not a misrepresentation of this system to pronounce it *materialism*, will be questioned by no intelligent mind. I speak of it thus, however, not invidiously, but merely to explain my use of the term in this treatise. But it is a gross absurdity for its advocates to reject as offensive the application of this term to their system. There is a great deal of such miserable chicanery in the present age. Men become advocates of certain views, which have always been known by a definite and distinguishing name; and yet, with a pusillanimity which is sadly in contrast with their professions of fearlessness and love of the truth, shrink from the frank and manly avowal of their position, and then, with no attempt to verify the charge, accuse every one of misrepresentation who, for distinction's sake, gives to their theory the name by which it ever has been known, and by which alone it can be intelligently distinguished. The time is past when any sensible mind will suffer itself to be influenced by a mere name. When, therefore, a man comes forward to assail the received doctrines of the Gospel, let him not shrink from the responsibility of his position, on the puerile and offensive plea that he otherwise will not be candidly heard. I have ever regarded this maneuver, and must still regard it, as a discreditable ruse for awakening an undeserved prejudice on the one hand, and for obtaining a blind sympathy on the other, to which the author, at least,

dreaming, and as we read in the case of visions) without the presence, as far as we know, of any material object." Of course, then, the appearance of Jehovah to Moses, (Ex. xxxiv, 5–8,) who both *saw* and *heard* him, was *material*, or only *imagined* on the part of Moses. So, too, in respect to the angels who appeared to Zechariah and Mary, and to the soldiers and women at the sepulchre. They were *material*, or only *imaginary*. To say these were *visions* is saying nothing to the purpose, unless by vision, in this sense, is meant the soul or spirit *perceiving*. Disembodied spirits and angels can and do see each other; and if so, why may not a spirit embodied in flesh sometimes also perceive, independent of the corporeal organs of perception and sensation? Will Dr. Whately please inform us! See Addison's Spectator, No. 110.

of such a movement, can have no just title. Truth is frank and fearless, and never can suffer in an encounter with error in a fair and open field.*

## § 7. *Doctrine of the Evangelical Churches.*

In connection with the foregoing summary of the Annihilationist views, it will be proper here to state briefly the doctrines of the Evangelical Churches on the subject of the soul's immortality. The whole may be presented in the following passage, which forms the thirty-second chapter of the Presbyterian Confession of Faith: "The bodies of men after death return to dust, and see corruption; but their souls, (which neither die nor sleep,) having an immortal subsistence, immediately return to God who gave them. The souls of the righteous, being then made perfect in holiness, are received into the highest heavens, where they behold the face of God in light and glory, waiting for the full redemption of their bodies; and the souls of the wicked are cast into hell, where they remain in torments and utter darkness, reserved to the judgment of the great day. Besides these two places for souls separated from their bodies, the Scripture acknowledgeth none. At the last day such as are found alive shall not die, but be changed; and all the dead shall be raised up with the self-same bodies, and none other, although with different qualities, which shall be united again to their souls forever. The bodies of the unjust shall, by the power of Christ, be raised to dishonor; the bodies of the just, by his Spirit, unto honor, and be made conformable to his own glorious body." See also Larger Catechism, questions 85, 86, and Shorter Catechism, question 37.

In chapter thirty-third it is stated also that at the day of judgment "not only the apostate angels shall be judged, but likewise that all persons who have lived upon earth

* The general reader may find in the Encyclopedia of Religious Knowledge, pp. 783–786, and in Buchanan's Modern Atheism, p. 192, and seq., a sufficient justification of our application of the term *Materialism* to the foregoing system.

shall appear before the tribunal of Christ. Then shall the righteous go into everlasting life, and receive that fullness of joy and refreshing which shall come from the presence of the Lord; but the wicked, who know not God, and obey not the Gospel of Jesus Christ, shall be cast into eternal torments, and be punished with everlasting destruction from the presence of the Lord and from the glory of his power." See also Larger Catechism, quest. 87–90.

Such are the received views of the whole evangelical Church: The Lutheran and the Reformed on the Continent; the Presbyterian, the Congregational, the Wesleyan, and the Episcopal Churches in England; while in this country all those denominations entertain the doctrine also, and as above expressed.*

### § 8. *The Position of Archbishop Whately.*

In consequence, however, of a turn which the discussion has recently taken both in this country and in Europe, we are under the painful necessity of here adverting to a matter connected with one of those Churches. I refer to the Episcopal. The doctrine of this branch of the Church of Christ on the subject before us has never been doubtfully expressed either in the writings of her representative sons, or in her standards. And yet a primate of that Church, and while remaining within her communion, has recently and repeatedly appeared before the public with a studied and labored assault upon her cherished principles in this matter. I have no disposition to meddle with the polity of the Church referred to; but as the procedure to which we advert (as will be seen in the sequel) has given an undue advantage to Annihilationists, it is our duty to refer to the subject so far as is necessary in order to place the matter in its true light before the public. That Dr. Whately has a right to assail, if he chooses, these or any

* "No article of any creed in Christendom is more universally or unhesitatingly held than that each individual enters, at death, upon an eternal state of retribution." (Bush on the Resurrection, p. 276.)

other doctrines whatever, no one will dispute; but that he either has or can have a right to enjoy the revenues of the Church, under the plea of receiving her doctrines, and under the pledge to defend them, while at the same time he is endeavoring to effect their subversion, every upright mind will most emphatically deny. The fact that others may have done the like before him, or that Paley's loose views of subscription might justify such a course, is (as his own "Logic" will tell him) neither excuse nor extenuation for Dr. Whately. If some have done the same thing, others can be named also who, when they were led to depart from the doctrines of the Establishment, and upon far less important grounds, have honestly abandoned her communion. The senseless outcry may be raised that this is unfavorable to freedom of discussion, (for "freedom of discussion" has been made to father many such proceedings;) but the question relates not to free discussion, but to moral integrity. And such theologastricism ought to be banished from among men.

Every book of the Annihilationists contains quotations from, and laudations of, Dr. Whately; and just in proportion as his course herein is indefensible and humiliating, do they laud him as one whose candor and fearlessness of con sequences have gained the ascendant of all selfish considerations.* And all this is made the basis for the most invidious insinuations against those who retain their principles and their integrity. In fact Dr. Whately has become their great authority. But to complete the portrait they have drawn from imagination rather than from fact; for so far from the love of truth leading Dr. Whately to disregard consequences, he stands before the world self-convicted, as one who persisted in receiving and enjoying the revenues of a Church whose avowed faith he was confessedly endeavoring to subvert. Certainly it was scarcely to be expected that in this age the humiliating example of Archdeacon Black-

* See, for example, S. I–VI, and in other places; D. 90, 96, 189, 190; H. 1, p. 189; M. 19, 25; H. 2, p. 65, 96; and B. 31, 65, 66, 74.

burne should find a counterpart among the dignitaries of the same Church.* I repeat the asseveration, that every man who lays claim to moral integrity ought to frown upon such a procedure. It is becoming of rather frequent occurrence; but the frequency can never divest the act of its odious character. The Socinians in Harvard might be named in illustration, and some recent cases also in the Presbyterian and other Churches. The same remarks apply also to the Rationalists in Germany, who likewise "dipped their hand in the dish" with the Church of Christ, at the same time that they were seeking to blot out her very existence. How nobly do the examples of David Simpson, Baptist W. Noel, and of thousands of others, contrast with that of such men?† But we need not dwell upon the

* Blackburne was author of the anonymous volume entitled, "Historical View of the Controversy concerning an Intermediate State," etc. London, 1772, (second edition;) a work from which the Annihilationists copy, as from a common stock, without acknowledgment; and throughout which the merest partisan appears, as usual, under the garb of an intolerant and proscriptive *liberality*, and with a fierce and almost ferocious zeal for *moderation*. Even the Socinians admit that his opposition to the doctrines of the Church of England, and his continuance in its connection, are "an anomaly not easily explained." See Collection of Essays, etc., by Dr. Jared Sparks, vol. i, p. 176. See also Robert Hall's views of such proceedings, in Works, ii, 320–323, 327; and Doddridge's, also, in the seventieth of his Lectures.

† The following remark of *Archbishop Magee* (a predecessor of *Dr. Whately* in the See of Dublin) is well worth pondering in this connection: "It is indeed," says he, "scarcely conceivable how a person in possession of a sane understanding can reconcile to himself subscription to the Articles of the Church, and rejection of the doctrines which those articles define." Now that the survivance and continuous activity of the human spirit of Christ between his death and resurrection infers that of his members, will not be denied, (on this point see § 33, subsection 14, *infra*;) nor will it be denied that both the *burial* and *descent of Christ into hades* are expressly taught in the Thirty-nine Articles, and also throughout the book of Common Prayer. The phrase, "*He descended into hell*," is therein explained by the phrase, "*He went into the place of departed spirits*;" and this very creed is not only repeated in the daily service, but committed and recited by every catechumen previous to confirmation by the bishop. It is, moreover, required to be repeated in "The Visitation of the Sick," and in the prayers offered on such occasions phrases like the following occur: "O Almighty God, *with whom*

subject. It is sufficient to add, in conclusion, that in proportion to the elevation of the position of him who is guilty of such a procedure, is the necessity for rebuke; for unreflecting minds are more influenced by the exalted *position* of such than by their arguments. And it may be mentioned in illustration hereof, that the Annihilationists do not rely for effect with the community so much upon the shallow sophisms of Dr. Whately, as upon his mere statements. His argument, of itself, carries but little weight, (and many of these writers far excel him in logical power and acumen;) but his statements, on account of his position in the Church, have an authority with the multitude, which the Annihilationists have shown that they well know how to make the most of.

*do live the spirits of just men made perfect, after they are delivered from their earthly prisons, we humbly commend the soul of this thy servant,*" etc. See also the Burial Service. How can any man entertaining the theology of Dr. W. conscientiously perform those services, or join in those sublime utterances of the *Te Deum Laudamus:* "The glorious company of the apostles praise thee. The goodly fellowship of the prophets praise thee. The noble army of martyrs praise thee?"

# CHAPTER II.

## THE ARGUMENT FROM REASON CONSIDERED.

### § 9. *Preliminary Considerations.*

THE discussion of the question respecting man's immortality, if limited to the announcements of Revelation, would be greatly narrowed, and the issue facilitated, so far as those are concerned who receive the Divine testimony. But as our antagonists do not confine themselves thereto, we cannot hope to do justice to the discussion without taking up the whole line of their argument, whereby they have sought to cast the shadows of uncertainty over the subject. Indeed it is impossible to over-estimate the importance to virtue and religion of the doctrine that the soul retains its conscious existence after death, for the knowledge of God and the immortality of the soul are most intimately associated as the primary foundation of all religion. Dissolve the connection between the present and a future life, and let it be supposed that after death man wholly ceases to exist, and that he shall live no more until the immeasurably distant period of the resurrection and general judgment, and a blow is at once struck which gives tranquillity to the impenitently vicious, and which at the same time robs the humble and faithful believer of the prospect which had cheered his spirit amid the sorrows of his wearisome earthly pilgrimage.* I admit that such considerations alone are not sufficient of themselves to set aside clear proof that the basis on which they rest is

* Dr. Whately labors to perplex this topic by mere metaphysical sophisms, and to prove that it is really a question of no practical importance whether our existence is or is not suspended at death. See Whately's Future State, pp. 74–78, 80–84, 88.

unsupported; but they certainly furnish sufficient reason to prompt a thorough examination of the claim by which that basis is sought to be invalidated.

## § 10. *The Question of Immateriality not important.*

In treating upon the subject of immortality, not a few of the defenders of the current views have perplexed both the question and themselves by claiming, as essential to the proper reception of the doctrine, that the soul should be conceded to be *immaterial* in the undefinable and so-called *philosophical* sense of that term. But we really know nothing of the essential properties of matter, and of course the term *immaterial* can convey no determinate idea. It is nowhere used in the Bible, nor has the cautious and profound Butler ever once employed it through his whole *argument.* The *idea* philosophically associated with the term is of modern origin, (for the ancient philosophers seemed to have no conception of it,) and was originated as an offset to the debasing material philosophy of Hobbes, Toland, and others. It is in no way required, however, in an investigation of the subject before us. *Corruptibility* and *incorruptibility* convey ideas which are not beyond our reach. But the same cannot be said of *materiality* and *immateriality* in their professedly philosophical sense.

If, however, in compliance with modern usage, the terms must be employed in this discussion, (for most of the authors to whom I reply are perpetually using them,) I wish it understood that they are herein employed, not in a philosophical but theological sense. By *material*, as applied to the soul, I mean *corruptible;* by *immaterial*, in the same application, I mean that the soul is a spiritual, incorruptible substance, of a nature similar to that of angels;* or, as Dr. Abercrombie defines the term, it may not be objectionable: "All that we mean or *can* mean by being *immaterial*, is that the phenomena of mind are entirely distinct from

* See E. 85, 136, S. 53, and D. 72, 73.

anything we know of the properties of matter."* But along with this explanation it ought to be repeated, that the doctrine of the soul's immortality neither depends on nor can be deduced from that of its immateriality, in the metaphysical sense of that term. And hence it is of no actual importance to religion. The Bible nowhere attempts to define the soul's essential nature and quality. The *body* or *flesh* (σῶμα, בָּשָׂר) is therein contrasted to the *soul* or *spirit*, and a different *origin* attributed to each. It likewise always distinguishes between them *as different substances*, attributes different *properties* and *operations* to each, and assigns to each a different *destiny* at death. And here the question as to its nature is left. For the things thus announced include all that it is needful for us to know at present in order to realize the importance of living for eternity.

### § 11. *Points involved in the True Issue.*

Three things are necessarily involved in the true idea of the soul's immortality: 1. The uninterrupted continuance of its substance; 2. The continuance of its life and self-consciousness; and consequently, 3. The lasting recollection of the soul itself, that its state or condition after death results from that state which preceded. Or, in the beautiful language of Isaac Taylor: "That which Christianity requires us to believe is the actual survivance of our personal consciousness *embodied*, and the perpetuity of our sense of good and evil, and our continued sensibility of pain and pleasure, and the unbroken recollection in another life of the events and affections of the present state. What Christianity decisively affirms is, that the LIFE—moral, intellectual, and active, or corporeal—is not commensurate with, or dependent upon, animal organization; but that it may, and that it will, spring up anew from the ruins of its present habitation. 'Destroy *this* body,' and the man still lives; but whether he might live immaterially is a mere question of philosophy,

* Inquiry, p. 35. Such appears to have been the idea, also, of *Cudworth*. See Intellectual System, B. 1, chap. 1, sec. 22 and 32.

which the inspired writers do not care to decide. This doctrine, concerning what is called the immateriality of the soul, should ever be treated as a merely philosophical speculation, and as unimportant to our Christian profession." *

§ 12. *The philosophical Arguments of the ancient Greeks.*

In considering the argument from reason, therefore, I shall pass without dwelling upon those philosophical arguments invented by the Greeks, and drawn from the ideas which they entertained of the essence of the soul; and also those metaphysical proofs upon which Plato and Cicero so abundantly and so beautifully expatiate. There may be force in them, but I shall not perplex the discussion with any such refined speculations, for after all they seem not to lead beyond the conclusion that the immortality of the soul is possible and probable, and in no way inconsistent with the nature of things.

§ 13. *State of the Question in respect to the Theory of the Materialists.*

It is a point, however, which must in the nature of the case be conceded by every one who is not a conceited sciolist, that reason cannot *prove* the soul to be corruptible or mortal. This plainly transcends the limits of man's intellectual powers. For how can any one go about to prove what this supposition must *logically and necessarily involve*, that the ultimate end for which man is here called into being is or may be attained in the present life? † Even the atheist, who pretends to believe that chance gave him his present existence, is compelled to admit that chance may make that existence immortal. Before we commence the direct argument, therefore, it may be well in this connection briefly to

* Physical Theory of Another Life, pp. 16, 17. See the subject of the above section very forcibly presented and illustrated in that almost forgotten, but excellent treatise, *Dilucidationes Philosophicæ*, by G. B. Buelffinger, pp. 384–396. Tubingen, 1725. See also Buchanan's Modern Atheism, chap. iv, sec. 3.

† See section 5, sub-sections 1, 2, and 7 above.

glance at some of the arrogant assumptions of Annihilationists on the subject. They claim that man is entirely material, and solely dependent upon his corporeal organization for all his sensations, feelings, thoughts, and mental developments. That at death he passes utterly out of all conscious being; and that in the resurrection *not the same soul* which previously animated his body is restored to him, but only a soul that is the same in kind; so that the soul *as such* is incapable of an existence separate from the body, and is never recreated nor returned to it again. It is a result of organization, and ceases to exist when the organism fails. If these things be so the soul of course is mortal, and the whole object of its creation or existence is attained in the present life.

The attempts at proof from reason and revelation, by which our opponents would establish this theory, we shall for the present omit to notice. But we would here, in passing, call their attention to a consideration or two which lie in the way of their conclusion, but which they either have not known, or they have thought it advisable to pass in silence. For if the soul is not really distinct from the body, then it is inseparable from the body, and of course essential to it as a body, as what is not distinct from body, properly speaking, is essential to it, and it is a contradiction in terms to say that a thing is ever without its essence. How then can it be known that after death our volitions and sensations cease? If a body *of itself* is susceptible of thought and sensation, it is always thus susceptible. If, for example, an atom of air, or of electricity, was ever destitute of sensation or thought, it is clearly impossible that becoming connected with something else should ever make IT *of itself* either think or feel; consequently as men do possess thought, it follows either that all bodies are thinking substances, or that the substance which thinks is truly distinct from the body.*

* Since we are informed by our Materialist friends that the doctrine of the soul's immortality is the foundation of spirit-rapping, and of all superstitions about ghosts, it may be of advantage for them to peruse the fol-

We are therefore certainly warranted by all the principles of correct reasoning to affirm the absurdity of the

lowing from Bayle. After referring to the puerile fears of Hobbes, of Malmsbury, about being alone in the dark, he says: "But you will say Hobbes denied the existence of spirits; say rather that he believed there are no substances distinct from matter. Now, as that did not hinder him from believing that there are many substances which design or do good or ill to others, he might and ought to believe that there are beings in the air, or elsewhere, as capable of mischief as the corpuscles, which, according to his system, form all our thoughts in our brain. How came these corpuscles to be better acquainted with the means of doing mischief than those of other beings? And what reason is there to prove that these other beings are ignorant of the manner of acting upon our brain, in order to make us see an apparition? These apparitions in dreams are very frequent, whether a man believes in the immortality of the soul or not. Suppose they should once happen to an incredulous man awake, as they do frequently in his sleep, we allow that he would be afraid, though he had ever so much courage. And therefore, for a stronger reason, we ought to believe that Hobbes would have been terribly affrighted by it.

"I have often wondered that neither Epicurus nor any of his followers should consider that the atoms which form a nose, two eyes, several nerves, a brain, have nothing more excellent in them than those which go to the making a stone; and therefore it is very absurd to suppose that every collection of atoms, which makes not a man or a beast, should be destitute of knowledge. He who denies the soul of man to be a substance distinct from matter *reasons childishly, unless he supposes that all the universe is animated, and that there are everywhere some particular thinking beings;* and that, as there are some which do not equal men, so there are others which exceed them. On this supposition plants and stones would be thinking substances. It is not necessary they should have a sensation of colors, sounds, smells, etc., but it is necessary they should have another sort of knowledge; and as it would be ridiculous for these to deny that there were any such beings as men, who do them a deal of mischief, who pluck them up by the roots, who cut and break them in pieces; as, I say, they would be ridiculous to deny this, under pretense that they do not see the arm or ax which smote them, so the Epicureans are most ridiculous in denying that there are beings in the air, or elsewhere, who know us, who do us sometimes evil, sometimes good, or who are inclined, some to destroy, others to protect us. I say the Epicureans would be very ridiculous to deny this, under pretense that they see no such beings. They have no good reason to deny witchcraft, magic, the larvæ, the specters, the lemures, hobgoblins, familiars, and other things of this nature. *It is more allowable in those who allow the soul to be distinct from matter to deny them, and yet I know not by what preposterous turn of mind they who believe the soul of man to be corporeal are the readiest to deny the existence of demons.*" (Crit. Dict., vol. iv, articles *Hobbes* and *Lucretius*.)

supposition that any substance which is unintelligent and insensible previously to organization, can become intelligent and self-conscious by organization, for organization alters not the nature and essence of things; consequently it does not at all follow that a substance which is endowed with essential activity, intellect, and volition, should lose all intellect, action, and volition, merely in consequence of being separated from another and utterly different substance to which it had been united, and which is naturally destitute of those attributes. In whatever way we may suppose it to be bound by the laws of that union for a time, there is no reason to suppose that it should still be subject to those laws, and that it should be unable to act or to think at all after such union is dissolved.

Should it be said, in answer to this, that the organization referred to is only a combination of different substances whose chemical affinities may, when brought into association, develop the laws of life, this would be a ridiculous evasion of the point; for according to this, those laws of life exist in matter itself, and only need an organic association in order to develop them. And yet, though in multitudes of instances the material organization, or combination aforesaid, remains the same immediately after death as immediately before it, all development of sensation and of the laws of life cease to be exhibited the moment that death ensues.

The material philosophy can furnish no satisfactory answer to this reasoning, and in view of it we may here advert to the annihilation theory a little further. Its advocates, as we have shown, frankly admit that the soul is wholly exterminated at death, and that the same soul is not necessarily restored to the body. The soul, they say, is merely the breath; and of course it would be absurd to suppose that man is to breathe over again after the resurrection the same breath which he now breathes. All thought, sensation, and being, therefore, utterly perish at death. How, then, is personal identity preserved? This question is a vitally important one in the discussion, and may be best viewed in the light of an illustration. An analogous illustration may be found in the production of sound by a bell. Suppose that yesterday such a sound was produced, which, after existing a short period, passed out of existence; then suppose further, that to-day a similar sound is produced; would it be proper to assert that the sound thus produced to-day is precisely the same which was produced yesterday? It would not, of course, be proper, for every child could see that they are numerically distinct and different. And though there may be points of resemblance, both numerous and striking, yet in no conceivable way can they be regarded as the same. Hence the sound produced to-day is an entirely new sound. Now apply this to the case in hand. At death the soul goes entirely out of existence. Its consciousness is extinguished, and it is *no more* in any sense of the word. But suppose that after it had been thus blotted out of being, God should produce another, as much like it as possible, and breathe it into the body at the resurrection? It is self-evident that this new soul is no more the same with that which existed previously than that the sound made from the bell to-day is the same which was produced from it yesterday. Are we to suppose then that a just God would, at the resurrection of the body, create a new soul, with new thoughts, and then hold it personally responsible and annihilate it for the acts of an old soul which existed and had been annihilated centuries before, and with whose acts it could have no more connection than Adam at the moment of his creation could have had with the previous acts of the fallen angels?

Some, who have evidently felt the force of such like considerations, have sought to escape from the absurdity by inventing the idea of the lethargic sleep of the soul, or the suspension of its consciousness between death and the resurrection. But how can this help the theory in question? If the soul thus sleeps, then of course it must sleep either *in* the body or *out of it*. If it sleeps in the body, then it would be well for our antagonists to make known the principle on which they venture to pronounce the body to be dead. If the soul is *the life* of the body, (as they affirm,) and if the soul remains in the body, then the life is in the body, and of course the body is not dead, for a human body cannot be both dead and alive at the same time. Hence it is wicked for our Materialist friends to bury their dead, inasmuch as it is wicked to bury any one with the life in him. Moreover, how can the soul sleep *in the body* when there is no body for it to sleep in? for instance, when the body, as in the case of Wyckliffe and the martyrs burned at the stake, has been utterly destroyed. The idea of sleeping in the body, when there is no body to sleep in, is an inconceivable absurdity. But if, on the other hand, the soul sleeps *out* of the body, then, of course, it is *separable* from the body, and consequently the whole materialistic theory, that it is merely a result of organization, and inseparable from the body, is unfounded and false.

There is an interesting corollary which here suggests itself, at which I shall just glance in passing. If the soul be merely the effect of corporeal organization, it of course partakes of the qualities of the body. Hence it partakes of the changes which the body undergoes in the attrition and replacement of particles. The change consequent upon such attrition and replacement is generally thought to be completed once in seven years. As the soul, therefore, is a constituent part of the material of which the body is formed, it changes along with the body, and of course its conscious personal identity must likewise change. For no man could rationally entertain the idea that a soul could be conscious of the truth and reality of a personal identity which had no existence whatever. If, for example, the aforesaid sounds of a bell were endowed with self-consciousness, it would be inconceivably absurd to pretend that the sound which was made to-day could be conscious of being the very same sound that was produced yesterday. Hence, therefore, according to this theory, every man has an entirely new soul once in seven years; and a man of fifty years has had seven, and a man of seventy, ten. The topic is suggestive of many other equally interesting reflections, but we must pass on to the positive argument.

§ 14. Argument I.—*The Nature of the Soul considered.*

Should we, for the sake of the argument, even concede the assumption that the soul is material, it would by no means follow from thence that it must necessarily be mortal, for matter of itself is not necessarily destructible. The idea of the nature of the soul, as presented in the traditions of all nations, and as contemplated by the great mass of the people in every age, is, that it is of a texture refined, ethereal, or spiritualized, and that the death of the body does not interrupt its conscious existence. The universality of this idea, independently of the sanction afforded it by the word of God, is, as Dr. Good well remarks, no small presumption of its being founded in fact.* As to the essence of the soul, however, (which Cicero seems to confound with its nature,) we shall say nothing, for on that subject we are willing to confess our ignorance. But as to its nature and attributes we may without presumption speak with confidence.

The soul is essentially active, and is therefore neither a result of organization nor a function of the brain. For, as already remarked, its attributes are entirely different and distinct from all the known attributes of matter, in whatever way matter may be supposed to be compounded or organized. Hence Dugald Stewart has justly remarked, that, "of all the truths we know, the existence of mind is the most certain." Our senses, so far as they relate to our physical organization, are dependent for their exercise upon impressions derived from external things. So that, for example, if light were annihilated, sight would necessarily be extinguished. But mind is not thus dependent on external things. We can, in all the intensity and vividness of present reality, recall the past, and anticipate the future; and there is every reason to believe that the soul would still retain

* Book of Nature, p. 331.

possession of its conscious existence, with the undiminished activity of all its powers, if the whole material universe were blotted out of being.

An illustration of this idea was some years since published in the medical journals, and is referred to by Dr. Abercrombie.*

A gentleman in France, through an attack of illness, lost every corporeal sense except feeling, and that continued only in one side of his face; and yet his mind was manifestly unimpaired, and his family acquired a method of holding communication with him by tracing characters upon the part of his face which retained its sensibility. Another fact of the same nature, respecting a youth in our own country, has been recently published. And how, I ask, will our antagonists explain such facts on the principles of their theory? How ineffably absurd would be the supposition that all the intellectual powers, the mental activity and volition, were dependent for their entire existence upon a piece of cuticle some two inches in diameter, which, of all the body, alone retained its sensibility, and that so soon as its susceptibility of sensation ceased all those powers should of necessity be blotted out of being? The fact is, however, wholly destructive of materialism; and even this mode of explaining it could not be resorted to without abandoning that theory.

But further. Agreeably to what are regarded as established laws of nature, we have, as already remarked, lost several times over, a great part or even the whole of our bodies, by that never-ceasing attrition or wearing away which is in every part. We can also easily recollect when our bodies were in bulk considerably less than now. Yet we feel most fully assured that we are now the very same beings that we were then; and if we look back upon any action of our childhood we are perfectly assured that we, and not another person, were the author of it. Hence it is clear that there is an obvious distinction between a living agent and a material body with which he may be associated or

* Inquiry, part ii, sec. 1.

connected. And if so, that material body may be removed and destroyed without at all impairing the consciousness of the living agent or any of its powers. The fact that in the one case this removal takes place gradually, by the attrition and replacement of particles, and in the other immediately, (as in death,) does not in the least affect the question. For we know that the loss of a limb, or even of all the limbs of the body, may take place suddenly without any impairing of consciousness. And in dying it often happens that the warmth of life has ceased in the whole body, (except in the region around the vitals,) which has become insensible and inactive, and this without at all impairing the consciousness or the intellectual powers. We find also within us a faculty to perceive objects in as strong and lively a manner without our bodily organs as with them, (things, too, which are equally the object of our desires and aversions,) as, for example, in dreaming. Now what have our external organs or our corporeal organization to do with this power? Plainly nothing. They neither assist nor hinder its exercise. How then or in what way could it affect this power, supposing all our bodily organs to be paralyzed or destroyed? * And then further. A mortal disease which by degrees consumes and prostrates the body, and finally destroys it, does not necessarily affect our powers of thought and reflection. While the body is thus consuming we can exert those powers as fully as ever, and even up to the very instant of death itself.

It were easy to expatiate on these considerations, but it is needless, for no candid mind that is capable of reflection will deny their force as arguments against the theory of materialism. But let us now consider the grounds upon which our opposers attempt to invalidate them.

The foregoing considerations completely obviate the objections urged by M. 24, 25; S. 6; D. 93–95, (and in other recent publications,) against this branch of the argument from reason, except in the instance of the attempted

* See Butler's Analogy.

*reductio ad absurdum* from the case of brutes;* but there is another objection insisted upon, and which calls for some notice in this connection. It is based upon a remark of Locke, that the soul cannot be essentially *active* because thought may be, and often is, suspended by sleep, swooning, and other causes producing apparent death. But the remark is based upon a mere assumption. Locke affirmed that *he* seldom or never dreamed, and thence inferred the suspension of his mental powers during sleep. The conclusion, however, confuses the very obvious distinction between *dreaming* and the *remembrance of dreaming*. Had he said, "I seldom have any recollection of having dreamed," he would have said all that the facts warranted. And he would, moreover, have avoided the confusion and contradiction in which he involves himself by his speculations on this subject. For example, he makes personal identity to consist entirely in consciousness, so that if our consciousness at any time ceases, our personal identity is destroyed, and we cease to be the persons we were previously. And yet in his speculations on the subject before us, he insists that consciousness ceases during sleep, and of course it follows that our personal identity is suspended every night. Locke knew, however, that if he did not dream, others did, and that, consequently, sleep does not necessarily suspend the mental powers.

In respect to his reasoning on the subject,† which prompted a careful examination of it in its application to my own experience, I am forced to conclude, after more than twenty years' close scrutiny, that the mind is never really inactive during sleep. In no instance have I ever been aroused, even from the profoundest slumber, without a full consciousness that during the sleep the mind was actively employed, and without being clearly cognizant of the thoughts which were occupying it previous to and at the moment of waking. But unless the dream itself aroused

* We shall consider this in the sequel.
† See Essay, B. II, chap. i, §§ 10–17.

me, I have generally found in such cases that the first impression which entered the mind from the external world, after I had become consciously awake, scattered those sleeping fancies so utterly that it was impossible even to tell what they were. If the thoughts, however, had been of a deeply interesting and exciting nature, their effect was in various ways clearly perceptible; but what they were I have frequently found it impossible to trace, and the remembrance of the fact that I had been thinking alone remained. And so, too, if the waking were gradual, the fancies and images would often vanish in the interval, leaving no legible trace upon the memory after I had become fully aroused. I thus refer to my own experience because I can speak positively in regard to it. But I have satisfied myself by conversation with numerous individuals that the same thing is true in regard to others.

That Locke, notwithstanding all his protestations to the contrary, did confound the distinction between *thought* and the *remembrance of thought*, is clear and undeniable. I admit that he did not remember the thoughts of his mind during sleep, and that the same may have been true in the other cases to which he refers; but I deny that their mental exercises were then suspended. I deny that any person is warranted on such grounds to assert that during his sleeping hours his mental operations are ever wholly suspended. Few men remember even what were their waking thoughts an hour ago, and it is with them a matter of inference that they did then think at all. Are we warranted therefore in the conclusion that at the time referred to they had no thoughts, and that the mind's activity was then suspended, because no perceptible traces of thought are left upon the memory? The conclusion in the one case is as sound as in the other.*

* Dr. Abercrombie (Inquiry, p. 218) says: "There can be no doubt that many dreams take place which are not remembered, as appears from the fact of a person talking in his sleep, so as to be distinctly understood, without remembering anything of the impression that gave rise to it." And were a somnambulist to deny that he ever walked in his sleep,

The same considerations will apply in reference to asphyxia, coma, and "trances," and suspension of vitality from drowning or from a stunning blow. There is under this head the most undoubted authentic testimony of facts, evincing that in these states the mental exercises are not necessarily suspended. As I shall have occasion to refer more particularly to the matter in another branch of the argument, it is sufficient here to remark, that the fact is established, beyond the power of any fine-spun philosophical theorizing to explain away, that none of these conditions necessarily involve a suspension of the activity or operations of the mind. It is no answer to such an argument to reply that in some such cases the powers of the soul *appeared* to be suspended, or that the mind itself did not afterward recollect its thoughts and feelings; for all this may be true, and yet it may also be true that the activity of the mind had not been suspended at all. A well-established veracious and positive statement in the matter is of more worth than a thousand that are merely negative.

## § 15. Argument II.—*The Nature of Human Aspirations and Desires.*

The immortality of the soul may be clearly inferred also from the nature of its aspirations and desires. These, though now affected by sin, (for man has fallen from his pristine state of holiness and peace with God,) were originally impressed upon our being by the Creator; for we find them as universal as the race of man. It is the nature of man to hope for and aspire after immortality, and many of the innate desires of his soul can find nothing in the present life which adequately corresponds to their nature, or by which they can approximate a full fruition.

We need not confine the argument, therefore, to the natural desire after immortality, for it is susceptible of a far wider application. Consider, for example, the desire

because he had no recollection of having done so, he would reason just as *conclusively* as Locke has done; but what would his conclusion be worth?

after knowledge. It is perfectly insatiable; for no sooner have we made one advance in science, or attained to one discovery, than we find our appetite whetted for a still farther advancement, and the desire for knowledge only increased. It is renewed with an ever-increasing vigor as often as it attains the object of its pursuit, while new wishes likewise perpetually spring up within the soul at every step of our advancement, and they thus accompany us from the very dawn of our earthly life until its close.

Since, therefore, these desires never end in full fruition here; since no object in this life can fully satisfy the longing aspirations of the soul, and since man is perpetually looking forward to anticipated fruition, are we to conclude that God has implanted them within us with no intention to gratify them, but merely to torment and make us miserable and discontented, as he must do if the theory of our antagonists be true? or shall we conclude that the present life does not limit the existence of man?

Can any one seriously suppose that of all God's creatures on earth, man should be the only one who possesses faculties without the power of obtaining the end for which those faculties were obviously given? or that he alone should possess an instinct without the power or opportunity of satisfying its instigations? as must be the fact if at death he passes out of existence. This indeed would be to render his condition more deplorable than that of the brutes themselves.* The silk-worm, for example, by the force of instinct, will spin its cone and shut itself up therein, and the moth, and butterfly, and dragon-fly, and myrmeleon formicaleo obey a similar instinct; but do we find the instinct ever disappointed? No, in no instance; and we are assured that a holy and good God would not give even to his meanest creatures such an instinct if it were not designed to be gratified. And would he thus care for the less and disregard the greater? Who can believe it? If, then, human existence is to terminate at death, why are there

* See Sturm, p. 197.

implanted within our souls desires boundless as infinity, and inclinations which nothing in this world can gratify? and why have we faculties which are ever grasping after something not to be found on earth? Has God then endowed us with these that they may be our tormentors, and so rendered our condition pitiable in proportion to our elevation above the merest insect in the scale of being? Atheism itself could suggest nothing more vile than this against the character of our Creator. Man therefore ceases not to exist at death.

The manner in which this argument, in its analogies and other branches, is attempted to be set aside by our antagonists, is not very favorable to their high assumptions of candor and logical acumen. They have labored the point with much earnestness, but with a success which will be apparent presently.*

At the outset these writers, in general, boldly deny that all nations believe the soul to be immortal, and adduce the testimony of Dr. Whately to sustain them in the denial, a matter which we shall fully consider in our next chapter. They affirm, likewise, that immortality is suspended upon conditions which render it merely contingent. This, however, is a fallacious attempt to connect metaphysics with the testimony of revelation on a point where the very conditions of the argument require that they should be separate. Such efforts to perplex a plain question do not evince an over-anxious desire to meet a fair issue. When, however, these writers come to present the argument itself, in order to give it a professed refutation, they state it in the following terms: "As employed by all who lay any stress upon it, it stands thus: all men are immortal, because they desire immortality." (D. 97.) In like manner S. 5 remarks: "This argument can avail nothing unless it can be proved that what

* See D. 95–99, 103, 104, and S. 5. As Mr. Dobney has labored the argument from reason more fully than the other writers of this sect, and as his work is their text-book, I shall throughout this branch of the subject bestow particular attention upon his lucubrations.

men desire they will possess." Such is their version. But let the reader turn to the argument as we have plainly and succinctly stated it, and then judge whether the above representation (unfair in the statement it presents, and false in the issue) is the result of misapprehension or intentional evasion. Its glaring unfairness would justify us in passing it without remark. We shall not do this, however, but proceed to meet the issue as they have presented it.

The whole corps of these writers concede that men universally desire immortality; but as an offset to this they affirm that "all, by the very constitution of their minds, desire happiness, yet multitudes neither are *nor will be happy.*" And moreover, that as this desire of happiness proceeds in like manner from the Author of the mind, if it of itself does not prove that all will be happy, so neither does the universal desire after immortality prove that all will be immortal. Such is their argument and analogy. But what is happiness? It is that state which is most agreeable to the nature of man as God *originally* created it. This, by the overtures of the Gospel to us in our probationary state, is put within the reach of human attainment. Of course, therefore, the force of the foregoing objection is this: that because the attainment of such a *state of being* is placed within the reach of man, and is the object of universal desire, (though "many *will not* be happy,") therefore *the continuance of our existence itself*, being a like object of desire, is also conditional. Such is the foggy atmosphere into which we are to be led in order to see the connection between a premise and conclusion which have not the slightest relation to each other. Does the human soul spontaneously shrink from the indulgence of its evil passions (the true and acknowledged ingredients of unhappiness) as it shrinks from the idea of the loss of being? This will not be pretended even by our antagonists. Why then should they attempt to perplex these plain distinctions?

Mr. Dobney (p. 99) endeavors also to point out an inconsistency in the above argument, from the fact cheerfully conceded by us, that the vicious would in general regard annihilation as a relief.* But this is equal to the rest of his logic. His argument, drawn out into a syllogism, would stand thus: All men desire a continuation of existence, and shrink from the idea of losing it. But the vicious, under the apprehension of a just judgment to come, and of eternal retribution for their crimes, would regard annihilation as a relief, and the prospect of it as an encouragement to persist in their sins. Therefore they contradict themselves who say that such depraved beings have a natural desire after immortality. Such is the miserable logic by which no small number of blood-bought souls have been led into the paths of ruin and of death.

The attempt to meet the argument from the analogies in nature (to which we have referred above) is equally evidential of egregious unfairness, or of a most imbecile logic. The real issue is this: God does not disappoint the instincts implanted in the lower orders of animated nature, and therefore it is not to be supposed that he would disappoint the native and instinctive aspirations of a higher order. In meeting this Mr. Dobney remarks that there are not many such cases in nature as the chrysalis, "while the overwhelming preponderance of facts is on the other side; and that, too, in reference to the higher orders of animals which, when they die, never present themselves again upon our path." (Pp. 103, 104.) Now does Mr. Dobney *know*

* They have always so regarded it. The profligate *Catullus*, (a proper representative of this class of character,) in writing to his mistress, could comfort himself and her in their iniquity, with the consideration that they should pass out of existence at death. He held precisely the Annihilationist psychology:

"*Vivamus, mea Lesbia atque amemus.*
*Soles occidere et redire possunt:*
*Nobis cum semel occidit brevis lux,*
*Nox una perpetua dormienda est.*"

This was all the consolation they needed to encourage them to continue in sin without apprehension of future consequences, and it is sufficient for wicked men now; for such never trouble their thoughts with the question whether the *righteous* shall live again. They need only to be per-

that these "other animals" have an instinct similar to that of those to which we have referred in the argument? If not, what have "the facts" in their case to do with the argument? And why will he persist to trifle in this manner?

He *next* objects that these analogies do not apply, for the chrysalis remains undecomposed and retains vitality, while the human *body* really dies and yields to corruption. Now the chrysalis, Mr. Dobney being judge, does retain its vitality until it "returns upon our path." And is it not puerile to pretend to meet such an analogy by saying that the human *body* does not retain its vitality? Who, pray, has ever said that it did?

The *last* objection is, that after the butterfly returns to life it comes to "a complete and final end." Admitted; but what has this to do with the argument or analogy? Does this fact conflict with any instinct implanted within the insect by its Creator? If not, in what way does the remark bear upon the question? And yet these are the best and most highly lauded specimens of Annihilationist reasoning on the subject.

## § 16. Argument III.—*The Powers and Capacities of the Soul.*

While we would not lay an undue stress upon the argument for immortality from the nature and reason of things, it could hardly be expected that in presenting that argument we should overlook the considerations suggested by the topic to which the present section is appropriated. The capacities of the soul, as illustrated by the sublime discoveries and noble inventions to which mind has advanced the arts and sciences, may surely be adduced in proof of its immortality; for who can suppose that such powers were conferred for the merely temporary use to which they are appropriated during the present brief span of our existence?

suaded that they themselves shall at length pass utterly out of being. And the doctrine of our annihilation friends comforts them with the assurance that their hopes are well founded, and will be realized.

Inferior animals, through their senses and instincts, may in such a term of life fulfill the purpose of their creation. But is it conceivable that the incomparably nobler powers of man, and "those thoughts that wander through eternity," can have no higher design than the instincts of the brute? and that in the same sensual world, and in a like groveling manner, (for this is even so if Annihilationism be true,) they are to fulfill the end or object of their existence? Can this be supposed in relation to any of the family of man? The supposition cannot be rationally entertained without the assumption that the vast and apparently unlimited capacities of the soul, and its capability for making a perpetual progress toward perfection, have been called into being by an all-wise Creator without an adequate object to be secured by means of them, and therefore that they have been bestowed to all intents and purposes in vain.

To illustrate: Even in the present fallen state of our nature, and when the soul is united to an unwieldy frame, there is no end to its desires after knowledge, and no exhausting its powers in the acquisition. Up to the very moment of death it is found to be still as capable as ever of augmenting its intellectual stores, and of pursuing those ardent and still increasing desires after both mental and moral perfection which hitherto had actuated it throughout its course. Death might, with some little show of reason, be deemed the end of those capabilities, if they were then as perfect in their development and aims as they could be. But who can seriously believe that such faculties, such transcendent capacities, found too in unimpaired and perfect existence at the last moment of their connection with this earthly life, should be called into exercise for no purpose that might not be equally answered by the groveling instincts of the brute? that a thinking, rational being, whose faculties have, till the moment of death, merely begun to develop their capacity and excellence, and who has just begun to look abroad upon the handiwork of his Creator, —that a being thus richly endowed, and capable of a continued progress in improvement, and of passing onward without limit or end, from one degree of perfection to another, should, at the bare commencement of its existence, droop and vanish away into utter nothingness? There is not in all the works of God a single analogy to sustain a supposition like this, and it is rather too much to ask reflecting minds to assent to it merely because it is demanded by the exigencies of a gloomy, ill-digested, and atheistic theory.

The offensive manner in which Mr. Dobney and his associates (in their effort to rebut these considerations) perpetually repeat the assertion that the advocates of immortality employ mere rhetorical flourishes in lieu of argument, merits a pointed rebuke. It is one of Mr. Dobney's frequently occurrent and very small attempts to enlist the sympathy of readers on his own behalf, and to awaken their prejudices against arguments which he is unable to refute. In an issue of such transcendent interest as the present, a course of procedure like this cannot be too strongly reprehended.

The true issue of the argument before us has been plainly stated. Does not the possession of such intellectual powers and capacities, they being moreover in the mere process of development, and before a thousandth part of their riches has been displayed, legitimately infer that the creature thus sublimely endowed by a wise and good God is not to pass from such a condition into nonentity? But Mr. Dobney, who has presented the strength of the negative side, (though he misrepresents the point really at issue,*) raises the following exceptions to the conclusion:

1. That "if some men have exhibited great capacities, it is an almost infinitesimally small proportion of mankind," and consequently, "if stress be laid upon the intellectual capacity exhibited by some, the same amount of stress may be fairly laid on the incapacity of others, to prove the opposite." The sophism here, however, consists in confounding the idea of *non-exhibition* of capacity with that of *destitution of capacity*,

* D. 99–103.

and is but another instance of a logic arrogant and presuming in proportion as it is helpless and imbecile. Are we to presume, then, that every characteristic tendency and potentiality of our nature must be everywhere efficaciously active, in order that its existence may be known or verified? Suppose that all men do not exhibit the capabilities referred to, what connection has this with the conclusion that man *as man* does not possess them? Were Mr. Dobney, for instance, to visit a manufactory of chronometers, in which he saw some score or two of the instruments measuring time, and some thousands of others lying upon the shelves in silence, would he be satisfied with the argument of an individual who might be present, and who should say to him, that "if the few watches which *are running* prove that watches in general are endowed with the capacity for measuring time, certainly the vast number of them which are *not running* prove *a fortiori* that watches in general have no such capacity?" The cases are parallel, so far as the point in question is concerned; but would Mr. Dobney regard such a conclusion as other than simply ridiculous? It *is*, therefore, a perfectly legitimate conclusion, that because a portion of our race has evinced the possession of the aforesaid high and noble capacities, therefore similar endowments belong to all men. Man is a species; and God has made *of one blood* all nations of men to dwell upon all the face of the earth. Then, further, Mr. Dobney misrepresents the argument itself to which he objects. That argument does not assert that all men have *equal* capacities of the kind referred to; but all men have *such* capacities, while the lower orders of animals have them not; all men are in *some degree* capable of progress in knowledge; of discovering, inventing, and achieving progressively till death; and to object, therefore, that *some men only* have *exhibited extraordinary capacities*, is trifling with the question.

2. His next objection is, that "it would be greatly more reasonable to suppose that God would connect *continued existence* with *moral* excellency rather than with intellectual

power," because an excellence which is merely intellectual is conceded to be inferior to that which is moral. But we may well ask, What has all this to do with the question relating to the capacities aforesaid? And how does the fact that continued existence *is* connected with moral excellence evince that it is not also connected with intellectual capacity? Such exceptions have the appearance of trifling with the issue. I would, however, in this connection, most pointedly deny the assumption of Mr. Dobney, that it is *more* reasonable, or reasonable at all, that continued existence should be connected with moral excellence rather than with intellectual capacity. The reasonable thing is that God should connect *happiness* with moral excellence in moral beings on whom he has bestowed such rich and noble endowments. And then further, as illustrating the vague and indeterminate conceptions with which Mr. Dobney has entered into the inquiry before us, it may be remarked that, according to the theory of himself and friends, God has not connected *continued existence* with either moral or intellectual excellence, or with anything else; for they hold that the existence of all men is interrupted, and that they pass utterly out of being during the countless ages which may elapse between their death and the resurrection. This he professes to entertain as his matured belief. Why then speak of *continued* existence being connected with anything whatever? This conscious want of resources, apparent at almost every step of the argument, must awaken astonishment in the reflecting mind that this writer not only should have ventured, in such circumstances, to assail the established belief on the subject before us, but that he should have presumed to call the attention of the religious world to his lucubrations.

3. The third objection of Mr. Dobney to the argument is, that "the progress of a vast majority of mankind is *downward, and rather from the man to the brute than from the man to the Divinity.*" Hence, if an upward progress proves a continuance of existence, a downward progress must prove the contrary. This, however, is a mere evasion. Mr. Dobney

speaks of *moral* progress, while the argument itself is concerned with *intellectual*. And then, moreover, nothing is said in the argument about progress *upward* or *downward*, but simply of the capacity for an onward or continual progress intellectually. The question stated by Mr. Dobney, however, resolves itself simply into this: whether God will have occasion under his government for the continuance in being of such lost and depraved creatures as those who die impenitent. This question has no relation to the point now before us; but we may have a word to offer on it in the sequel.

### § 17. *Capacities of the Brute Creation, and the Relation of this Topic to the Argument.*

The *last* objection which is presented by Mr. Dobney, and which all these writers perpetually and with no little assurance reiterate, is, that the foregoing argument proves too much, because, if legitimately carried out, the conclusion from it must be that brutes too are immortal, since some of them, it would seem, are capable of acquiring knowledge from instruction imparted by man, and also from their own experience. And as we know not what may be the extent of their capacity for such intellectual progress, if the aforesaid capacities prove the immortality of mind, they must in like manner prove the immortality of all minds.

I am not unwilling to concede to the premise of this argument that it presents a difficulty which is made the most of by our opponents.* It is likewise presented with great force, and for a similar purpose, by Voltaire,† and Bolingbroke,‡ and by other infidels without number; while Socinus and many of his followers took the ground that brutes are *rational* creatures, and that they were *destroyed in the deluge for their own sins*,§ so great was his hatred of the doc-

* See A. 109–114; D. 93–95 and 100–103; R. 9–12.

† Philosophical Dict., vol. i, pp. 29–32.

‡ Works, vol. iii, p. 528.

§ See his *Responsio ad Puccium*, Opp., tom. ii, pp. 257–369. Many of the ancient philosophers maintained that beasts have rational souls, an opinion which I cannot see how our Annihilationist friends can reject,

trine of the imputation of Adam's guilt, as entertained by the Reformed Church. Nor can I perceive how Mr. Dobney and his coadjutors can logically avoid coming to a similar conclusion (and the reader will, I hope, pardon my referring to such a side issue in this connection) in respect to the moral responsibility of the brute creation; for they maintain, and greatly insist upon the distinction, that the endurance of actual pain or suffering is not essential to the endurance of punishment. In other words, that it is not necessary that the subject of punishment should continue in existence during its infliction.* Hence, say they, "when the sinner is annihilated, or everlastingly deprived of existence, he is everlastingly punished." And all this they aver in immediate connection with the perpetually repeated affirmation that man

inasmuch as they strenuously assert the doctrine that there is no difference between the nature of the soul of a beast and that of a man, (though Christ has said that a man is *much better* than a brute.) *Anaxagoras* placed the difference in this, that men are able to explain their mental operations, and beasts are not. *Pythagoras* and *Plato* held the same views, while *Porphyry* allowed them not only reason, but the faculty of making their reasonings understood; and adds that *Apollonius Tyaneus, Melampus, Tiresias, and Thales* actually knew and understood their language. *Strato* and *Ænesidemus* may likewise be considered as advocating the rationality of beasts, for they taught *that sense could not subsist without understanding*. We are told, also, that *Parmenides, Empedocles*, and *Democritus* taught that all beasts are endowed with the faculty of understanding. *Galen*, too, seems to have been substantially of the same mind, and maintained that they "possessed that reason which is attributed to a soul;" while *Xenocrates*, the Carthaginian, supposed that they had a religion, and were not without the knowledge of God.

At the late annual meeting of the Association for the Advancement of Science, held in Boston, Mass., an interesting paper was read by Dr. Gibson on the language of animals. He stated that every variety of animated being possesses some means of intelligible communication. Each creature, by sounds or signs of correspondence, has a language understood by its own kind, and sometimes learned by others. Emotions of caution, affections of fear, of joy, gratitude, and grief, are disclosed by single tones of voice, or by impressive gestures, to signalize feelings strictly comprehended and often answered. Insects and birds, fish and beasts, thus express themselves in distinct languages, signed, spoken, and sung, seen, heard, and felt. See an interesting view of the subject in *Bayle*, Crit. and Hist. Dict., Art. *Pireira* and *Rorarius*.

* See M. 11, 12, 52; S. 83; H. 1, pp. 136, 137; A. 105.

is not naturally immortal, and that the sinner has no claim whatever to live everlastingly. Hence, it of course follows that as brutes (possessing as they do, according to our antagonists, intellect of the same order as the human) are at death forever blotted out of being, *they too are everlastingly punished*, but whether innocently or otherwise we leave the objector to determine. I advert to the point, however, merely to apprise our antagonists of what they are too prone to disregard, that it would not be amiss for them occasionally to make a *homeward application* of certain objections which they are rather fond of parading.

But what is the real force of the argument against the immortality of man, derived from this source? "Suppose," as Butler remarks, "the invidious thing designed in such a manner of expression were really implied, as it is not in the least, in the natural immortality of brutes, namely, that they must arrive at great attainments, and become rational and moral agents, even this would be no difficulty, since we know not what latent powers and capacities they may be endowed with." "We find it to be a general law of nature, that creatures endowed with the capacities of virtue and religion should be placed in a condition of being in which they are altogether without the use of them for a considerable length of their duration, as in infancy and childhood, and a great part of the human species go out of the present world before they come to the exercise of these capacities in any degree at all. But then the natural immortality of brutes does not in the least imply that they are endued with any latent capacities of a rational or moral nature, and the economy of the universe might require that there should be living creatures without any capacities of this kind."*

A careful examination of the facts in the case will also evince that, in the aforesaid objection, much is taken for granted that is wholly destitute of proof. Some popular writers denounce it as a shallow philosophy which denies to the

* Analogy, Part I, chapter i.

brute an intellect *the same in kind* as pertains to man,* and assert that "the principle is of *the same kind*, though under a less active and elaborate modification." But what are the data which warrant asseverations like these? What is meant by "*kind* of intellect?" and who has sufficiently explored the intellectual world, and the essence of mind, to justify the utterance of such a dogmatism? or the assertion that there is not between the mind of man and the minds of brutes just that difference *in kind* which constitutes the distinction between a mortal and an immortal nature? If reference for proof be had to the attributes or manifestations of each, it is just on this ground that we affirm an immeasurable distance between them.

The difference between instinct and reason is palpable and universally admitted. And facts alone, therefore, which are supposed to indicate the existence of reason, are all with which we are concerned in this discussion, for they are the only facts to which intelligent men among our opponents profess to appeal.

What then are those manifestations of mind in the brute which are supposed to identify him with man in point of intellectual capacity? "He has reason," it is said, "and memory, and is capable also of learning from experience and from instruction, and therefore there can be no *radical* difference between the mind of man and that of the brute." Now, as it is confessedly beyond our power to explore the *essential nature* of the intellectual world, there is but one method by which to determine the point before us; we must mark the phenomena of each of these orders of mind, with their ascertained characteristics, and from these conclude respecting the nature and attributes of each, and their likeness or unlikeness. And if this method evinces that while brutes possess some qualities of mind in common with man, they are utterly destitute of others, and those the very ones which invest him with the grandeur, the responsibilities, and the destiny of a moral being, the conclusion

* See, for example, Dr. Good's Book of Nature, p. 381.

is fair and legitimate, that the difference between the two orders of mind is radical, and a difference, not in degree only, but in kind and in nature.

Now in contemplating these orders of mind there is one marked difference which will at once occur to the careful observer, and which can indicate nothing less than a radical difference in kind between them. The human intellect is of such a nature that, universally among men, there is an aptitude or susceptibility of receiving like instruction, and of making any attainments in theoretical and practical knowledge which have been made by others of the race; but the moment we cast our eye over the manifestations of mind in the brute creation, we find an absence of everything of the kind. The wasp or hornet could never, by any process, be taught to make wax or honey, or to construct the honey-comb; nor the bee to manufacture the paper which is made by the hornet or black wasp, or to construct a nest like the hornet; nor, like the mason or blue wasp, to form a cell of clay, and after depositing an egg therein, fill up the cell with insects, and seal it at the top that the young wasp might possess a supply of food until able to provide for itself. Illustrations of the same truth can be adduced from all the tribes of animals, and they prove a radical difference between the orders of mind referred to.

Then, further, that some of the tribes of animals, such as the horse and cow, the dog and the elephant, are endowed with a species of reason, is evident from the manifestations they evince of possessing that attribute. The dog also gives evidence of dreaming while asleep. But there are limits obvious and marked beyond which this ratiocinative faculty in them is incapable of being instructed. The horse, for example, will give various proofs that in many respects his mind is capable of a reasoning process, yet let him become somewhat entangled in his harness, and though the bare lifting of a leg would disentangle him therefrom, he will yet stand plunging and kicking till he has lamed himself or exhausted his strength; and his reason, whatever may be its nature or quality, not only fails to suggest to him this simple method of obtaining relief, but he is incapable of being so instructed as to adopt it in like circumstances at any other time. Illustrations of a similar character may be obtained from well-ascertained facts in the history of other animals. But the moment we pass from these manifestations to contemplate the exercise of reason in man, we find a radical and immeasurable distance between them. Even a little child, brought into circumstances analogous to those in the case of the horse, could be easily taught to extricate himself, not only then, but to apply the knowledge in all similar circumstances into which he might be brought. And this, moreover, is universally true of human nature.*

It were easy to extend these and other not less forcible considerations to any length in illustration of the question, but the above are sufficient for the argument. Brutes have the faculty of sense, by which they perceive through its bodily organs (according to the adaptation of each of them) the qualities of certain objects in the material world. They have feelings excited within them through the perceptions of this faculty, and by the spontaneous action of their organism, as in hunger, thirst, and the like. They act under the impulsions of these feelings in reference to the objects the perception of which impresses them; but here their mental operations cease in respect to them. The difference, therefore, between the mind or soul of a brute and the intellectual capacity of man, is just what the inspired writer declares it to be, (Eccles. iii, 21,) and is sufficient to constitute the dividing line between the heirs of immortality and the mere creatures of time.

### § 18. Argument IV.—*The Existence of Conscience in Man.*

Whether *conscience* (*con* and *sci-re*, to know, to be privy to) be an original faculty of our nature, or only the general principle of moral approbation or disapprobation ap-

* See section iv of Isaac Taylor's Introductory Essay to Edwards on the Will, for this and additional illustrations of the point.

plied to our actions and affections, or whether our ideas of right and wrong are obtained through a single faculty, or from the various powers of the understanding and will, is a question of no practical importance to the argument. Nor is it of any importance thereto whether conscience is regarded as either a faculty, or power, or feeling, or sentiment. The admitted fact of its existence in man is all that the basis of the argument requires.

When a man has perpetrated what he feels to be wrong, the consequent pain, grief, and indignation which are aroused within him are altogether different from what he experiences when he incurs unavoidable insults, misfortunes, or calamities; for in that case he feels that he has brought upon himself an evil which he might have avoided; and no mere skeptical philosophy is able to override or even displace this impression, unless the heart or moral nature itself has become obdured by continued and voluntary persistence in wrong. If then the soul be merely the result of material organization, (as the Materialists affirm,) the existence of conscience becomes unaccountable, as in that case *freedom* (the *τὸ αὐτεξούσιον* of the Greeks) can really have no existence, since all our mental operations being indeed and in fact *necessary* and unavoidable, it is impossible that there should exist any consciousness that they are otherwise, as we cannot be conscious of the actual existence of that which does not exist. Hence *remorse*, in the proper sense of the term, becomes an impossibility, as is indeed admitted and maintained by leading Materialists. It is obvious, therefore, that the faculty referred to does not exist in matter, but must be traced to some other source or basis in our being.

The fact, however, of the existence of conscience in man is and has been admitted from the earliest ages. And to its existence is to be traced the idea of the Stoics, that virtue and vice are their own reward. Even infidels and atheists are compelled not only to admit its existence, but to acknowledge its power. Associated with the freedom of the will, it is the very ground and center of man's moral nature. It is first occupied in ascertaining our duty before we proceed to action, then in judging of the actions themselves when performed. It is one grand peculiarity of man, ever pointing to and prophesying of the future. As Young remarks:

> "Conscience of guilt is prophecy of pain,
> And bosom counsel to avoid the blow."

A technical definition is of no consequence, therefore, so long as the actual existence of the thing itself is admitted and its power felt and acknowledged. The very etymology of the word imports a double or joint knowledge, a knowledge of a Divine law or rule, and also of a man's own action, and so is properly the application of a general law to a particular instance of practice.* In its offices, therefore, conscience appertains to the subject of right and wrong, merit and demerit, obligation, etc., and of course its peculiar province is the action of the will in respect to the idea of right and wrong, praise and blame.

The fact that it is more or less under the control of our faith, and that in some instances it has become obdured or perverted, so as to decide erroneously, does not in any way affect the issue of the argument. That issue is based upon the admitted fact of its existence, and that in its nature it is anticipatory both of reward and punishment. Its greatest power is often felt in the hour of death. Fearful forebodings then harass the guilty soul. Hence the question arises, Are these anticipations or forebodings (based as they are in man's moral nature, and owing as they do their very existence to the Almighty Creator) to be regarded as false? as they must be if the soul at death goes out of existence. We shall advert to this again in the next argument.

* We have referred to this etymology above. It is, moreover, worthy of remark that *conscientia* is a literal translation of συνείδησις, and that both terms plainly imply something more than *simple knowledge*, *scientia*, εἴδησις. The prepositions *con* and σὺν, signifying *with*, imply here, as above stated, a *conjoint knowledge*, or, as the full word means, *knowledge in common with another*.

Our opponents do not trouble themselves with this argument, though Dr. Chalmers has presented it with much force in his works, (vol. xi, p. 62,) and M'Cosh has admirably elaborated it in his "Method of the Divine Government, Physical and Moral."

## § 19. Argument V.—*Perplexing Anomalies of the Present State of Things.*

The last argument which we shall present on this branch of the subject is taken from the disordered state of the moral world, and the unequal distribution of good and evil in this life, all of which evince the absurd consequences of denying the soul's immortality, and of asserting that a future state of existence is conditioned on the conduct of the rational creature itself. That God is the moral governor of the world can be really denied by none but atheists. Even Paine not only admitted the fact, but affirmed that there is a particular Providence over the affairs of men.

Now it is obvious that the present state of things does not accord with a perfect moral administration, unless we regard it as merely a part of a great whole, and only the beginning of what is to be fully developed in a future state of being. All moral distinctions seem to be confounded by the manner in which men of different characters are treated; "all things come alike to all; there is one event to the righteous and to the wicked; to him that sacrificeth and to him that sacrificeth not; to him that sweareth, and to him that feareth an oath." Eccles. ix, 2. There are also "just men unto whom it happeneth according to the work of the wicked. Again, there be wicked men to whom it happeneth according to the work of the righteous." Eccles. viii, 14. The lot of the righteous is often such as we are assured the lot of the wicked shall be, and *vice versa.* Nor can this matter be explained and justified on the assumed principle (see D. 106–109) that virtue and sin are their own reward, for what then becomes of the truth that sin is pleasant to the depraved heart, and that its *pleasures* may be enjoyed? (Heb. xi, 25,) and that self-denial is required to abstain therefrom? (Psalm lxxxiv, 10; Luke ix, 23; 1 Cor. xv, 19.) But further: How would such secret retribution answer the public ends or design of God's moral government, and vindicate his character and uphold the authority of his law? And let it be remembered, also, that much of that which is thus called the recompense of virtue and vice arises from the conviction that there is a future state. Take away that idea, and many a wicked man would cease to be troubled on account of his crimes.*

Hence, therefore, as there is no regular or adequate distribution of rewards and punishments in this world, and as the moral character of God requires that there should be such a distribution, so it follows that there is a future state of being in which such distribution shall be recompensed, both to the evil and the good; and not only may the aspirations of good men be referred to in support of this conclusion, but also the fearful apprehensions and anticipations of the wicked, when a sense of guilt or remorse for any evil action has taken hold of them. There is a realization of moral responsibility in such cases, and an apprehension that the soul shall, in a future state, eat the fruit of its own doings, and reap what it has sown. No man can divest himself entirely of all apprehension of future retribution,

* An instance of what frequently occurs in this respect is related by the Rev. Warren G. Jones, and may serve as an illustration of the truth of the above statement. "An aged Sabbath-breaker, when I (says Mr. Jones) asked him one Sabbath morning what he expected would become of him, replied, '*Why, I hope to be annihilated!*' and in that hope he went on sinning till he died, and thus obtained (according to Annihilationism) the accomplishment of his wicked desire." See J. T. 38. So too, *Hierocles*, in his commentary on the Golden Verses of Pythagoras, says that "the wicked man would not have *his soul to be immortal*, (*ἀθάνατον εἶναι τὴν αὐτοῦ ψυχὴν*,) that so he might not abide under punishment." And Socrates says: "If death be extinction, or freedom from all evils, this will be *good news to the wicked*." (*In Phædone.*) Dionysius Halicarnasseus, the celebrated historian, also observes that, "if the soul, when separated from the body, perishes, it is not easy to discern how good men can be happy, who receive no fruit of their virtue here, but often perish by it." (Antiq., lib. viii, p. 539.)

or of that anticipation of something after death which leads men

> "To rather choose to bear those ills they have
> Than fly to others that they know not of."

They themselves, therefore, are conscious that they do not meet the full recompense of their crimes in this world. These anticipations are common alike to the pagan and the Christian world. And as God has not implanted them within the soul merely to delude and deceive us, so they are a proof that it shall pass into another state, where those apprehensions shall be realized, and where exact justice shall be done to the evil and the good. Such distribution, therefore, according to the innate conviction of all men, is merely deferred until man shall have passed through his present state. This conclusion cannot be avoided, and hence it is manifest that there is a future state for both the righteous and wicked. This is the only solution that presented itself to the mind of Asaph, (Psalm lxxiii,) and the only satisfactory solution that can present itself to the mind of any man.

Mr. Dobney, though he has not by any means stated the argument in its real strength, yet confesses that it is the strongest and most satisfactory argument that reason can adduce, (p. 105,) and is willing that the conclusion, "*there remains therefore another state in which all shall be adjusted*," shall stand as a logical conclusion from "*good reasoning*." He justly concedes this to the argument, for what man of but moderate intelligence and reflection can concede less. Let us therefore now attend to the methods by which he endeavors to obviate its application to the point we are maintaining.

His *first* exception is based upon the distinction which he makes between a *future state* and *immortality;* as man may live in a future state and yet not live forever. He therefore admits that the argument renders a future state "probable, even in a high degree," but claims that it does not show that man must live *forever*, in order that the anomalies of threescore years and ten might be rectified. (Pp. 105, 106.)

As my design here is to consider the theory of our Annihilation friends, I shall not stop to claim for this argument more than is thus conceded. How, then, does this concession bear upon the theory of Mr. Dobney and his friends? They maintain that the wicked are to be annihilated. This annihilation takes place *at death*, from which, some of them say, the wicked are not to be raised, though the majority maintain that while the wicked are annihilated *at death* they are to be hereafter raised from the dead in order to be annihilated over again.* Now, let it be here observed, 1. That while the argument *confessedly* renders a future state of retribution in the highest degree probable, there is not the least principle in nature which would lead to the supposition that in that state of being our existence is to terminate. A future state of existence being granted, therefore, the burden of proof is with those who affirm that our existence will then terminate. Then all analogy is against it. If in this world our existence is not terminated, but survives all the changes through which we pass, and to which we have referred above, it is fair to infer that it will continue in that state upon which we confessedly enter at death.

Further, experience teaches that matter is imperishable. No process is known by which it can be annihilated, nor can the least conception be formed even of the possibility of its annihilation. It is still imperishable, though undergoing unnumbered changes in the processes of solution, evaporation, rarefaction, decomposition, and combustion, for these processes themselves are merely the effects resulting from the changes which have already taken place, and which indicate that the new combinations have been completed. And this being so, how infinitely more probable is it that the mind, which directs and controls the activities of matter, and *confessedly survives the stroke of death, is likewise imperishable?* To affirm of the less that it is *imperishable*, and of

* A few references will suffice. D. 111, 164, 165, 185; C. 21, 22; Has. 25, 38; S. 14, 64; E. 234, 239; H. 2, p. 93, note; H. 1, p. 120, 142; A. 96, 115.

the greater that it is *perishable*, would be to array one's self against all the dictates of reason. Mr. Dobney's attempted distinction, therefore, between a future state and immortality, is of no consequence here.

But, 2. This very distinction, as made and applied by Mr. Dobney, is based upon an equivocation. He maintains that something less than eternity (by which he means unending duration) would be sufficient to rectify all the anomalies of the present state, thus confounding the idea of rectification with that of the non-existence itself of the subject who is to receive it. He moreover assumes (and this is the basis of the objection) that time may be compared to eternity. But suppose, for illustration, that man's probationary state in this world should continue a thousand, or a thousand million years, that period would still bear no more proportion to the eternity which shall succeed than the period of seventy years would bear to it, and the objection, therefore, would be equally plausible in that case as in this. If the objection proves anything, therefore, it must prove that rational creatures can never be justly placed in a state of probation.

3. The aforesaid argument, as already remarked, is conceded to teach a future state for the reward of virtue and the punishment of vice. Now the theory of Mr. Dobney and his friends logically denies, save by a vain disclaimer, a future state *to the wicked;* for to call that a future state which consists merely in being raised from the dead in order to be deprived of future existence, is an abuse of language. Mr. Dobney and his friends affirm that man passes from conscious existence into nothingness at death, and that the doom of the wicked is privation of existence (if, indeed, they are raised from the dead) after the resurrection; so that if they are not raised from the dead, the argument which is admitted to teach a future existence is falsified; and if, on the contrary, they are raised merely to be deprived of future life, where is there any future existence for them? They have no existence between death and the resurrection, and after the resurrection they have none; for these writers, *una voce*,

teach that immediately after the Lord accepts the righteous at judgment, he sweeps the wicked into the process of utter extermination. Mr. Storrs, indeed, says that he does not know how long they may be in undergoing annihilation; but as the Annihilationists maintain that not torment but privation of being is the penalty of sin, it is plain, on their own showing, that the wicked, in strictness and propriety of language, *are wholly deprived of a future state of existence;* for to call that a state of existence which consists in undergoing the process of extermination by consuming fire is simply theologastrian.

I need say but little as to the character which these views attribute to God. The penalty of sin, say our opponents, is privation of being, and not suffering or torment, and the wicked are utterly deprived of existence at death. Why not let them remain then in non-existence? They sin not, if annihilated, between death and the resurrection; and why bring them into being again merely to make them perish over again? What should we think of a ruler who, after hanging a man, would resuscitate him merely to hang him over again? And then, if the anomalies of the present life are rectified, as these men assert, by the salvation of the righteous and the annihilation of the wicked, and if not suffering but privation of existence (*mera annihilatio*, as some of the Socinians express it) is the design of God in inflicting the penalty, then of course those anomalies would be wholly rectified by raising from death the righteous and rewarding them, and permitting the wicked to remain annihilated. The idea that these disorders would be better rectified merely by annihilating the wicked over again is sheer absurdity. And hence the foregoing admission of Mr. Dobney is fatal to his whole theory. He *admits* that the argument fairly proves a future state of the wicked, and his theory *denies* that there is substantially any such state for them.

4. In this same connection he throws out an intimation or two which evince a consciousness on his part that the theory of which he is the advocate is only in the process of its prac-

tical development. I can, however, notice them but briefly. And *first*, he denies that God is under obligation to inflict upon the wicked *all* the evil that justice would allow him to inflict, and denounces the idea that infinite or perpetual suffering can be due to a finite agent, however vile he may be. The parentage of this sentiment it is not difficult to trace. Well has Isaac Taylor remarked: "Every one who has reflected maturely upon the workings of the human mind, perceives that, whether the fact be confessed or concealed, the stress of the controversy concerning the divine mission of Christ pends upon the doctrine of future punishment. The affirmations of our Lord and his apostles on this subject, though they fall in with the smothered forebodings of conscience in every man's bosom, give a distinct form to apprehensions from which the mind strives, by all means, if possible, to escape, and which it will never cordially admit, until the moral faculties be rectified. *The quarrel of the world with Christianity comes to its issue upon this doctrine of future retribution.*"*

Now it is only from the word of God that we know what the claims of Divine justice are against the sinner. Those claims are made known not only by the law directly, but by the threatenings of God against sin; and if God is not obliged to execute what he has threatened, but may remit as much as he pleases of the punishment thus denounced, it is plain that he is really under no obligations to execute his threatenings at all; so that if annihilation be the penalty against sin, he is not bound to execute it, and Mr. Dobney and his friends have therefore no real grounds of assurance that the wicked shall be annihilated.

That God may remit his threatenings in relation to man in the present world is most certainly true; for here they are mostly conditional, and mean no more than this: I will punish you if you do not repent. (See Jer. xviii, 7, 8; Ezek. xviii, 32; xxxiii, 8–11.) This is as it undoubtedly should be in a state of probation. But to extend the idea

* Saturday Night, p. 219.

from a probationary to a retributory state, is at war with all the principles of reason. The cases, so far from being in any way analogous, are as opposite as hell and heaven.

Now it will be conceded that God's threatenings against the *finally impenitent* are but the expression of his justice against unrepented sin. As we are not therefore to suppose that those who die impenitent will repent and be converted *after death*, so if their punishment, as denounced by justice, be remitted either in part or in whole, we must conclude that either God has changed, or that when he uttered the threatening he did not design to inflict it. Mr. Dobney and his friends may take either alternative.

I shall not here pursue this topic further than to remark, that either God may justly inflict upon the wicked what he has threatened, or it is unjust for him to do so. If he may justly do all that he has threatened, then Mr. Dobney's declaration *is false;* but if it be unjust, then we are of course either under no obligation to believe the word of God, in which those threatenings are recorded, or we are obliged to believe that God will act unjustly. Should it be said by these men that the finally impenitent deserve more than God will inflict upon them, I should like to learn by what rule their desert is ascertained, if it be not by the law of God. And if the law of God is to settle it, then the exception is a mere quibble, for God will certainly execute the penalty of the law. And let our antagonists likewise remember that the wicked are to have "judgment *without mercy*." Jas. ii, 13.*

5. The other intimation of Mr. Dobney presents an equally striking exhibition of his theological sympathies. In such terms as the following he lauds the men (and their doctrine) who taught that virtue and vice are their own reward: "Some of the *loftiest and purest minds* of antiquity," "men of *noble* spirits," "the *elevated* doctrine," "such *noble* spirits," "the conclusion would have been *nobly denied* by some of the *very best* men that antiquity can produce." And all this

* See Part III, infra, in which this whole subject is thoroughly considered.

on two pages! This "*elevated* doctrine" which teaches that depraved and polluted men may indulge in whatever iniquity they choose, provided they are willing to endure the *qualms* of an obdured conscience, has found "*noble*" advocates also in our own day, who, on this basis, have contended that *all* men, without exception, are received at death to the pure bliss of heaven. They will doubtless be pleased with Mr. Dobney's eulogy.

### § 20. *Conclusion of the Argument from Reason.*

The manner in which our antagonists treat the argument from reason for the immortality of the soul, is a fair subject for animadversion. They at the outset adopt the material philosophy, with its endless concatenation of unimaginable absurdities, and assume that its principles are consistent with and based upon the dictates of reason. This assumption we of course deny, and sustain the denial by a thorough investigation of the real facts in the case. When this is done they thereupon vary their ground of assault, quote eminent writers who have asserted that the immortality of the soul cannot be *demonstrated* by the light of nature alone, and then accuse us of being conscious that revelation does not clearly teach the doctrine, as otherwise we should care nothing about the argument from reason. If, on the contrary, however, we consent to dispense with the argument from reason, and appeal to revelation alone, they thereupon assume that we are conscious that reason does not sustain the doctrine, as otherwise we should not have abandoned an appeal to her decisions. Thus, whether we employ or dispense with the argument, our antagonists pretend to find ground for triumph in this controversy. To give such a procedure a name would be a work of supererogation in the estimation of an intelligent reader.

Now let us understand the matter fully before we proceed. I care but little, intrinsically, for the argument from reason in its *positive relation* to this inquiry. But it is of use in other important relations to it. For example, the

Materialists (those who reject the Bible as well as those who profess to believe it) assume that reason is silent on the subject, and from that assumption infer that the doctrine in question is false. We meet them here and disprove both their assumption and inference. But in every case where they are willing to rest the decision of the question on the testimony of the Word of God, we are willing to dispense entirely with the argument from reason. Written revelation is abundantly clear, and to it we of course make our ultimate appeal. The reader will not therefore misunderstand our design in this chapter in employing the argument from reason, or in our contemplating it under a somewhat varied aspect in chapter iii, for the unfair procedure of our antagonists in this controversy renders it necessary; and to them we now commend its issues, (in its relation to their own theory,) as fairly presented by us in the foregoing pages, while we proceed to consider, in its relations to the subject, the next great division of the argument.

# CHAPTER III.

## THE TESTIMONY OF THE NATIONS CONSIDERED, AND OBJECTIONS TO THIS PORTION OF THE ARGUMENT ANSWERED.

### § 21. *Early Knowledge of the Doctrine—Explanation of 2 Timothy* i, 10.

It will be of course admitted by all who believe the Bible, that God in the beginning made known to our first parents the principles of moral and religious obligation. Religion, as Butler remarks, could only have entered the world by revelation, for nothing could have rendered man so enlightened hereon as the Scriptures represent him to have been in the first ages of the world, but such a revelation, or divine communication, teaching him what was his original, whither his end, the duties demanded of him, and the terms on which God would proceed with him in justice or mercy.*

Such being the undisputed fact, we may fairly conclude that whatever we find on this subject among the nations which answers to the *written* revelation of God's will, must owe its origin not to human speculation, but to the aforesaid original communication from God to man. Before the flood he conversed with Adam, Abel, Enoch, and Noah; and after it with Abraham, Jacob, etc. (Heb. i, 1; Jude 14, 15.) With Adam he conversed immediately after his creation. The first words of the serpent to Eve prove her knowledge of him; and Cain, after his sin, "went out from the presence of the Lord." Nor could Enoch and Noah have walked with him without a distinct and accurate knowledge of his will.

* See on this subject also the works of Dr. Ellis on the Knowledge of Divine Things, and Whence cometh Divine Knowledge?

It is usual with our antagonists, however, to represent as in conflict with this statement, the declaration of the apostle in 2 Tim. i, 10, that "life and immortality are brought to light through the Gospel." They attempt no thorough exegesis of the passage, but dissever a part of it from its proper connection in the paragraph, and deduce from that part of it their unwarrantable conclusions, and so attempt to array an inspired declaration directly against the clearest possible array of undisputed facts. A signal instance of such procedure is found in the recent work of Archbishop Whately. In pp. 13–27 of his "Future State" he speaks as follows: "We are told by the Apostle Paul (2 Tim. i, 10) that it is 'our Saviour Jesus Christ that hath abolished death, and brought life and immortality to light through the Gospel;' that it is to him, and to him alone, that we owe this revelation—'the bringing in of this better hope'—(as it is expressed in the Epistle to the Hebrews.) That neither Jew nor Gentile had, or could have, an assurance of a future state but through the Gospel, is a truth so plainly taught in Scripture, and so fully confirmed by what we read in other books concerning the notions formerly entertained on the subject, that its having been doubted or denied by any Christian is to me a matter of unfeigned wonder. There are, however, not a few who do deny or overlook this truth, I mean who maintain, or who take for granted, that the doctrine of a future life was revealed to the Jews, and was discovered by the ancient heathens, and *consequently* (for there is no avoiding that *consequence*) that Jesus Christ *did not* 'bring life and immortality to light,' but merely gave men an additional assurance of a truth which they already knew." "It was then Jesus Christ who brought 'life and immortality to light,' and founded the doctrine, not on ingenious philosophical arguments, nor on obscure traditions of which no one can tell the origin, but on the authority of his own assertions, established by the miracles he wrought, and especially by that splendid one of rising himself from the dead, as the 'first-fruits of them that slept,' to confirm his promise to his disciples that he would raise up also at the last day his faithful followers. On the nature of that future state which he *then revealed and proved*," etc., etc. The same substantially is repeated in D. 167–176, and others.

That a celebrated scholar should, in this age of philological and critical learning, hazard a criticism like the foregoing, and deduce such conclusions in the very face of the most undeniable facts, is truly a matter of astonishment. Had Dr. Whately only consulted the Apocrypha, he would have found, in its clear and unequivocal announcements of immortality and of a resurrection, that his conclusions were utterly fallacious; or had he reflected that these doctrines were familiar to the Jews when Christ first appeared among them,* he might have been led to spare his expressions of surprise. In the passage on part of which he offers the foregoing comment, there is a clear reference to the fact that from the earliest ages (as the phrase means in Greek usage) God had given us grace in Christ Jesus, (v. 9,) and also that this grace was manifested by Christ, "who abolished *death*, and brought life and immortality to light through the Gospel." The term death here refers to Gen. ii, 17, and means the penalty of the Divine law. It was incurred by Adam, and through him brought upon all the race. The record of its *abolishing* is also given in Gen. iii, 15, the *proto-evangelium*, as it is rightly named. And by this abolishment our forfeited life and immortality were brought to light, or brought again within our reach, and hence we read that the people of God, under all the former dispensations, were justified by faith and died in faith. Compare John i, 9.

The attempt to restrict the term *Gospel* to the period of

* See John v, 39. So, too, *Tacitus*, speaking of the Jews, says: "They think that the souls of those who perish in battle or by punishments are eternal. Hence their contempt of death." *Numenius*, also, who flourished under Antoninus Pius, (in his lib. 1. *De Bono*,) places the Brahmins, Jews, and Egyptians among the nations who entertain the doctrine of Platò on the Immortality of the Soul. See the note of Grotius on Matt. v, 20.

our Saviour's advent, and subsequent thereto, must furnish matter of surprise to any one conversant with the Bible. The mere quotation of a passage or two, and a reference to a few others illustrating the subject, are all that will be necessary to set this subject in its true light. "And the Scripture foreseeing that God would justify the heathen through faith, *preached before the Gospel unto Abraham.*" Gal. iii, 8. Paul, likewise referring to the rebellious Jews who perished in the wilderness, expressly says: "For unto us *was the Gospel preached* as well as unto them." Heb. iv, 2, 6.* Compare also Gen. xxii, 18; Heb. xi, 13, 39, 40; 1 Pet. i, 10–12; John viii, 56; Luke ii, 29, 30; x, 24; Gal. iii, 7–9, 14–18.

The Gospel in its true and proper sense is a revelation of the grace of God to fallen man through a mediator.† Hence the original, ἐυαγγέλιον, signifies good news, or glad tidings.

In its true as well as technical sense, therefore, it imports

* The peculiar idiom in this passage is of frequent occurrence in the Scriptures. See, for instance, Psalm lx, 5; Mark xvi, 6; Acts v, 30; x, 19; xv. 11; 2 Cor. viii, 21; Heb. xi, 40.

† The truly profound Pascal, speaking on this subject, says: "That religion which consists in the belief of man's fall from a state of glory and communication with God, into a state of sorrow, humiliation, and alienation from God, and of his subsequent restoration by a Messiah, *has always been in the world.* All things else have passed away, but this, for which all other things exist, remains. For God, designing to form for himself a holy people, whom he would separate from all other nations, deliver from their enemies, and lead to a place of rest, promised that he would do this, and that he would come himself into the world to do it; and he foretold, by his prophets, the time and manner of his coming. In the mean while, to confirm the hope of his elect through all ages, he continually exhibited this aid to them in types and figures, and never left them without some assurances of his power and willingness to save; for at the creation of man Adam was made the witness and depository of the promise of a Saviour to be born of woman. And though men, at the period so near to their creation, could not have forgotten their origin, their fall, and the Divine promise of a Redeemer, yet since the world in its very infancy was overrun with every kind of corruption, there were however, holy men, as Enoch, Lamech, (Gen. v, 25–31,) and others, who with patience waited for that Saviour who had been promised from the beginning of the world." (Thoughts, chap. iv, section 5.)

the whole scheme of mercy and salvation toward man from the moment of its first announcement. Christ is its author, and by it he has brought life and immortality to light. He brought it to light first to Adam, then to Abraham and others, and finally appeared on earth incarnate, and more fully declared and confirmed its truth by his teaching and miracles, and death and resurrection; and this is just what Paul asserts in the passage under consideration. And the rays of this Gospel, thus originally announced to our first parents after the fall, continued for many ages to give light to the nations, until wholly obscured by sin, and sensuality, and materialism.

The statements of revelation on this subject ought certainly to be sufficient for any serious mind. They inform us that when Adam, our covenant head and representative, proved unfaithful to his trust, and by obeying the suggestions of Satan became his servant, (see Rom. vi, 16,) and thus virtually surrendered to him that government of this world which had been entrusted to him, (Psalm viii,) Satan usurped the dominion, and so erected his own kingdom here. Matt. xii, 26; Luke iv, 5–7; Col. i, 13; Acts xxvi, 18; Heb. ii, 14, 15, (where κράτος, translated *power*, means *kingdom* or *dominion*. Compare Matt. xxii, 32,) and is thereafter recognized as the prince or "god of this world." John xiv, 30, and xvi, 11, and 2 Cor. iv, 4; Eph. ii, 2. The original constitution provided for the continuance and propagation of the human race irrespective of their obedience, (Gen. i, 28; compare also iii, 16;) and thus the world and its inhabitants, being severed from God and his favor, were brought under his displeasure, and became slaves and instruments of Satan. Hereupon, and in accordance with the covenant of redemption, the world with all its interests was immediately placed in the hands of the Son of God, who became our Mediator and second Adam, for the purpose of abolishing all these operations of Satan, (1 John iii, 8; Isa. xlix, 24, 25; liii, 12,) and to subvert his kingdom and restore earth to its pristine state; and this he will ultimately accomplish, (Rom. viii, 19–23, and 2 Pet. iii, 9–17,) and then render it back to the immediate government of God. 1 Cor. xv, 24–28.

This work he at once commenced by denouncing Satan, and promising a deliverer to man. (Gen. iii, 14–24.) Thus life and immortality were, through him, brought again to light, and within our reach. The world is therefore Messiah's world, and all its interests are at his disposal. The offer of deliverance could come only through him, and in consequence of his intervention on our behalf. And all revelations and dispensations previous to his advent were only preparations for his manifestation to men as their Prince and Saviour, God manifest in the flesh.

In exact agreement with this representation we find, even according to the admission of learned infidels themselves, advocates, too, of the material philosophy, the doctrine of the soul's immortality known and believed by mankind in the earliest ages of the world. *Lord Bolingbroke*, for instance, declares that "the doctrine of the immortality of the soul, and a future state of rewards and punishments, began to be taught before we have any light into antiquity. And when we begin to have any, we find it established that it was strongly inculcated from time immemorial, and as early as the most ancient and learned nations appear to us."* *Volney*, too, who maintained that "the soul is but the vital principle which results from the properties of matter," admits that all the earliest nations taught that it survived the body and was immortal.† "This doctrine," says he, "was taught in India, Siam, Ceylon, Japan, China, etc., by Beddou (Zoroaster) 1027 years before Christ; it is found in Orpheus, Pythagoras, and the Indian gymnosophists. Pythagoras lived in the ninth century B.C.," and Orpheus much earlier; and the Egyptian priests recite that Hermes, as he was dying, said: "I have hitherto lived an exile from my country, to which I now return. Weep not for me. I ascend to the celestial abode where each of you

* Works v, 237. † Ruins of Empire, pp. 157–160, 162.

will follow in his turn; there God is; this life is only death." Volney avers that Hermes lived upward of a thousand years before Christ. These admissions are important in this connection, and their number could be increased almost indefinitely from the writings of both ancient and modern opposers of the doctrine of immortality.

Another point, which demands a brief notice in this stage of the argument, is, that the doctrine of *incorporeal substances* was clearly understood and announced by the ancients. This is most amply demonstrated by Cudworth,* and it is unnecessary here to do more than merely refer to it. The opinion that there was no other substance than that which is palpable and material, was directly opposed by the best of the ancient philosophers, and "condemned for a piece of sottishness and stupidity." Plato expressly asserts the existence of a substance distinct from body, and which he sometimes names *incorporeal substance*, *οὐσίαν ἀσώματον*, and sometimes *intelligent substance*, *οὐσίαν νοητήν*, in opposition to the other, which he names *sensible*, *αἰσθητήν*; and in this matter Aristotle plainly agrees with his master, and asserts that *there is another substance besides sensibles.* In *some* of their schools it was a sort of maxim that whatever is incorporeal must be destitute of perception and pleasure, (as having no sensuous organs,) a maxim which Epicurus endeavors to make the most of, and which Aristotle seems to have sometimes admitted; and hence that declaration in his Nicomachian Ethics, so often referred to by Dr. Whately, who endeavors to deduce such unwarrantable conclusions from it as we shall see on a future page. How extensively this doctrine of incorporeal substances was entertained by the philosophers both before and after Plato, may be seen in the passages of Cudworth mentioned above.

It has been asserted, and the Annihilationists have made the most of it, that with the ancients the doctrine of the

* Intellectual System of the Universe, chap. i, sec. 18–22, 41, 42. Works, vol. i, pp. 70-76, 110, 111.

soul's immortality was always associated with that of its pre-existence and transmigration. This however is untrue. In the later schools of philosophy these ideas became associated, and the one was regarded as implying the other; but it was only after they had adopted the notion that the soul was sempiternal, being a part or particle of the Divine substance. Now Pherecydes Syrus, as Cicero plainly informs us,* was the first who taught that the souls of men were eternal: *Animos hominum esse sempiternos.* He was the master of Pythagoras, and from this sentiment was evolved the doctrine of transmigration. In the same sense also *Laertius*† intimates that Thales (who was cotemporary with Pherecydes) was thought to be the first who held that the souls of men were *immortal*, using ἀθάνατος in the sense of *sempiternus*, employed by Cicero, and also as related to the Divine nature. But previous to this we never find immortality associated with transmigration. A single fact will illustrate this: Homer, who so fully expresses the popular idea of the immortality of the soul, yet never in any way, either directly or by implication, intimates anything concerning transmigration. There is not the slightest trace of it in his works. But Virgil, his copyist, who lived after this idea had gained entrance into the schools of philosophy, gives it a full expression; and hence, therefore, we may see why our blessed Saviour, and his apostles and evangelists, who address themselves not to the philosophers, but to the popular mind, always in their teachings take for granted that the doctrine of the soul's immortality is true, and that those to whom they in the main addressed themselves recognized it as true. And whatever may be the explanation of the strong fact that all nations entertained the firm conviction that this doctrine is true, whether they obtained it from tradition or from reason, or from a consciousness of its truth, the fact itself is undeniable, as we shall now proceed to show.

* Tusculan Quest., lib. i, cap. 16.

† Lib. i, sect. 24.

## § 22. *Specific Testimonies.*

*Diodorus Siculus*, cotemporary with Julius Cæsar, declares (lib. 18, cap. 1) that Pythagoras and others of the eminent naturalists, (φυσικῶν,) taught that the souls of men are immortal.

*Lactantius*, speaking of *Zeno*, the founder of the Stoic philosophy, says that he taught that "the abodes of good men in Hades (*inferos*) were distinct and separate from those of the wicked; the former inhabiting pleasant and delightful regions, while the latter suffer punishment in places horrid and dark!"*

*Tertullian* also remarks that the Egyptian *Hermes* taught that the soul, when departed out of the body, still retains its distinct and separate existence.†

*Empedocles* also (according to Clement of Alexandria,‡) taught that "if we live holily and justly we shall be happy here, and more happy after we have departed hence: μακαριώτεροι δὲ μετὰ τὴν ἐνθένδε ἀπαλλαγήν: having our happiness not necessarily confined to time, but being able to rest in it permanently forever; enjoying intercourse with other immortal beings," etc.

The *Meheshtani*, who were disciples of Zoroaster, believed in the immortality of the soul, in rewards and punishments after death, and in the resurrection of the body; at the time of which resurrection all the wicked would be purged by fire, and associated with the good."§

The philosophical *Xenophon*, who was born B. C. 450, thus expresses the sentiments of Cyrus, when dying, as addressed to his sons: "Do not think that when I have finished my life among men I shall cease to exist. During my past life you saw not my soul, but by its actions you learned that it existed. I never, my sons, was persuaded that the soul lives only while inhabiting a mortal body, and dies when it has departed thence."¶

* Divin. Instit., lib. vii, cap. 7, page 369. † De Anima, cap. 33.
‡ Stromatum, lib. v, page 722.
§ Zend Avesta, as quoted by Jahn, Arch., sect. 314. ¶ Cyropædia, lib. viii.

*Socrates*, the father of Grecian wisdom, and the greatest of all the philosophers, taught in the fullest manner the same doctrine. As he was about to drink the fatal draught which the executioner had given him, he expressed his unwavering conviction of this truth, and his full expectation of meeting the souls of the mighty dead of former times. His words as recorded by Plato, (*Phædo*,) and addressed to *Simmias* and *Cebes*, are as follows: "If indeed I had no expectation of going to those gods who are both wise and good,* and then to men who have died, but who are happier now than those who still live on earth, I had done wrong in not viewing with anxiety the approach of death; but now, believe me, I hope to arrive among good men. This, however, I would not positively affirm. But be assured that I would affirm (if I may affirm anything of this nature) that I shall go to gods who, as rulers, are truly good. For these reasons I am not therefore concerned as I otherwise should have been, but fully expect that there remains something for those who have died, and something much better for good men than for the wicked, as has been said of old:" *ὥσπερ γὲ καὶ πάλαί λέγεται.* Dr. Whately's remarks on this testimony will be noticed in the sequel.

The views entertained on the same subject by *Plato* are too well known to require to be specified. Cato the Younger, (a Stoic,) after reading with great attention his book on the soul's immortality, committed suicide in order to rid himself of the burden of the present life, and to enter upon the life to come.

*Ælian*, another pagan philosopher of a later date, narrates that a person who was sorely tormented by a disease, being asked if he were willing to die, replied: "Why not? I indeed delight in the thought of being separated from the body; for then I shall be with Pythagoras and Homer, and all the great and virtuous men who have gone before me."

*Cæsar*, speaking of the Druids, or ministers of religion

* Such undoubtedly is the force of the words *παρὰ θεοὺς ἄλλους σοφούς τε*, etc., as employed in such a connection.

among the ancient Gauls and Britons, says: "Among their leading doctrines is this, that the souls of men do not perish at death, but pass from one body to another; thus they inspire the people with courage, and raise them above the fear of death."*

*Lucan* the poet (who was slain by Nero) says of the Druids:

> "Thrice happy they, beneath their northern skies,
> Who that worst fear, the fear of death, despise.
> Hence they no cares for this frail being feel,
> But rush undaunted on the pointed steel;
> Provoke approaching fate, and bravely scorn
> To spare that life which shall so soon return." †

*Plutarch* taught also that "it is absurd to imagine that souls are made only to blossom and flourish for a day in a tender and delicate body of flesh, and then to be immediately extinguished on every slight occasion." And that "the same reasons confirm the providence of God, and the permanency of the human soul, and that the one of these cannot be maintained if the other be denied; and that since the soul exists after death, it is probable that it partakes of rewards and punishments."‡

*Dionysius Halicarnasseus*, the historian already referred to, says: "If, along with the dissolution of the body, the soul also, τῆς ψυχῆς, whatever it may be, is dissolved, I know not how those can be supposed to be happy who have enjoyed no advantage by virtue, but have perished on account of it."§

*Maximus Tyrius* also says: "What the multitude call death is but the beginning of immortality, and the birth into a future life." "The soul having put off this earthly body becomes a demon," *δαιμόνιον*;¶ a word which, though employed only in an evil sense in the holy Scriptures, signifies among the Greeks an intermediate being between men and the gods, and may be either good or evil.

*Herodotus* also, (the father of history,) who flourished

* De Bell, Gal., lib. vi, 13. † Pharsalia, i, 806. Rowe's Translation.
‡ Opp., tom. ii, p. 560. Francof, 1620.
§ Antiq., lib. viii, p. 539. ¶ Dissert, 27.

B.C. 450, referring to the same subject, says: "The Egyptians, who first taught that the soul of man is immortal, say that when the body is dead the soul enters into some other living creature, as it is born in that succession which is continually coming into existence; but when it has gone through creatures of land and sea, and through birds, it returns into a human body, newly born."*

*Strabo*, who lived at the beginning of the Christian era, speaking of the ancient Brahmins, says: "According to Megasthenes, they discourse much on death, for they regard our present life as merely the state of creatures fully conceived, and death as a birth to that which is really life; a life of happiness to those who have cultivated wisdom. Hence they are studious to prepare for death."†

*Cicero* also strongly maintained the doctrine of the soul's immortality, and its separate existence after death, asserting, too, that such was the belief of all nations. He regarded the doctrine of future retribution as consequent upon that of the soul's immortality, and as deducible from the attributes of God, and the condition of man's life on earth. A brief passage or two will suffice from his writings. In his Tusculan Questions, after referring to and condemning the views of the old materialist philosophers, he adds: "But the views of the others may afford hope, (if perchance this pleases thee,) that souls when they have passed out from their bodies, can enter into heaven as their dwelling place."‡ Then in his tract on Old Age, he says: "But if I err in believing the souls of men to be immortal, I am willing to err,§ nor while I live would I wish to have the delightful error removed. And if I shall feel nothing when dead, as is thought by some minute philosophers, I am not afraid that dead philosophers shall laugh at me for the error." In connection with the foregoing positive testimonies, we may here adduce facts also of another descrip-

* Lib. ii, sect. 123. † Lib. xv. ‡ Lib. i, c. 11.

§ *Lubenter erro.* Why is this always preposterously translated "*I err willingly?*"

tion, and which furnish a further illustration of the same point. For example, the testimony incidentally afforded by the ancient and universally practiced art of magic has no little weight. Of course, this art presupposes the existence of spiritual agents; though, in its widest sense, *magic* is the art of performing something which surpasses the natural powers of men, by the aid of superior spirits.* Its first inventor, according to Pliny, was Zoroaster, who practiced it among the Persians;† and its practitioners professed to hold converse with the dead, and even to make them appear, all of which supposes, of course, the universality of the belief that man ceased not to exist at death.‡ The same remarks apply also to *necromancy*, the art of learning the secrets of the future by conjuring up the dead. This too was generally practiced among the Orientals.§ The intelligent reader will not misapprehend the point which these facts are designed to illustrate. For the question is not how these processes may be explained, or whether they were not sheer "*humbuggery*," (to use a very expressive Americanism,) for all this may be admitted without in any way affecting the issue. The true point is this: These arts were universally practiced, and flourished greatly among all the ancient pagan nations; but as the very existence of those arts depended upon the recognition of the soul's immortality, so the fact that they universally prevailed and flourished clearly infers the universal belief of that doctrine. Then, again, the whole system of heathen mythology is based upon the same doctrine. Take, for example, the sacrifices and divine honors paid to heroes and great men after death, a practice so prevalent in every nation of antiquity except the Jews. Prayers and sacrifices were offered to them, which of course presupposes the full

* Knapp. Theol., p. 205. † Nat. Hist., lib. xxx, c. 1.

‡ See Homer, Odys. de Circe; Virgil, Ecl. viii, 69, seq., and Æn. iv, 487, seq.

§ See Homer, Odys. 11. Comp. also 1 Sam. xxviii, and Psalm viii, 19, along with Lev. xx, 27, and Isaiah xxix, 4. The Jews always practised it when they fell into idolatry.

conviction that their souls still existed. So too the descriptions and allusions to the subject in their approved writers evince the universality of the same belief. But on this topic it is needless to enlarge, and I shall proceed to cite a few more specific testimonies.

*Sir William Temple*, speaking of the ancient Goths, Vandals, Lombards, Huns, etc., says: "It is certain that an opinion was fixed and general among them that death was but the entrance into another life; that all men who lived lazy and inactive lives and died natural deaths, by sickness or by age, went into vast caves under ground, all dark and miry, full of noisome creatures, usual in such places, and there forever groveled in endless stench and misery. On the contrary, all who gave themselves to warlike actions and enterprises, to the conquest of their neighbors and the slaughter of their enemies, and died in battle, or of violent deaths upon bold adventures or resolutions, went immediately to the vast hall or palace of Odin, their god of war, who eternally kept open house for all such guests, where they were entertained in perpetual feasts and mirth," etc.*

*Hyde*, in his learned History of the Religion of the Ancient Persians,† says: "Some of them believe that the souls of the blessed were translated to the sun. Such was the opinion entertained by the Manichæans and other heretics. But the orthodox, as appears by the inscriptions in their cemeteries, asserted that after death the soul ascended to God, where it enjoyed a state of quiet repose until the resurrection; that it was then reunited to a body, and returned to this earth, which would at that time be renewed and purified; for the Indo-Persians profess to believe that the earth is to be formed anew at the general judgment. Upon the *judicial bridge* which extends over the gulf of hell, two angels were always stationed, having a pair of scales, in which the merits and demerits of men

* Essay III, Heroic Virtue.

† Cap. xxxiii, p. 491. See this and other testimonies in Abercrombie's Sermon on the death of Alexander Hamilton.

were carefully weighed; if the latter preponderated, they were cast down into the regions of misery; but if the former, they proceeded onward to Paradise."

*Sir William Jones*, speaking of the *modern* Persians, states that from time immemorial that numerous sect whose teachers are now known by the name of *Sùfis*, held that the human soul is an emanation from the Divine essence, which for a time is separated therefrom by its union with matter, but will return again to its original source; and that the chief good of mankind in this transitory world consists in as perfect a *union* with the Eternal Spirit as the incumbrances of a mortal frame will allow.*

The doctrine of the *modern* Brahmins concerning the nature of the soul is, according to *Mr. Wilkins*, thus delivered in the Bhăgvăt-Gēeta: "Thou grievest for those who are unworthy to be lamented, whilst thy sentiments are those of the wise men. The wise neither grieve for the dead nor for the living. The man who believeth that it is the soul which killeth, and he who thinketh that the soul may be destroyed, are both alike deceived; for it neither killeth nor is killed. How can a man who believeth that this thing is incorruptible, eternal, inexhaustible, and without birth, think that he can either kill or cause it to be killed! As a man throweth away old garments and putteth on new, even so the soul, having quitted its old mortal frame, entereth into others which are new. The weapon divideth it not, the fire burneth it not, the water corrupteth it not, the wind drieth it not away, for it is indivisible, inconsumable, incorruptible, and it is not to be dried away; it is eternal, universal, permanent, immovable; it is invisible, inconceivable, and unalterable; therefore believing it to be thus, thou shouldest not grieve."

*Purchas*, a most laborious researcher, gives the following account (which he published in 1625) of the belief of the Africans on the coast of Guinea in relation to the same subject: "We asked them of their belief, and what opinion

* Asiatic Researches, vol. ii, p. 62.

they had of divers things, as first, when they died, what became of their bodies and souls? They made us answer that the body is dead, (dies;) but they knew not what any resurrection at the latter day meant, as we do; but when they die they know that they go into another world, but they know not whither, and that therein they differ from brute beasts; but they cannot tell you to what place they go, whether under the earth or up into heaven; but when they die they used to give the dead body something to carry with him, whereby it is to be marked that they believe that there is another life after this, and that there they have need of such things as they have here on earth."*

In like manner *Edwards*, in his History of the West Indies, speaking of the negroes brought from the Gold Coast of Africa, says: "They tell me, likewise, that whenever a considerable man expires, several of his wives and a great number of his slaves are sacrificed at his funeral. This is done, say they, that he may be properly attended in the next world. This circumstance has been confirmed to me by every Gold Coast negro that I have interrogated on the subject, and I inquired of many."†

*Dr. Robertson*, speaking of the American Indians, says: "With respect to the other great doctrine of religion concerning the immortality of the soul, the sentiments of the Americans were more united. The human mind, even when least improved and invigorated by culture, shrinks from the thought of dissolution, and looks forward with hope and expectation to a future state of existence. This sentiment, resulting from a secret consciousness of its own dignity, from an instinctive longing after immortality, is universal, and may be deemed natural. Upon this are founded the most exalted hopes of man in his highest state of improvement; nor has nature held from him this soothing consolation in the most early and rude period of his progress. We can trace

* Purchas's Pilgrims, Part II., lib. vii, c. 2, sec. 4, p. 943.

† Hist. of West Indies, B. IV, c. 3. See Dr. Abercrombie's excellent sermon referred to above.

this opinion from one extremity of America to the other; in some regions more faint and obscure, in others more perfectly developed, but nowhere unknown. The most uncivilized of its savage tribes do not apprehend death as the extinction of being; all hope for a future and more happy state, where they shall be forever exempt from the calamities which embitter human life in its present condition."*

*Peter Martyr*, speaking of the arrival of Columbus on the shores of Cuba, mentions that an old Indian chief, aged about eighty years, came forward and addressed him thus: "We have been told that with your powerful army you have made a rapid progress through all those lands with which heretofore you were unacquainted, and that you have greatly terrified the people who inhabit them. Know then by my exhortation and admonition, that for the souls of men departed from their bodies there are two different ways of destination: the one dark and horrible, prepared for those who disturb and annoy mankind; the other pleasant and delightful, appointed for those who, during life, have loved the peace and tranquillity of nations. If you will remember that you are mortal, and that future retributions are reserved for every person, proportioned to his present actions, you will make no one unhappy."†

*Captain Cook*, in his account of the Friendly Islands, says: "The inhabitants have very proper sentiments about the immateriality and immortality of the soul. They call it life, the living principle; or, what is more agreeable to their notions of it, an *Otooa;* that is, a divinity or invisible being. They say that immediately upon death the souls of their chiefs separate from their bodies and go to a place called *Boolootoo*, the chief or god of which is *Goolcho*. As to the souls of the lower sort of people, they undergo a sort of transmigration."‡

*Mr. Anderson*, in his account of Otaheite, says: "The in-

* History of America, B. IV, c. 7. *Works*, p. 842. London, 1831.

† Lib. iii, Dec. 1, p. 43, anno 1574.

‡ B. II, cap. 11, vol. i, p. 405, anno 1785.

habitants believe the soul to be immaterial and immortal."*

It were easy to add indefinitely to these testimonies; the foregoing are, however, sufficient.

But we are told that the doctrine of the soul's immortality could only have arisen from the speculations of men of genius; and that it was introduced by legislators to console mankind under oppression, or deter them from crime by motives drawn from future retribution. If this be so, how happens it that the doctrine has been universally held by all nations and in all ages? How happens it that it has found its way into the deserts, and has been diffused alike over the South Sea Islands and those of the Pacific; over Lapland and Asia, and the nations of benighted Africa? The nations of the Society Islands entertain it, and those too of the Friendly Islands; the New Zealanders also, and the inhabitants of the Pelew Islands, with the wild tribes of Kalmuc Tartary, and all the wandering tribes which have peopled and do still people the continent of America.

> "E'en the poor Indian, whose untutor'd mind
> Sees God in clouds, and hears him in the wind,
> Whose soul proud science never taught to stray
> Far as the solar walk or Milky Way;
> Yet simple Nature to his hope has given
> Behind the cloud-topp'd hill an humbler heaven,
> Some safer world in depths of woods embraced,
> Some happier island in the watery waste,
> Where slaves once more their native land behold," etc.†

To what then is all this to be ascribed? The idea that legislators or philosophers originated the doctrine is sheer absurdity.‡ The belief of it by these untutored tribes can-

* B. III, cap. 9, vol. ii, p. 164. † Pope.

‡ See the latest attempt to justify this puerile conceit in a work recently published by Mr. C. F. Hudson, called "Debt and Grace." (Pp. 276–282.) A *learned* work this! It informs us that *Achilles* commanded the Greeks at Troy, or else that *Thersites* was a *myrmidon*, (p. 273;) that *Seneca* the moralist and *Seneca* the tragedy-writer were the same person, (pp. 281–282;) and that the celebrated reformer, *David Pareus*, was a Romanist, (p. 258.) It misquotes *Aristotle*, and misconstrues him most ridiculously, (pp. 274–5;) shamefully misrepresents *Witsius*, (see title-page, and compare

not thus be accounted for. While they every day see their companions and neighbors die, they never see the pale corpse revive from its corruption. Is it pride that cherishes the fond anticipation? But is it pride that leads the unhappy African to plunge into the waves during the middle passage, or take his life when on the plantations, that he may return to his country only to be captured a second time? Is it pride, when in other nations (for example, in the Islands of Otaheite) the hope is restricted to a renovation of the same life that they had already led on earth? Can any reflecting mind entertain such a sentiment? No; there is no sufficient solution of the problem presented by these masses of universal testimony but the admission of the fact that *the soul is immortal*, and that there is in the breast of every man a consciousness of this truth.* In no other way can that vast array of facts in the case be fairly and candidly met, and rationally explained.

### § 23. *Issue presented by this Argument.*

I will now briefly state the issue which this argument presents, and then the exceptions taken to its conclusions by our antagonists.

*All nations have received the doctrine of the soul's immortality.* This universal belief, therefore, had some adequate origin; I will not say that mere unassisted reason taught it,

p. 420;) repeats the blunders of *Blackburne* in accusing *Luther* of holding the sleep of the soul, (pp. 258, 259;) falsifies the views of the German theologians, (p. 353;) and performs a vast number of other gyrations equally remarkable, and which it would take a pretty large volume to expose. The book has some good points, but the material is utterly in a crude and undigested state. It is entitled to little or no authority on the question before us, for no dependence can be placed upon the accuracy of its averments.

* The learned reader will be pleased to see in this connection the following: "*Omni antem in re consensio omnium gentium* LEX NATURÆ *putanda est.*" "*Natura ipsa* de animorum immortalitate *tacita judicat.*" (*Cicero*, Tusc. i, 13 sq.) So too even *Seneca*: "Quum de animarum æternitate disserimus, *non leve momentum apud nos habet consensus hominum*, aut timentium inferos, aut colentium." (*Epist.* 117)

but I do say that if mere reason did not, then either it originated from a convincing universal consciousness of its truth, or it was originally revealed to the human race, and has been handed down in the traditions of all nations. If pure, unassisted reason taught it, then of course it is not contrary to, but consistent with reason. If a universal consciousness of its truth originated the belief, then of course the conviction is based in nature itself, and is the impress of the seal of the Creator; and if it was originally revealed to mankind, as it undoubtedly was, (see § 21,) then of course God is its author. These are the facts, and here is the issue which they present.

But let us now turn our attention to the exceptions taken to this argument by our adversaries. As we may suppose, it has greatly perplexed their ingenuity, and they are even divided sadly as to the principle upon which it should be met. Some of them, for example, deny the facts *in toto*, while the others freely admit them all, and in view of them claim that the doctrine is thereby proved to be of pagan origin. We shall attend to each of these objections, for each has an important bearing upon the general result.

### § 24. *Their Denial of the Facts.*

We might naturally suppose that it would require no trivial amount of courage to come forward and deny the very existence of any such facts as those which we have so fully presented in the fore-cited instances; and in view of such denial we might be tempted to draw a very obvious conclusion as to the intelligence or honesty of the individuals who assume this position; but here at the outset we shall say nothing on the subject, but permit our antagonists to speak for themselves.

Mr. Storrs says: "There is *no evidence* that all nations and people believe it. There is evidence to the contrary;" and then referring to a passage from Socrates, in which he is represented as saying that most men believe that the soul will be annihilated as soon as it parts from the body, he adds: "Here the fact is brought out that, so far from its being a general belief that the soul is immortal, the exact reverse was true in Socrates' day." And then, after referring to the Sadducees, he adds: "Hence there is no truth in the argument that all nations and people have believed in the immortality of the soul." (S. 5.)

Another of their writers thus speaks: "I question the assertion on which the argument stands. As far as my knowledge reaches there never was, *in the absence of revelation*,* a general belief in, much less a desire for, immortality. In ancient classic lands no such belief existed," and in evidence he adduces Mr. Storrs's quotation from Socrates.†

In the same train Mr. Dobney follows thus: "I must profess my conviction that the only proper answer to the present argument is a denial of the premise, for surely if there were no such universal belief in the heathen world, *and in the absence of revelation*, it were a little too much to expect me to account for it."‡

All these writers quote Dr. Whately "as a witness *eminently entitled to profound respect*,"§ and the unfortunate "Essay on a Future State," by that celebrated prelate, is made to sustain unassisted the whole burden of annihilation authorship touching this question. We shall therefore permit the archbishop to speak for himself, for in showing the inaccuracy of his statements we shall of course show the inaccuracy of all.

"When we find Socrates," says Dr. Whately, "and his disciples represented by Plato as fully admitting, in their

* But if revelation does not teach the doctrine, how is the universality of its prevalence among Christian nations, and the Jews, to be explained by *the presence of revelation?* Will our opponents answer this question?

† M. 25, 26. ‡ D. 97.

§ D. 96. Mr. Dobney quotes Dr. Leland as saying that Cicero admitted that *in his day* the doctrine was denied by philosophers and learned men; but Mr. Dobney's optics alone can discover what this has to do with the fact that *originally*, and before the Epicurean philosophy came into vogue, all nations entertained it.

discussion of the subject, that 'men in general were highly incredulous as to the soul's future existence,' and as expecting that it would at the moment of our natural death 'be dispersed,' as he expresses it, 'like air or smoke, and cease altogether to exist, so that it would require no little persuasion and argument to convince them that the soul can exist after death, and can retain anything of its powers and intelligence;' when we find this, I say, asserted, or rather alluded to, as *notoriously the state of popular opinion*, we can surely entertain but little doubt that the accounts of Elysium and Tartarus were regarded as mere poetical fables, calculated to amuse the imagination, but unworthy of serious belief." "So far, indeed, were the promulgators of Christianity from finding the belief of a future state already well established, that they appear to have had no small difficulty in convincing of this truth *even some of their converts*."

In the same style Dr. Whately continues, and denies that the doctrine was ever generally admitted among the ancient philosophers. He specifies Aristotle, also, as utterly rejecting it, and as treating it with pointed contempt. Such is, in all its strength, the objection to the foregoing argument, and we shall now proceed to consider to what extent it may be regarded as strengthening the hands of our opponents.*

As to the attempt of Dr. Whately thus to drag Aristotle,

* Dr. Moore, of England, in one of that popular series of his works recently republished by the Harpers, thus refers to Dr. Whately's connection with the Annihilation theory: "A name famous in the subtleties of logic is associated with the defense of this notion, but it appears as if it had been with a total abandonment of his accustomed acumen, and in a desperate hope of modifying the objections of Materialists to the broad and unaccommodating language of revelation. It is a grief of soul to see the benevolent efforts of a lordly spirit so completely defeated by the extravagance of his ready accommodation *to those spiritual paupers who so sturdily ask charity because they have no faith.* Not being able to discover the least glimmering of reason to infer from the words of the Bible, or its spirit, that man dies with his body, the gifted writer referred to met the smiling skeptic half way, with a surmise that as the body seemed so essential to action in this world, it might be the appointment of Omnipotent Wisdom to keep the soul in a sound sleep somewhere until the resurrection, when it would find itself suitably provided with

the pupil of Plato, into such a connection, and to represent him as treating the doctrine of immortality with pointed contempt, the reader may know what to think of it presently. Had he said that the views of that prince of philosophers were not at all times logically consistent on the subject, he would have asserted *the utmost* that facts will even appear to justify. It is apparent to any reflecting mind, that in the topics on which Aristotle treated, in the works which have come down to us, there was little call or occasion for him to present *his own views* of the doctrine in question; and a single illustration will show the egregious unfairness of Dr. Whately in this whole procedure. Sir Robert Boyle, a philosopher but little inferior to Aristotle himself, has, like him, treated in his philosophical works* on a vast range of topics under the general heads of physics, pneumatics, natural history, medicine, etc., furnishing him with frequent occasion to refer to or remark upon the subject in question; and yet, unless I greatly err, there is but a single mention of his views on this subject, (except in two or three theological tracts, in vol. ii, 229–280,) throughout the whole of his three volumes. Suppose, now, that an individual should undertake to prove from that fact that this pious and warm-hearted Christian philosopher disbelieved the doctrine of the soul's immortality, he would act as fairly as Dr. Whately has acted, and merit the same consideration.

In this illustration, however, it is admitted, for argument's sake, that Dr. Whately's statement on the subject is correct. But this is not the fact, for in the treatise *De Anima*,† after remarking that the powers of the mind

a machinery to work with. *But this purposeless slumber of the soul served only to excite the greater ridicule of the unbelieving and profane, while deepening the sorrow of the devout;* for the notion seemed to imply that the Maker of all worlds, being deficient in materials to employ human and departed spirits, laid them by in dormant idleness until a new organization could be conveniently arranged for their use, which might be after indefinite ages had rolled over their transmuted dust." (See "Man and his Motives," by George Moore, M.D., pp. 41, 42.)

* I refer to Dr. Shaw's edition, in three volumes, quarto. London, 1738.

† Lib. iii, cap. 5.

and body are very different, Aristotle proceeds to illustrate the statement by referring to the senses of smell, hearing, and sight, "which," says he, "may be so overwhelmed and confused by too intense a manifestation of their objects as to be unable to act; while, on the contrary, the mind can as easily, and even more easily, from the elevating influence of the object, conceive of and contemplate the greatest objects, as those which are less. It would appear, therefore, that while the sentient part of man is not capable of being separated from the body, *the mind itself is separable*," *τὸ μὲν γὰρ αἰσθητικόν οὐ κἄνευ σώματος ὁ δέ νοῦς χωριστός*; a plain sanction of the doctrine of his master, Plato. In the third book of the same treatise he also extols Anaxagoras for designating the mind as something *pure and unmixed with anything*, (*νοῦν ἀμιγῆ*.) It is true that both Atticus and Origen accuse him of doubting or denying Plato's doctrine; but Plutarch, a true philosopher, and a far more competent witness, represents him as teaching that "Death pertains not to the soul, but to the body alone, for there is no death to the soul." *θάνατον εἶναι μόνον τοῦ σώματος, οὐ ψυχῆς, ταύτης γὰρ οὐχ ὑπάρχει θάνατος.**

In exact accordance with this, he, when elsewhere speaking of the necessary qualifications or pre-requisites of the body, in order to its occupancy by the soul, says: "Men are as careless on this subject as if it were even so that, according to the Pythagorean fables, any soul might enter into any body; on the contrary, every animal as it has its proper species, so it has its appropriate form; but those who teach otherwise speak as if one should affirm that the skill of a carpenter entered into a flute, for every art must have its proper instruments, and every soul its proper body."† While he here, therefore, allows the doctrine of pre-existence, he repudiates the fable of Pythagoras, that

* De Placit. Philos., lib. v, cap. 25. The remark of Hippolytus, charging Basilides with "*teaching the doctrine of Aristotle, the Stagyrite*, respecting the immortality of the soul," likewise deserves attention. Basilides taught the doctrine of the soul's separate and continued existence.

† De Anima, lib. i, cap. 3.

the soul of a beast might enter a human body. Then, in another part of his works,* wherein he treats the question of the pre-existence of souls, and also whether both the sensitive and rational souls pre-exist before they enter the human body, he concludes by saying: "It remains therefore that only the rational or intellectual soul enters from without, as being of a nature purely divine."

Such are the deliberate and matured views of this philosopher in respect to the nature of the soul; and what then is the amount of the declaration in his Nicomachian Ethics, to which we have referred already, and of which Dr. Whately and the Materialists endeavor to make so much? In the chapter in which it occurs,† Aristotle is treating of *courage*, and the passage referred to reads as follows: "What sort of fearful things, then, has the courageous man to do with? the greatest: for no man is more able than he is to undergo terrible things; but death is the most terrible of all things, *for it is a limit, and it is thought that to the dead there is nothing beyond, either good or bad,*" *φοβερώτατον δ' ὁ θάνατος· πέρας γάρ καὶ οὐδὲν ἔτι τῷ τεθνεῶτι δοκεῖ, οὔτε ἀγαθὸν, οὔτε κακὸν εἶναι.*

This, then, is a fair rendering of the famous passage which, according to Archbishop Whately, is to reverse all the other statements of Aristotle, and at once turn over to the Materialists and Annihilationists the prince of philosophers, who held that the human soul was *particula animæ divinæ.* He moreover gives an import to the language which the words will not bear, when he charges Aristotle with here affirming that "death is the complete and final extinction of existence, *beyond which there is neither good nor evil to be expected,*" words which belong to Dr. Whately, and not to Aristotle. But in precisely the same manner in which he here refers to the opinions of others respecting death, he likewise, in this same ethical treatise,‡ refers to the subject again as follows: "For if there is some good

* Generat. Animal., lib. ii, cap. 3. † Nicom. Eth., lib. iii, cap. 6.
‡ Lib. i, cap. 10.

and evil to the man who is alive and who is not aware of it, there may be supposed to be some to the dead man also, as honors and dishonors, and the good and evil fortunes of children generally." Let the whole paragraph, however, be carefully read.

It seems, however, impossible to obtain from the former of these passages any idea as entertained by Aristotle *himself* respecting the soul. The word translated "*it is thought*" may refer to his own view, but does not necessarily refer to it; but even should it be so regarded, nothing would be proved more than an inconsistency—a Homeric nod—making little against his more full and elaborate declarations elsewhere given. And it is simply absurd to attempt, by this questionable interpretation, to offset, not only those fuller statements, (see also those found in his Ethics, lib. i, c. 8 and 10,) but also the emphatic declaration of Plutarch, above given, or that of the author of the life of Pythagoras, quoted by Photius, and in which he expressly affirms that "with one consent both Plato and Aristotle agree that the soul is immortal, though some, not fathoming the profound mind of Aristotle, suppose that he held the soul to be mortal." *κὰν τινες εἰς τὸν 'Αριστοτέλους νοῦν οὐκ ἐμβαθύνοντες, θνητὴν νομίζουσιν αὐτὸν λέγειν.*

And now, with respect to the much insisted on argument from the case of Socrates, and which, on Dr. Whately's authority, is, and long has been, doing its evil work in the minds of men, I shall not pause to inquire how, or on what principle the meaning of a passage which obviously refers not to the common people but to the philosophers, and not to the world at large but to Attica, and not in the remotest sense of it to *previous* ages, but to Socrates' own times, has become so extended as to constitute a valid objection to the foregoing argument, and to include not only the Athenians, but mankind at large; not only Greece, but all nations; and not only the age in which Socrates lived, but all preceding ages. The inquiry might be interesting, and the topic itself would furnish a fair theme for pointed animadversion, especially in such a case as the one before us, where a writer professes to have examined a subject *de novo*, and under that assumption, and by a most partial and distorted view of facts, undertakes to effect a change in the minds of men on subjects deeply affecting their welfare through eternity.

As to the expressions quoted from Socrates and Cebes, I had intended to lay them before the reader, and to show, by a thorough criticism, how utterly unfair is the construction put upon them by Dr. Whately and our opponents.* But admitting for the argument's sake that they refer, not to the generality of those philosophers with whom Socrates was conversant, but to the generality of the men of Attica, upon whom he had so assiduously labored to inculcate his philosophy, how does this possibly touch the issue of the argument before us? In what way can it be made to affect at

* Dr. Whately will, I have no doubt, fully believe me when I say that it is inexpressibly painful to my feelings to be compelled thus to refer to a gentleman and a writer for whom I have, through the most of my life, entertained a high admiration and regard. In reference, however, to the matter here in discussion, I would ask him in all earnestness whether there either is or can be any grammatical or rhetorical propriety in attempting to construe, according to a strict literality of the words, that common phrase of Socrates—"*as most persons think*," or "*as most men believe*"—and of every body else, and on which the Doctor's statement is based? It occurs, unless I greatly err, several times even in the *Phædo* itself, and such expressions are common to all nations and times, and no one ever dreams of understanding them literally. In familiar conversation we say, for instance, of any given statement, "*everybody believes it*," "*all persons think so*," at the same time that we know that not one person out of a thousand of mankind believes or thinks anything about the matter, and we mean no more by it than that most of our acquaintances who have expressed themselves on the subject think or believe so. Socrates, in this familiar and cheerful conversation with his friends, could have meant nothing more, and I am persuaded that his words would never have been regarded as meaning anything more, or as presenting an offset to his deliberate and serious asseverations above referred to, had it not been for a total misapprehension of the real import of 2 Tim. i, 10. But let the reader consult Grotius, in Matt. v, 20, and the *Harmonia Apost.* of Bishop Bull, *Dissert. Post.*, cap. x. Compare, likewise, Grotius *De Veritate Rel. Christ.*, lib. i, cap. xix, usque ad xxiv.

all the testimony of preceding ages, and of other nations? and how then does it in any way conflict with the truth of the statement that all nations *originally* entertained the doctrine of immortality? Few works on the art of reasoning can be studied with more advantage than Dr. Whately's Logic, and few men in their reasonings have more fully than he set at defiance all its principles. But a heavier charge than that of employing an infirm logic lies against Dr. Whately in this matter. He certainly knew of the frank and full declarations of Aristotle himself, and of Socrates, and of others of the very philosophers referred to, that previous to their own times, and from the earliest ages, this doctrine was universally received by mankind: why then, in a professed discussion of such a topic, should he thus keep it in the background? The subject is an extremely painful one, and I shall not dwell on it. I submit a few facts to the reader, and appeal to his judgment in the matter.

*Socrates*, for example, says, in a passage which we have quoted above, that he fully expects that there is something to be enjoyed by those who are dead; and that, *as has been taught in ancient times*, ὥσπερ γὲ καὶ πάλαι λέγεται, "it is much better for good men than for bad." So, too, in his apology to the judges, he thus refers to the same doctrine: "If the things which are told us are true," εἴπερ τὰ λεγόμενα ἀληθῆ ἔστιν; wherein he evidently refers to some ancient traditions which were regarded as sacred or divine. And *Plato*, in writing to Dion, says: "We ought always to believe *the ancient and sacred words*, which teach us that the soul is immortal, ἀθάνατον ψυχὴν εἶναι, and that it hath judges, and suffers the greatest punishments *when it is separated from the body*;" and in his *Timæus* also, where he speaks of "those endless punishments which attend the remains of unhappy men; and all those torments, which I highly applaud the Ionic poet *for recording from ancient tradition*, in order to cleanse and purify the mind from vice."

*Aristotle* also, as quoted by Plutarch, speaking of the happiness of men after their departure out of this life, represents it *as a most ancient doctrine, so ancient that no man knows when it began, or who was the author of it*, and which had been handed down by tradition from the remotest ages. *Plutarch* also, in his consolation to *Apollonius*, declares that it was "so ancient an opinion that good men should be recompensed after death, that he could not reach to either the author or original of it." *Polybius* also states (lib. vi, cap. 54) that "the ancients with great wisdom propagated the doctrine of a future state, and particularly of future punishment;" while *Cicero* also says of the immortality of the soul, that "it has been held by the best authors; and that *all* the ancients (*omni antiquitate*) *agreed to it* who were more worthy of credit, and the more likely to know the truth the nearer they approached to the first rise of mankind, and to their divine original;" and he argues from the consent of all nations concerning it: *consensu nationum omnium*. *Seneca* also, in a passage cited above, (sect. 23, note,) admits the same *universal consent*, and states that it is of no small importance in the argument. And now, in view of all these facts, I would merely ask, What are we to think of the aforesaid denials of Dr. Whately and our antagonists, that there is any evidence of the existence of such universal consent?

It is related in the Hindoo mythology that *Bistnoo*, having created a large serpent and a tortoise, placed the earth upon the head of the serpent and stood him erect upon the tortoise, (see *Theol. et Philos. Indica*, by A. Duperron, tom. i, 657, 683.) The resting-place of the tortoise, however, was found to be by no means answerable to his responsibility. So with the present annihilation theory. It rests upon the serpent, and the serpent leans for support upon Dr. Whately, (who represents the tortoise,) and Dr. Whately, as we have seen, *rests*, if the Hibernicism may be pardoned, *upon nihility*. His whole statement and argument on the subject before us are utterly destitute of foundation; and I trust he will have the candor and Christian principle to arrest the evil which they still are effecting, by promptly retracting both.

We shall now proceed to consider the other ground of exception to the foregoing argument.

### § 25. *Their Admission of the Facts.*

I have, in the beginning of this chapter, briefly pointed out the manifest origin of this universal belief in the immortality of the soul. In later ages the doctrine became greatly obscured by philosophical speculation. Until, anterior to the time of Christ, the prevalence of the Epicurean philosophy had well nigh, among the learned men of the Greeks and Romans, blotted it out of existence. The rest of the nations however continued to receive it.

It is of no consequence how the nations and people whose testimony we have cited above defined the *soul* or *spirit* of man, or what they thought of its *materiality* or *immateriality*, (in the philosophical sense.) It is enough for our argument that they held it to survive the body, and that it is immortal. It is not at all necessary that they, any more than we, should know precisely how to describe and define its essence; and all objection to the argument therefore on this ground is puerile.

In reply to our argument, while some of our opponents, as we have seen, totally deny the facts on which it is based, others frankly admit them to their fullest extent, and on the ground of this admission denounce the doctrine as of pagan origin. Their books are filled with such denunciations, and we shall here present a specimen of them. They have had, from the bold impudence with which they are made, considerable influence upon the minds of the illiterate, and hence the importance of giving them a particular notice.

One of the writers referred to, in his reply to Mr. Lee, says: "(Mr. Lee) has proved, overwhelmingly and incontestibly proved, the PAGAN ORIGIN *of the popular doctrine of immortality!* He has triumphantly sustained the very position we have long maintained, namely, *that the immortality of the soul is pagan in its origin, and was generally believed among pagans*." "If he receive *the pagan idea of immortality*, he must take along with it the pre-existence of souls." "*The pagan tradition of the soul's immortality* not only renders null and void the resurrection," etc.* Again: "The notion that there is life in the soul of the wicked, or a principle that cannot die, was taken from the Platonic philosophers, and was introduced into the Church as a Scripture doctrine in the third century." "It originated in heathen philosophy, and was grafted on to Christianity to its immense injury."† So, too, in another work, extolled by our opponents as a *wonderfully learned* production,‡ we have the following *polite* remarks: "The pagan philosophic theology of the present day." "It is absurd and wicked to infer that it (the soul) is immaterial and immortal, to favor a pagan fable," etc. "The pagans originated the idea of the immortality of the soul." "Christians have adopted these fables, and inserted them into their creeds."§ This writer is peculiarly gross and indecent in his vituperation of the doctrine on the same assumed ground. But we have presented a sufficiency of such wretched stuff.

The avowed basis of all these vituperative scurrilities is, that the doctrine referred to was received and taught by the nations (as above shown) who were not favored with a written revelation. We have sufficiently explained how the doctrine originated among them; but we shall not trouble our readers by exposing the fallacy of the inference, *that because the nations entertained the doctrine they therefore originated it.* We shall merely invite our antagonists to an application of the principle *to their own theory.* It is a poor rule, says the proverb, that will not work both ways; and if the recognition of the doctrine of immortality by the

* See A. 44, 45, 55. † S. 82.

‡ "A David to slay Goliath," "a standard work," "three years were spent upon it," etc., etc.; see B. 44.

§ See E. 3, 10, 39, 42, 43, 134, 230, etc. See also H. 1, pp. 118, 135; and H. 2, pp. 83, 85, 91.

best and purest minds of antiquity proves it to be of pagan origin, what conclusion shall we draw from the fact that the very doctrine of our opponents respecting the mortality of the soul originated with the ancient Epicureans and Atheists, and has ever since been maintained by Atheists, Infidels, Socinians, Universalists, Nothingarians, etc. But let us here briefly refer to its paternity, and trace its genealogy down to the present time. A *Historia Dogmatis* may be of no little service to our antagonists, for their works generally afford the best of evidence (notwithstanding their prodigious pretensions to the contrary) that, believing "much study to be a weariness to the flesh," they are inclined to get along with as little as possible.*

Early, in the Grecian states, philosophy began to array itself against the universally received doctrine of the soul's immortality. The professed and distinguished tenet of some sects of philosophers was, that the soul was mortal and died with the body. Such were Democritus and his followers, the Cynics, etc., and especially the wide-extended

* In the preceding section we have had several interesting specimens or illustrations of this in the case of D., M., and S., and the writings of the sect contain many more equally interesting. S., for example, evinces his familiarity with Rabbinic lore, by always calling the *Gemara* the *Germara;* see no less than four such instances on a single page in his Appendix, p. 15, 21st edition. The manner in which they quote *Hebrew* is truly edifying, see E. *passim;* and their quotations from the Greek, and especially their use of the letters in spelling the words, may yet revolutionize Hellenistic orthography. See, for example, F. 17, and J. T. 36. The old philosopher, "Hobbs," is also uniformly divested of one of the letters of his name, (pp. 30, 36, etc.) And in one of their *latest* publications, Locke, the metaphysician, is uniformly transformed into "*Dr. J. Lock, Esq.*, the great mental philosopher and Christian," "Dr. Lock," "Dr. John Lock's Question," etc. B. 36–38. In the same work "The *Calde*, or Babylonian Targums," are referred to, (p. 62;) while the first President Edwards is occasionally mentioned, who, as appears from this book, wrote a reply to Dr. Chauncey some thirty years after his own death. How they will reconcile *this fact* with their denial of the separate existence of the soul, is not for me to say. But the above specimens, and thousands of others that can be adduced, evince that these writers are not disposed to over-estimate the importance of literature; and who can tell but that they are preparing to renounce formally all connection with it, on the ground that it is a "relic of barbarism."

sect founded by Epicurus. Plutarch, in speaking of the sentiments of these two philosophers, mentions that they "*taught that the soul is corruptible and perishes with the body*," precisely the doctrine of our Annihilationists.

*Epicurus* was the most determined foe to the doctrine of immortality. He taught that the soul was a subtile elastic gas, composed of the most sublimated parts of the atmosphere, and introduced into the system in the act of respiration, and hence that it must be material and mortal. It comes, says he, from a material source, exists in a material system, is nourished by material food, grows and is matured with the material body, and declines with its decline, and hence must die when it dies.

The atheist *Lucretius*, his follower and fervent admirer, taught the same doctrine in his celebrated poem, *De Rerum Natura.*

*Bayle** portrays their theory briefly as follows: "Death disunites the parts of these bodies, but destroys nothing of their substance. Those that the earth supplied are restored to the earth, and those which descended from the regions of the ether ascend thither again." These very terms are employed by our Annihilationists in depicting their theory. (See § 5.)

*Dicæarcheus* also, an eminent Peripatetic, to whom Cicero so frequently refers, (in *Tuscul. Quæst*, lib. i,) wrote several books to prove that the soul is mortal and dies with the body. *Pliny* the naturalist also thus teaches the same: "All men are in the same condition after the last day of their life as before the first, nor have they, after they are dead, any more sense either in body or soul than before they were born."† *Seneca*, too, teaches that death is alike the end of, and release from, all our pains and sorrows; for the evils of this life do not extend beyond it. It replaces us in the same tranquil state in which we were before we were born."‡ It will doubtless be very gratifying to our

* Crit. Dict., Art. LUCRETIUS.

† Hist. Nat. lib. vii, cap. 55.

‡ In Consol., ad Marciam, c. 19.

opponents, to see how thoroughly their fundamental principles were discovered and reasoned out without the aid of revelation by these eminent philosophers. We might in like manner quote *Galen*, who declares that he "violently suspects that the essence of the soul is corporeal, because in all its powers and operations it depends upon the dispositions and temperaments of the body;" and in like manner we could adduce the *high* authority of *Hobbes*, *Toland*, etc., but we shall present an instance or two from more modern times.

The *profound Voltaire* has defined and illustrated the same doctrine in his usually *convincing* style. The following are a few extracts from his writings on the subject.* He says: "My being rewarded or punished after death, requires that something which feels and thinks in me must continue to subsist after me; now, as no part in me had any thought or sense before my birth, why should it after my death? What can this incomprehensible part of myself be? Will the humming of the bee continue after the end of its existence? Thus the *soul* itself, which signifies our memory, our reason, our passions, is only a bare word." Then, after employing sundry of the very same illustrations which we find in the works of our Annihilationists, he thus proceeds: "How can I be rewarded or punished when I shall cease to be myself, when nothing which constituted my person will be remaining?"

The equally profound *Volney*, the atheist, also denounces as "*profane inventions*" the immortality of the soul, its transmigration to places of pain or pleasure, its resurrection, the final judgment, good and bad angels, etc.; and in reference to the first of these he reasons as follows: "The soul is but the vital principle which results from the properties of matter, (see § 5 above,) and from the action of the elements in those bodies where they create a spontaneous movement. To suppose that this product of the play of the organs, born with them, matured with them, and which sleeps with them, can subsist when they cease, is the

* Philosophical Dict., vol. i, pp. 42–48. London, 1775.

romance of a wandering imagination." "Solomon, who lived one hundred and thirty years before Pherecydes, treated it as a fable."*

Such then is the paternity and development of this *interesting* speculation which our Annihilationists now advance as the teachings of the word of God. Let it not be supposed, however, that they are so vain as to imagine themselves to be the first who have attempted to engraft it upon Christianity, for they do not claim this honor. The Socinians of the sixteenth century for a long time strenuously persevered in making the same experiment, and in fact, as we shall hereafter see, our Annihilationists are indebted to them for many of the criticisms on the texts of Scripture which are urged against their theory. They taught expressly that "man by death undergoes such a total dissolution (*annihilatio*) as to be altogether nothing, except that his spirit, as a kind of wind or breath, returns to God, for that breath is a kind of virtue or efficacy derived from him. Hence, souls after death have no sensation, and really do not in themselves subsist." Like our Annihilationists, they did not all entirely agree in their views, but such was the prevailing doctrine. Their modern disciples also advocate the same. Dr. Priestley's views are sufficiently known. And *Mr. Belsham*, with his peculiar and characteristic modesty, speaks upon the subject as follows: "No well-informed observer of the phenomena of human nature *can believe* that the soul is capable of perception and activity in a state of separation from the body. To maintain this would be to maintain a doctrine contradicted by reason, by analogy, *and by uniform and universal experience.*"†

The modern Universalists have made similar attempts to

* Ruins of Empires, pp. 122, 162, 163, 227. Dublin, 1811.

† "Summary View," etc., p. 178. Boston, 1808. Mr. Belsham had a peculiar way of illustrating the truth of the maxim, *Omne tulit punctum, qui miscuit utile dulci.* But whose "uniform and universal *experience*" does he refer to in the above extract? Perhaps our antagonists may try to tell.

engraft the theory on Christianity. For example, *Abner Kneeland*, (who subsequently adopted it in its full development, and became an atheist,) while pastor of a Universalist church in Philadelphia, thus taught: "Although the consequences of death would have been eternal had it not been for eternal life, yet the consequences would not have been eternal misery, but an eternal extinction of being; for death is an extinction of life. Hence natural death puts an end as much to moral death as it does to natural life, because a man cannot be even *carnally minded* in a state of natural death." He adds also in a note: "It will be perceived here that the author does not believe in an intermediate state of conscious existence between death and the resurrection, and of course death to him is an extinction of being, and all his ideas of a future state of existence are predicated on the glorious doctrine of the resurrection. This point will not be labored in these lectures; but if any one thinks otherwise, he is requested to read attentively Dr. Priestley's Disquisition on Matter and Spirit."* So too *Mr. Ballou* says: "The doctrine of a future state of retribution must owe its origin to some other source than the Holy Scriptures, and to some other wisdom than that which is from above."† Their *great* critic *Balfour* also says: "No sacred writer mentions an *immortal* soul." "There is no *immaterial*, *immortal* soul which lives in a conscious state of happiness or misery in a disembodied condition. This doctrine has been the fertile source of much error and human misery." "The doctrine of the immortality of the soul seems to have had one common origin among the heathen." "But it may be asked, Is not the doctrine of the soul's immortality revealed in the new Testament? No; for if it was taught there, it would be no revelation from God to the world, for it was a popular doctrine among the heathen nations many centuries before the Christian era. With more propriety it might be said, the heathen

* Lectures, p. 48. Philadelphia, 1824.

† Collection of Valuables, p. 304. Montpelier, 1836.

revealed this doctrine to God, than that God revealed it to them."*

But it is not necessary to continue these references and quotations. Let the reader consider, however, that such is the doctrine (heathenish and atheistic in the highest degree) advocated most strenuously by the Annihilationists, who at the same time denounce the precious truth of God as pagan, popish, and what not, and who are scattering through this country and Europe their crude productions, assailing in the most scurrilous manner the doctrine of immortality, and all who entertain it, while the doctrine which they themselves advocate is the miserable offspring of heathenism and atheism.

## § 26. *Conclusion.*

The following fact, while it serves to conclude the foregoing argument, may also appropriately introduce the argument from Scripture upon which we enter in the next chapter.

The apostle, in Titus i, 2, refers to a very ancient revelation of the doctrine of immortality. His words are very remarkable: "God promised eternal life, *πρὸ χρόνων αἰωνίων*, before the endless ages," a phrase on which we shall have occasion to remark more fully in the sequel. A similar phrase occurs in 2 Tim. i, 9, where it is said that God "gave us grace *in Christ* before the world began," not "*on account of* Christ," as some shallow critics would

* Inquiry, pp. 143, 146, 342, 343. Boston, 1832. The reader will observe the beautiful consistency between the above statement and that of Dr. Whately. The argument from the Testimony of the Nations must, at any rate, be "squelched" in some way, but these writers cannot exactly agree upon the mode. Dr. W. says: "The doctrine of the soul's immortality was not known to the heathen, since if it was known to them *the New Testament does not reveal it.*" Mr. B. says: "The doctrine was a popular belief among the heathen, and therefore *the New Testament does not reveal it.*" So that the argument is answered on the ground that the New Testament both contains, and does not contain the doctrine. *Query.* Would it not be an improvement of this reasoning if the conclusion of the arguments were employed as the premises, and the premises as the conclusion!

render it, (for ἐν *never* has that sense in connection with a proper name,) but *by* Christ. The promise was to us, fallen creatures, by Christ. It was a promise of the immortality which we had forfeited, and of course it contemplates the period of time subsequent to the fall, and at the very introduction of the Gospel (Gen. iii, 15.) And hence Chrysostum, Theodoret, and Œcumenius seem to express the exact idea, ἄνωθεν ἐξ (ἀπ') ἀρχῆς, *from the beginning*. The grace devised for us in the eternal covenant was thus at the very beginning made known to us by Christ. Here then was the origin of the aforesaid universal belief. And how beautiful and interesting is the illustration of its universality and antiquity, which is, as above remarked, presented by those wonderful productions of Homer, the earliest of the Greek writers! He lived before the Greek philosophy was cultivated, and of course before the atheistic notions of Protagoras and Epicurus were dreamed of. And hence in his doctrine respecting the soul there are no metaphysical speculations; nothing respecting its materiality, past eternity, pre-existence, transmigration, or of its being a portion of the soul of the world, or an emanation from the Deity. His ideas of it were obviously not the result of reasoning or speculation, but the remains of this early and universal tradition; a tradition so emphatically referred to by Socrates and Aristotle, and still later by Cicero and Seneca, as above shown.

# PART II.

IN WHICH THE ARGUMENT FROM THE SCRIPTURES IS CONSIDERED, AND ALSO THE VIEWS ENTERTAINED ON THE SUBJECT BY THE ANCIENT JEWS AND CHRISTIANS.

---

## CHAPTER I.

### TERMS EXPLAINED: ARGUMENT FROM THE OLD TESTAMENT.

§ 27. *Terms Explained.*

In treating the Scripture argument, our opponents uniformly endeavor to attach a sense peculiar to themselves, and which the exigences of their theory demand, to several important Scriptural terms; and as this is a subject which radically concerns their exposition of texts, it will be proper, before we proceed with the argument itself, here at the outset to notice a few of the more important of those terms, and the use which they endeavor to make of them. From the positive dogmatic tone of assurance with which they treat the topic, it is apparent that our opponents think themselves wiser than the rest of mankind, simply because they differ from them in their views of these and other topics. What they profess to offer in justification of their own strange use of the terms, will be fully considered when we come to examine their *argument from the use of words*; all that is necessary here is that, in connection with the Scriptural argument, we present also a brief exposition of these terms as employed in the Bible.

1. *Death* is a term which is perpetually occurring in their sermons and writings. Their manner of using it is as follows: The law of God denounces the penalty of death for sin, and as death is a cessation of existence, and as the penalty of death is inflicted upon man, so man is mortal, soul and body, and soul and body alike must cease to live. I shall not here remark upon the strangely illogical character of this argument any further than its use of the term death is concerned. And, first, this usage confounds all those clear and obvious distinctions which the Gospel makes on the subject of human salvation. If the penalty of the law is death, in the sense of annihilation of both soul and body, let it be remembered that those who believe in Jesus and receive him as their Saviour, are saved from the penalty of the law, in strictness of speech, for "there is *no condemnation* to them who are in Christ Jesus." Rom. viii, 1. And certainly Enoch, Elijah, and Moses, at least, were not annihilated. But this usage necessarily confounds the believer with the impenitent, and utterly annihilates the existence of both between death and the resurrection.

But, secondly, death, in the Scriptural sense of the term, and as related to the subject before us, does not imply an actual cessation or even suspension of existence; and our opponents ought not to theorize on the subject, but confine themselves to the clear representations of the word of God. Let us briefly consider a few examples of the use of the term; and to give our opponents all the advantage they could desire, we shall select also one or two instances of its use when applied to subjects which confessedly are not endowed with immortality. Take then the example of the seed-corn sown in the earth. Our Saviour says: "Except a corn of wheat fall into the ground AND DIE, it abideth alone; but *if it die* it bringeth forth much fruit." John xii, 24. And in referring to the same matter, Paul, addressing a skeptic, says: "Thou fool! that which thou sowest is not quickened, *except it die*." 1 Cor. xv, 36. Now in these passages the term death is used in its obvious and ordinary import; and yet it does not imply even a suspension of vitality, for through the whole process of *death* the living germ retains its vital power unharmed. The outer coat molders away, but the principle of life is still there, vital and active. So too in the case of the devil and his angels; the curse of God, or the penalty of the law, has been inflicted upon them, but they still live; that death has not suspended their existence, for they believe and tremble, and are reserved in chains of darkness until the judgment of the great day. Why then should the existence of the spiritual part of man's nature be suspended by an infliction of the same penalty? But it is not; for Christ expressly asserts the fact when he said that Lazarus *died* and was carried *by the angels* into Abraham's bosom, and that the rich man *died and was buried;* and in hell he lifted up his eyes, *being in torments.* Now it is of no consequence to the argument whether this be a parable or not; for, be that as it may, the language here employed by Christ evinces that the term death, as applied to man, does not even suppose a suspension of conscious existence. Why then should these men attach to that term a meaning which is wholly foreign from the Bible, and then apply their unfounded and false definition to prove that the soul of man shall be blotted out of being? In the whole Bible there is not an instance in which the term *death*, as applied to either human or angelic nature, imports a loss of conscious existence. See also §§ 44, 45, 46, *infra.*

2. They employ similar equivocations respecting the term *life.* The Holy Spirit employs the term often in the sense of simple *existence*, and also uses it to signify *well-being*, as when Christ is said to have brought *life* and immortality to light. In the *former* of these senses it is used in such passages as the following: "The moving creature that hath *life.*" Gen. i, 20. "God did send me before you to preserve *life.*" Gen. xlv, 5. "The breath of the Almighty hath given me *life.*" Job xxxiii, 4. See also Job iii, 20. The same usage obtains in the New Testament. Christ says: "Take no thought for your *life.*" Matt. vi, 25. Can this possibly

mean that men are to take no thought for their salvation? So also says Peter: "The time past of our *life* may suffice us to have wrought the will of the flesh." 1 Pet. iv, 3. This use of the word is of frequent occurrence.

In the *latter* of these senses it is employed in such passages as the following: "I have set before thee *life;*" that is, God's favor, blessing, etc. Deut. xxx, 15, 19. "Thou wilt show me the path of *life.*" Ps. xvi, 11. "Righteousness tendeth to *life.*" Prov. x, 16; xi, 12; xix, 23. "The fear of the Lord is a fountain of *life.*" Prov. xiv, 27. So, too, all through the New Testament. "If thou wilt enter into *life.*" Matt. xix, 17. "Ye will not come to me that ye may have *life.*" John v, 40. "Narrow is the way that leadeth to *life.*" Matt. vii, 14. "That believing ye might have *life* through his name." John xx, 31. "Shall reign *in life* by one, Jesus Christ." Rom. v, 17. "To be spiritually minded *is life.*" Rom. viii, 6. "Christ, who is our *life.*" Col. iii, 4. "He that hath the Son hath *life.*" 1 John v, 12. Now our opponents are compelled to admit that in all these passages the term *life* is employed to signify salvation, or eternal happiness. And yet in all their discussions they never once even allude to the fact that the term is employed in the Bible in these two senses. The point is a most vital one in this controversy, and enters into the very heart of the great question as to what the Scriptures teach respecting the soul's immortality; and yet, without exception, the teachers of annihilation keep in the background the truth that the word in the Bible is employed as it is in common conversation in these two distinct senses. And on the ground of their most unfair and garbled presentation of the matter at issue, they quote passages in which the term *life* in the sense of *eternal happiness* is employed, and apply them as though the term had no other meaning than that of *simple existence* itself. Now why should men thus conceal the truth from their readers or hearers, and in a matter, too, of such immense importance to their eternal welfare? What can they hope to gain either for themselves or others by such shameless perversions of the word of God? It is a striking truth that these two terms alone, when understood in their Scriptural sense, sweep away utterly from all its muddy moorings the whole annihilation theory. In fact, it is actually based upon a most shallow perversion of them.

3. There is a similar equivocation in their use of the term *immortality.* They perpetually repeat that immortality came by Jesus Christ alone, and that therefore those who do not receive Christ as their Saviour cannot be partakers thereof, and consequently must be blotted out of being. Now this is trifling with the use of language; and the whole argument is based upon a confounding of *mere existence* with *eternal well-being.* I have above pointed out the clear distinction which the Bible makes on this subject, and need not here repeat it. We owe our entire existence to Christ as our Creator; but to say that we owe it to him as our *Redeemer* is an abuse of language. It might with the same propriety be said that man's mortal and material body came by Christ, *as our Redeemer*, as to say that the immortal spirit thus came by him. It is impossible to imagine how a serious and thoughtful mind can confuse such obvious distinctions.

4. In their management of the Scriptural argument there is another procedure on the part of our antagonists which should be here noticed, and by which they endeavor to perplex the plainest testimonies. For example: where a plain spoken text is adduced by us, and which leaves no tangible ground of escape for the Annihilationist, he endeavors to bedim the luster of its testimony by referring to some of those expressions in Proverbs, Ecclesiastes, and Job, relating to the dead and death, taken from the *popular* language of the Orientals; thus sanctioning the preposterous absurdity of endeavoring to explain the clear announcements of the New Testament revelation by the confessedly obscure teachings of the Old, and making the Old Testament the key to the New, instead of the contrary. And thus all their proof texts, with two or three exceptions, are derived from the Old Testament; and all this, at the same time that no peo-

ple on earth are louder in their professed attachment to the Gospel as a clear, and full, and glorious revelation. To see persons with such loud-sounding professions perpetually going back to the confessedly most obscure book in the Bible, (Ecclesiastes,) in order to obtain light that they may explain the clear revelations of the Gospel, is certainly a most *edifying* spectacle. But to the point. In the Old Testament the dead are said to be inactive, and to know not anything, etc. It is an Oriental idiom, simple and beautiful, by which things are described from their appearance. Neither the Jew nor Arabian ever misunderstands such language. The man, to all appearance, in death becomes inactive; ceases to mingle any more in the affairs of this life; all his thoughts and plans in respect to this world have perished; he knows not anything; all appearance of sense and knowledge is gone. Such is the appearance presented by death; and hence death is described in language which presents this idea and expresses this appearance. So, too, the dead are said to *sleep*, because there is a striking apparent resemblance between death and sleep.* Not only the Orientals, however, but every nation has adopted such language on the subject, notwithstanding their belief in the soul's uninterrupted immortality. Even our American Indians employ it; although in speaking of one who is dead they say, "He will now see his father, his grandfather," etc. We, too, in our popular language, employ the same terms on the same subjects, and speak of the *sleep* of death, and of the destruction which it brings. Such language is found even in our devotional hymns:

"Their hatred and their love are lost,
Their envy buried in the dust;
They have no share in all that's done
Beneath the circuit of the sun."

Suppose, now, that hereafter a person should undertake to prove that the evangelical denominations of this age held the doctrine of the soul's mortality, and in proof of his as-

* See section 36, sub-section 11, *infra*.

sertion should cite such language as the above, how much would his argument be worth? Why full as much as that of the Annihilationist, derived from similar expressions in the Bible. Even the unlettered savage would scout such argumentation; and every man would at once see the folly of attempting to make mere popular language, which is often expressive of only the outward appearance of things, the foundation of any such assertion or argument.

The entire procedure of our antagonists in this matter is singularly unfair and disingenuous. They pretend to have great reverence for the Gospel and to value its clearness, and yet go to the most obscure book in all the Bible, and one which they are totally unable to explain, in order to elucidate the clear announcements of the New Testament, and then attempt to erect, on mere popular language and Oriental idioms, an argument which is to neutralize all the clearest declarations of the Gospel itself. Such is Annihilationism.

### § 28. *Relation of the Old Testament to the New.*

But let us now proceed to consider the Scripture argument itself.

That the Jews possessed a knowledge of a future state will be questioned by no candid and intelligent mind; but that the Old Testament contains an announcement of this doctrine, equally full and clear as that which is contained in the New, will not be pretended. This doctrine was undoubtedly conveyed, though in terms of comparative obscurity, in numerous passages of the law and of the prophets. "Still, it must be admitted as natural to suppose that the doctrine declared by Christ on this subject would be, in the main, a fuller and clearer enunciation of the very doctrine so darkly intimated in the Jewish Scriptures; or, in other words, that the fundamental truth which entered into his disclosures on this head would be that of the *immortality of man; that death was not a complete victory over life; that notwith-*

*standing the triumph of the grave, that which constituted his real, essential being, survived the dissolution of the body, and subsisted forever in a state of happiness or misery in another world.* This would form the burden of his teachings."* To infer, however, that because the ancient Church possessed not the clear knowledge of all that the New Testament has revealed on this subject, she therefore had no knowledge on the subject, is the fatuity of imbecility.

The relation which the Old Testament sustains to the New seems to be, in the general, but inadequately appreciated. There is clearly an aspect in which, as a religious constitution, or as a full and complete revelation, it is represented as imperfect, (2 Cor. iii, 6, seq., and Heb. viii, 6, seq.,) as first rudiments, (Gal. iv, 3–9,) or as a stage in religious education which the Christian is supposed to have passed over, (Gal. iii, 23, seq.,) and as relating in some particulars to matters which have formally (or as relates to the mere letter) ceased to be obligatory. (Heb. viii, 13; 2 Cor. iii, 11.) And all this, moreover, in perfect consistency with the fact that Christ and his apostles refer to its precepts, ordinances and prophecies, as the basis of their arguments, (Luke x, 26; xvi, 29; xx, 37, 42; xxiv, 25–27, 44–47; John v, 39, 46; Acts ii, 25–31; xxviii, 23; see also the Epistles;) regard its teachings as those of God himself, (Matt. xv, 4–6; Acts iii, 18, 21; iv, 25; 1 Cor. ix, 8; Heb. i, 1; iii, 7; x, 15; 1 Pet. i, 10–12;) and establish its validity, and recommend its use, (Matt. v, 17; Luke xvi, 17, 29; 2 Tim. iii, 14–16; 2 Pet. i, 19.) Hence, therefore, the religion of both Testaments is one.†

* Professor Bush, Anastasis, p. 141.

† Bishop Bull, after treating this topic with his usual ability, remarks: "Verbo dicam: Lex carnaliter et secundum literam spectata nec spiritualem justitiam exegit, nec vitam æternam promisit: *Spiritualiter vero considerata erat ipsissimum Evangelium;* nec de eâ hoc modo sumptâ, controversiam hîc ullam movet Apostolus." *Harmonia Apost. Dissert. Post*, cap. x, sect. 8. "Præterea floruerunt singulis seculis in populo Judaico Viri Dei ac Prophetæ cœlitus edocti, quos, inter tot arcana ipsis patefacta, Mysticum hunc Legis sensum penitus ignorâsse, nihilque de futurâ vitâ intellexisse, nemo prudens suspicabitur." *Ib., sect.* 10. And

They differ in this: that the former points to Messiah as yet to come, while the latter proclaims that he has come; and consequently the New is the key to the Old, and must open for us the true import of its teaching.* And if, as our opponents, with pretended exultation, affirm, but little is said therein of the separate state of the soul, it might be useful for them to remember, also, that as little is said of the resurrection. But even placing the question on a historical basis, it were idle for them to deny that the Israelites, after sojourning so long in Egypt, had a knowledge of the immortality of the soul; for Herodotus expressly affirms that the Egyptians, from the earliest times, maintained that doctrine, and that they were THE FIRST who defended it.† Compare Acts vii, 22.

In our references to the views entertained of the soul's immortality by the nations, we made no allusion to Christians, Jews, and Mohammedans, for they all have had access to the word of God. It however devolves upon those who deny that the Bible teaches that doctrine to explain how it has thus always and universally been regarded as announcing the soul's uninterrupted immortality. There have been, it is true, sects among Pagans, Mohammedans, Jews, and Christians, that have attempted to explain away the doctrine, but

Grotius, likewise, after referring to 2 Mac. vii, as illustrating the sentiments of the Jewish nation on the subject of a future life, remarks: "Statum piarum animarum post mortem ab horto illo in quo Adam initio constitutus fuerit, גן עדן, Hebraicè; Græcè *παράδεισον* appellarunt, ut apud Philonem etiam Josephum videre est: At statum post resurrectionem excellentiori vocabulo dixerunt Hebraicè מלכות אלהים aut מלכות השמים, Græcè *βασιλείαν τοῦ Θεοῦ* aut *βασιλείαν τῶν οὐρανῶν*, quo pertinet inter cætera locus ille Sapientiæ, *Δίκαιοϊ*, etc. (He quotes *Wisdom* v, 16, 17.) And that the Jews in the time of our Saviour regarded their Scriptures as revealing the doctrine of eternal life, cannot be questioned. See John iii, 39.

* See that admirable little tract of *Francis Junius*, entitled *De Politiæ Mosis Observatione*, in which that most learned and truly great theologian has treated the question as to what should be observed and what not observed therein by the people of God after the formal proclamation of the Gospel. *Leyden*, 1602. See some excellent thoughts also in Am. Biblic. Repos., xi, p. 234.

† Lib. ii, sect. 123.

such exceptions only confirm the rule, and render it necessary for those who deny the soul's immortality to meet the argument derivable from this source. The fact, moreover, that this doctrine was universally, and from the earliest ages, received by the nations, evinces also why the Scriptures do not announce it in the form of a positive and direct affirmation, but on the contrary everywhere proceed upon the assumption that it was believed and acknowledged. Such announcements, under such circumstances, were unnecessary, and the absence of them evinces, in the clearest and most pointed manner, that no such theory as Annihilationism was entertained (except by the Sadducees, whom the Saviour refuted by a reference to the Old Testament) by those to whom the prophets and apostles addressed themselves. But let us now proceed to consider

### § 29. *The Old Testament Argument.*

That the ancient Jews, and also the patriarchs, had a knowledge of the doctrine of immortality is evident:

1. From the distinction which is made between the subterranean residence denominated *Sheol*, שְׁאוֹל, and בּוֹר, *the grave*, or place for the body, denominated קֶבֶר. (Gen. xxviii, 5; xxxvii, 35; xlix, 33; l, 2–10; Numb. xx, 24–26; Deut. xxxiv, 7; xxxi, 16; 1 Kings ii, 43.) The writings of our antagonists teem with idle and illiterate discussions of *Sheol* and *Hades*, but they carefully avoid any mention of the obvious and forcible argument deducible from this distinction.

2. That the Jews believed in the existence of the spirit after death is evident from the credit which they, in common with other nations, (see § 22,) were disposed to give to the art of *necromancy*, by means of which the *spirits of the dead* were thought to be summoned back to the present sphere of existence. (Levit. xix, 31; xx, 6, 7; xxvi, 27; 2 Kings xxiii, 24; 1 Chron. x, 13; Isaiah xix, 3; xxix, 4; lvii, 9. Compare Zach. xiii, 2–6.) Moses enacted laws

directly against this art. "There shall not be found among you a consulter with familiar spirits, a wizard, or a necromancer." Deut. xviii, 9–12. How fully it was entertained in Saul's time appears in 1 Sam. xxviii, 3–10. Now it would be sheer absurdity, as *Jahn* remarks, (to whom I am much indebted in this section,) to suppose that persons who did not believe that departed spirits continued to exist, should invoke them, and give full credit to the ability of non-existing spirits to reveal the mysteries of the future.

The belief of the ancient Hebrews on this subject, therefore, was that the *spirit* at death is received into *Sheol*, (ἀδης,) their name *for the kingdom of the dead*, and which is represented as a large subterranean abode. (Gen. xxxvii, 35. Compare Numbers xvi, 30–33, Deut. xxxii, 22.) The term, as we have seen, is carefully distinguished from that by which they designate the receptacle for the body, except in cases where the former sense includes also the latter, and means simply the receptacle for departed spirits without reference to their state. Thus, for example, the rich man and Lazarus were both represented as in *hades*. And into this abode the wicked are said to be driven suddenly, their days being cut short, while the righteous descend into it tranquilly and in the fullness of their days.

This spacious dwelling-place for the departed is sometimes described as dark, sorrowful, and inactive, (Job x, 21; Psa. vi, 5; lxxxviii, 11, 12; cxv, 17; Isaiah xxxviii, 18;). and then again as full of activity, (Isaiah xiv, 9, seq.,) and its inhabitants are represented as possessing more than human knowledge. (Job xxvi, 5, 6; 1 Sam. xxviii, 7.) In this abode the *departed spirits* rejoice in that rest so much desired by the Orientals, (Job iii, 13,) and there the living hope to see once more their beloved ancestors and children. (Gen. xxxvii, 35. Compare Gen. xxv, 10; xxxv, 28; xlix, 29; Numbers xx, 24–26; 1 Kings ii, 10, 11.) And there, also, the slave is at length freed from his master, and enjoys a cessation from his toil. (Job iii, 13–19.)

3. The same truth is also apparent from that often-occur-

9

ring phrase translated "being gathered to his fathers," or "to his people," or, more correctly, "entering into their habitation or abiding-place." (Gen xxv, 8; xxxv, 29; Numbers xx, 24, etc.) Take now, for illustration, the first of these: "Then Abraham gave up the ghost, and *was gathered to his people.*" What, then, is this *gathering?* Does it relate to the body or the soul? It cannot refer to the body, for while his body was buried in the cave of Macpelah, in Canaan, his fathers were buried afar off; Terah in Haran, in Mesopotamia, and the rest of his ancestors far off in Chaldea. Of course, then, this gathering relates not to the body, but to the soul; *he was gathered to the assembly of the blessed, and thus entered his habitation.* In precise accordance with this idea Job, speaking of the ungodly rich man, says: "The rich man shall lie down, [that is, in the grave,] *but he shall not be gathered.*" Job xxvii, 19. So, too, says Jeremiah, (chap. viii, 2; xxv, 33,) "They shall not be *gathered nor buried,*" making this obvious distinction between being *buried* and being *gathered* to the good.

There are other expressions, which are employed both in the Old and New Testaments, which it may be important to consider here. They properly belong to the Old Testament argument even though they may be employed or referred to in the New also. We shall adduce some of them, therefore, in this connection, before we proceed to the critical examination of particular passages. For example:

4. The word *spirit* is frequently employed in the Old Testament in such a sense as necessarily to convey the idea of the separate existence of the vital principle in man. A single instance must here suffice, for we shall have occasion to refer to others hereafter. In Psa. xxxi, 5, David says: "Into thine hand I *commit my spirit.*" This is uttered in view of the separation of soul and body, and may be illustrated by Psa. xxiii, 4: "Though I walk through the valley of the shadow of death, I will fear no evil: for thou art with me; thy rod and thy staff they comfort me." Now, in the New Testament, we find the same expression used by our

blessed Redeemer, when just about to enter the same dark valley: "Father, into thy hands I commend my spirit." Luke xxiii, 46. (Compare 1 Pet. ii, 23.) In the same manner the proto-martyr Stephen, when in similar circumstances, addressed Christ: "Lord Jesus, receive my spirit." Acts vii, 59. (Compare also Eccles. viii, 8; xii, 7.)

Now who will doubt that these words have a meaning, or that they express the truth, or that they who employed them knew what that meaning was? One who used the expression was an inspired prophet, another was Jesus Christ himself, and the other was Stephen, "*a man full of the Holy Ghost.*" I ask, therefore, Do the words refer to the body? No man can entertain such a thought. What then do they refer to? What was it that the inspired prophet and our dying Redeemer besought God to receive? What was it that the expiring Stephen committed into the hands of the Lord Jesus? (Compare 2 Tim. i, 12; iv, 7; 2 Pet. i, 14.) Was it the breath? Can any one suppose that they wished to commend to God the last portion of the air they breathed? No serious mind could trifle thus with these affecting and solemn expressions. What was it then? The mere life which passed into nonentity at death? And can any one suppose that they would have commended to God a nonentity? This would be a shameless trifling with sacred things. There is therefore but one answer to the question: they commended to God just what they express, *their spirit*, (רוּחִי, *τὸ πνεῦμα μου*. See Luke viii, 55,) when it should leave the body and enter into *Sheol* the world of spirits. Hence the existence of the spirit is not interrupted by death. The spirit of man is therefore not annihilated, but survives the dissolution of the body.

5. An equally forcible expression, conveying the same idea, is also frequently employed in both the Old and New Testaments, in which the death of any person is called "a *giving up of the ghost.*" Our Annihilationists consider this a "*very awkward* expression,"* and certainly it fits their theory very

* See H. 2, p. 65, and A. 93.

awkwardly. The phrase, however, exactly expresses the idea of the original. Thus of Jacob it is said, "He yielded up the ghost." Gen. xlix, 33. Job also says "man giveth up the ghost." Job xiv, 10. Jeremiah also employs the same idiom to express the idea that spiritual life had departed from the ancient Church: "She hath given up the ghost." Jer. xv, 9. It is frequently employed also to express the precise idea of what takes place at the death of mankind. See Job iii, 11; xi, 20; xiii, 19; Gen. xxv, 8, 17; xxv, 29. So too in the New Testament, "Jesus cried with a loud voice and yielded up the ghost," or dismissed his spirit, *ἀφῆκε τὸ πνεῦμα*. (Matt. xxvii, 50; Mark xv, 37, 39; Luke xxiii, 46; John xix, 30.) So too of Ananias and Sapphira, (Acts v, 5, 10,) and of Herod, (Acts xii, 23,) it is said, they *gave up the ghost*. The idea is found expressed almost in every variety of form throughout the Scriptures, and the phraseology is that which has been chosen by the Spirit of God. It can therefore, confessedly, convey no false idea, when taken in its plain and obvious import. And now, in connection with this expression, place one or two passages which shall be the subject of critical remark hereafter; for example, Gen. ii, 7: "God breathed into his nostrils the breath of life, and man became a living soul;" or the following, which, like the above quoted, are descriptive of what takes place at death. "Then shall the dust return to the earth as it was, and the spirit shall return unto God who gave it." Eccles. xii, 7. "Who knoweth the spirit of man that goeth upward, or the spirit of the beast that goeth downward to the earth." Eccles. iii, 21. Here, then, the idea in the foregoing passages is not only expressed, but the import of the language is made known by the God who cannot err. At death the *body*, the בָּשָׂר, the *σάρξ*, the *σῶμα*, is separated from the נֶפֶשׁ the רוּחַ, *πνεῦμα*, *ψυχὴ*, the *soul* and *spirit;* (for in the Hebrew and Greek these words are often used interchangeably, as they are in our own language;) whereupon the body, which contains all that was taken from the dust, is given back to the dust, or the material elements, and consequently, if the soul were mortal it too would be given up to the dust, it would return also to the earth. But God affirms that it does not return to the earth; and therefore it is distinct from the mortal and perishable part of man.

6. The same truth which is found thus didactically expressed, shines forth gloriously also in innumerable places in the devotional compositions of the Bible. A single illustration will suffice to suggest to the attentive reader a multitude of others which it will be unnecessary here to adduce: "*Thou shalt guide me with thy counsel and afterward receive me to glory.* Whom have I in heaven but thee? and there is none upon earth that I desire besides thee. *My flesh and my heart faileth; but God is the strength of my heart, and my portion forever.*" Psa. lxxiii, 24–26.*

That reference is here made to a future state, none will deny who can understand the language and scope of the Psalm. (See vs. 16, 19; compare also Psalm xvi, 5, and Job xix, 25–27.) Now when do heart and flesh fail in the sense here expressed? It is of course at death, for the ex-

* The distinction referred to above may serve to explain a matter upon which many critics have evinced more wit than wisdom. For a century past, whenever a critic upon the Psalms would wish to make a formidable appearance of liberality, he begins by saying: "Cocceius found Christ *everywhere* in the Psalms, but Grotius found him *nowhere*." This remark of course affords the critic a fine opportunity for making a display of his own judiciousness in avoiding both these extremes, and of adding a few words also on the subject of fanaticism and unbelief. It is time, however, that this senseless tirade should cease. I am no admirer of Cocceius, but every one can see that in the notes referred to he is speaking not only of Christ as the Redeemer or Prophet, *but of the doctrine respecting him*, and which has ever been the basis of all vital godliness. Every expression of true piety, therefore in the Psalms, (and elsewhere in the Bible,) *must relate directly to Christ*, (comp. Heb. xi,) and of course where such an expression occurs, it is perfectly proper to regard it as a reference to Christ. (See my work on the Resurrection, pp. 143, 144.) It is just as proper to say that such passages refer to Christ, as to say that the righteous under the Old Testament were justified and saved by Christ. In the case of Grotius the matter was different. He was looking for formal predictions of Christ, and not for expressions which implied a practical recognition of him as man's Redeemer and hope. Had he sought for the latter there would not have been so much apparent difference between Cocceius and himself.

pression, "Spent is my heart and my flesh," (see Heb.,) is an idiom importing the *failure* which then takes place. Of course, then, when (or if) these fail, says the Psalmist, "God is still my strength and my everlasting portion." Now can any one reconcile this declaration of the Psalmist (whose heart and flesh have failed) with the Annihilationist idea that God *was not then* his support and portion, and is *not now* his portion, and *will not be* his portion through the myriads of ages which may intervene from the present time until the resurrection? Can any supposition more directly contradict the passage than this?

7. The plainness with which the doctrine is announced in the Old Testament appears also from the fact that Paul argues from Gen. xlvii, 9, and other places, in which the patriarch calls this life *a journey*, that the pious men of the former dispensations expected to enter upon a happier state at their dismissal from the body. (Heb. xi, 13–16.) This idea was constantly present to their minds. So with Abraham, (Gen. xxiii, 4;) David also, (Ps. xxxix, 12;) and so, too, referring to the Jewish nation, he says: "We are strangers before thee, and sojourners, as *were all our fathers.*" 1 Chr. xxix, 15. See also Levit. xxv, 23, where God addresses them "*as strangers and sojourners.*" Ps. cxix, 19. The Jews always entertained this idea. Thus, for example, Philo (*De Confus. Ling.*) says: "According to Moses all the wise men are strangers, who look upon heaven as the city wherein is their dwelling-place, and the earth as the place of their pilgrimage."

The expression *τὰς ἐπαγγελίας*, *the promises*, (Heb. xi, 13,) which these patriarchs had not received, cannot relate to temporal good.* The term, by a metonymy of the adjunct, is employed for *the things promised;* and those things they had not received, but saw therein in all their fullness afar off. Those only who *died in faith* are here referred to, and not such as *died in unbelief*, (see chap. iii, 18, 19; iv, 2, 6, 11. Comp. Ps. xcv, 7–11;) and of course others are included be-

* See Whitby, *in loco*.

sides Abraham, Isaac, and Jacob, (see ver. 39,) as, for example, Abel and Enoch, to whom no temporal promises are said to have been made; and yet they all alike *departed from this world* in faith, Enoch retaining his body, and the rest separated from theirs. The promises, therefore, relate to the glories of the world to come, and shall be manifested *in all their fullness* at the resurrection, (ver. 35,) at which time the victors shall all alike be crowned, (ver. 40,) and in the presence of the assembled universe.

The same idea of the present life being a pilgrimage is also occasionally referred to in the New Testament. See 1 Pet. i, 17; ii, 11.

Such then has ever been the view of the Church of God. The idea that life is but a journey cheered the early patriarchs in all their lonely wanderings; and hence, at their journey's end, the Holy Spirit taught them to expect the resting-place for which they were contented to resign their all on earth. And now I ask: *Have they not arrived at their journey's end?* Are not their journeyings over? Yes, and they have been ended for thousands of years. Is then their journey concluded, and has it been concluded for thousands of years, *and they not yet arrived at home?* Can any serious mind believe that such is the meaning of the Spirit of God? I know it has been asserted by the old Socinians, and repeated by Dr. Whately and the Annihilationists, "that as those who are annihilated are not conscious of the lapse of time, it is all the same to them." But can any sober mind entertain the thought that these faithful followers of God, after performing their wearisome pilgrimage, their sad and toilsome journey through this wilderness, are not yet arrived at home? and that instead of the blessed light of a Father's smiles, and the sweet companionship of kindred spirits, they have found a universal blank, and have been blotted out of existence? Are such the expected joys, such the hopes, by which the precious Gospel is to cheer us amid life's crushing sorrows, and persecutions, and bitter tears?

8. But not only does Paul argue from such passages that

the pious patriarchs entered their rest at death, but our blessed Redeemer, in reply to the Sadducees, also refers to the Old Testament as teaching the same great truth. He quotes Exod. iii, 6, and pointedly censures his adversaries for neglecting to perceive the true import of that passage. In this passage Jehovah says: "I am the God of Abraham, of Isaac, and of Jacob;" that is, *I am their protector and the object of their worship and adoration.* Now these words were spoken to Moses long after the death of those patriarchs. How, therefore, was Jehovah *then* their God, and the object of their worship, if they were blotted out of existence at death? Could their dust and ashes worship him? If not, then they still were living, though their bodies had moldered away ages before. And hence Christ, in his argument against the Sadducees, (who were the Annihilationists of that day,) referring to the fact of the continued existence of those patriarchs, adds the impressive words, "*for God is not the God of the dead, but of the living;*" who still live to him, (as all the dead do,) though they have ceased to live among men. (Matt. xxii, 23–33; Luke xx, 27–38.) So too our blessed Saviour is said *to live to God* after he ceased to live among men. (Rom. vi, 10. See the Greek in both places.) The passage, however, in Matthew and Luke will be the subject of critical investigation when we come to consider the New Testament argument.

### § 30. *Examination of particular Passages.*

We shall not detain the reader any longer by these and similar considerations, but shall at once proceed to the examination of those proof-texts of the doctrine of immortality which are found in the Old Testament, the testimony of which our opponents endeavor to neutralize. We shall confine our attention mainly to these, without attempting to enumerate all the passages in which the doctrine is inculcated.

1. In Gen. i, 26–28, we have a statement of the fact that God created man; and a declaration of man's superiority to

other *living creatures* in the fact that he was created to have dominion over them. Such was his state before the fall; but since he became a sinner, and has rebelled against God, he no longer has *this* pre-eminence over them. His authority has disappeared, and is, in effect, renounced by them. (Eccles. iii, 19.) All alike are called to endure pain, and misery, and death.

In Gen. ii, 7, however, we have the fact described, the existence of which is simply declared in chapter 1: "And the Lord God made man out of the dust of the ground, and breathed into his nostrils the breath of life; and man became (or was thereby constituted) *a living soul.*" לְנֶפֶשׁ חַיָּה, *εἰς ψυχὴν ζῶσαν.* See also ver. 18, 19, and Psa. viii, which relate to his pre-eminence over the creatures. Here, then, it is distinctly stated that after God had created from the dust of the ground the *corporeal part* of Adam, *the soul was added*, which was, of course, not produced from the earth or elements as the body was. If, therefore, the soul was not formed from the same material as the body, on what principle can it be said that it shall perish with the body? That it does not, however, is plainly stated, for, referring to this very fact of man's original creation, the Spirit of God says that at death "the dust returns to the earth as it was, and the spirit returns to God who gave it." Eccles. xii, 7. And that the soul or *spirit*, the רוּחַ, is not the result of organization, as the Annihilationists pretend, (see § 5, *supra*,) is clear from the fact that in such a case it would, of course, be as much the product of the dust of the ground as the body itself, and that the body itself would be *in the same sense* as the spirit, *given by God;* but the inspired writer here makes a clear distinction between the *forming* of the body and the *giving* of the soul. Of course, therefore, *the soul is separable from the body*, and the annihilation theory is consequently false. But let us now hear our antagonists on the subject.

They come down upon this passage in a perfect avalanche of snow, ice, stones, sticks, mud, and noise. And if the reader desires to see in full what they offer, he may find it in, C. 14–16, 44, 46; D. 112–120; E. 32, seq.; G. 3, 4; H. 1, pp. 115–117; J. T. 11–14; M. 17–20. They advance not one new idea, and their criticisms, if they may be called such, have been answered a thousand times. Mr. Dobney, as usual, leads the van, and, in common with most of them, considers the passage in connection with Gen. i, 26, 27.

In collocating these passages his first aim is to prove that man was not created immortal; and all these writers reiterate the assertion that "*immortality was contingent upon obedience*," as though they were uttering some important proposition which involved the real issue in the controversy. Thus, while Mr. Dobney explains *the image of God* in man to be "intelligence, self-consciousness, and a moral nature capable of rational happiness, and of ruling over the *inferior tribes* (the irrational creatures) as their lord," he denies that he was created immortal, and the rest of these writers all reiterate the denial. There is here, however, an equivocation which is unworthy of a Christian teacher. I know of no approved theological writer who denies the above proposition. All with one voice declare that our first parents were created amenable to law, and that exemption from its penalty was contingent upon their obedience. And I am persuaded that Mr. Dobney and his friends can produce no instance among such writers in which this is questioned. Why then should he represent us as entertaining views the reverse of this?

Now, the penalty of the law is death; that is, the curse, wrath, displeasure of God, separation from his gracious and sustaining influences, (Gen. ii, 17; Ezek. xviii, 20; Rom. vi, 23, and Gal. iii, 13;) and thus our first parents died the *very moment* they sinned, for they thereby at once incurred the displeasure and curse of God. Consequently man lost his immortality. Death seized upon both body and soul, and God subsequently ordained (Gen. iii, 19) that the body should return to dust and the soul pass into the eternal world. (Eccles xii, 7.) Thus *as man* he truly died, and his nature as man was dissolved.* He would have been immortal as man had he obeyed, but he disobeyed, and thus forfeited the favor of God, and should forever have lost it had not the intervention of Christ prevented. Such is and ever has been the doctrine of the Christian Church, and any attempt of our adversaries to make a contrary impression should be met, not by argument, but by a pointed reprimand.

The equivocation of the Materialists in their use of the term immortality in this connection is obvious. We employ it in relation to man *as man*, and say that *as man* he lost his immortality. They, on the contrary, while professing to use the term as we do, apply it specifically to the component parts of man, and claim that *each part* lost its immortality. Now is this an honorable procedure? We grant that man *as such* lost his immortality, while they claim that his *spirit* lost it. Their proof is, first, that *he died.* But death, as we have shown above, (§ 27, 1,) is perfectly consistent with the continuance of the conscious personality. The fallen angels, moreover, incurred the penalty of death, and their conscious existence is not interrupted. Man died; but this proves not that his conscious existence has been interrupted. As man he has ceased to exist; but this proves not that his spiritual nature has ceased to exist. Their *second* proof is that *he returned to dust;* in other words, the nature given him became dissolved. Death, so to speak, brought him back to his original state when God completed his work by endowing it with a spirit. As man his nature was dissolved. He returned to dust, and the spirit returned to God who gave it.†

* We shall hereafter treat upon corporeal death in its relation to the penalty in Gen. ii, 17.

† Rev. J. Panton Ham, of Bristol, England, fully sustains this remark. In his "Life and Death," p. 120, he thus speaks: "When I say that the human mind is *dissolved*, I neither affirm nor imply that the components of man's compound being are annihilated. All that I state in the text is, that since neither the body nor the soul, but *the union of both*, is the man, therefore the *disunion* of these constituent parts of *the man*, is the dissolution *of the man*, neither of these constituent parts, that is, neither the *soul* nor the *body*, is separately the human personality: their *separate des-*

In the same sense the dead are said to sleep in the dust, (Dan. xii, 2,) and to be in their graves, (John v, 28, 29,) because they cease to be men at death; their nature is dissolved, nor shall they be men again until the resurrection. Hence, too, *David* has not ascended into the heavens, (Acts ii, 24,) and the proof which the apostle adduced of this was, that his sepulcher still retained his body. The spirit of David was not David, (in the sense in which the apostle used the term,) and David, soul and body, had not ascended as Christ had. I am aware that in some instances, as we shall see hereafter, the term soul is employed for the *person*, and in others that the term *body* alone is thus employed; it is so in all languages. But I now refer to language as used in its strict philosophical import, and nothing therefore can justify the aforesaid equivocations of our antagonists on the term immortality. But let us now hear their attempted explanation of Gen. ii, 7.

Mr. Dobney thus professes to represent the strength of our argument from this passage for the immortality of the soul: "He, it is said, has emphatically *the breath of life*, and he alone is made *a living soul*." Mr. Ham follows his

*tiny* is *therefore* of no practical interest to our race." This preposterous conclusion may evince to the reader how much it must have cost Mr. H. to admit the premises. I may here remark, that the arrangement of God respecting man's return to dust, (Gen. iii, 19, and Heb. ix, 27,) being subsequent to the abrogation of the Edenic dispensation and the covenant of works, and also to the appointment of a Saviour, it is perfectly gratuitous to assert that this *return to dust* is exegetical of "*dying thou shalt die*," in Gen. ii, 17. I shall refer to this matter again in a future chapter. But for aught that appears to the contrary, the infliction of the penalty threatened in Gen. ii, 17, is perfectly consistent with the uninterrupted existence of man *as man*, (that is, soul and body united,) for he could as properly have then endured that penalty (which is the curse or displeasure of God) as the sinner can endure it in his proper personality after the resurrection. And his exclusion from the tree of life (Gen. iii, 22, 24) was designed, not to prevent his recovering the *favor* of God, (which it were absurd to suppose,) but that he might not, by partaking of it, perpetuate his present existence, and so frustrate God's gracious arrangement for terminating his new probationary state in a world of suffering and sin, and for furnishing him with the renewal of his physical nature by a resurrection.

footsteps closely, and even copies him largely without acknowledgment. M. follows in the same course, and asserts that "man in Eden was a candidate for immortality," and that "after his sin he was debarred from the tree of life, lest he should eat of it and live forever;" that is, of course, live forever in his then state without a separation of body and soul. And he quotes Archbishop Whately as denying that man "was originally created of an immortal nature." S., on the same subject, with his usual decency, says that the devil preached the immortality of the soul when he said, "Ye shall not surely die," intimating that we deny that Adam did die. In like manner E. represents us as basing our whole argument from this passage on the expression that man had *a living soul*, and that therefore his soul was immortal. So, too, of the other writers above referred to. Then, after having thus stated the argument, they proceed to answer it by showing first, that all other animals are called *living souls;* and secondly, that all other animals have the *breath of life.* And having with great parade effected this, they triumphantly announce that the passage in question furnishes no ground for supposing the spirit of man to be immortal.

It seems out of character to enter into thorough philological criticism with such men, for they cannot understand it. But we shall endeavor to make the subject as plain as possible, and not refer to the original oftener than is absolutely necessary. The expression וַיְהִי הָאָדָם לְנֶפֶשׁ חַיָּה is literally, *and the man was for a living soul.* The Chaldee translates it, "*and it* (that which God breathed into his nostrils) *was in man for a speaking spirit.*" The idea in the original is sufficiently obvious: God had made the body of the man out of the dust of the ground, as the animals had been made. But as yet man was only their equal. But more than this was needed; an intelligent governor over them was required; and hence something was to be added to the mere animal life, derived from the dust of the ground. Had man remained as he then was he would have been as unfit to be their governor as the orang-outang. Hence in his case God did what was done in no other instance of all the animal creation. He imparted to him directly (*breathed into his face, countenance*) a principle of intelligence. *Then his creation was complete*, and he, too, took his place as a living, moving creature upon the earth. It seems impossible to mistake the obvious sense of the passage.

It will be apparent to all, therefore, that the emphatic word, as discriminating man from the other animals, is נָפַח, *he breathed*—breathed into him this vital principle endowed with intellect and intelligence.* The attempt made by these writers at the *reductio ad absurdum*, pretending that we are compelled to take the word as employed in this instance as we do when it is employed of a creature, and that therefore we are to suppose that God has lungs, etc., can influence none but grossly ignorant minds. God, in speaking to men, must employ *human* language, for man can understand no other. And shall we therefore attribute to him everything which the same language imports when applied to man? and so conclude that God has arms, feet, nostrils, hands, etc. These men know better. Why, then, do they attempt thus to impose upon the illiterate? And now I ask, What have the objections of Mr. Dobney and his coadjutors to do with this argument? They reply to our criticisms that other animals are said to have the *breath of life*, and that they are called *living souls*, all of which we most freely admit, for we have always taught the same thing. But let our adversaries show a solitary instance in which it is said that God, in creating other animals, constituted them living creatures by *breathing* into them the breath of life. If Mr. Dobney can do this, let it be done. If he cannot, then we must charge upon him and his friends a culpable equivocation in pretending to meet the issue which is presented by the aforesaid argument.

The usage of the word (נָפַח) cannot be mistaken. As used in the text it is descriptive of *imparting* the immortal spirit; so elsewhere it is employed to express its *departure* from

* See in this connection our remarks on Zech. xii, 1, in § 30, 6, *infra*.

the body at death, as in Jer. xv, 9: "She hath *breathed out* her spirit." In the one case the body *receives* that which in another case it *upyields.* The word (except sometimes perhaps in Pual and Hiphil) has always reference to some actual substantial existence; as, for example, imparting, dismissing, bringing it to bear upon something else, etc., and never in the sense of merely developing, without such agency, qualities already possessed by the object. Thus, Ezek. xxii, 20: "To *blow the fire upon it.*" Ver. 21: "I will *blow upon you* in (with) the fire of my wrath." xxxvii, 9: "Come, O Spirit, and *breathe upon* these slain." Hag. i, 9: "I will *blow* it away;" that is, with the blast of my indignation. Isa. liv, 16: "The smith that *bloweth* the coals;" that is, kindles them by an increase of air. Jer. i, 13: "I see a pot which is *blown upon;*" or, under which the fire is kindled by a blast of wind. Job xx, 26: "A fire *not blown* [not kindled by being blown upon] shall consume him." Job xxxi, 39: "If I have caused the soul of the owners to *breathe out;*" that is, if I have made them to grieve or caused them to die. But the usage cannot possibly be misunderstood, and it is utterly subversive of the idea that imparting the soul to man was merely the starting of his corporeal organs into operation. (See § 5.) Such a criticism would indeed (as Luther says, *in loco*) lead one to suppose that there is no difference, *inter hominem et asinum.* In fact even this *is* asserted by J. T., 33–35, and others of our antagonists. And if politeness should require that we admit the proof to be conclusive in their own case, and to accept as analogous the instance recorded in Numb. xxii, 30, (to which, however, they do not refer,) we must protest against their attempt to extend any further its application to the human race. Now the Bible is *a unit,* and its testimony is to be taken *as a whole* in relation to the subjects on which it treats. Whatever is obscure in one part of its great moral teachings is always made clear in other parts. And I conclude these remarks by requesting the reader to consult for himself a portion of its testimony on the fact announced in Gen. ii, 7.

See, for example, Job xxxiii, 4; Eccles. iii, 21, xii, 7; Isa. lvii, 16; Zech. xii, 1; (with Psalm xxxiii, 15, *Heb.*;) Heb. xii, 9; Matt. x, 28; Numb. xvi, 22; xxvii, 16.

2. There are several other passages sometimes referred to in this discussion, as, for example, Psa. xc, 10, (where, however, the phrase "it is soon cut off" cannot be sustained by a thorough exegesis;) Gen. xxxv, 18, where, speaking of Rachel's death, the phrase occurs: "While her soul was in departing;" Job xviii, 18, where it is said of the wicked that he shall be "*chased out of the world;*" and of man, Job xiv, 20: "Thou changest his countenance *and sendest him away*," referring to death. It is impossible to imagine that these and a multitude of similar phrases could ever have come into existence and use, except on the supposition that the soul or spirit is really separable from the body. Certain it is that our antagonists, with their view of the matter, would never have originated them, for no ingenuity can make them fit the materialist scheme. There is one passage, however, upon which I shall offer a remark. It is Gen. xxxvii, 35, in which Jacob says: "I will go down in to the *grave* (sheol) mourning for my son." The LXX here render *sheol*, *ᾅδης*, and the Latin Vulgate, *infernus;* and such is undoubtedly its import here, and not *grave*. Jacob had not the slightest idea of having his body laid side by side with that of Joseph, which he believed to have been devoured by wild beasts. Hence, says he, "I will go down into *sheol* to my son." Nor can it be successfully denied that this is the true rendering of the Hebrew phrase. Consequently this passage clearly intimates the separate existence of the soul after death.*

The objection to this, that the term *sheol* sometimes means the grave, is a mere evasion, for how does the fact that this is *sometimes* its import prove that such is its meaning here? In § 29, 1, I have referred to this matter briefly, and I would here add a word respecting the usage

* See Wolzogenius, p. 684; Knapp, Theol., p. 458; Bretschneider's Dogmatik, II, 372, 373.

of the term among the Hebrews. It is sometimes, as above remarked, employed to designate *the grave*, as in Gen. xliv, 29, 31; Job xxiv, 19; Psalm cxli, 7, and perhaps some other places. Its more general import, however, is the receptacle for the living intelligence, or immortal part of man, after death. Hence it is *distinguished from the grave*, (see § 29, 1,) as in Job xxvi, 6; Prov. xv, 11; xxvii, 20. "*Sheol* and *destruction* (the receptacle for the body, *in which it perishes or is destroyed*) are before the Lord," and "are never full." And hence it is represented as a kingdom, full of life and activity, (Isaiah v, 14; xiv, 9–20; Ezek. xxxii, 21, 27;) into which all the living are also represented as passing at death. See 1 Sam. ii, 6; Job vii, 9; xiv, 13; xvii, 13, 16; Psalm xxx, 3; Eccles. ix, 10; Isaiah lvii, 9; Ezek. xxxi, 15, 17; Hosea xiii, 14; and also Psalm lxxxvi, 13, which is an instance of ellipsis: "Thou hast delivered my soul from [going down into] the lowest hell;" and hence, finally, the phrase *to descend into sheol* is applied to both the good and evil, though not in the same sense: to the *good*, Gen. xxxvii, 35; xlii, 38; Psalm xvi, 10; xlix, 15; Isaiah xxxviii, 18; to the *evil*, Numb. xvi, 30–33; Psalm xxxi, 17; lv, 15; and in relation to the wicked it is moreover expressly stated that they are visited with retribution, or enter a world of woe in sheol. (Job xxi, 13; Psalm ix, 17; Prov. v, 5; ix, 18; xxxiii, 14; Ezek. xxxi, 16.)

These things will render apparent why whole generations are spoken of as *sleeping with their fathers*, (Judges ii, 10.) They all pass into the kingdom of the dead.

3. We shall therefore omit noticing a number of other passages in the Pentateuch, and historical books, and Psalms, etc., and pass on to consider Eccles. iii, 21: "Who knoweth the spirit of man that goeth upward, and the spirit of the beast that goeth downward to the earth."

The Hebrew term for spirit in this verse is רוּחַ in both instances; and unless I greatly err, this is the only instance in which *ruach* is predicated of the interior nature of a beast. The writer, as is evident from verse 18, is, in this whole passage, describing the state of doubt and perplexity through which he had formerly passed in relation to the whole subject here specified, (verses 18–21,) and which *then* led him to say, " Wherefore I perceive that there is nothing better," etc. The verse before us (21) should undoubtedly be translated as a question,* and the doubt here expressed as it relates to the spirit of man, is of course not answered at once, as the writer is here describing the perplexities through which his mind had been passing. In this perplexity he attributes to both man and beast a *ruach.* When, however, his mind is at length relieved, he answers the question in relation to man, and tells what became of his *ruach* at death, (chapter xii, 7.) But he never again attributes a *ruach* to beasts, as he had done in his season of doubt, and never mentions the matter again. He gives no answer to the question as it relates to them, (see also Job xxxiii, 28, 30; xxxiv, 14;) for as he confirms the statement that the *ruach* of man goeth upward, so we may regard him as tacitly confirming the statement also that what he called the *ruach* of the beast *goeth downward.* See the word as used in Deut. xx, 20; xxviii, 43, 52; Isaiah xxxii, 19; xxxiv, 7; Zech. xi, 2.

The term רוּחַ is of extensive application in the Hebrew, as also its corresponding term in Greek, πνεῦμα. It frequently is used in the sense of wind or air, (Gen. viii, 1; Numb. xi, 32; 2 Sam. xxii, 11; Job xli, 16.) Hence it signifies also *breath,* (Gen. vii, 15; Job ix, 18; Psalm civ, 29; Eccles. iii, 19.) It is also used in the sense of animal life, (Job vi, 4; x, 12; Psalm lxxvi, 12;) and of man's spiritual nature, as in Eccles. xii, 7; Zech. xii, 1; and in innumerable places. So too it is often a designation of God himself, (Gen. vi, 3; Numb. xi, 29; 2 Sam. xxiii, 2; 1 Kings xviii, 12; Job xxxiii, 4.) In like manner it is frequently used in the sense of *personal agent,*† or intelligent

* See Stuart, *in loco.*

† We shall treat upon this more fully in Part III, chapter ii.

creatures. Of the *evil spirits*, for instance, (1 Sam. xvi, 14–23; xviii, 10; xix, 9; 1 Kings xxii, 21–23; Zech. xiii, 2; Matt. x, 1; Luke x, 20;) and of angels, (Psalm civ, 4; Heb. i, 14;) and also of disembodied human spirits or ghosts, (Job iv, 15; Luke xxiv, 39; Acts xxiii, 8, 9; Heb. xii, 22, 23; 1 Peter iii, 19.) This of course settles its import as applied to *creatures endowed with intelligence;* and its application to man in the text evinces the separability of the spirit from the body, and the uninterrupted continuance of its self-consciousness. We shall have occasion to refer to this passage again in the sequel.

4. The next passage which we shall examine is Eccles. xii, 7: "Then shall the dust return to the earth as it was; and the spirit shall return to God who gave it."

It is impossible to mistake the import of this passage. At death *all of our nature* which is dust returns to the earth *as it was*, but *the spirit*, which consequently is not from the earth, "*goes forth*," as the Psalmist expresses it, (Psalm cxlvi, 4,) and *returns to God*, that is, passes out of a state of probation, into a state of retribution, (comp. Luke xvi, 22–23,) and is disposed of by him according to its moral condition and desert. (Verse 14.) That *returning to dust* is not the same thing as *returning to God*, will be admitted by all, and therefore the spirit does not perish with the body, but is separable from it, and survives the stroke of death.

There is also in the verse itself a striking intimation of the *object* of this return. Of the body it is said, "The dust returns to the earth *as it was*." But *the spirit does not so return*. It has acquired a moral character, and so is changed from what it was when first created, and given to man.* It therefore returns to God, *not as it was*, but to receive according to that which it has become.

It may well be supposed that this passage is rather a per-

* The reader may find some striking passages from Homer, Euripides, and others, on this subject, in Grotius on Gen. iii, 19, and in his *De Jure Belli ac Pacis*, lib. ii, cap. xix, sec. 2, p. 279.

plexing one to the Annihilationists, and the reader will perhaps be gratified to see their *elucidation* of it. It is as follows: "Eccles. xii, 7, says, the *ruah* goes to God who gave it. Now if God intends to restore this *ruah* to the man, so that he may live again, where does God bring this ruah from? We shall see that *it is not the* SAME RUAH, *but ruah of the same kind*, though perhaps less diluted with atmospheric air." (E. 88, 89.) The light which this *profound* psychological remark sheds upon the passage is so great as to render the object of vision altogether invisible. The proof by which he sustains the point is Ezek. xxxvii, 5–13: "Prophesy unto the *wind*," and "Come, O wind," phrases in which רוּחַ refers to the Holy Spirit, according to Job xxxiii, 4. Their other *expositions* are as follows: "The spirit (breath, life, for so the original word signifies) shall return to God who gave it. This is as true of the wicked man as of the good, and it just as truly proves universal salvation as it proves that a man is *alive* when he is dead." "Let me ask, was it [the spirit] in a conscious state *before* it was given? If not, how can it be proved that it *was* in a conscious state *after* it returns? I do not see but we might as well argue that because the body has feeling while we have life, it must have feeling after it returns to dust." (S., Append. 17, 25.) In other words, if the soul had no consciousness before it was created, why should it have after it leaves the body? And this remark, silly as it is, is constantly repeated by these men. See H. 1, p. 120, and H. 2, p. 86.

Another of their writers thus explains the passage: "When man dies, that which came from the earth returns to the earth, and that 'breath of life' which God 'breathed into his nostrils,' returns to him in the expanse of heaven." (A. 32.) And again on page 73: "The fact of the spirit returning to God who gave it, does not prove its consciousness or happiness. '*He gathers to himself the breath of all flesh;*' but must we thence infer that the breath is conscious?" It is not a new thing for these writers to invent

Scripture, and then quote and apply it, as in the foregoing instance. If A. has no Bible, he ought to apply to the Bible Society and get one. We may next expect to have them quote *that other passage:* "He tempers *the wind* to the shorn lamb," and then criticising it as follows: "*Wind* here is *ruach* in *the original.* Lambs therefore have *ruachs* tempered, that is, *adapted* to their nature. Hence, if men are immortal, lambs must be." This is a far better argument than many which they urge.

C. 35, 36, criticises the passage as follows: "If the spirit here spoken of means the immortal spirits of men, it proves too much for the advocates of *immortal soulism* generally; for it proves the spirits of wicked men go to the *same place* [is God a place?] at death that the spirits of the just do." "If any man is Christ's, then he has the spirit of Christ, which returns to God who gave it; this is a never-dying spirit." I hope the reader will not require of me to explain these *profound* observations.

H. 1, p. 120, after quoting the text, thus comments upon it: "But this language is rather confirmatory of the opposite view, that *in the disjunction of the constituents of man's conscious being he ceases to be such a being.* The body, or *the dust*, returns to the earth *as it was*, and the spirit in like manner returns to God *as it was* before he gave it." Here is another instance of a gross attempt to manufacture Scripture. The idea expressed in the phrase, "*as it was*," as applied to the spirit, is in no way suggested either directly or by implication. Why should these writers thus trifle with sacred things, and with the souls of men! The inference, too, that because the soul separates from the body at death, it therefore loses its consciousness, is a fair specimen of Annihilationist logic, the premise being in no way connected with the conclusion.

The same writer, in his other work, thus refers again to the passage. After quoting and commenting on Gen. ii, 7, he says: "God breathed into man, and so kindled the human mechanism with life; and when man dies, this gift of life—this breath—returns to God who gave it." (H. 2, p. 86.) And he here repeats also the puerile remark above referred to respecting the consciousness of the soul previous to its creation.

M. 23, after quoting the passage, thus speaks: "It contains no proof of the soul's immortality. Certainly it establishes the doctrine, to which I fully subscribe, that the human spirit survives the stroke of death, as you see illus trated in the parable of the rich man and Lazarus."

Such is the exposition of these critics:* contradictory, subversive of each other and of all correct principles of hermeneutics, and of a character which would disgrace a freshman. I have presented them thus fully that it might be seen with what weapons and with what success these men endeavor to set aside the plain testimony of God's word on the subject before us. As to their dominant exposition that *the breath* returns to God who gave it, what does it mean? *The breath is the air we breathe*, a material substance. In what sense then does the air we breathe return to God at death? But it is a waste of time to press the matter further. That the soul not only survives the stroke of death, but still lives, understands and feels either the favor or displeasure of God, is clear from this text and the context; for immediately after uttering the former, the writer makes, in verse thirteen, an application of the truth to men, and then, in verse fourteen, gives the reason why the soul must at death return to God: to wit, *that it may be judged.*

5. Another passage which announces the doctrine of immortality is Haggai ii, 23: "In that day, saith the LORD of hosts, will I take thee, O Zerubbabel, my servant, the son of Shealtiel, saith the Lord, and will make thee as a signet: for I have chosen thee, saith the LORD of hosts."

It is conceded that Zerubbabel may have been a type of

* Mr. Dobney has not favored us with his views of the passage, if he had any in relation to it.

Christ. The word "*son*" here stands for *grandson*. Compare Daniel v, 2; xviii, 22. He returned from the captivity to Jerusalem at the beginning of the reign of Cyrus, who committed to his care the sacred vessels of the temple. (Ezra i, 11.) He laid the foundations of the temple, and restored the daily service. (Ezra iii, 8, 9; Zech. iv, 9, etc.) In consequence of his faithfulness, God addresses him in the above-cited passage, in which he promises to take him to himself, and make him as a signet, when desolation should sweep over the earth during the coming centuries, and while the thrones and kingdoms of the heathen should be subverted and destroyed.

The passage may be illustrated by Zech. iii, 7, in which God thus addresses Joshua, the companion of Zerubbabel: "If thou wilt walk in my ways, and keep my ordinance, then thou shalt also judge my house, and shalt also keep my courts, *and I will give thee places to walk among these that stand by.*" (Comp. chapter i, 9–11; iv, 14; vi, 5; Luke xxi, 36; John xiv, 2; Heb. xii, 22, 23; Rev. v, 9–14.) This last expression, "*among these that stand by*," as illustrated by these references, is very striking, but its import is at once settled by a reference to the original, בֵּין הָעֹמְדִים, *with those who stand in my presence.* Thus the seraphim are said to stand *in the presence* of Jehovah, (Isaiah vi, 2;) and the angel in Isaiah lxiii, 9, is called *the angel of his face.* So also Gabriel is said to stand *in the presence* of God. (Luke i, 19.) See also the Hebrew usage in 1 Kings x, 8, and 2 Kings xiv, 11. And according to their mode of speech, *to see the face of the king*, and *to stand in his presence*, mean the same thing (comp. Matt. xviii, 10; 1 Sam. vxii, 6, and also xxv, 27) in the Hebrew.

The figure employed (in Haggai ii, 23) to evince to Zerubbabel how highly God regarded him, is that of a signet, חוֹתָם, (a seal, especially one set in a ring,) from חָתַם, *to seal, to confirm.* (See Daniel vi, 17.) And a striking illustration of the force of this figure is given in Jeremiah xxii, 24: "As I live, saith the Lord, though

Coniah, [for Jeconiah, the *yod* being dropped, to signify the diminution of God's regard for him,] the son of Jehoiakim, king of Judah, *were the signet upon my right hand*, yet would I pluck thee thence." (See Solomon's Song viii, 6, and Luke xv, 22.) Nothing therefore could more forcibly express the idea of favor or regard than such a figure as the one employed in our text; and thus at death was Zerubbabel to be received into God's everlasting favor, and like Joshua, be admitted among those who stand in the presence of God.

This exposition is in no way affected by any theory respecting Zerubbabel's typical character. Adam himself was a type, and so was David. But this interferes in no way with their own proper personality, or with the promises made to them as individuals. And if Zerubbabel's faithfulness in the discharge of his duties renders him in any sense a type of Christ, how should this prevent his faithfulness from receiving its promised reward? The overthrow and punishment of the kingdoms referred to, moreover, took place previous to the advent of our Saviour, and during all those political convulsions Zerubbabel was to be as the signet on Jehovah's right hand; and as he could be such in no sense if he were blotted utterly out of existence, it is clear that he still existed after he had passed away from earth. And that the ancient Jewish Church regarded the passage as teaching this great truth, will not, I think, be questioned.*

6. The last passage which I shall adduce in this branch of the argument is Zech. xii, 1: "The burden of the word of the Lord for Israel, saith the Lord, which stretched forth the heavens, and layeth the foundations of the earth, and formeth the spirit of man within him." The *burden of the word*, as it is literally, is, by hypallage, *the word of the Lord concerning the burden;* a sorrowful word, or

* In a future chapter we shall dispose of the cavil of our antagonists, that the early Jews had no adequate conception of the doctrine of immortality.

address concerning the destruction or utter overthrow of the enemies of the Lord.

The author of this prophecy, and the protector of his people, (of whom the prophecy speaks,) is Jehovah, whose power to protect them is here illustrated by three exhibitions of it, evincing both the power and the will of God: He *stretched forth the heavens, laid the foundations of the earth, and formed the spirit of man within him*, and therefore as he is *willing* to protect his people, and *able* also to protect them, they may fully rely upon his protection. The manner in which he will protect them is also stated particularly in verses 2–9.

That there is here a direct reference to the operation described in Genesis ii, 7, will be questioned by no one. The three great operations of the Creator are here enunciated: The stretching forth of *the heavens*, the creation of *the earth*, and of *man*. He himself enumerates them as those signal displays which evince his power to be such, that every one whom he promises to protect may with the fullest confidence trust in his protection. What then, according to his own statement, is the signal feature about the creation of man which thus wonderfully displays the Creator's omnipotence? Is it the formation of the body from the dust of the earth, and starting it, like a machine, into operation? as our Annihilationists assert. No, by no means; but it is, as he himself avers, *the formation of the spirit within man.*

Here then we have the inspired record, or God himself, explaining the meaning of the phrase "*breathed* into his nostrils the breath of life." God declares this to be *the formation of the spirit within him*, and to be such a work of almighty power as to be worthy of being classed with the production of the heavens and earth. It was therefore the creation of *a new substance*, a spiritual existence, a greater work than the production of the *visible creation*, (for this specification is the *climax* of the period,) and is as much more glorious a work than the creation of matter, as a spiritual, immortal substance is more glorious than that which is only material.

By what word then does he explain this operation called *breathing into his nostrils* the breath of life? Is it a word which may be interpreted as the mere starting into operation a machine already manufactured? or is it a word which imports the bestowment of existence? This question the reader shall decide. The word is יָצַר, and he may consult it in Genesis ii, 7, 8, 19, (πλάσσω, lxx,) and in Psalm xciv, 9, "*formed* the eye;" also Psalm lxxiv, 17, "*made;*" Isaiah xxii, 11, "*fashioned* it," κτίζω; Isaiah xxvii, 11, "He that *formed* them." It is also employed in the sense of *Creator* of all things, (Jer. x, 16; li, 19; Isaiah xliii, 1; xliv, 2, 24.) It is also used to signify a *mental* creation, or a plan formed in the mind, (2 Kings xix, 25; Psalm xciv, 20.) These things can leave no doubt as to the import of the word when used as it is in the text; for, as applied to the production of the *spirit* of man, it has the same force and significance as when applied to the creation of an angel, or of the human body itself. And I repeat it, that nothing can be a more preposterous contradiction to the idea here presented than to suppose that the climax, the antecedents of which are the creation of the heavens and the earth, should express no more than the mere starting into operation a piece of machinery already formed and prepared. Such an act would be no proof of omnipotence at all; yet such an anti-climax must be supposed, or the Annihilation theory respecting the creation of man is utterly false.

The formation of the spirit of man is thus rendered prominent among the works of Omnipotence, says Hengstenberg,* "because this is the ground of the absolute and constant influence exerted upon it by Him who turns the hearts of kings as waterbrooks;" and the argument in its application here is, Surely the Creator of the spirits of men (Numbers xvi, 22, and xxvii, 16) is able to strike with

* Christology, ii, 202.

madness the hostile cavalry, (verse four,) and to inspire his people with courage, (verse six.) In the same manner precisely is the omnipotence of God predicated on his being *the former of the hearts of men.* (Psalm xxxiii, 15.) With the Hebrews the *heart*, לֵבָב, is the seat of the feelings, affections, and emotions. See Judges xvi, 15: "Thy heart is not with me;" and Deut. iv, 29; vi, 5; Psalm civ, 15; cix, 16. Hence the prayer of David, Psalm li, 10, (comp. 1 Kings iii, 6; ix, 4.) Thus does God regard his creative operations in respect to man's spiritual nature as furnishing an incomparably grander display of his all-sufficient power than that furnished by the creation of the whole material universe; an idea which utterly annihilates the philosophico-theology of the Materialists.

A single other passage is all that we shall adduce in further illustration of the idea here presented. In Isaiah xlii, 5, we have the same three predicates joined together as in the text, the enunciation of which is, in like manner, intended to accredit the assurances which Jehovah has given in the context: "Thus saith God the Lord, he that created the heavens, and stretched them out; he that spread forth the earth, and that which cometh out of it; he that giveth *breath* (נְשָׁמָה, πνοή, LXX) unto the people upon it, and spirit (רוּחַ, πνεῦμα) to them that walk therein." Here then is the same idea as in Zech. xii, 1, and the same remarks apply to it. And as though to guard us against the pagan theory of our Annihilationist antagonists, who make the breath and spirit the same thing, God here makes a plain and pointed distinction between them.

Thus then Zech. xii, 1, must ever stand as God's own eternal protest against the soul ruining errors of our antagonists. It is utterly destructive of their whole theory respecting the inseparability of the soul from the body, and the soul being merely the result of organization. In fact, the word translated *within him*, בְּקִרְבּוֹ (from קֶרֶב, *medium*,) is of itself sufficient in this connection to sweep away the whole fable. The remark of Calvin expresses its sense precisely: "When he says *in the midst* of him, he teaches that the spirit dwells within; for we know that *our body is as a tabernacle.*"

This passage, and Haggai ii, 23, our antagonists are in the habit of passing in silence; hence we cannot edify our readers by any speculations of theirs on the subject.

7. I shall here offer but a single remark respecting the translation of Enoch and Elijah, though I had designed to treat it more extensively. Our antagonists admit that these holy men were removed from earth without suffering death, and no Christian can call this in question. See 2 Kings ii, 11; Matt. xvii, 3; Gen. v, 24; Heb. xi, 5. The impression respecting the immortality of man, which their translation has ever made upon the ancient Church, is also well known, for the Jews understood thereby that man continued to live after his removal from this world. The question then is, Were these facts calculated to originate and foster such an impression?

The ancient Church of course knew that man was created immortal, and that sin brought the displeasure of God upon him, and that instead of continuing immortal he returned to dust. See § 30, 1. But here were men who, though they had sinned as other men, left the earth without returning to dust. It was seen that all ceased to live on earth, but these two were removed in an unusual and wonderful manner. Other saints died in faith of a coming Saviour; these were translated by faith. They were translated, not for any merit of their own, but for Christ's sake. It was a benefit they received for his sake alone. If on this last point the ancient Church had not the clear views possessed by the Christian Church, it is sufficient for the argument that *we* know the statement to be true.

Wherein, then, would it be likely to occur to the pious Jew or Patriarch, was the difference between the condition of the pious dead and the translated? Could it be that one had his existence perpetuated, while the other was for myriads of ages utterly blotted out of being? the one to continue to exist, and the other to be deprived of existence? That they did not receive such an impression we know; but the question is, not *what* impression they did obtain, but whether such an impression was more rational under the circumstances than the one they did receive? Could they have possibly believed that men who were alike dear to God, and alike saved by the intervention of his Son, (to whom they had all alike been given in covenant, as the reward of that intervention,) should receive such different treatment at his hands? It is no answer to this to say that the question might be asked why all were not alike translated; for the difference between being thus translated and being blotted out of existence, is by no means to be compared to the comparatively slight difference between such translation, and the separation of soul and body, in order that the soul might enter upon its rest. The question then returns, and our antagonists may well consider it.

I have in this statement referred to the ancient Church. But whatever force these considerations had upon the minds of good men then, no one can doubt their real force when contemplated by the fuller and clearer light of the New Testament. And the plain inference is, that no such difference can be made by God in the treatment of his redeemed, leaving the great mass of them (though pardoned, regenerated, and accepted) to endure for myriads of ages "the full penalty" of a law from whose curse they had been delivered, and delivering others from the curse utterly and forever.* But we shall now proceed to consider the teachings of the New Testament respecting the uninterrupted immortality of the soul.

* The reader will perceive that I employ here the phrase "full penalty of the law," *ex concessu*. Our adversaries affirm that extinction of being is the full penalty.

# CHAPTER II.

## ARGUMENT FROM THE NEW TESTAMENT: DOCTRINES WHICH INFER IMMORTALITY.

### § 31. *Preliminary Remarks.*

I DEFER to a future chapter the consideration of those passages (chiefly derived from the Old Testament) on which Annihilationists profess to rely in support of their views, and shall now proceed to examine the statements of the New Testament on the subject under discussion. With respect to the testimony of the Old Testament, all the attempts at argument of our opponents have failed to invalidate it in the slightest degree; and they have not even undertaken to meet fairly the issue which that testimony presents, so that the texts hitherto examined unite in arraying themselves in direct hostility to their speculations.

Yet these are the men who perpetually denounce the doctrine of the soul's immortality as "a pagan fable," and who scruple not to assert such things as the following in relation to the view of it entertained by the Church at large. I give a few extracts from one of their most popular writers, and *ab uno disce omnes.* He commences his book with an extract from Archbishop Whately, in which it is *denied* that "the immortality of the soul, as a disembodied spirit, is revealed in the word of God," and *asserted*, also, that "no such doctrine is revealed to us." And feeling thus encouraged in his aspersions of the received doctrine, he remarks: "Here philosophy has for many ages usurped the chair of the Great Teacher, and her voice has prevailed above the voice of Him that speaketh from heaven. Here the authority of Plato transcends the authority of Christ, and the dogmas of the Academy the doctrines of the Bible." "The separate existence of the human soul, its immateriality, immortality, and conscious personality, are, I believe, the labored cogitations of human reason, unblessed with, and, alas! despite of the teachings of revelation. They are, in my humble opinion, neither more nor less than the perpetuation of Platonic theories in the Christian Church," etc. (H. 2, p. 66.) We are accused also of relying on "*dubious portions* of the sacred writings, which looks, to say the least, very suspicious." (P. 75.) "That system, however, can have but little support, and must be of very doubtful merit which clings so tenaciously to *ambiguous texts*," (p. 90;) "and therefore the charge of our Lord is painfully applicable to every advocate and promulgator of the popular theory: 'Ye do make void the law of God through your traditions.'" (P. 91; see also p. 85.) But on p. 83 we have the following, which concentrates into a focus all the invectives of this advocate of the Annihilation scheme:

"The popular presentation of Christianity is defective and unintelligible; a system of detached and incongruous doctrines, which necessarily fail to produce an enlightened and vigorous piety. The great bulk of most evangelical congregations is composed of persons who are totally unable to explain the relations of the several articles of their inherited creed. There they exist, stored up in motley group in a tenacious memory—a doctrinal mosaic—an awkward complication of the teachings of God and the traditions of men. The understanding can make nothing of them; its attempts have been so often baffled that it has foreborne to attempt. By the interpolation of these traditionary dogmas, every cardinal truth of revelation has been displaced, or put in a false light. The landscape of infinite love is blotted by dark and unnatural shadows; 'men' appear 'like trees walking;' indistinctness and disorder are everywhere introduced. Some cardinal truths, and among them the *first* and *chief*, immortality, the gift of God through Jesus Christ, is entirely rejected! The central sun of the doctrinal system being gone, all other truths have lost their orbit, and move in eccentric and confused course. Divines have labored again and again to reduce this wild confusion to order, but in vain. The ancient regime can only be restored by the reinstation of the sun of the system, life in Christ, and the abandonment, once and forever, of the presumptuous claim to the soul's immortality."

The foregoing extracts are specimens of the style of these writers in the premises, and express the views which they perpetually advance in relation to the doctrines which they assail. The reader will have them in view while we proceed to consider also the argument from the New Testament Scriptures.

The whole of the New Testament is to be regarded as containing the express teachings of Christ on the subject as delivered either in person or by his apostles. But before we proceed to a formal examination of specific passages, which have been the subject of dispute between us and our opponents, we shall invite attention to a few considerations bearing upon the doctrine itself, which the materialistic critics find it very convenient to lose sight of.

### § 32. *Doctrines which infer Immortality.*

1. All the passages in the Old and New Testaments which speak of the present existence of a hell for wicked men infer the doctrine of the soul's uninterrupted immortality; for it is not to be supposed that hell should be created, and exist for thousands and myriads of years without an object. Hence the doctrine of the Annihilationists necessitates, in those who receive it, the denial of a hell; and of course every passage in the Bible which proves the present existence of a hell for wicked men, proves likewise the Annihilation theory to be false.

Should it be replied to this, that hell may have been created for the fallen angels, I admit that it may have been; and I am willing that our opponents should avail themselves of this reply, for this is conceding the *present existence* of hell. It is conceding also that it is not inconsistent with God's goodness to punish sinners before the day of final judgment; that is, during the ages which intervene between the fall and the judgment, and that, too, without any design of bringing them to repentance or to mercy. And further, if the present existence of hell is conceded, the fact of its being created for sinful angels is not inconsistent with the doctrine that the spirits of wicked men may also be banished thither at death. (Luke xvi, 23, 24.) So that, even admitting the above reply, the argument would still stand thus: every passage of Scripture which proves the present existence of a hell for wicked men, proves likewise the Annihilation theory to be false.

Now in the Old Testament the fact of the present existence of such a place of retribution is repeatedly asserted. A fair and candid exegesis of the following texts cannot develop any other signification: Job xxi, 13: "They spend their days in mirth, and in a moment go down to *sheol;*" that is, suddenly pass into a state of retribution. So, too, Psalm ix, 17: "The wicked shall be turned into *sheol.*" Of course retribution is here referred to; for if sheol meant the grave, and did not import something peculiar and specific in relation to the wicked, the discriminative designation here made would be inappropriate; for the righteous, no less than the wicked, are turned into *sheol*, in the sense of *grave*, or mere *state of the dead.* The original term translated *turned*, שׁוּב, (ἀποστρέφω, LXX,) cannot be explained to mean "*hurried with violence*, as by desolating judgments," etc., for it has no such meaning. The English word exactly expresses its import; so that there is no way to escape from the obvious conclusion that the wicked at death enter into a state of retribution.

Another passage, teaching the same truth, is Prov. v, 5,

where, speaking of the lewd woman, it is said: "Her feet go down to death; her steps take hold on *sheol*." In this place, as in the last, our translators have properly rendered *sheol* by *hell;* for the phraseology expresses distinctly the idea of retribution, by the discrimination of character which it marks, and which is the basis of the admonition given in the context. The objection of Universalists, that the language is employed to "express the premature or sudden death of a lewd woman," is ineffably preposterous. For to whom is it addressed? Not to the woman herself, nor to women at all. It is an admonition of Solomon to his *son* to shun all intercourse with bad women. The same idea is expressed in Prov. ix, 18: "But he knoweth not that *the dead* are there, and that her guests are in the depths of *sheol*." The word translated *dead*, רְפָאִים, is very remarkable in this connection. In its general import it means *living beings*, *mighty ones;* and there seems to be here a striking reference to the mighty fallen spirits which the penal infliction of the law had cast down to Tartarus. (2 Peter ii, 4; Jude 6.) *They are there*, and thither, too, is the destination of all the guests of the adulteress. See also the Hebrew of Prov. ii, 18; xxi, 16; Isaiah xxvi, 13, 14; xxx, 33; xxxiii, 14; Psalm xxi, 9.

The same doctrine is taught also in Prov. xxiii, 14: "Thou shalt beat him with the rod, and shalt deliver his soul from *sheol*." Parental faithfulness cannot deliver from the grave, but it may deliver from hell. *Sheol* therefore here refers to the retributions which overtake the wicked in the state of the dead, and forever.

The same truth is brought very fully and frequently to light in the New Testament. The present existence of hell is affirmed in every way by which such an idea can be conveyed, as in 2 Peter ii, 4; Jude 7; Luke xvi, 23, 24, already referred to. So too in the phrase, "*Is* hewn down, and cast into the fire." (Mat. iii, 7–12; vii, 19.) See also Rev. xx, 10: "The lake that *burneth* with fire and brimstone." Mark ix, 43: "Where the worm *dieth* not, and the fire *is not quenched.*" Jude 13: "To whom *is reserved* the blackness of darkness forever." (Comp. 2 Peter ii, 17.) "In danger of hell fire." Matt. v, 22. The same idea of a present hell is conveyed also by metaphorical language; as, for example: "*Set on fire of hell;*" (James iii, 6,) an expression which would be without meaning if hell had no existence.*

In view of these passages, I repeat therefore the question, Is hell now in existence? If it is, (and they prove it to be,) then what is the use of it? Where is there any more difficulty in admitting that wicked men should, before the day of judgment, suffer its torments, than that sinful angels should? If the one reflects against the goodness and compassion of God, does not the other equally? How then does the theory of Annihilation relieve, as it pretends to do, the character of God? But I would advise our opponents not to be troubled about the character of God. He is able to take care of it, and will do so. Every text, therefore, which announces the present existence of hell, is a proof that the Annihilation theory is false.

I might remark here further, that this theory necessitates the denial of a hell either now or hereafter. For since mankind pass out of existence at death, the wicked of course have nothing to do with hell between death and the resurrection; neither have they anything to do with it after the resurrection; for immediately after the conclusion of the process of judgment, they undergo the process of being annihilated over again. So of course this theory utterly obliterates the doctrine respecting hell in its relation to impenitent man, and thus proves itself to be false.

2. All the texts which speak of the present existence of heaven, (the region of the blessed,) in like manner prove the Annihilation theory false. For if this theory be true, then Christ is now and ever has been, and ever will be, until the resurrection at the last day, without his redeemed. In his intercessory prayer (John xvii) he prayed that his suffering

* In Part III this subject will be more fully considered.

followers might be with him in glory; but that intercession, it would seem, has not been regarded. When he was about to be taken away, he comforted them with the assurance that it would be but *a little while*, and promised that he would come again and receive them to himself; told them not to let their hearts be troubled, for that he would come and take them to the mansions in his Father's house. *But nothing of all this has yet been done if the Annihilation theory be true.* Instead of being gathered home to their Saviour's arms, they have been blotted out of being, and of all the many mansions in heaven which he at such a cost obtained for his redeemed, none are inhabited except by those of them mentioned in Matt. xvii, 3; xxvii, 52, 53; Heb. xi, 5; and though his grievous sufferings for their redemption were endured so many centuries ago, the first note is yet to be struck in heaven by the blood-washed throng. Can any sober man, with the Bible before him, believe these things to be taught therein? The bare supposition would seem like an insult to any candid and intelligent mind; and yet these things are so, or the Annihilation theory is false.

The present existence of heaven is asserted in the clearest manner, both directly and by implication. It is plain from the translation of Enoch and Elijah, and of those who arose with Christ. These writers, at least some of them, make a distinction between Paradise and heaven, and assert that these translated and raised saints are in Paradise. I shall not stop to dispute this point, so long as they admit also that it is a place of happiness; nor have I the slightest objections against employing the term Paradise to designate Abraham's bosom, or the state of the righteous dead antecedent to the resurrection. The existence of such a place of blessedness is all that I claim, and the name by which it is designated is of comparatively small account.

The fact that there is an angelic heaven will not, I suppose, be disputed; (see Isaiah vi; Luke i, ii; x, 13; Matt. iv, 11; xiii, 39, 49; xxiv, 36; xxvi, 53; Acts vii, 53; 1 Tim. v, 21; Heb. i, 14;) nor can it be denied that the righteous among men stand related to heaven as a dwelling-place. (Luke xvi, 22; Rev. vii, 15, 17.) Hence also we have such expressions as the following: "Lay up for yourselves treasures in heaven." Matt. vi, 20. "*Our citizenship* (*πολίτευμα*, *civitas cujus jure fruimur*) is in heaven; from whence *also* we look for the Saviour, the Lord Jesus Christ." Phil. iii, 20. "Your names *are* written in heaven." Luke x, 20. "Ye *have* in heaven a better and an enduring substance." Heb. x, 34. "The first born which *are* written in heaven." Heb. xii, 35. "Provide yourselves bags which wax not old; a treasure in the heavens that faileth not. For where your treasure *is*, there will your heart be also." Luke xii, 33, 34. So too in all those passages in which the Lord speaks of our death as the time in which he comes to call us to account, and in view of it urges us to be prepared for that event. See Luke xii, 35–48; Matt. xxv, 13; Mark xiii, 37; Acts xx, 31; and so in passages almost innumerable.

When Jesus therefore says, "In my Father's house *are* many mansions," (John xiv, 2,) and again, that these mansions, or this kingdom, was prepared for the righteous from the foundation of the world, (Matt. xxv, 34,) he affirms directly the present existence of heaven as the dwelling-place of the righteous. Hence the patriarchs recognized its present existence, "and sought a city which *hath* foundations whose builder and maker is God." Heb. xi, 16. It is in this heaven, and among these many mansions which had been prepared from the foundation of the world as the kingdom of the redeemed, that Jesus went to prepare for the reception of his faithful disciples, that they might be with him when they had passed away from earth.* And the very fact that he specifies this as an immediate reason for his going away, proves the immediateness of that preparation, whatever it consisted in, and consequently that it was for his disciples when death should close the scene of their labors on earth.

* Comp. Luke xxii, 28–30.

Hence too the clear distinction between the Church militant and triumphant, the Church on earth and in heaven, which is observed in many passages, (some of which we shall critically examine presently,) and also in the Apocalypse, where reference is made to periods of time antecedent to the resurrection, and in which the redeemed are represented as before the throne, with harps in their hands, and singing a new song. (Rev. iv, 8; v, 9, 12; vii, viii, etc.) And in Rev. xviii, 20, the departed spirits of the prophets and apostles are thus addressed in relation to the destruction of mystical Babylon: "Rejoice over her thou heaven, and ye holy apostles and prophets." Of course, then, they were able to rejoice, which they could not have been, had they at death ceased to exist. Paul also thus refers to both parts of God's ransomed Church: "Jesus Christ, of whom the whole family in heaven and earth is named." Eph. iii, 14, 15. And in Col. i, 20: "And having made peace through the blood of his cross, by him to reconcile all things to himself; by him, I say, whether they be things in earth or things in heaven." See also Gal. iv, 26. Now what *things in heaven* are they for whom peace has been made by the blood of Christ, and which have been by him reconciled to God? They certainly are not angels. Who then are they that are now in heaven, whom Christ has thus redeemed and reconciled, and who receive from him, as the Saviour, their name? They of course are from among men, for he died for man alone, and not for other intelligences. (Heb. ii, 9–18.) "The whole family" of the redeemed, who have died on earth, are consequently there, and therefore the soul does not perish at death. See also Heb. xii, 22–24.

3. The same truth is announced also in all those passages which declare of the faithful believer that he shall *never* perish. See, *e. g.*, John x, 28: "I give unto them eternal life, *and they shall never perish*," (*καί οὐ μὴ απόλωνται εἰς τὸν αἰῶνα.*) It is impossible to employ a stronger expression than is here used to signify the very opposite of the Anni-

hilation doctrine, which teaches that man does utterly perish at death. The two ideas are in perfect antithesis to each other. See also John iii, 15, and iv, 14. The same idea is also expressed in such passages as John v, 24: "Verily, verily, I say unto you, he that heareth my word, and believeth on him that sent me, *hath* everlasting life, and *shall not come into condemnation*, but is *passed from death unto life*." Now *everlasting* life is of course an uninterrupted continuance of life. And this life is here begun; the believer here *hath* it, and *is passed* from death unto life. But the Annihilationists affirm that the life here begun does not thus continue, but is wholly interrupted and abolished between death and the resurrection, and that the believer does come into condemnation, and suffer the penalty of the law during that period as fully as the unbeliever himself, for that penalty takes as full effect upon the one as upon the other. This is also directly the reverse of Paul's statement, that "there is *no condemnation* to them that are in Christ Jesus." Rom. viii, 1. In like manner says John: "We know that we *have passed from death unto life*." 1 John iii, 14. Nothing can be stronger than the original expression here used.

4. The same conclusion follows also from the fact that the believer is regenerated, or receives a new spiritual nature in this world. (John i, 12, and iii, 3–8.)

With this nature the law has nothing whatever to do in the way of penalty, because the believer who is thus renewed is quickened together with Christ, (Eph. ii, 4, 5,) and is *begotten again* by God the Father, (1 Peter i, 3; James i, 17, 18;) and the old man, to which alone the penalty applied, is crucified and destroyed. (Rom. vi, 6.) Hence they are dead to sin, but *alive unto God* through our Lord Jesus Christ. (Verse 11.) They have put off the old man with his deeds, and put on the new man, (Col. iii, 9–11,) and old things are passed away, and all things are become new, (2 Cor. v, 17.) Hence also God's image is re-enstamped upon them, and they are *made partakers of a divine and heavenly nature*. (Eph. iv, 24; Col. iii, 9–11;

2 Peter i, 4.) Now as the penalty of the law cannot reach this renewed nature, (Rom. viii, 1,) it cannot, if retained, suffer death; therefore it is called the *incorruptible seed*, "being born again, not of corruptible seed, but of *incorruptible*." 1 Peter i, 23. The word is ἀφθάρτος, which is translated incorruptible in 1 Peter i, 4, and 1 Cor. ix, 25, where it relates to the heavenly inheritance. The same word, with the same import, is moreover applied to the renewed nature of the believer in 1 Peter iii, 4, and to the body of man when hereafter raised from the dead, 1 Cor. xv, 52, and also to God, Rom. i, 23.

Such then is the nature begotten in the believer at his renewal or regeneration. It is of *immortal* seed, and this seed remaineth in him, (1 John iii, 9,) and is itself expressly affirmed to be immortal, as immortal as the body itself shall be after the resurrection, as immortal as heaven itself, and it shall exist while God himself endures. The bare attempt to reconcile all this with its annihilation would be the extravagance of folly. The penalty of the law cannot reach it, for it is not under the curse; death cannot affect it, for it is in the fullest sense *immortal*.

5. The same conclusions follow also from the believers' justification. It takes place in this world, and relieves him from the penalty of the law; for this justification is a release from condemnation, and an acceptance of the sinner as righteous, through and for the sake of Jesus Christ. They are therefore absolved from sin, condemnation, and death, on account of that perfect satisfaction which he rendered to the justice of God, "being justified freely by his grace, through the redemption that is in Christ Jesus." (Rom. iii, 24.) See also Isaiah liii, 11; Rom. v, 9, 19; x, 4; 1 Cor. i, 30; 2 Cor. v, 21.

That they are absolved from sin and death appears from such passages as the following: "Through his name whosoever believeth in him shall receive remission of sins." Acts x, 43. "There is no condemnation to them." Rom. viii, 1, 34; Col. ii, 14. "By him all that believe *are*" (not, *shall be* hereafter, but now *are*) "*justified* from all things," etc. Acts xiii, 39. On the contrary, those who are of the works of the law, and reject the Gospel offer of salvation, *are* now under the curse. (Gal. ii, 16; iii, 8–12; Phil. iii, 9.)

Now is it conceivable that the children of God, after being thus finally freed from the curse of the law, should endure it, nevertheless, by being utterly annihilated between death and the resurrection? Such a supposition confounds their condition with that of the condemned sinner, and is contradicted by every passage which proclaims their full and free justification in this world.

6. The same conclusions follow from what is said in the Bible respecting their adoption, which is that act of God by which he adopts as his children all who are justified. Hence it is said of them: "Ye have received the spirit of adoption, whereby we cry, Abba, Father." Rom. viii, 15. "Hereby know we that we dwell in him, and he in us, because he hath given us of his Spirit." 1 John iv, 13. Thus they become the sons of God as truly as by an original creation in righteousness and true holiness, (Luke iii, 38; Job xxxviii, 7;) and being accepted through Christ, it is obvious that the penalty of the law has no more to do with them than it has to do with Christ, or than it had to do with angels and men before they had sinned. Death, in the sense of the penalty, can never reach them, and they are of course delivered from the wrath of God. (Gal. iv, 4–6; Heb. ii, 10.)

Hence they are expressly named "the *sons of God*," (Phil. ii, 15;) "Behold what manner of love the Father hath bestowed upon us, that we should be called the sons of God," (1 John iii, 1;) "*heirs of God*," (Romans viii, 17; Gal. iii, 29; iv, 7; Tit. iii, 7;) and the "*household* or family *of God*," (Eph. ii, 19;) and subjects of angelic ministration. (Heb. i, 14.) And all this takes place in the present world. *In this world* they become sons and heirs of God, the household of God, and are delivered from the curse or penalty of the law, all of which is utterly irreconcilable with the idea that they suffer the curse of the law, and *perish* at death in the sense of being blotted out of existence; for if they are thus annihilated, they of course cease to be the sons of God, and the Spirit's work is wholly interrupted.

Here it will be in place to notice one of the multitudinous errors of our opponents, which result from their odd conceptions of the teachings of God's word. If, for example, as we have shown, they find words used in two senses in the Bible, and their theory requires that those terms should have but *one* sense attached to them, they are careful to refer only to passages in which the usage seems to be favorable to their theory, and represent this as the only true sense of the term. So too in relation to the subject before us: they find the word *adoption* used in connection with the resurrection, and therefore endeavor to keep out of view all such passages as the above, in which we are taught that in the present life the believer is adopted into the family of God. They quote, for example, 1 John ii, 2, "*When he appears* we shall be like him, for we shall see him as he is," as though it taught their doctrine, though in the very clause preceding this we have the words, "*Now* are we the sons of God." Then, too, they quote Rom. viii, 23: "But ourselves also, which have the first fruits of the Spirit, groan within ourselves, WAITING FOR THE ADOPTION, to wit, the redemption of the body;" from which they reason that the adoption is yet future, and will not take place until the resurrection, a most lame and impotent conclusion. Paul here expressly explains what he means by the future adoption: "*The adoption*, TO WIT, *the redemption of the body*." *The soul* (when the body is in the grave) is already redeemed, and the redemption will be consummated when the body shall be released from the grave. Hence it is the body alone to which he thus refers as being then redeemed. And this passage itself, therefore, is a full proof of the falseness of the Annihilation scheme, which would have the soul likewise to be then redeemed out of the grave.

As I have shown on pp. 294, 295 of my little treatise on the Resurrection, the New Testament announces a two-fold adoption or filiation. The one takes place here, the other at the resurrection. So Christ our Head was the Son of God when he came into this world, and yet he was powerfully manifested to be such by his resurrection from the dead. (Rom. i, 4.) Thus, too, the *manifestation* of the believer's adoption will take place at the resurrection, when the body is "loosed from the bands of death." The obvious distinction, therefore, between *adoption* and the *manifestation of adoption* utterly destroys the argument of our opponents.

7. The same conclusions follow from what is said in the Bible respecting the believer's *union with Christ.* It is as intimate as that of the vine and its branches, and as that which exists between the body of man and his head. (John xv, 1–5; Eph. iv, 15, 16; v, 30.) Hence they are denominated "those that are *alive from the dead.*" (Rom. vi, 12, 13.) They partake of the *living bread and never die; never see death.* (John vi, 50; viii, 51; xi, 26.) And yet they do suffer death in the sense of a separation of soul and body. But they *never die* in the sense of enduring the wrath of God, or the penalty of the law. See Ezek. iii, 18; xviii, 4; xxxiii, 18. (Comp. ch. iii, 21, and xviii, 9, 17, 19, 21, 22.) But as they do suffer the aforesaid death, that death is not *the* death threatened by the law, and consequently it can in no way interfere with the continuance of that life which they derive from Christ. *They die*, and yet in the higher sense of the term *they never see death.* Their union with Christ is therefore never interrupted by death, for they are alive from the dead; they are the members of Christ's body, the branches of the vine, and while he lives they shall never cease to live, (1 Cor. xii, 27; Eph. i, 22, 23;) and of course, therefore, to say they are blotted out of being at death is false.

The same train of remark may be pursued in respect to many other particulars, but it is needless. Every doctrine of the Gospel arrays itself against the theory in question; and there is not even one passage of Scripture which its advocates attempt to produce in their favor which, if fairly interpreted, does not bear directly against them. Even those expressions so often pleaded by them, in which death is spoken of as a *sleep*, refute their theory; for it is impossible to predicate sleep of that which has no existence. If therefore the person *sleeps* in death, he of course still exists. We shall not, however, pursue this line of argument, but proceed at once to the consideration of those passages whose testimony our opponents have endeavored to neutralize.

# CHAPTER III.

## THE NEW TESTAMENT ARGUMENT CONTINUED.

### § 33. *Examination of Particular Passages.*

1. THE first passage in the catalogue is Matt. x, 28: "And fear not them which kill the body, but are not able to kill the soul; but rather fear him which is able to destroy both soul and body in hell." These words of our Lord he repeated *on another occasion*, as follows: "And I say unto you, my friends, be not afraid of them that kill the body, and after that have no more that they can do. But I will forewarn you whom ye shall fear: fear him, which after he hath killed hath power to cast into hell; yea, I say unto you, fear him." (Luke xii, 4, 5.) This clear announcement of the separability of the soul from the body, and of the fact that the death of the body does not involve the extinction of the soul, has perplexed our opponents not a little, and we shall now proceed to notice what they have to offer in view of it. Their comments may be found in S. 50; D. 209, 210; H. 2, p. 87; A. 74–76; G. 21, 22; M. 39; E. 38, 39, 170, seq., and 224, 225; F. 16–21, and J. T. 71. And so completely does it haunt the imagination of these writers, that one of them (E.) gives it no less than *three* distinct and formal explanations in his book, at each time repeating the same ideas, and seeming to be wholly unconscious that he had uttered them before. Let us therefore hear him first: "Matt. x, 28, has been often quoted as favoring the separate existence of the soul; but when properly translated, and compared with the parallel account of Luke, it does not furnish

the shadow of a shade of support to the pagan fable." Then after quoting Luke he adds: "The meaning undoubtedly is, that wicked men can only destroy the present being of the righteous, and that God could raise them up again; but if they apostatize to save their present lives, that God was *able* (which implies that he would do it) to destroy their entire being in Gehenna." Then after quoting a silly rendering of the passage by some obscure, illiterate blunderer, he adds: "It is evident that Luke understood a man's soul to be himself, nothing more, nothing less; and although he was a doctor, he evidently had not graduated into the pagan philosophic theology of the present day."*

Mr. Dobney pursues substantially the same train of remark. He says that Christ here teaches that it is in the power of God to kill or destroy the soul, as the body is destructible, and that *on this very account* we are to fear God more than persecutors, who are not able to kill the soul, but could only destroy the body. In other words, he

* In respect to this handsomely printed volume, ("Bible *versus* Tradition,") which the Annihilationists are zealously endeavoring to circulate through the country, I would here add a single remark. Two men claim its authorship, and its production is said to have cost them three years of incessant labor. It is however one of the grossest instances of deception ever palmed upon the public. Its authors claim a thorough knowledge of Hebrew and Greek, and pretend to quote them with a vernacular fluency; but the ignorance of the matter which they perpetually exhibit is so palpable and gross and ludicrous, as to leave not a particle of doubt that they are unacquainted with even the veriest rudiments of those languages. Their style is one perpetual strain of low ribaldry, and is throughout so like the pot-house indecencies of Paine's "Age of Reason," as to remind one constantly of it, and awaken the impression that these men must have selected that work as their model, or *beau ideal* of what a work like theirs ought to be. As to their literary claims, it is not too severe to remark, that had they studied ignorance as a profession their book could be presented as furnishing triumphant evidence that they had graduated with the highest honors. Yet these are the men who perpetually assail, in language that would disgrace a savage, the precious truths of the Gospel, and glory in it, when they succeed in perplexing the unlettered believer, or in sweeping away the consolation of the aged and infirm poor, or in crushing the cheering hopes of the Christian when his spirit is about to wing its way to the eternal world.

sets before his hearers, as a fearful warning, the idea of an entire destruction of their whole conscious being, a motive which he would not have set before them if no such thing could be justly apprehended. Such, in brief, is his exposition, the entire force of which rests upon an equivocation on the word *destroy*, a matter which we shall fully consider hereafter. It will be observed, however, that D. here contradicts E., who, as above shown, denies that this passage teaches the separability of the soul from the body.

We shall next hear Mr. Ham. He quotes the passage with the following remark: "The following passage has been urged in proof of the separate state of the soul as a conscious and *indestructible* being;" after which, in his usual style of evasion, he proceeds to play upon the word *indestructible*, intimating that we teach that the soul is indestructible even by God himself. I shall not attempt to designate by its appropriate cognomen such puerile trifling. He then adds: "Nothing more is implied than that the soul is *distinct* from the body," and at the same time denies that "the disembodied soul is the conscious personality of the being man." "Such a distinction as that which is commonly claimed for it is purely gratuitous. How can it be logically affirmed from the above words, that the *soul* of man is the *personality* of man, capable of existing and acting distinct from the body?" In reply to this attempt at ratiocination, I would here remark, 1. This writer admits that the soul is distinct from the body. 2. That man possesses *conscious personality*. 3. He admits that this conscious personality does not belong *to the body* as such, for it ceases at death though the body may continue to exist. We come therefore to the conclusion that this self-consciousness either appertains to the soul or spirit, which is admitted to be distinct from the body, or that it results from the simple union of soul and body. If it does not belong to the spirit or soul, (for I employ both words in *this connection* to signify the same thing,) then of course it results simply from the union of soul and body; and by consequence, the union of two impersonal unconscious things results in conscious personality; an absurdity too preposterous for even our opponents seriously to maintain. But on the contrary, if conscious personality be not the result of such union, and does not appertain to the body, then it does, as Christ here teaches, appertain to the disembodied spirit. And of course the annihilation theory is false. But let us hear Mr. Ham further.

He next proposes to ascertain the meaning of *soul*, and cites for this purpose the passage which we have above quoted from Luke xii, 4, 5, and then adds: "In *this* record of our Lord's words, the peculiarity of the expression in Matthew's Gospel, upon which so much stress is laid, is altogether absent, the word *soul* does not appear." He evidently wishes here to make the impression that Luke and Matthew refer to the same occasion, when in fact they refer to two separate occasions on which Christ spoke these words. He distinctly uttered each expression as reported by both the evangelists. The remark of Mr. Ham, however, that the word *soul* does not appear in Luke's record, is worthy of the theory which requires such aid. Admitting that the word is not expressed, it is implied in the plainest possible manner. The term *kill*, as it relates here to the power of both man and God, has reference to the *body*, as even our adversaries must confess; for they do not hold that the soul is first killed by the Lord, and then cast into hell, but that it is killed by being cast into hell. This being so, therefore, what is the import of these words from Luke? "Fear him which, *after* he hath killed [that is, the body] hath power to cast into hell." Cast *what* into hell? The body? But that has been disposed of, and this casting into hell is to take place while the body is slain. Of course then it can refer only to the soul. And this proves, moreover, that the soul is the conscious personality. For if it were not conscious it would of course be but like the body after death. And if so, why fear its being cast into hell? To cast a dead body into hell would matter but little, so far as feeling or sensation is concerned; and if the soul too were senseless or unconscious after separation from the body, it would matter as little where it was cast; and the fact, therefore, that Christ admonishes us on this ground to fear God, evinces that after the death of the body the soul is susceptible of happiness and misery, and that there *now* exists a hell for impenitent men.

Our author next quotes Matt. xvi, 25, 26, to prove that the word *soul* in the above texts means simply *life*. "Whosoever will save his *life* shall lose it; for what is a man profited if he shall gain the whole world and lose his own *soul*," etc.; upon which he remarks that it is the same word in the Greek which is here rendered by both life and soul, and then with some low flings at our English translators, this writer exclaims: "Why not preserve the same rendering throughout. There is evidently no reason why *one* Greek word, occurring four times consecutively, should be translated by *two* different English words." This is the language not of the scholar, but of the pretender to scholarship. I need, however, spend but little time upon it here, for the passage will come up in another connection. Any one who will open his Greek Testament at John iii, 5–8, for instance, will find the word πνεῦμα employed *five* times consecutively, and yet it is translated by two English words, *spirit* and *wind*, and who ever dreamed of faulting the translation on that account? Even Dr. G. Campbell, whose claims to uniformity in his translation are presented and insisted on *ad nauseam*, so renders it. So too Castalio, Beza, Piscator, the German and French versions render it, without ever dreaming of Mr. Ham's profound principle of criticism. As to the word ψυχή, in Matt. xvi, 25, 26, it is of little consequence to the argument how it is rendered. It does not, however, become such *scholars* as Mr. Ham and his adherents to sneer at the venerable authors of the best translation of the Bible that ever was made. Luther, in the passage referred to, translates ψυχή as they do, though our opponents pretend that he believed in the *sleep* of the soul.

The word πνεῦμα has two meanings, *spirit* and *wind*, and to prove that it means spirit in twenty places, does not prove such to be its meaning in the twenty-first. So, too, ψυχή may mean both *life* and *soul.* And now suppose we admit it to mean *life*, in Matt. xvi, 25, 26, and how does this prove it to mean life also in Matt. x, 28? The bare idea of drawing such a conclusion is ludicrous, and such precisely is the miserable equivocation of Mr. Ham. It is followed also by an attempt to paraphrase the verse upon these principles; but we think we have given the reader quite enough of this author on this passage.

F., A., G., S., (as above referred to,) follow in the same train of remark, and need no separate notice. J. T. and M., however, suggest and insist on another exposition, (recommended also by G.,) which, as it is the last and most lauded effort of the criticism of this school, we must lay before the reader. J. T. shall state it, as he expresses it, in the most forcible manner: "Although wicked men and devils can extinguish this life, and reduce the being of man to dust, they have no more that they can do; they cannot prevent the resurrection, and therefore cannot *destroy* our being or life. In consequence of the provision made in Christ for the resurrection of every human being from the Adamic death, those who can *kill the body*, take this life, ONLY SUSPEND OUR BEING UNTIL THE RESURRECTION; THE DEAD IN ADAM ARE NOT DESTROYED." (The italics and capitals are the author's.)

By such a method therefore is this plain-speaking text to be silenced: man cannot destroy our being but only suspend it until the resurrection. But how does such a criticism help the matter in respect to their theory? They teach that to kill the body is to kill the soul. What then does our Saviour mean when he says: "Fear not them that kill the body, but *cannot* kill the soul?" Even on their own principles, persecutors cannot kill *either body or soul*, save only *till the resurrection;* and in the same sense precisely, therefore, in which they kill the body, they likewise kill the soul. This criticism therefore is simply foolish, and renders the Saviour's language unmeaning.

And here I would take occasion to explain a procedure adopted by all these authors. It may be called the introduction of the *democratic principle* into criticism. For example, a few of the texts are produced in which the soul is declared to be immortal. But instead of attempting to explain those texts in accordance with their theory, our opponents go to work and collect twice the number of passages in which the word soul is employed to designate the body, or the natural life, etc. And having done this, the texts which we adduce as teaching the doctrine of immortality are considered as *outvoted*, perhaps by two to one. Such a procedure may do very well at an election, but it does not answer in the interpretation of language. I know not which of their critics originated this profound principle of hermeneutics, for they all adopt it.

The efforts of our opponents, therefore, to neutralize the testimony of our Saviour in Matthew x, 28, and Luke xii, 4, 5, have not rescued their scheme from the death-blow he there deals against it. The import of his words cannot be mistaken. He expressly asserts that man consists of both soul and body, *καὶ ψυχὴ καὶ σῶμα*, and that the soul survives the body, and continues in a state of consciousness when separated from the body; for while he admits that men can kill the body, he denies that they can kill the soul, which could not be true on the theory of our opponents, that both soul and body perish together at death, and therefore their theory is false.

The Saviour's argument is, Know therefore that ye possess immortal souls, which come not under the power of men, but are subject to the power of God alone. Let not your faith therefore fail at the threats of men. Their power extends to the body only, and not beyond the present life; therefore, I say unto you, fear God, who, when the body is killed, can cast the soul into hell—the God who has power to destroy both soul and body in hell. Even Slichtingius can obtain no other meaning from these words. He says: "God is much more to be feared than men, if they command anything contrary to God. He can hinder them, and they can do only what he permits. And if he permits them to kill the righteous, they cannot affect their interests after death. But God has power, not only in respect to the body and the present life, but also over the soul after the death of the body, (*sed etiam in animas post corporis mortem,*) and can afflict them with a much more grievous death than that of the body."* Grotius, too, remarks that "Christ, in chapter five, spake of the punishment of the body in hell, but now he adds that God is able to destroy the soul also. By the word *soul* we are not to understand the life of the whole man, of which any one may deprive us, but that more noble substance which, in connection with the body, constitutes the man, and which in other places is called πνεῦμα, or spirit." *Christ* "does not repeat the word *kill*, which he made use of in the first member of the sentence, but employs the word destroy, which has the signification of torment, (*quod cruciatus habet significationem.*") See Grotius in Matt. x, 28.

That the Jews thus understood the language of our Saviour is perfectly obvious. Their own writings evince it. In the Apocrypha, for instance, we find such words as these: "Thou, O Lord, hast the power of life and death. Man may kill through malice; but when the spirit is gone forth it shall not return; neither shall *he* call back the soul that is received; but it is impossible to escape thy hand." (Wisdom xvi, 13–15.) So too in the work *De Rationis Imperio*, attributed to Josephus, one of the sons of Eleazar says: "We do not fear him who appears to be able to kill the body, τὸ σῶμα; for Abraham, Isaac, and Jacob receive those who die for the law; but great danger of eternal torments is the allotment of the soul, τῆς ψυχῆς, who violates the commands of God."† Again, in a quotation by Buxtorf, they say: "Man fears that an earthly ruler, who

* In 1 Peter iii, 15. † Cap. xiii.

may die to-morrow, should punish him: why then does he not fear Him in whose hands his soul is, both in this life and in the life to come?"

This text, therefore, must continue to stand as the testimony of the Son of God in favor of the soul's immortality, and his solemn condemnation of the soul-ruining errors of the annihilation and Sadducean doctrine.

2. The next passage to which we invite attention is Matt. xvii, 3: "And behold there appeared unto them Moses and Elias, talking with Him." (See verses 1–9, and Luke ix, 28–36.) The passage refers to Christ's transfiguration. Moses and Elijah appeared to him in the presence of his three disciples. Elijah had been translated, and of course appeared in the body in which he left the earth; but Moses had died and was buried, and as his body had never been raised from the dead, he of course appeared as a disembodied spirit. This being so, the theory which teaches that the soul perishes with the body, or that it is not possessed of conscious personality, and is incapable of happiness and misery, is false. What then have our opponents to say to this argument? for they must meet it, or renounce their theory. Let us hear them.

S., App., pp. 10, 11, says: "It is said Moses and Elias appeared with our Lord at his transfiguration, and therefore they must have been in a conscious state. That I admit. Elijah was translated and did not die. As to Moses, it seems likely that he was raised from the dead;" and to prove this to be "likely," he refers to Jude 9, and to the fact that Moses was an eminent type of Christ. (Deut. xviii, 15–18.) And to prove that Christ was not the first born raised from the dead, he refers to the widow's son, raised by Elisha, and to those raised by Christ. D. 137, passes it with the remark that "Moses died and was buried, yet he appeared on Tabor with Elijah, and he was *visible, or embodied.*" This is most uncandid. Why not meet the question honestly? To predicate *embodiment* of this *visibility* would prove that the disciples thought Christ to be an *embodied spirit* when he walked on the water, and when they saw him after his resurrection; and that the chariot of fire and horses of fire mentioned in 2 Kings ii, 11, were *embodied;* and the angels which appeared to Zacharias and Mary, and to the shepherds, and to the woman at the sepulchre, *were embodied.* But it is needless to pursue this further. One thing however is to be observed, namely, both these writers admit the *reality of the appearance of Moses* on this occasion. H. 2, pp. 90, 91, reasons on the case as follows: "The appearance of Elijah in this memorable scene can cause no surprise, since we are informed that his, like Enoch's, was an exception to the common lot of men. And the presence of Moses is *no proof* that he still exists, or that he ever existed as a *disembodied spirit*, for in that scene he appeared as a *glorified body.* He died in the land of Moab; God buried him; and if it could be shown from the Scriptures that he still lives, it would contribute nothing to the popular faith. I would, however, simply remark on this event; that there is no inconsistency in supposing that Moses should be raised from death, in his spiritual body, in order that he might be present on this august occasion." "There is no reason why *Moses should not put off his glorified form, and return again to the quiescence of the grave*, until the resurrection of the saints, since Christ only assumed temporarily *his* glorified form, and divested himself of it when he left the mount. The case of Moses is materially different from that of the prophet Elijah. The former, unlike the latter, died and was buried; and it seems necessary on this account to suppose that Moses returned again after this event to the state of death," etc. If this theory be true, then of course Moses has suffered death twice, once in a mortal, and then in an immortal body, an idea which I shall leave to speak for itself. Then again, this writer speaks of *Moses* himself *putting off* his form, his glorified form. Now according to his own expressed doctrine, there is no such thing as self-consciousness separate from the body. The *form* of Moses was therefore *Moses himself*, and consequently a form may divest itself of itself. It is perfectly absurd therefore for our opponents to pretend to use such language. It must be entirely abandoned by them, or the theory of annihilation must be given up. I need scarcely pause to point out the strange error into which Mr. Ham has lapsed, in endeavoring to trace an analogy between the case of Moses and that of Christ. He would have us believe that Christ's body was glorified, and that he divested himself of that glorified body when he descended from the mount. The chief objection which I have to this statement, however, is that it is not true. *The shining of our Saviour's face* on this occasion (Matt. xvii, 2; Luke ix, 29) no more proves that he had "*put on*" a glorified body, than the same thing in the instances of Moses and Stephen (Exod. xxxiv, 30–35; Acts vi, 15) proves that they were invested with such bodies. Mark distinctly refers the *transfiguration*, or μεταμορφώθη, to the *raiment*. His face shone as the sun, and *his raiment*, ἱμάτια αὐτοῦ, became white as snow. Mark ix, 2, 3. (Comp. Matt. xvii, 2; Luke ix, 29.) Even the phrase ἐν ἑτέρᾳ μόρφῃ, *in another form*, (Mark xvi, 2,) is to be referred solely to his raiment, as Grotius remarks: *Habitu alio quam quo uti solebat;* and Piscator: *alio habitu seu vestitu.*

The aforesaid writers, S., D., and H., therefore admit the reality of the appearance of Moses on this occasion. The following, however, take different ground. A. 76, after quoting the words that *Moses himself* appeared, says: "It follows, therefore, either that Moses was raised from the dead, or that the whole affair was merely a *vision*, in which absent things or persons were represented as being present." J. T. 59, reiterates this idea. E. 162–169, repeats the assertion, and denies that Moses personally appeared. He says: "Moses was not there, except in vision." "Moses, Elijah, and even Christ, were glorified at that time, *only in appearance*, for special objects." "Moses might have been raised for this special occasion, but not in his incorruptible or immortal nature, which he could only have in appearance; and if such were the case, which we think not, then he died again." C. 34, 35, is so pressed with the argument that he thus speaks: "In the first place, this account furnishes us no evidence that either Moses or Elias was ever on that mountain." "The whole was a vision."

We might properly leave these writers to settle the matter as to the reality of this transaction between themselves. I would remark, however, that such equivocations on the word *vision* are contemptible. Is *vision* always opposed to *reality?* And did Zacharias then only *imagine* that he saw and conversed with the angel of the Lord in the temple. (Luke i, 22.) Did the women at the sepulchre only *imagine* that they saw the angels? Did Paul only *imagine* that the Lord met him on the way to Damascus? (Acts xxvi, 19.) It may be easily supposed where such a principle must lead. It is true Jesus said "Tell the vision to no man, till the son of man be raised from the dead," (Matt. xvii, 9;) but this language is fully explained in Mark ix, 9: "He charged them that they should tell no man *what things they had seen;*" and in Luke ix, 36, also.

But in order to constitute this a mere representation of unreal things, how shall we draw the line between the real and the unreal? Christ and his three disciples certainly ascended the mountain. He certainly prayed, and while at prayer his countenance was changed. Does the reality then stop here? If so, how were the disciples placed, so as to witness the representation? We read that they slept. Did they then witness it in their sleep? On the contrary, it was after they awoke from their sleep that they saw the glory of Christ, and the two men who talked with him. (Luke ix, 32.) And did Peter desire that three tabernacles should be erected, two of which should be for the accommodation of unreal appearances? And was the great fear of the three disciples based upon a mere shadowy, unreal representation? But it were a waste of time to pursue this matter.*

Such then are the efforts of these men to get rid of the testimony of this passage, which, like the preceding one, is utterly fatal to their theory. Their evasions are of not the slightest account, and do not in the least relieve the system. The argument stands thus: Moses was present on the occasion referred to. He was present therefore either as a disembodied spirit, or he had been raised from the dead, and was in possession of a glorified body. He had died and was buried, (Deut. xxxiv,) and in the time of Christ he was still dead. (John vi, 49, 58.) If he had been raised from the dead in a glorified body, then it cannot be true that Christ is the first-born from the dead, (Col. i, 18;) or the first-fruits of them that slept (1 Cor. xv, 20, 23;) or that his resurrection from the dead proved him to be the Son of God, and the true Messiah. (Rom. i, 4.) The evasion that others had been raised from the dead by Elisha, and by Christ before he suffered, bears not upon the point. They were not glorified as Moses was, if he were raised; they were raised again to this present and mortal state of being. So that Christ was the first-fruits of those who shall be raised to immortality, to die no more. (See Rom. vi, 9; Acts xiii, 34.) Therefore the body of Moses had not been raised when he appeared in glory with Elijah; and consequently he appeared as a disembodied spirit, the representative of the happy state of those who die in the Lord.

Again: so far as the express testimony of inspiration is concerned, the assumption of Professor Bush, that Elijah had lost his body, and appeared on the mount with Moses as a disembodied spirit, (that is, so far as a material body is concerned,) is equally rational with the assumption of our opponents, that the body of Moses had been raised and restored to hi n. The one is just as good as the other, and just as free from all rational or Scriptural support. And by

* One of these writers, (A. 76,) asserts that *Josephus denies that Moses died.* This is false. See his Antiquities, b. iv, chap. viii, sec. 49.

way of offset to the statements of those who have supposed that Moses was thus raised from the dead, I will conclude these remarks with a quotation from the "*Gospel History*" of Mr. Thompson, the Unitarian: "These are called *men*, as if the sacred writers would guard us against the false notions of some, that they were angels or aerial phantoms. Many are inclined to believe that the spirits of men are some indescribable things, or nothings, between death and the future general resurrection; but all antiquity believed in a corporeal form, and existence obtained immediately after death, which Paul, in 2 Cor. v, expressly affirms to be his own faith and hope. The appearance of Moses and Elias confirms the doctrine of an intermediate state, and refutes the fable of the soul-sleepers." "The impenetrable barrier is passed; a light seems to dart from heaven to disperse the thick clouds that hang over the valley of the shadow of death, and we are admitted into the presence of the Judge of the world, and see with the eye of faith the spirits of the just made perfect, before we are called upon to resign this corruptible body to the shroud and to the tomb. Where the spirits of the departed exist, what their condition, or what their laws of consciousness or means of happiness, man must die before he can ascertain. But it is not improbable that the invisible world is so mysteriously connected with this visible, diurnal sphere, that the cessation of our consciousness as to present things is but the commencement of our consciousness of all those unknown realities of the other world." See pp. 200, 201. Mr. Thompson, however, should have credited this last passage to Rev. Mr. Townsend, Harmony of the New Testament, "Notes," p. 115.

3. Our next passage is Luke viii, 54, 55: "He took her by the hand, and called, saying, Maid, arise! *And her spirit came again*, (καὶ ἐπέστρεψε τὸ πνεῦμα αὐτῆς,) and she arose straightway." Now that the maid was really *dead*, in the true sense of that term, will not be disputed. See verses 49, 53. Nor was the language of Jesus, in

verse 52, designed to convey any other idea, as is clear from John xi, 11, 14; and therefore to attempt to explain this language by expressions which import only the restoring of a *living* person to his vigor, as in Judges xv, 19, is simply absurd, and merits no notice. A similar passage occurs also in 1 Kings xvii, 20, 22: "Let, I pray thee, the soul of this child return unto it; and the soul of the child returned, etc." I shall not weary the reader therefore by quoting the Annihilationist criticisms on the text, as they are all based upon the shallow sophism above referred to.

Grotius, commenting on the passage, says: "Luke adds the phrase, '*and her spirit returned*,' that he might, *en passant*, teach that the human soul was not a mere result of corporeal organization, (*κρᾶσις*,) nor anything which might perish with the body, but something subsisting by itself, (*αὐθυπόστατον τί*,) which after the death of the mortal life is elsewhere than where the body is." And even the Socinian, Wolzogenius, himself a soul-sleeper, is so pressed with these considerations that he comments on the passage as follows: "The spirit, that is the soul, (*anima*,) which had been separated from the body, again entered into the body. Hence it may be seen that the human soul is a substance, or a thing subsisting by itself, (*rem per se subsistentem*,) which after death exists in another place than in the body." It is unnecessary to add anything to these remarks.

4. We next invite the reader's attention to the statements of Christ respecting the rich man and Lazarus. We need not quote it all, as the passage can be easily referred to, and the following verses present the main issue: "And it came to pass, that the beggar died, and was carried by the angels into Abraham's bosom. The rich man also died, and was buried; and in hell he lifted up his eyes, being in torments, and seeth Abraham afar off, and Lazarus in his bosom." Luke xvi, 22, 23. By *Abraham's bosom* the Jews (to whom of course Christ addressed these words) understood the resting-place of the righteous dead. The word translated

*hell* is ᾅδης, a term equivalent to *sheol*, and means the place of departed spirits without reference to their state. Consequently it may be employed to designate, in connection with a qualifying term, either the place of future happiness or of torment: as in these verses, "He lifted up his eyes, (in *hades*,) *being in torments*."

There has been much dispute as to whether the Saviour here spoke a *parable* or related a matter of fact. The dispute, however, presents no true issue, for many of his parables are relations of actual occurrences; and in fact all of them are taken from things as they then existed. That this was an actual occurrence seems certain from his manner of introducing it: "There was a rich man, . . . there was a *poor man* (πτωχὸς) named Lazarus;" and from the fact, moreover, that he never employs *a proper name* in fictitious narrative, or in any of his narratives which are conceded to be parables in the true sense of that term. The question, however, is one of no practical importance, though our opponents pretend that everything depends upon it, to this extent at least, that if they can only prove it to be a parable they have divested it of all its impressive significancy in relation to a future state. Now it is a just rule of interpretation, in reference to the practical parts of the sacred Scriptures, that whatever impression is thereby uniformly made upon the minds of unsophisticated and pious readers is the impression which was designed to be conveyed by the Spirit of God. And this rule applied to the passage before us can leave no doubt as to its true import. Admitting, therefore, that it is a parable, the question for our opponents to settle is this: Whether Christ would, by a parable, teach what evidently intimates, and supposes, and irresistibly conveys to the pious, unsophisticated mind, the impression that the existence of the soul is not suspended at death, when in fact death does really suspend it? Or, in other words, Is it proper to regard him who is Truth itself, as conveying false impressions to mankind under the guise of a parable? But let us now hear what our opponents have to offer on the subject.

It may be found in full in C. 25–34; S. 20–22; App. 14–17, and 27, etc.; D. 137, 239; H. 1, pp. 139–141; H. 2, p. 74; A. 82–84; G. 18, 19; Has. 40; M. 23; E. 214, 125; B. 61–64, and J. T. 66–70.

Some of them go *very far back* to find a starting-point for their exposition. Thus C: "By reading the 15th and 16th chapters of Luke it will be seen that this parable was spoken in reply to an accusation made by the Pharisees and Scribes against our Saviour. The accusation was, 'This man receiveth sinners, and eateth with them.'" Luke xv, 2. "Now any one can at a glance see that it was spoken in direct reference to what is mentioned in Luke xvi, 14–18, and as an admonition against the conduct there condemned." C. next gives his exposition thus: The rich man represents the Jews; the beggar represents sinners who "came begging a few crumbs of the bread of life." The death of the beggar is the sinner's *dying* to sin, and he lives in Abraham's bosom, that is, becomes an heir to the promise through faith. The *great gulf fixed*, which no one can pass over, is the gulf between Jew and Gentile, which neither can pass to the other, etc., etc.

S. explains it three several times, and with more actual ability than all the rest of them put together. He says: "Its design is, to illustrate the folly and danger of seeking our good in this life. There are other points, namely, 2. To expose the deception common among the Jews, that they should be sacred because they were the children of 'Abraham.' 3. That this life is the only time to secure salvation, and the certainty of perishing without hope if this period is neglected. 4. The sufficiency of the means now employed to turn men to God, and hence the folly of supposing that some other means would be more effectual. They would not be persuaded though one rose from the dead. But does this prove what is to be the punishment unto which the rich man is reserved? Certainly not." Both he and C. and H., however, translate the expression *ἀπέθανε δὲ καὶ ὁ πλούσιος, καὶ ετάφη. Καὶ ἐν τῶ ἅδῃ επάρας τοὺς οφθαλμοὺς αὐτοῦ,* thus: "*The rich man died and was buried in hell, (the grave;) and he lifted up his eyes.*" The reader may guess from this what *Grecians* these critics are.

Mr. Storrs also says that the rich man refers to the Jews, and Lazarus to the Gentiles; and this allegorical sense most of them put upon it in the *general.* But even if this were admitted, it would not affect the real merits of the question, as to the actuality of the facts selected for illustration, any more than the fact that the parable of the sower illustrates the preaching, etc., of the word, would prove that the things mentioned in that parable were not in accordance with actual occurrences.

D. does not seem disposed to trifle on the subject, and in reference to the passage thus remarks: "Our Lord shows an ungodly man in a state of wretchedness after death. How long it would last is not estimated. It is true there was no hope for him. He could not buoy himself up with the prospect of restoration to enjoyment. But whether that torment should endure forever, or would ultimately destroy him, the parable does not intimate. It teaches a terrible and hopeless state for the wicked after death, and that is all." But this "*all*" is considerable for a man to admit who elsewhere perpetually denies a conscious state of existence between death and the resurrection.

H. "readily admits that we have here some apparent countenance of the popular doctrines;" and he gives the same exposition substantially as S., above, and like D., denies that the fact of the rich man being in torments, proves those torments to be eternal. A. makes the rich man represent the Jews, and Lazarus the Gentiles. G. says: "It must be admitted that *a part* of our Lord's representation of the state of the rich man and Lazarus seems to favor the opinion of conscious happiness and misery *immediately* after death, especially the request of the former, that Lazarus should be sent to his father's house. The *entire* representation, however, is far from sustaining such an opinion." "By what process of reasoning do we infer the conscious misery of a *disembodied spirit* from the declaration that a man 'lifted up HIS EYES' in hell, and felt 'HIS TONGUE' tormented in the flame?" Such is the objection perpetually harped upon by these men, and its fairness is on a par with the rest of their criticisms. No one ever drew such an inference as G. here represents. The premise is this: *The rich man died, and was buried;* his body had lost all sensation; and yet in hell and in torment he lifted up his eyes. Therefore he was *still alive,* though his body was dead. He was in a world adapted to his *spiritual nature.* Fire in hell need not be *earthly* fire; (nor the water in heaven earthly water; see Rev. vii, 17;) and as it *did torment* him, we are taught that there is a fire adapted to spirit as well as to matter. So the rebel angels find it, and those who deride the declarations of the Son of God, and trifle with his language, may yet find to their cost, if they repent not, that such is indeed the fact. (Mark viii, 38.) And as to *tongue, eyes,* etc., they are perfectly proper in such a connection, as the spirit or soul of man retains its proper human form after it has left the body, as is clear from Matt. xvii, 3. In Revelation, *passim,* also, the same idea is presented in every form. The redeemed are refreshed with living *waters,* have *crowns* of glory, and palms in their *hands;* they stand round about the throne, and also *sing* the praises of redeeming love. Whatever, therefore, these terms may import as applied to a spirit, they of course are sufficiently appropriate to justify the use of *tongue, water, eyes,* and *finger,* as applied to the departed spirits of both Dives and Lazarus, as the passages referred to in Revelation i–xviii, all relate to events which are to transpire antecedent to the general resurrection.

M., speaking of Eccles. xii, 7, says: "It establishes the doctrine, to which I fully subscribe, that the human spirit survives the stroke of death, *as you see illustrated in the parable of the rich man and Lazarus.*" While E. makes the rich man represent, not the Jewish nation, but the priesthood, and Lazarus the Gentiles, B. makes the rich man "denote the Jewish nation, *or* the priesthood, *or* both combined;" *his death*, the destruction of the political and ecclesiastical state; *torment in flame*, the misery they endured as a nation; their *looking to Abraham* for relief is their relying on the law instead of Christ, etc. Lazarus symbolized the Gentiles and publicans, who were looked on as "dogs" by the Jews. Abraham's bosom is the Gospel Church, into which Peter and Paul were special angels to transport them. J. T. repeats the same view; thus making Lazarus to be both dogs and beggar, and lick his own sores.

Such are the vain struggles of our opponents with this impressive portion of God's truth.* They are wholly subversive of each other, and yet all alike maintain the "parable" to be plain and obvious in its import.

The objection which they and the Universalists are perpetually repeating, that this same "parable" is found substantially in the Gemara of Babylon previous to the time of Christ, *may evince*, though not necessarily, that it is not an actual history; but that objection is fatal to their theory. Its import in the Gemara (and that it was understood by all the Jews as teaching a separate state and punishment between death and the resurrection) will not be questioned even by our opponents. If, therefore, Christ adopted it, and employed it without any implied or expressed dissent from their explanation, then that explanation is the true one beyond doubt. He and the Gemara both relate it as an actual occurrence, and of course intended distinctly to convey the doctrines which facts so presented irresistibly teach.

That it is *susceptible* of an allegorical explanation (and

* I had intended also to lay before the reader the spectacle of the Universalist struggles with the same passage, as contrasted with those of the Annihilationists, but have neither leisure nor space for it. The reader may, however, do it for himself by turning to Ballou and Whittemore on the Parables; Smith's Universalism, pp. 106–110; Kneeland's Lectures, p. 202; Balfour's Inquiry, pp. 74–84. Both sides deduce conclusions which destroy each other, and yet both unite in virulently assailing the evangelical view.

this is the amount of what our opponents can offer in favor of their expositions) proves nothing at all, for there is not a passage in the whole Bible which may not be allegorised. And what should we think of the individual who from this fact would conclude and insist upon it that such allegorical meaning was consequently the true one? On this principle all the foregoing expositions of our adversaries must be true, though destructive of each other.

Such then is their exposition of this passage, and we shall conclude with a brief review of it.

The question whether it is a parable or a veritable history was early discussed in the Church. Justin Martyr, Eucherius, and Theophylact, and, in later times, Lightfoot and Whitby, asserted that it is a parable; while Irenæus, Tertullian, Origen, Clement of Alexandria, Chrysostom,* and more lately Calvin and others, maintain that it is a history. Tertullian (De Anima, c. vii,) says: "You will perhaps say, It is parabolical and fictitious. But why then is the name Lazarus therein employed if it were no real thing? *Et quid illic Lazari nomen, si non in veritate res est?* But even though you believe it to be a parable, it must still be in accordance with the truth; *testimonium veritatis.*" So too speaks Irenæus, (Adv. Haer., lib. ii, c. xxxiv:) "In the narrative which is written concerning Dives and Lazarus;" *in enarratione quæ scribitur de Divite et de Lazaro.* So too Origen speaks of "The rich man punished and the poor man refreshed in Abraham's bosom before the end of the world, and therefore before the resurrection;" πρὸ τῆς συντελείας τοῦ αἰῶνος, καὶ διὰ τοῦτο πρὸ τῆς ἀναστάσεως. But these extracts are sufficient. In later times Grotius and Rosenmuller adopted the view of the author of the *Responsio ad Orthodoxos*, that it is a *hypotyposis*, or narrative in which something real is de-

* Euthymius, one of the fathers, expressly affirms that the narrative is historical, and that he had the rich man's name, *Nineusis*, from a tradition of the Jews; that he lived in the time of Christ, who therefore does not mention his name.

picted in colors of probability. But the matter simply comes to this: If it be historical, then it is a narrative of *what has been;* if a parable, or hypotyposis, then it is an illustration of *what does occur*, and of what may therefore be regarded as an example.*

The same narrative, as above remarked, is found in the Talmuds, both of Jerusalem and Babylon, with a slight variation. As therein presented it is as follows: "There was a good man and a wicked man, both of whom died. The good man had no funeral rites celebrated, but the wicked man had. After their death, one in a vision saw the good man walking in the midst of gardens, and near pleasant fountains; and the wicked man, with his tongue

* In Dr. Whately's criticisms on this narrative we have a further illustration of his wholly inadequate preparation, in a literary and critical point of view, for entering thoroughly and intelligently into the discussion of those weighty themes upon which he has undertaken to speculate. He asserts, without any qualification whatever, that "*all* allow that the narrative is a parable, that is, a fictitious tale formed in order to teach or illustrate some doctrine; and although such a tale *may* chance to agree in every point with matter of fact, with events which actually take place, there is no necessity that it should." W. 56. The parables of our blessed Lord are therefore "fictitious *tales*," according to this dignitary! Paine was equally fond of using the word "*tale*" in reference to the Gospel narratives, and it would do Dr. Whately no harm to read the severe but merited rebuke given him by Bishop Watson for employing such a term in such a connection. But what shall be said of Dr. Whately's assertion that *all* allow the narrative to be a parable? Let the reader consider it in the light of the facts presented in the foregoing exposition, and then make up his own mind in view of it. Dr. Whately had either examined the subject or he had not. If he had, *he knew of the facts above stated.* If he had not, why did he venture upon such an assertion, and then make it the basis for an insinuation that nothing can be certainly known from parabolic illustration? On p. 58 he likewise thus speaks on the subject matter of the narrative: "Indeed, the very circumstance of the torturing *flames* implies, literally, the presence of the *body*, and therefore cannot be literally true of a state in which the soul is *separate* from the body." That is, in other words, because there are "torturing flames" adapted to a material body, "therefore it cannot be literally true" that there are also torturing flames adapted to the spirit. To call such argumentation puerile would be to eulogize it. It would be bad enough on any subject; but to introduce it on the topic before us is egregious trifling. See in Matt. xxv, 41; Rev. xx, 10, whether there is not a fire adapted to spirits.

hanging out, at the bank of a river, endeavoring to touch the water but could not." From this the reader may judge how perfectly idle is all the talk and noise of our opponents, based upon the fact that "this *parable* is found in the Gemara."

We need not hesitate, says the profoundly learned Storr,* "to found an argument on the phrase ὑπὸ τῶν ἀγγέλων, he was carried *by the angels*, since there is nothing in all the structure of the narrative to render that addition necessary, the narration being perfectly complete without it. There could therefore be no reason why our Lord should have mentioned the conveyance of the soul of Lazarus to Paradise *by a company of angels*, except a design to signify some circumstance of the blessedness of the pious dead. Nor can his intention be to convey a *general* notion by this special illustration; for that it was by the *providence* of God that Lazarus was brought to Abraham's bosom, is so evident that the phrase ὑπὸ τῶν ἀγγέλων, if designed to convey that meaning, would have been perfectly needless. Hence we may believe (nor does any objection arise from the nature of the thing itself, as certainly the ministration of angels (Heb. i, 14) is of all things least incredible in that most important change of our condition) that our Saviour intended to point out, in the example of the dying Lazarus, the manner in which the Divine providence is exercised toward the good in the hour of death." The truth of these admirable remarks appears to be self-evident.

It was the doctrine of the Jews that God employed angels to convey to Paradise the souls of the righteous at death. Thus they relate respecting Moses, that at the moment of his death God said to Gabriel: "Go and bring to me the soul of Moses!" And it is added: "God took hold of him, and put him under the throne of glory; nor is the soul of Moses alone treasured up under the throne of glory, but there also are placed the souls of other just persons." Comp. Rev. vi, 9.†

* De Parabolis Christi, sec. 20.

† See Lightfoot, in Luke xvi.

By Abraham's bosom they meant Paradise. The three names, *Garden of Eden*, *Abraham's bosom*, *and Paradise*, were employed by the Jews as synonyms, to express the condition of the blessed between death and the resurrection. Wetstein, from the Chaldee paraphrasts and other Jewish writings, shows that it was a tradition of the ancient Jews, that the souls of the pious are at death carried by angels into Paradise. See Wisdom iii, 1–3; and comp. Luke xxiii, 43, and 2 Cor. xii, 1–4. They also say: "On the day that the Rabbi died, R. Ada ben Ahava said, '*This day he sits in Abraham's bosom.*'" "God took Abraham and planted him *in Paradise*." "When our master, Moses, departed *into Paradise*, he said unto Joshua," etc., Then again say they: "He (Moses) is *in heaven* ministering unto God." So too in the *Jerusalem Talmud*, it is said of Rabbi Judah, when he died, that "*he is carried by angels;*" but the *Babylonian* has it, "He is placed *in Abraham's bosom.*" They also represent the mother of the noble martyr (2 Mac. vii,) as saying to him just before his death, "Go thou, O my son, to Abraham thy father, and tell him," etc. (Comp. Matt. viii, 11; John i, 18; xiii, 23.) But it is needless to detain the reader any longer on this passage.

5. The next passage to which we invite attention is the following: "But as teaching the resurrection of the dead, have ye not read in the book of Moses, how in the bush God spake unto him, saying, I am the God of Abraham, and the God of Isaac, and the God of Jacob? *God is not the God of the dead, but of the living; for all live unto him;* ye therefore do greatly err." I give the whole statement, as presented by the three evangelists. See Matt. xxii, 23–33; Mark xii, 18–27; Luke xx, 28–38.

When we come to consider the Annihilationist "arguments," we shall take occasion to refer again to a part of this passage. My object at present is to view it in a single aspect. The Sadducees believed that man ceased utterly to exist at death, and consequently they denied his resurrection. Their denial of the resurrection was of course based upon this belief. Hence, if this could be disproved they must give up their doctrine, as the foundation on which they denied the resurrection would be utterly swept away; for, granting that the soul continued to exist after death, they had no conception that it would forever remain separated from the body, the body being a part of the man, and of course belonging to him *as man*. If death was not annihilation, therefore, and if man must live forever, they saw that he must live forever *as man*, and consequently that a reunion of soul and body must at some time take place.

Hence our Saviour pursued the line of argument that he did. Had he designed merely to establish the revival of the body, he could have referred to the case of Enoch, whose translation clearly announced that man was not destined to lie forever in the cold obstruction of the grave. But he aimed at something more; for had he simply proved a future resurrection, the Sadducees would still have objected, as the Annihilationists now do, that there was no such thing as a spirit. (Acts xxiii, 8.) While if the existence of the spirit after death is proved, the resurrection, as they viewed the matter, followed of course. Our Saviour therefore, in order at once to disprove their views on both these points, refers to Exodus iii, 6, 16, (comp. also Acts vii, 32, and Heb. xi, 16,) which affirms that God was *still* the God of Abraham, Isaac, and Jacob, though they had been long dead, and upon which he also remarks that "*God is not the God of the dead*," (in the sense in which the Sadducees used the term dead, for how could he be the God of that which had no existence?) "*but of the living*;" and then, directly in the very face of their theory, he adds, "for ALL live unto him;" that is, So far is man from ceasing to exist at death, as ye Sadducees pretend, that, even though they have ceased to be seen on earth, all that are dead still live to Him.

The import of the expression, "I *am* the God of Abraham," etc., can hardly be mistaken: *I am their protector, and the object of their worship.** And as this was spoken long after the death of these patriarchs, he could not *then* be their protector, and the object of their worship, if at death they had ceased to exist. For to claim to be the protector of that which has no existence is as complete an absurdity as it would be for a man to proclaim himself the protector of a house which had been destroyed by fire. Hence, as He was still their protector, *they still existed.* And hence too, in the narrative of the rich man and Lazarus, Abraham, who also was dead, is introduced as in full possession of his conscious personality; a representation which would never have been made, if the annihilation theory be true, as it must necessarily lead to serious error.

The remarks of our opponents on this passage are, from first to last, beneath criticism. They may be seen in C. 36; S. app. 12; D. 153–160; H. 2, pp. 73, 74; A. 77–82; E. 152–154. There is not one attempt to grapple with the argument, except by evasions and equivocations of the most puerile character. I will refer to those however which have an air of plausibility.

And first: It is claimed by them that the clause in Luke, "*For all live to Him,*" (πάντες γὰρ αὐτῳ ζῶσιν,) is the key of the whole passage; meaning, as they say, that though these patriarchs are dead and extinct, they yet live in the purposes of God, who calleth things that are not as though they were. Thus E. says: "They are alive in the purpose and in the vision of God." "Mark, God is not the God of the wicked dead, but of the living saints." But if the wicked are raised, even if only to be annihilated over again, how is it that they are not as much alive in "the purpose and vision of God" as these patriarchs themselves? But it is obvious that *for* (γὰρ) is here explanatory, and denotes *how* God is the God of the living and not of the dead; they all are alive *to him,* (αὐτῳ,) though they be dead *to men.* He could not be their God if, in the Sadducean sense, they

* See Knapp's Theology, p. 458, and section 29, sub-section 8, *supra.*

were dead or extinguished. They are withdrawn from human sight and observation, but yet they live. Thus too it is said of Jesus, even after his resurrection, that he "*liveth unto God.*" Rom. vi, 10. And of course, therefore, those who are said to live to God are not supposed to be less alive than they were when they lived to men.* Then further: In what were these patriarchs distinguished from others if they all were extinguished at death? Relationship is expressed in these words:† for as there cannot, in the proper sense of the term, be a father without children, nor a king without people, so neither could God be the God of these patriarchs unless they were then existing. (See Rev. vi, 9, 10.) And so too, if God intended to say to Moses what the annihilation theory makes him say, it of course would have been, "I *was* the God of Abraham," etc., and not "I *am*," etc. (Comp. Exod. vi, 3.) The same idea is illustrated also by the language which God employed in relation to the Abrahamic covenant. (Gen. xvii.) He promises not only to be Abraham's God, but that he *will be* the God of his seed. Now it is just as true that this seed "lived in the affections and purposes of God," as it could be true that the patriarchs thus lived if they ceased to exist at death. And yet God does not say, *I am* the God of thy seed after thee, but, *I will be their God.* See also Gen. xxviii, 13–15, in which, in the address to Jacob, God employs the emphatic language, "I am the God of Abraham thy father, and the God of Isaac." Isaac had not yet died, and yet in precisely the same sense that God was his God, he was also the God of Abraham; whereas, if the annihilation theory were true, the only appropriate language would have been, I *was* the God of Abraham thy father, and I *am* the God of Isaac. But the verb of existence is not expressed in the Hebrew, thus evincing that in the same sense he was the God of both.

Mr. Dobney remarks that "a modern teacher would find no argument at all for a resurrection, *as we commonly*

* See Cudworth, ii, 238.

† See Calvin in Luke xx, 37.

*understand it*, in the phrase quoted by Christ, but only for the continually conscious existence of the patriarchs." But when Mr. Dobney made this assertion *he knew* that modern teachers *do find* such an argument in those words, and that they rely on those words as teaching irrefragably the doctrine of the resurrection. Had the Sadducees, moreover, known of that modern theory of Swedenborg, which teaches that the separate state of the soul is the *perfect state* for which God created man, they might have objected that the argument did not establish the resurrection. But as this theory had not been broached among the Jews, they were silenced by the argument.

Mr. Ham remarks that the only states referred to in the language of our Lord are the *present* and the future resurrection state; thus, in his peculiar style of logic, assuming the point to be proved. Now the intermediate state, as I have shown above, is clearly referred to in the words, "I *am* the God of Abraham," etc., and "God is not the God of the dead, but of the living; for all *live* to him." But having thus assumed the point, he thus reasons: Had our Lord taught the doctrine of the conscious disembodied soul existing in a state intermediate between death and the resurrection, it would have been more to the purpose of the Sadducees to have inquired, What relation does this woman sustain to her seven husbands *now?* In other words, Mr. Ham has so clear a conception of what Christ taught respecting the state and condition of the disembodied spirit, as to perceive that marriage pertains not only to persons in the body but also to separate souls! The Sadducees were incapable of such folly. From their question, *Whose wife shall she be?* and from our Lord's reply, *In the resurrection they neither marry nor are given in marriage*, their true sentiments appear. They supposed that *the resurrection of the body* must necessarily infer the continuance of the marriage relation as it *here exists*. Hence their attempt at the *reductio ad absurdum*. But Mr. Ham turns that into an inquiry for information, which was merely designed to convict of absurdity a doctrine which they despised. But suppose they had even inquired, Whose wife is she *now?* how would this have proved the doctrine absurd which they were endeavoring to subvert—the doctrine of the resurrection of the body? It is difficult to characterize such criticism. And yet such are the quibbles of this *body of critics* on the passage in question.

To conclude. The immortality of the soul being demonstrated, the resurrection of the body clearly follows, because the word of God deduces the latter from the former and immediately conjoins them. The Jews regarded the question relating to the two *as one*, in this sense, that the one being granted the other necessarily follows; then the justice of God demands that the soul should receive, in connection with the body, its desert. The works of God, also, (that is, creation, redemption, and sanctification,) respect not only the soul but the body. Hence, therefore, the argument in this passage stands thus: God is not the God of the dead, but of the living; but he is the God of Abraham, Isaac, and Jacob; therefore Abraham, Isaac, and Jacob are not dead in the sense in which ye Sadducees employ the term, but living; and consequently they shall, at some future time, arise from the dead, and with them the rest of mankind.* Thus is the doctrine of the resurrection invincibly established upon the basis of the soul's immortality.

6. Our next passage is Luke xxiii, 43: "Jesus said unto him, Verily I say unto thee, to-day shalt thou be with me in paradise." The Greek, which I purposely present without pointing, is *εἶπεν αὐτῷ ὁ Ἰησοῦς ἀμὴν λέγω σοι σήμερον μετ' ἐμοῦ ἔσῃ ἐν τῷ παραδείσῳ.*

The struggles of our opponents with this passage may be witnessed in C. 38–40; S. app. 8, 9; H. 2, pp. 75, 76; A. 84–86; G. 21; E. 159–162; F. 21–23; J. T. 66. Mr. Dobney seems to have wisely concluded to say nothing on the subject.

* See Schmidtii, Colleg. Biblicum, ii, p. 380.

The text itself requires not much commentary to elucidate its import, and I shall therefore merely call the reader's attention to the efforts of our opponents to divest it of its significancy, for this process will sufficiently elicit its true sense. Their *first* objection is the following criticism on the word "to-day."

C. remarks: "Luke xxiii, 43, is often quoted as conclusive evidence that the righteous, at death, go immediately into heaven to dwell with Christ. But strange as it may appear, this evidence hangs on the position of the little comma placed before the word to-day, making the word to-day qualify the verb *shall be* in the second member of the sentence. Now, suppose we move the place of the comma, so as to make it read, Verily I say unto thee to-day, shalt thou be with me in paradise. This destroys the evidence that good men go to heaven at death. Now the location of the comma is no part of inspired testimony, but a thing of modern invention. But, says one, if the word to-day is made a part of the first member of the sentence, and qualifies the *verb say*, instead of *shall be*, it is not good sense, for the thief could not think Christ was saying it yesterday or to-morrow. This leads us to examine more closely the word. It is not a noun in the original, but an adverb, *sēmeron*, and *does* qualify the first expression, "*I say*," and is the same in other instances translated *now*, [where is the proof of this in the New Testament?] which is frequently used without the least regard to definite time. As if I should say to my opponent, *Now* you are mistaken with regard to what the Saviour said to the thief. Here I do not use the word *now* to let my opponent understand he was not mistaken yesterday, to-day, or to-morrow, but to give a force to that indicative form of expression. This appears to be the use of the word *sēmeron* in the text. 'Now, verily, I say unto thee shalt thou be with me in paradise.' When? Listen to the thief's prayer: 'Lord, remember me when thou comest into thy kingdom.' Not when thou goest into thy kingdom at death, but when thou comest into it." The same pointing is insisted on by S. and by A., who also add: "The Lord has not even yet come into his kingdom, and consequently the thief's desire has not been realized;" which G. also asserts, and expresses a doubt whether the passage is genuine. E. further denies that paradise has *now* any existence, or that it will have, until it is located in the new earth, and consequently that neither Christ nor the thief could then have entered it. "How could either Christ or the thief be in paradise that day, when paradise does not yet actually exist?" But of this more presently. F. and J. T. speak in the same strain, whom H. follows, by denying that there is any congruity between the request of the thief and the reply of Christ, if that reply means that he shall go immediately to heaven; and he explains the passage thus: "As if Christ had said, I will remember you when I come in my kingdom, for *this day* you shall be among those of whom *it is written*, Blessed are the dead which die in, or with, the Lord." Mr. Ham does not say, however, *where* this passage was *then* written. See note in § 37, sub-sect. 2.

The reader will have perceived how these writers contradict each other in their criticisms on the word "*to-day*." But as we shall have occasion to refer to this again, we shall now confine our remarks to those who assert that this word qualifies the verb "*say*," instead of "*shall be*." And in support of this they quote such passages as Deut. xi, 1, and Gen. ii, 4, 17, in order to prove, what no one will deny, that the term *day* does not always mean a natural day.

These objections, the learned reader is aware, have been copied from critics of former times, and are still occasionally insisted on by one or another who might know better. The reply of Grotius and Wolzogenius, which I here subjoin, has never been met, however, as it ought certainly to have been, before any man laying claim to common honesty should undertake to repeat the objection. Grotius remarks as follows: "Σήμερον, (*to-day.*) They have acted most basely (*pessime*) who have joined this word with λέγω, (*I say*,) or have explained it to mean after the resurrection. Christ promises more than had been asked. *Thou askest*, says he, *that I may remember thee hereafter, when I shall receive possession of the kingdom; I shall not postpone so long the answer to thy prayer; but within this very day I shall bestow upon thee a part of the first fruits of the hoped-for felicity. Die then without apprehension, for divine consolations await thee immediately after death.* The word to-day is emphatically spoken, (ἐμφατικὸν,)" etc. These positions are fully sustained in his admirable note on the passage, in which also he remarks, "that no one can deny that the thief, as he was a Jew, having heard the name גַּן עֵדֶן (*Garden of Eden*, or *Paradise*) thus emphatically connected with the designation of time, *to-day*, death too approaching, understood that state in which it was the persuasion of the Jewish people that the souls of Abraham, Isaac, and Jacob then existed." The remarks of the celebrated Wolzogenius are equally unanswerable, and in his case the more remarkable, as he was a strenuous advocate for the sleep of the soul. He says: "*To-day.* This adverb is not to be connected with the preceding, thus, *I say to thee to-day;* (which the Syriac version also expressly repudiates;) neither is the sense, *To-day*, that is, after my resurrection, (*post resurrectionem meam*,) thou shalt be with me in paradise. But Christ promises to the thief more than he had besought; as if he had said, You ask that I will at some time remember you when I shall receive my kingdom. But I affirm to you that I shall not delay so long the fulfillment of your supplication; but to-day, that is, in this very day, so soon as you have passed from this life, you shall be with me in paradise. There is, according to Jewish usage, a singular emphasis in this adverb *to-day*," etc. He also proves by invincible arguments that the Jews distinguished "the state of paradise, into which pious souls enter at death, from the resurrection state," and adds: "As Christ therefore here wished so to speak as that the thief understood what he said in accordance with the meaning attached to such language by the Jews, why surely since he made mention of paradise, and had also named the time, *to-day*, and as he was even then with him in the agony of death, it is certain that the thief could have understood nothing else by paradise than that state or place into which the Jews believed that the souls of Abraham, Isaac, and Jacob, and of the rest of the pious, were conveyed at death. This therefore is what Christ would say: 'Not only when I come in my kingdom will I remember thee, but even now, to-day, thy soul shall be with me in the place, and with the congregation of the righteous.' For Christ did not vainly, and without cause, add the word *to-day*."

These criticisms, substantiated as they are by irrefragable proof, cannot be gainsayed. I would add, however, in reply to the remarks of our opponents on the *pointing* of the text, that ὅτι, *that*, is obviously always *understood* in such a connection, if it be not expressed. The plain construction is, Verily I say unto thee, *that* to-day thou shalt be," etc.*

Ὅτι is frequently expressed where such a collocation of words is found; as, for example, in Mark xiv, 30; Luke xix, 9; but it is, as every tyro knows, full as often understood as is the Hebrew כִּי, the German *dass*, and the English *that*, especially after verbs of declaring. See, in the Greek, Heb. iii, 7; iv, 7; James iv, 13. Hence, too, though expressed in the Greek text, it is often omitted in translation, as in Luke iv, 21, and xix, 9. In fact not one instance can be found in the inspired Scriptures of any such usage of the word σήμερον as these men so arbitrarily and ignorantly attempt to fix upon it in this instance.

The attempt to justify their procedure by the remark

* The old Syriac version, which appears to have been made previous to the death of the Apostle John, expresses the particle: "Verily, I say unto thee *that* to-day thou shalt be with me in paradise." This of itself is sufficient to demonstrate the relation of σήμερον to ἔσῃ.

that the "pointing is not inspired," amounts to nothing; for surely that fact does not give them liberty to turn the Scriptures into nonsense by placing points anywhere. I will here present two or three analagous instances, and let any competent reader take his Greek Testament and examine them. We will first take Luke xix, 5: "Zaccheus make haste and *come down for to-day*, *I must abide at thy house.*" The collocation of words is just as it is in Luke xxiii, 43. Is, then, the idea that Zaccheus must come down to-day, and then go up and stay there the rest of his life? or to-morrow? So too in such passages as Heb. iii, 7: "The Holy Spirit *saith to-day*, If ye will hear," etc.; and Heb. iv, 7: "As it is *said to-day*, If ye will hear," etc. Now it would be just as senseless to insist that these passages should be *thus translated and pointed*, because "pointing is not inspired," as it is to say, for the same reason, that the analagous passage in Luke xxiii, 43, *may* be pointed as our opponents pretend. See also James iv, 13: "*Ye who say to-day or to-morrow*, we will go," etc. The above instances however are sufficient.*

The reference to the passages in Deuteronomy, where Moses says: "I command thee *this day*," etc., as illustrative of the term *to-day*, as here used, evinces the extremity to which our opponents are reduced by this text. For in his prayer the thief had expressed *a time:* "Remember me *when* thou comest," etc. And in Christ's reply the term *to-day* responds to the *when:* you ask me to do it *hereafter*, but I do it *now*. It is true the poor penitent did not ask to be remembered that *day*, as our opponents assert; but does this hinder that Christ should give him more than

* Several writers of the Romish Church adopted this criticism, to whom *Bellarmine* replies as follows: "This exposition is perfectly ridiculous, for why should the Lord say, 'Verily, I tell you *to-day?*' Could not the robber see that he was speaking to him that day; and besides, who does not see by the adverb *to-day*, the reply is given to the adverb *when?* The true exposition, therefore, is that of Theophylact, Ambrose, Bede, and others, who by paradise understand the kingdom of heaven." De Beat. Sanct., lib. i, cap iii.

he asked? Did the poor publican ask to be "justified," and made a child of God, with all the fullness and promptness with which his prayer was answered? Did the prodigal son ask to have a ring on his finger, and shoes on his feet, and to be clothed in the best robe his father possessed? And was his prayer therefore not answered because he got more than he sought? Was there "*a want of congruity* between the prayer and its answer?" But such objections are purely theologastrian.

Our opponents also ask: "Why, if the thief believed the doctrine of the soul's immortality, did he not ask to be remembered by Christ immediately after death?" But this is merely an objection *ab ignorantia.* He asked to be one of the subjects of Christ's kingdom, and surely this included everything. Paul affirms of himself that he labored and toiled so that he might "*attain to the resurrection of the dead.*" Yet he does not consider this as at all inconsistent with an earnest *desire to depart and be with Christ.* If, from a deep sense of unworthiness, the thief thought himself unfit to be associated with Christ, this has nothing to do with the import of the Saviour's language. We know not fully what were the thief's theological views previous to this, his conversion, though he of course was familiar with the figures, etc., of the Jewish language; he may have been a Sadducee, or a "*Nothingarian.*" But it is not *his* language, but that of the Saviour, with which the argument before us is concerned.

Another objection which they bring is on the very verge of blasphemy, and well nigh charges the Saviour with uttering a falsehood. C. denies that the thief died on the same day with Christ, and asserts that Christ died on Thursday, and was in the grave all of Friday and Saturday. Others repeat the same idea. It is needless, however, to notice these reckless assertions, except by remarking that in Mark xv, 42, and xvi, 9, it is emphatically stated that he was crucified on Friday. It is evident also from the fact that the Jews themselves would have put him to death, as they did Stephen, had it not been the day of the passover, when it was not lawful for them to put any man to death. The blunder of C., and others of our opponents, arose from their being ignorant of the fact that while Matthew, Mark, and Luke, who wrote mainly to Jews, calculated the time from evening to evening, according to the Jewish method; John, who wrote long after the Jewish believers ceased to be a majority in the Church, calculated his time by the Roman or Asiatic method, from midnight to mid-day, and from mid-day to midnight. But it is useless to spend more time upon this objection. Mr. Ham, and others of the chief writers of this sect, assert that Christ and the thief died on the same day.

Their *third* objection is that paradise is an ambiguous term, and consequently the language of Christ to the malefactor is ambiguous, "on account of *our* ignorance of the precise sense to be attached to the word paradise." So speaks Mr. Ham, and he further denounces the argument as based upon a "dubious portion" of Scripture. An equally able writer, (F. 22,) however, says in the most emphatic manner, "paradise, remember, *is where God resides*." "The thief died that day." E. also says that the word is used but three times in the Bible, (Luke xxiii, 43; 2 Cor. xii, 4; and Rev. ii, 7,) and that paradise does not now exist. Thus they hallucinate.

The question, however, is not whether the term is ambiguous to these writers and their coadjutors, but whether it was ambiguous to the Jews in the time of Christ? That it was not, any one can satisfy himself by merely referring to the quotations from the Talmuds, as given by Grotius and Wolzogenius *in loco*. The Jews understood by it, as employed in this connection, the resting place of the souls of the righteous between death and the resurrection. And as to the term being used nowhere in the Bible except in the places above named, the reader may judge for himself what profound critics these are, when I assure him that פַּרְדֵּס is found in Neh. ii, 8; Eccles. ii, 5; and Cant. iv, 13.

The remark that paradise *does not exist*, in the sense in which the word is employed in the New Testament, is equally profound. Luke xxiii, 43, asserts its existence in the clearest manner, as Christ and the thief were both in paradise on the day they died. Paul also asserts that he was caught up into paradise, (either in the body or out of the body,) and none but an Annihilationist can imagine that the Apostle could have been conveyed into a place that had no existence. And Christ also expressly declares that the tree of life *is* in the midst of the paradise of God, (Rev. ii, 7,) language which can convey no other idea than that paradise has a present existence.

Their *last* objection is that Christ was not in paradise, or heaven, until after his resurrection. See E. 159, 160; G. 21; A. 85; J. T. 66; and S., App. 8, 9. Here too they are expressly contradicted by others of their writers: F. 22; H. 2, pp. 75, 76. Those, however, who maintain the first proposition quote, to sustain them, John xx, 17: "*Touch me not, for I have not yet ascended to my Father*," a passage which we shall therefore briefly examine.

This exposition is directly contradicted by the words of Christ in John xvi, 16, in which he tells his disciples that *at his death* (comp. verses 17–28,) he should go to the Father. Even Archdeacon Blackburne is compelled to admit that these words teach that Christ ascended to heaven in the interval between his death and resurrection. The same idea in substance, as we have seen, he expressed to the dying malefactor. Mary, to whom he speaks in John xx, 17, doubtless knew of his words in both these instances, and that in the former instance he expressed his intention of returning again to the Father after his resurrection, and that then his disciples should meet him on earth no more. Now the words translated *I am not yet ascended*, are οὔπω αναβέβηκα, the preterite for the present, according to the usage illustrated by Glassius, Philol. Sac., lib. iii, tract iii, can. 46, 47; also by Viger, De Idiotis. Græc, c. v, sec. 3; (see also Annotationes Hermanni, in Vigerum;) and by

Winer, p. i, sec. 41. Now every tyro knows that in composition ἀνα has very frequently the force of *again.* Βαίνω alone means simply *to ascend; ἀνὰ adds* a shade of meaning. Thus, Matt. iii, 16, "Christ *went up again,* or returned." Matt. xiii, 7: The thorns which had been cut off in order that the seed might be sown *sprang up again.* In referring also to our Saviour's frequent ascent into mountains, the same word is used. "He went up *again* into a mountain." Matt. v, 1; xiv, 23; xv, 23. It is in like manner employed in referring to his frequent visits to Jerusalem. "He went up *again* to Jerusalem." Matt. xx, 17, 18; John v, 1. "We go up *again.*" Mark x, 32. See also Mark vi, 51; Luke ii, 42; ix, 28; x, 31; xix, 28; John vii, 8, 10, 14; and so too in multitudes of instances, where the idea, though not expressed in the translation, as it is in the Greek, is clearly implied. Now this same composite term is used in our text. And as Mary had doubtless heard of his remarks above referred to, no term can be more proper: "Touch me not, for I do not yet ascend again to my Father."*

These words, therefore, clearly imply such an ascent between his death and resurrection, according to chap. xvi, 16, and so teach the very doctrine which our opponents endeavor to disprove by quoting them.

The import of the phrase *touch me not,* μή μου ἅπτου, is sufficiently plain. Ἅπτομαι refers to the method of evincing respect among the Greeks and Orientals. It was to fall down before a superior and embrace, or even kiss his feet.

* Or if the perfect tense be contended for, it will amount substantially to the same thing. "I have not yet ascended again (that is, since my resurrection) to the Father; but I am now about to ascend." There is no impropriety in admitting that during the interval of the forty days between his resurrection and final ascension, in the presence of his disciples, the Saviour may have frequently ascended to the abodes of the blessed. (See my work on the Resurrection, pp. 336–338.) I have translated the idiom literally, merely to exhibit the precise shade of meaning conveyed by the original; though, of course, as every one knows, an idiomatic expression can seldom be felicitously transferred from one language into another.

See Luke v, 8; vii, 38; 2 Kings, iv, 27; compare also Josephus, Antiq., vi, c. xiii, sec. 78, and vii, c. xi, sec. 2. The idea therefore is, Do not cling to me as though you supposed that I shall now at once depart from earth; I do not yet ascend again to the Father. But go and tell my brethren that, having now arisen, I *shall* [the present for the future] ascend again to my Father, etc. I have here translated the ἀνὰ, though the sense is sufficiently clear, even in our own idiom, without it.

As the Jews therefore employed the terms Abraham's bosom, Garden of Eden, and Paradise, as synonymous, and were accustomed to say of the good man when dying, "*To-day he shall rest or sit in the bosom of Abraham*, (whence arose also the Chaldaic saying: "*Seek Paradise, the glorious country of the soul*,") and as Christ used this language in that sense in which the thief, who was a Jew, could understand him, so Luke xxiii, 43, must ever stand as a clear announcement of the uninterrupted immortality of the soul. The assurance given to the expiring penitent was also backed by that most solemn form of asseveration, ἀμην, (from the root אמן, *to be true and faithful*,) which the Scripture employs when it would affirm anything in the most direct and earnest manner. It is even employed also as one of the names of Christ: "The *Amen*, *the faithful and true witness*." Rev. iii, 14. Well therefore might the dying but penitent thief rely on the assurance thus given; nor is the hope misplaced which now cheers the expiring saint, that when the agony of death is past, he too shall meet his faithful and beloved Redeemer in paradise.

7. The next passage to which we shall invite attention is Luke xxiv, 36–39: "And as they thus spake, Jesus himself stood in the midst of them, and saith unto them, Peace be unto you. But they were terrified, and affrighted, and supposed that they had seen a spirit. And he said unto them, Why are ye troubled? and why do [such] thoughts arise within your hearts? Behold my hands and my feet, that it is I myself; handle me, and see; for a spirit hath not

flesh and bones as ye see me having." See also Job iv, 13–17; Matt. xiv, 26; Mark vi, 49. That the basis of the fear here mentioned, as associated with this sudden appearance of Christ, was the belief of the Jewish doctrine of the immortality of the soul, will not be questioned, for they saw and recognized his form.

I refer to this passage particularly to illustrate the manner in which our opponents openly falsify the Scriptures in order to get rid of their testimony. E. 100, for example, thus quotes and remarks upon it: "Luke xxiv, 37: 'They supposed that they had seen a spirit.' Verse 39: 'It is I; for a spirit hath not flesh and bones.' In this place Griesbach puts *phantasma* in the margin, which doubtless is the true reading." This is one of the many false statements which this illiterate production is scattering through the country. The same assertion is also made by A. 60, an equally reckless and illiterate work. Griesbach, on verse 37, notes that φάντασμα, though suggested as a reading *in that verse*, is yet *without authority, and is to be repudiated;* while in respect to verse 39 no such reading had ever been suggested, so that in both these verses πνεῦμα (spirit) is the undisputed reading. No censure can be too severe upon men who can thus falsify the express declarations of God's word in order to deceive the unwary.

S., App. 13, supposes that *spirit* here does not mean the spirit of a man, and adds: "*Angels are spirits*, but have not a body of flesh and bones." H. 2, p. 88, with his usual learning, maintains that the reference "is *not* to the *human* spirit, but merely to spiritual existence;" and as Christ does not use the "possessive pronoun," and say "*my* spirit hath not flesh and bones," he cannot admit that here is any proof "of the theory of disembodied human existence." Such passages, says he, merely imply "the existence of *other beings*, who are called *spirits*."

That the Jews believed the soul survived the body and might become visible, (1 Sam. xxviii,) no one acquainted with their theology will deny; and such was their belief in the time of Christ. The disciples retained this doctrine during the whole time of their intercourse with Christ, and though early expressed by them, (see Matt. xiv, 26,) he never corrected "the Pagan fable," and "false and pernicious delusion," and "wicked superstition," as our opponents name it, but permitted them to entertain it fully. And even now, after his resurrection, their minds are still influenced by the same ideas, and yet he gives not the slightest intimation that they are inaccurate. A fact which, of itself, fully demonstrates the annihilation theory to be a false and pernicious delusion.

In the passage before us he appeared to the eleven, and addressed them with his usual and well known salutation, "*Peace be unto you.*" They saw him distinctly and clearly before them. They had entertained doubts, however, as to whether he were really risen from the dead; and as he now appeared in their midst after they had fastened the doors, they supposed that his *material* body could not come thus amongst them unperceived. Their doubts as to his actual resurrection were revived, and in their fear they cried out, supposing that, after all, he was only a spirit. The reader can decide whether, under such circumstances, it is supposable they could have believed that what they saw before them might have been any other spirit than his own. He replies to the thoughts which were rising in their hearts by saying, "*Handle me and see.*" Of course, therefore, they had recognized *the form*, and needed only to be assured of the reality of his corporeal presence.

In his reply the Saviour confirms their belief in the reality of the disembodied state of the human spirit, from the fact that he did not, by assuring them that all such fears were ungrounded, correct the impression which they entertained. Our Annihilationists, with the views which they profess, would doubtless have done so at once, for they are continually asserting this in every variety of form. They would have corrected it at the fountain head, especially if they had known, as Christ did know, that multitudes of his most devoted followers, in every age, would rely upon this fact as conclusive evidence that the human soul exists when separated from the body. Why then did not our blessed Saviour thus correct it, as they would certainly have done? There is but one satisfactory answer to this question, namely, *the views which these men entertain and advocate are the reverse of the truth;* for it would be the most infamous blasphemy to pretend that they are more zealous than Christ or his apostles were in removing error and inculcating the truth.

8. I have already referred to the language of Stephen in Acts vii, 59: "Lord Jesus receive my spirit;" and to the similar language of our blessed Saviour when dying. (Luke xxiii, 46.) I here introduce it again, merely to expose the manner in which our opponents endeavor to evade the testimony furnished by those passages.

C. 44 says: "On a careful examination of the text, it does not appear that he [Stephen] prayed to the Lord to receive it [his spirit.] The record states: Then they [the Jews] ran upon him, [*reviled* and *ridiculed* him,] and cast him out of the city, and stoned him. Now it seems it was the same *they* that *ran upon him*, and calling upon God, and saying, Lord Jesus, receive my spirit. But it may be asked why the Jews should say, Lord Jesus, receive my spirit? Only by mocking the confidence of Stephen in the Saviour," etc. In that *profound* treatise, the "Bible *versus* Tradition," E. 98 says: "*The grammar of the text charges the saying*, 'Lord Jesus, receive my spirit,' *upon the wicked Jews*, and afterward records what Stephen did and said." To justify this criticism, the authors of this book make a show of quoting the expression itself in Greek.

The original here has no various readings in MSS., and is as follows: *καὶ ἐλιθοβόλουν τὸν Στέφανον, ἐπικαλούμενον καὶ λέγοντα.* Κύριε Ἰησοῦ, etc. This language is of the plainest and simplest form and character; nothing therein is in any way involved. The word for *they stoned* is plural, and expresses the act of the Jews; while the word for *invocating*, or *calling upon God*, is *singular*, and relates directly to Stephen; nor is there the remotest possibility of mistake in the matter by any one who understands the language sufficiently to distinguish a plural form from a singular. What then is to be thought of the assertion that "the grammar of the text charges upon the wicked Jews" the *calling upon God?* One of two things is true in relation to it; either it is another instance of those reckless misstatements of which the book "Bible *versus* Tradition" is so full, and which appear .to be designed to deceive the unwary; or it is declarative of the real amount of knowledge possessed by the authors of that book, who, while they profess to quote Greek and criticise it as though it were perfectly familiar to them, do not even understand the merest rudiments of the language. Whichever of these alternatives be chosen, the public will be at no loss how to appreciate the claims of such writers to be intelligent and conscientious advocates of truth.*

Wolzogenius thus comments on the passage: "*Receive my spirit:* even that nobler part of the substance of man, now about to be separated from the body." One meaning alone could have been by the Jews attached to the words of Stephen, (see Wisdom iii, 1, 2,) and that is apparent upon the very surface of the expression. He, too, by being filled with the Holy Ghost, was secured from error. Now he could not have commended his spirit to Christ, if he believed either that he had no spirit, or that it was annihi-

* I am the more particular in calling attention to this work because it is regarded by many of this sect as their ablest production, and it is well calculated to deceive the unwary and ignorant. ,They call it "a two-edged sword;" it is recommended in the most laudatory terms, and circulated by their agents through the length and breadth of the land. They assert that the evangelical clergy are afraid to read it, and that if Dr. Beecher had only possessed a copy of it, his mind would have been so fully relieved by its perusal that he would probably not have published his "Conflict of Ages." They affirm too that the editors of our religious press are afraid to notice it; yet I hesitate not to repeat, that a more grossly illiterate publication has not been issued from the press in modern times.

lated or perished with the body at death, and never revived again except in conjunction with the body itself; for in this case the soul is of no more importance than the body, and it is even of less value, according to E., who asserts that *it is of no consequence what becomes of it.* See § 5, *supra.* The fact, then, that Stephen, under these circumstances, did discriminate between soul and body, and that his anxiety in the hour of death related to the former instead of the latter, establishes beyond cavil itself the separate existence of the soul.

I add here a single remark in reference to the language relating to our blessed Lord in the hour of death. Our opponents take no notice of the different terms in which the Holy Spirit has recorded the idea thus presented. Mark and Luke both say *ἐξέπνευσε*, *he expired*, or *died.* John (xix, 30) says, *παρέδωκε τὸ πνεῦμα*, *he yielded up his spirit;* while Matthew (xxvii, 50) expresses the idea in the most emphatic manner: *ἀφῆκε τὸ πνεῦμα*, *he dismissed his spirit.* The intelligent reader will know how to appreciate the fact here presented as connected with the question of the soul's separate existence.

9. I have but a single remark to offer on our next passage, (Acts xxiii, 6–8,) in which it is expressly mentioned as one of the errors of the Sadducees that they denied the existence of human spirits: "For the Sadducees say that there is no resurrection, *neither angel nor spirit*, *μηδὲ ἄγγελον μητε πνεῦμα.* Now that the Sadducees did not deny that man before his death possessed a vital and intelligent principle, which is called the soul or spirit, all will admit. What then was their error? They denied the existence of the human spirit in a separate state; for by *spirit*, as here distinguished from *angel*, is beyond question meant the departed spirit of man. Our opponents meddle not with this text, and therefore we need offer nothing further upon it.*

* "Paul said he was a Pharisee, in the midst of an assembly of Pharisees and Sadducees. He intended to save his life by it. Did he

10. The next passage to which we invite attention is 2 Cor. v, 1–9: "For we know that if our earthly house of this tabernacle were dissolved, we have a building of God, a house not made with hands, eternal in the heavens. For in this we groan, earnestly desiring to be clothed upon with our house which is from heaven; if so be that being clothed we shall not be found naked. For we that are in this tabernacle do groan, being burdened; not for that we would be unclothed, but clothed upon, that mortality might be swallowed up of life. Now he that hath wrought us for the self-same thing is God, who also hath given unto us *the earnest of the Spirit. Therefore* we are always confident, knowing that while we are at home in the body we are absent from the Lord, (for we walk by faith and not by sight.) We are confident, I say, and willing rather to be absent from the body and to be present with the Lord. Wherefore we labor, that whether present or absent, we may be accepted of him."

The paragraph of which this passage is the conclusion commences at chap. iv, 17, and its connection therewith is so obvious that nothing but carelessness in dividing the New Testament into chapters could have occasioned the separation.

If this passage contained all that the word of God has taught on the subject under discussion, one might suppose that it was of itself sufficient to settle the question of the soul's conscious existence after the dissolution of the body. A few remarks upon it therefore are all that can be here required.

lie? He was, in the sectarian sense, a Pharisee and not a Sadducee. This was solemnly affirming for them in all the points designating their peculiarity on the Sadduceean hypothesis. I offer it now in confidence as a conclusive argument against destructionism, against Sadduceeism, against materialism in every form of it. The resurrection of the dead, the existence of angels and spirits, and the everlasting existence of man, either in happiness or misery, were the whole constituents of a Pharisee. Paul affirmed these to be true when he solemnly declared that he was, in opposition to the skepticism of the Sadducees, a Pharisee in faith and by descent; not merely the son of a Pharisee, but a Pharisee himself." See "Life and Death," by President Campbell, of Bethany, Va.

I have remarked that the passage is, by an arbitrary division, severed from its proper connection with verses 17 and 18 of the previous chapter. In verse 1 the apostle directly refers to the afflictions mentioned in those verses, and the obvious connection is the following: "But even if those afflictions should come to the worst and destroy our life, yet we know that when this tabernacle, this earthly tent, is taken down, we have an eternal mansion in the heavens which shall receive us." And in enlarging upon this thought, he adds that the desire of the soul is not so much to be *unclothed* as *clothed upon* with its house from heaven, (and to which he had referred in his former epistle, 1 Cor. xv, 35–55,) that so it might neither *be** unclothed nor continue naked. "Hence," says he, "we groan and desire, not so much to be unclothed as to be clothed upon with that heavenly body, that so mortality may be absorbed (not *by death*, as some think it to be, but) *by life*." In other words, while death, though it unclothe us, is desirable amid our afflictions, (Phil. i, 21,) as it will bring us into the visible presence of our Lord; yet, as the soul in its separate state is unclothed, we still more desire our final triumph over death and the grave; and to this we look forward steadily, for we have received the Spirit as a pledge or earnest that it shall be achieved. (See Rom. viii, 23; 1 Cor. xv, 54; Rev. vi, 9–11.) Both ideas, therefore, are here advanced: first, that the soul, when its earthly body dies, shall enter the heavenly mansion, (John xiv, 2;) and secondly, that it looks forward notwithstanding to its reunion with the body, when that body shall have been raised and glorified, or when it has become a spiritual body. For the separate state of the soul, however blissful and perfect, is still, in a sense, an unnatural one; as it was not created for a separate existence, and it is not in accordance with that of our Redeemer, and hence the soul still looks forward

* That *εὑρίσκω* has this sense is plain. See Matt. i, 18; Luke ix, 36; xvii, 18; Phil ii, 8; iii, 9; Heb. 11, 5.

to it, and desires the period when it shall be fully like him.*

In this passage, as in Phil. i, 23, there is an obvious antithesis: *to be with Christ* is contrasted with *our continuance in this world.* And hence, while we are at home, or sojourn in the body, we are absent from the Lord. But how

* "The Church now in heaven is not in its fixed and ultimate, but in a progressive, subordinate, and preparatory state. The state in which they are in is in order to another. In the employments in which they are now exercised, they look to that which is still future, to their consummate state, which they have not yet arrived at. Their present happiness is, in many respects, subordinate to a future, and God in his dealings with them has a constant and perpetual respect to the great consummation of all things. So it is both with respect to the saints and angels; all things in heaven and earth, and throughout the universe, are in a state of preparation for the state of consummation; all the wheels are going, none of them stop, and all are moving in a direction to the last and most perfect state. As the Church on earth is in a state of preparation for the resurrection state, so is that part of the Church which is in heaven. It is God's manner to keep things always progressive, in a preparatory state, as long as there is another change to a more perfect state yet behind. The saints in this world are progressive, and all things relating to them are subordinate and preparatory to the more perfect state of heaven; which is a perfect state, in that it is a state of freedom from sinful and uneasy imperfections; but when the saints are got to heaven, there is another great change yet behind; there is yet another state, which is that fixed and ultimate, and most perfect state, for which the whole general assembly both in heaven and earth are designed, and therefore they are still progressive. Not but that I believe the saints will be progressive in knowledge and happiness to all eternity. But when I say the Church is progressive before the resurrection, I mean that they are progressive with a progression of preparation for another and more perfect state; their state is itinerary, viatory; their state, their employments, their glory and happiness, are subordinate and preparatory to a future, more glorious state." (President Edwards, Works, vol. viii, p. 539. New York. 1830.) See also the remarks of Müller, in "Doctrine of Sin," ii, pp. 333-337; and Calvin Instit., lib. iii, cap. xxv, sec. 6. And for the earlier view see Tertullian, De Anima, cap. lviii; Chrysostom on Philippians, and Augustine De Civitate Dei, lib. xx, cap. ix, and also xv. See also his De Genesi, lib. xii, cap. xxxv. He sometimes carried his view of the subject almost to extremes, as in De Civ. Dei, lib. xii, cap. ix; and in Enarrat, in Ps. 36, Conc. I, sec. 10. But his object here was evidently to free himself from the imputation of entertaining the doctrine condemned by Justin Martyr and others, to which reference will be made in another chapter. See also Ambrose, De Cain et Abel, lib. ii, cap ii, sec. 9.

can we be absent from him when "to live is Christ?" and when every true believer walks with him, and enjoys a consciousness of his presence? To this inquiry, which could not but suggest itself in this connection, the apostle answers substantially, that though this is even so, yet while in the body, we being absent from the Lord, it is *by faith* that we thus walk and enjoy his presence, and not by sight, (2 Cor. iv, 18;) but when *absent from the body* we shall enjoy his *visible* presence; we shall walk *by sight and not by faith.** And thus clear is it that the soul in its separate state shall be in the full possession of its native powers.

In the application of the argument furnished by this passage against the theory of our opponents, it is sufficient to remark that the apostle affirms that what he here announces is matter of absolute knowledge. "*For we know* that if our earthly house of this tabernacle were dissolved, we have a building of God, a house not made with hands, eternal in the heavens." For the pious soul, therefore, there is not only this earthly tabernacle, but a heavenly mansion, and when the former is dissolved, the latter shall be its dwelling-place. (John xiv, 2; Heb. xii, 22–24.) Nothing can be more directly contrary than this, to the notion that the apostles and primitive believers expected no happiness until the day of the resurrection. For why long to put off this earthly tabernacle, wherein they could be so useful in doing the work of Christ, when they knew that by dying they could be brought no nearer the fruition of future bliss? For in that case death, so far from being *gain*, as Paul calls it, (Phil. i, 21,) would, on the contrary, be inestimable loss, depriving the believer of opportunities for usefulness, and of making still higher attainments in the divine life, all of which every Christian feels to be truly dear to the heart. And it may be further remarked, that according to the theory of our opponents there is no such thing as being, in any sense, *absent from the body.* The

* See "Essays on the Second Advent," etc., by Rev. J. W. Brooks, Essay viii, p. 87.

soul is inseparable from the body, and of course perishes with it, and exists not again until the body is reconstructed at the resurrection. There cannot be a more direct antagonism than this to the language of the apostle in the foregoing passage.

The expositions which our opponents give of this text are not only contradictory to each other, but absolutely beneath criticism and unworthy of notice. The reader, if so disposed, may consult them in C. 40; D. 160–164; H. 1, p. 116, and H. 2, pp. 78–80; A. 87–89; G. 19; F. 2–6, and 8–11; J. T. 31; E. 156; W. 115–119; and Hud. 255–256.

11. The next passage is 2 Cor. xii, 2–4: "I knew a man in Christ above fourteen years ago, (whether in the body, I cannot tell, or whether out of the body, I cannot tell; God knoweth;) such a one caught up to the third heaven. And I knew such a man, (whether in the body or out of the body I cannot tell; God knoweth;) how that he was caught up into paradise, and heard unspeakable words, which it is not lawful for a man to utter."

That the statements in this passage inevitably imply, in the mind of their author, a full belief of the *separability* of the soul or spirit from the mere corporeal frame or body, no serious mind will venture to call in question. A man who believes that the soul is only the result of corporeal organization, could not employ such or similar language in conveying his views; and the passage must stand as an eternal protest against the attempts now being made to harmonize Divine revelation with the material philosophy.

The apostle here distinctly avers that he was caught or snatched up to (ἡρπάγη ἕως) the third heaven, and *into* (εἰς) paradise. On this point he is direct and positive, and expresses no doubt whatever. He knew the man (that is, himself) who was so caught up. He does, however, express a doubt whether it were in the body or out of it; and hence it is obvious that he might have been conveyed thither in either of these methods, or as well in one way as in the other. And he further affirms that during this rapture or transportation he heard unspeakable words, which plainly infers a full consciousness on his part while the rapture continued; and it is, moreover, implied in the phrase, "which it is not lawful for a man to utter," that he still retained those unspeakable words in his remembrance.

The effort of Slichtingius and others to represent this *vision* (see Matt. xvii, 9, for the import of this word, and § 33, sub-sec. 2, above) as of the same character as that of Ezekiel (xi, 24; xxxvii, 1) and John, (Rev. xvii, 3; xxi, 10,) is without the slightest reason, as a mere perusal of those passages will show. In these instances all is expressly said to be done ἐν πνεύματι, *in the spirit;* but nothing of this kind is intimated in the case of Paul. In verse 1, he indeed speaks of "visions and revelations of the Lord," but he refers them to what he saw during this rapture. And then, further, he confesses that he cannot tell whether he was then in the body or out of it; whereas in all mere visions, properly so called, the soul continues in the body; and he moreover avers that he *heard there*, that is, *in paradise*, unspeakable words. Of course, then, he was *there*, as above remarked.*

The question has been raised whether the apostle here speaks of more than one rapture. The opinion of all the ancients, as Whitby remarks, seems to be that he was taken up at different times into different places. *Irenæus* says that "he was caught up into the third heaven, and was again carried into paradise." *Tertullian* speaks in the same manner; and *Epiphanius* asks, "Who can endure the notion of *Origen*, which placed paradise in the third heaven?" That the raptures were distinct seems probable from verses 1 and 7, in which the apostle speaks of *visions* and *revelations*. *Methodius* inferred the same also from the repetition of the phrase "*whether in the body*," etc., which would have been unnecessary concerning one and the same

* See Dr. Whitby's commentary on this whole passage.

vision. "For hence," says he, "the apostle intimates that he had seen two great visions, being twice caught up, first into the third heaven, and then into paradise." This point, however, is of but little moment to our argument, one well-established instance of the kind being as good as a thousand.

It is obvious, therefore, from this passage, that the soul may exist separate from the body, and that in the separate state it may retain its capacity to witness and understand celestial things; since, were the soul inseparable from the body, the apostle never could have entertained a doubt whether, during the rapture, he was in the body or out of the body.

Our opponents do not seem disposed to meddle with this passage. Dr. Whately and Mr. Hudson pass it in silence, and the Annihilationists touch it only *currente calamo*, and offer nothing which calls for reply. A. 89 seems out of patience with it; and S., Append. 13, utters childish nonsense. H. 2, p. 89, says: "It will suffice to remark that Paul *could not mean* that his soul was his conscious personality, capable of a separate existence apart from his body, and that in this disembodied state he might have been 'caught up to the third heaven.'" And E. 154 says nothing that has not been fully met in the foregoing exposition. As to the rest of the Annihilation family now existing, they follow the example of Dr. Whately, and preserve silence on the subject. Nor have the Materialists and soul-sleepers of former times fared any better in their attempts to set aside this testimony.

Dr. Priestley, however, assails it with his usual intrepidity, and says that the apostle here refers to a vision, "in which he was in paradise, which is the place of the virtuous dead;" but that "it by no means follows from this representation that there is any such place as this paradise, or general receptacle of the dead." This truly is to interpret Scripture with a sledge hammer.

Archdeacon Blackburne, a "soul-sleeper," and the last of our opponents to whom we need refer, says, in reference to the passage: "St. Paul was taken up into paradise, but whether in the body or out of the body he could not tell. Paradise, therefore, for anything this apostle knew, might be a receptacle for *bodies* as well as souls."* This vulgar sneer, to which I refer, however, only to show to what extremities our opponents are driven in their efforts to set aside the inspired testimony, will have but little weight with those who reflect that Enoch and Elijah, and our blessed Redeemer, and those mentioned in Matt. xxvii, 53, had all, in their bodies, preceded the apostle to paradise, or the third heaven. Had Dr. Blackburne read only the candid note of Slichtingius on the passage, he would have blushed, if that were possible, at this abortive attempt at ridicule.

12. The next passage to which we shall call attention is Phil. i, 21–24: "For to me to live is Christ, and to die is gain. But if I live in the flesh, this is the fruit of my labor; yet what I shall choose I wot not. For I am in a strait betwixt two, having a desire to depart, and to be with Christ, which is far better. Nevertheless, to abide in the flesh is more needful for you."

In the verse which immediately precedes this passage, Paul had expressed his earnest hope and expectation that Christ should be magnified by him, whether through life or through death. He adds, in verse 21: "For to me to live is Christ, and to die is gain;" or, as it would be better rendered: "*For to me, in both life and death, Christ is gain;*"† that so Christ may be, as he truly is, the subject of each member of the passage, and not merely an attribute of the first. It were easy to establish the justice and propriety of this criticism on purely philological grounds, as well as from the analogy of faith; but it is not required in

* Intermediate State, p. 283.

† Since writing the above, I perceive that the old English translation named "The Geneva Bible," sustains the criticism. It renders the passage: "For Christ is to me, both in life and in death, advantage." Several good MSS. support the following reading: "For to me, either life or death is a desirable gain."

this connection; for so far as the present discussion is concerned, we are willing the passage should stand as it does in our most excellent version. The reader, however, who may feel interested in the inquiry, can consult the note of Calvin *in loco.*

Christ is, therefore, says the apostle, "gain to me while I live; and this is the fruit of my labor. For if I live, what else is my life but Christ, that I may hope in him, preach him, honor him, serve and worship him; that is, express Christ in all my actions, and say and do all things to the glory of his name. He is gain also to me when I die, for then I shall be absent from the body and present with him, and shall rest from my labors; and hence I am in a strait between the two; for I have a desire to depart and to be with him, which for me is far better; and yet I am willing to remain here, or abide in the flesh, and labor for Christ, and to do you good; for this is more needful for your welfare. And I am willing to forego the bliss of heaven for a season in order that I may be a benefit to you. Thus life and death being good, and each to be desired, I know not which to choose." Such is the plain and natural import of the paragraph. But we shall now notice the manner in which it is treated by our opponents.

H. 2, pp. 68, 78, in explaining it, shows how death was *gain* to the apostle; and yet, on p. 70, quotes many texts to prove that death is the penalty of the law, and the most terrible of all things to man.

G. 20 says: "The apostle does not affirm that he expected to be with Christ *immediately* on his departure, though such would be a fair construction of his words, if it were not a violation of the general tenor of Divine truth on this subject." F. 11-14 explains it thus: "Between living and dying on one hand, and departing on the other, Paul was in a strait, and not between living and dying." By departing he means going to Christ after the resurrection; so that, according to this writer, Paul was in a strait whether he should now live or die, or *now* depart some thousands of years in advance of the march of time. The reader will judge whether such an idea were likely to enter the mind of an intelligent man. E. 139, however, says: "Mark, reader! he was perplexed between the TWO, whether to choose life or to choose death; they were both equally indifferent to him." Thus they hallucinate. Several of them likewise endeavor to show, in utter violation of all grammatical usage and propriety, that the *gain* refered to in verse 21 is gain to Christ, and not to Paul.

A. 91, E. 145, and Hud. 256, 257, endeavor to render verse 23 as follows: "For I am in a strait betwixt two, having a desire to *return*, and be with Christ, which is far better." But to return whither? How is this to be explained unless on the principle asserted in the "Conflict of Ages?" and surely these men do not entertain that idea, as it would utterly destroy their materialism. Ἀναλύω is employed only in one other place in the New Testament, (Luke xii, 36,) and though there translated "return," it properly means *depart;* they wait till their Lord shall *depart* from the wedding, *and come and knock* to be received. And so the noun ἀναλύσις, used only in 2 Tim. iv, 6, means simply "*departure*," since our opponents can hardly suppose that Paul there says, "the time of my return [that is, of my resurrection] is at hand." But ἀνα, in composition, is not always to be translated, as every one knows; (see, for example, Matt. ii, 14; iv, 1; xiv, 19; Luke ii, 22; xiv, 10; Acts xx, 3; xxii, 13;) though it may impart a shade of meaning in most cases.

The above-named writers, however, and all the others, (see A. 90; C. 40; S., App. 9, 21, 22; W. 84, 85, 89,) unite in assuming the position on the subject which is presented as follows by its two ablest advocates, John Crellius and Dr. Priestley. Crellius says, in almost the very words of Archbishop Whately: "Because the time between death and the resurrection is not to be reckoned, therefore the apostle might speak thus, though the soul has no sense of anything after death." Priestley says: "The apostle, con sidering his own situation, would naturally connect the end of this life with the commencement of another and a better, as he would have no perception of any interval between them. That the apostle had no view of any state short of the coming of Christ to judgment, is evident from the phrase that he makes use of, namely, *being with Christ*, which can only take place at his second coming. For Christ himself has said that he would come again, and that he would take his disciples to himself, which clearly implies that they were not to be with him before that time."*

Now the strait in which the apostle felt himself to be was, whether he should *then* choose that life which would still enable him to do many things for Christ and his suffering members, or that life which was consequent on a departure from the present life, and which would bring him to be with Christ. It was a present strait in which he stood, and a choice of then existing alternatives. And the contrary idea asserted by our opponents, that the choice was whether he should *now* live on and toil and suffer, or *now* depart and be with Christ after the resurrection, when the resurrection was yet thousands of years distant, is simply absurd. For so far from these presenting an alternative, the one does not in any way conflict with the other, since his living on earth any length of time could in no way affect his being with Christ after the resurrection, and could neither hasten nor retard that event. And for the same reason the alterna-

* The assertion in this last sentence is thoroughly demolished by Dr. Knapp, as follows: Speaking of John xiv, 1–7, he says: "Neque est, quod nos offendant verba, *παλιν*, *ἐρχομαι*. Quo enim sensu hæc dicantur, id vel ex commate 23, intelligi potest; *si quis me amat—eum Pater meus amabit; atque ad eum veniemus, et apud eum habitabimus*. In eandem quoque sententiam idem ille vs. 21, dicit; *Ἐμφανισω αὐτῳ ἐμαυτον*, *præsentem me ipsi exhibeo*. Vid. Es. 57, 15. Nempe sacri Scriptores, æque ut exteri, Deum iis *appropinquare* vel *adesse*, Deum ad eos *venire* vel *redire* perhibent, quibus propitius est, quos adjuvat, aut singulari aliquo benevolentiæ suæ documento dignatur. Comp. Exod. xx, 24; Psa. lix, 20; lxiv, 4; Hos. vi, 3; Zach. ii, 10, 11; Matt. xviii, 20; 2 Tim. iv, 17; Apoc. iii, 20."—*Scripta varii Argumenti*, tom. i, p. 286.

tive could not be whether he should still live, and labor, and suffer for Christ, or depart into unconscious, joyless nothingness; for, *first*, he always esteemed it a high privilege to live and suffer for Christ, (see verse 29,) and secondly, he who so loved his brethren that he could wish himself accursed that he might thus save them, would never have felt himself in a strait if called to choose between living and laboring for them, or abandoning their service for a condition in which he could neither do them good, nor enjoy the presence of his Saviour. And of course the oft repeated remark of Dr. Whately and the rest of this school, that the soul would be unconscious of the lapse of time, has no bearing on the question. The point is, simply, could a man of Paul's self-sacrificing spirit, and of his intense love for souls, and for the promotion of God's glory, be in any strait whether to choose a continuance of life with those glorious privileges, or an utter extinction of being for all coming time.

The same truth is evident from many other considerations. 1. It is evident from the fact that he could *say*, "*for me to live is Christ;*" and if during the long term elapsing between death and the resurrection (whether he should *feel* it or not) his conscious union with Christ was to be interrupted and broken; then, as already stated, death, so far from being *gain* to him, must prove to be inestimable loss, by depriving him of all opportunity for serving, and glorifying, and enjoying Christ. To be thus deprived of that sweet communion and intercourse which he possessed while here, and to receive nothing in lieu of it save what a stone would possess, could this be *gain* to him, a gain to be greatly desired? If so, on what principle? The same argument which would prove it gain in such a case, would prove it gain on the supposition that the extinction of being should continue for billions of ages; for he would be no more conscious of the lapse of time in the one case than in the other.

2. Why then, we ask, did Paul and the primitive Chris-

tians view death with pleasure? Why were they willing to be absent from the body, if their happiness were deferred till the last day? Why wish for death, and consequently to be deprived of all their privileges and blessings, when death could bring them no nearer to bliss, since they had nothing to expect till the consummation of all things? For a man to wish to be deprived of great privileges and blessings, without the possibility of obtaining through the privation any manner of advantage, either for himself or others, would be evidence of sheer insanity.

3. A further remark, which evinces the folly of the Materialist notion that Paul here refers to his being with Christ after the resurrection, is, that he places the expressions *continuing in the body*, and *abiding longer in this world*, in antithesis to the expression, *to depart and be with Christ.* But his abiding in the flesh could in no way delay his being with Christ, according to this theory, even if he had lived a thousand years longer on earth.

It is obvious, therefore, that if the apostle had regarded death as suspending his opportunities for glorifying and enjoying Christ, he would, so far from desiring it, have been loth to depart on that very ground; and as he did desire death, he consequently entertained no such notions as those of the Annihilationists.

The same considerations apply also against the doctrine of the soul-sleepers, and they also effectually dispose of the objections from the cases of Hezekiah, Lazarus, Epaphroditus, etc., who viewed death as forever cutting off all further opportunity for usefulness in this world of probation. Hezekiah, it is true, grieved at the thought of dying at the time specified. But this makes as much against the idea that annihilation may be desirable to a good man, as that it may be otherwise. But the child of God would choose to abide in the flesh for the good of men, and to promote the glory of Christ, quite as much as to seek his own enjoyment in heaven, and must often, therefore, realize the very strait which Paul here describes.

13. Another passage, and one on which we need offer but a few remarks, is Heb. xii, 22, 23: "But ye are come to Mount Sion, and unto the city of the living God, the heavenly Jerusalem, and to an innumerable company of angels, to the general assembly and Church of the first-born, which are written in heaven, and to God the Judge of all, and to the spirits of just men made perfect."

By consulting the whole paragraph, it will be seen that the apostle here is comparing the privileges and enjoyments of the believers, under the new economy, with those of the Jews. The Jew approached and contemplated material and earthly forms, the types of what was to come; but the Christian approaches, contemplates, and enjoys the spiritual and celestial. We are come to Mount Sion, the heavenly mount, the heavenly Jerusalem, or the city of the living God, of which the earthly Jerusalem was but an obscure type; and to the innumerable company of angels; to the Church of the first-born, whose names are enrolled in heaven;* and to God, the Judge of all, (that is, of both the living and the dead;) and to the spirits (not to men in the flesh, who are never so named, but to the *spirits*) of the just made perfect.

The apostle, therefore, here asserts the delightful truth that the kingdom of Christ exists both on earth and in heaven, and that to enter it by accepting the offer of life through "Jesus the Mediator," brings us into connection, not only with the people of God on earth, but with the angels and ransomed spirits who are already gathered home into heaven. For that the departed saints do dwell with angels in heaven is evident from Eph. iii, 15: "*The whole family* in heaven and earth;" in exact accordance with the passage before us, which teaches that angels and departed spirits are of the family of God in heaven; and penitent, believing men are of his family on earth. The spirits of the departed saints are called spirits of the just

* See the very remarkable notes of Crellius on this passage, both in his Commentary and Paraphrase, in Pol. Frat., tom. iii.

made perfect, because they appear in the robe of Christ's righteousness, and are justified, (see Rev. iii, 18; vi, 11; vii, 14; xix, 7, 8,) and are freed from the body of flesh with all its infirmities, and from the guilt and pollution of sin. And hence it is obvious that the soul or spirit still lives when the body is dissolved, otherwise it could not be said, in any sense, that believers here are "come to them," or brought into union with them; for how could there be any union with them if annihilated? And it is further evident from the fact that these departed spirits are said to be made perfect; for how could a living, acting, perceiving spirit be made perfect by dropping into either a sleep of insensibility, or into annihilation? Can a soul which has been living a life of faith, and advancing in holiness, be said to be brought into a state of perfection by being utterly extirpated or annihilated? The idea is monstrous.

Our Annihilation friends prudently say but little on this passage. Priestley's remark is inane and not worth quoting, while of all the late Annihilation authors none refer to it save H. 2, p. 88, A. 36, and G. 22.

H. finds the passage "highly oratorical," and not to be treated with "critical severity." And whatever may be the meaning of the passage, he finds that "it is sufficiently clear that in it is no declaration that 'the spirits of just men are their *conscious personalities*.'" "The phrase 'the spirits of just men made perfect,' is obviously an example of the figure synecdoche, in which the *entire nature* of the human being is expressed by a term which signifies only a part." "All the particulars referred to are *future* and *not present*." So that when the apostle here says (v. 2–4) Christians are come "to Jesus the Mediator of the new covenant, and to the blood of sprinkling," he means not that they have already, in this world, come to Jesus and received forgiveness through his blood, but that they shall do this after their resurrection. But enough of this. A. says that he apprehends that the phrase "the spirits of just men made perfect," "applies to persons raised from the dead, and not to men in the flesh;" which is substantially the same idea as the above. G. also repeats the idea. In fact this is all that their theory will permit them to say on the subject. Calvin's note *in loco* is well worth consulting.

14. The next passage to which we shall call attention is 1 Pet. iii, 18–20: "For Christ also hath once suffered for sins, the just for the unjust, that he might bring us to God, being put to death in the flesh, but quickened by the Spirit: by which also he went and preached unto the spirits in prison; which sometimes were disobedient, when once the long-suffering of God waited in the days of Noah, while the ark was a preparing, wherein few, that is, eight souls, were saved by water."

The connection of this passage with the subject under discussion will be seen by a critical examination of its principal words and phrases.

And, *first*, the reader will please to observe that in the phrase "put to death in the flesh, but quickened by the Spirit," *θανατωθεὶς μὲν σαρκὶ, ζωοποιηθεὶς δὲ* [τῷ] *πνεύματι*, the assumption that *spirit* here refers to the Holy Spirit is unfounded, and entitled to no consideration whatever. The article (τῷ) before spirit is, moreover, spurious. Let it be noticed, too, that the prepositions in both branches of the clause are supplied by the translators. The prepositions to be employed, therefore, in transferring the import of the clause into any other language, are purely a question of exegesis. The idea simply is, that "Christ had indeed suffered the stroke of death in the flesh, but survived that stroke in the spirit." The word "quickened" gives a sense which is not supported by the language of the apostle. The old word "*quick*" (as Horsley remarks, Ser. *in loco*) presents the exact sense. "Being put to death in the flesh, but quick (alive) in the spirit, in which he went and preached," etc.*

* An effort has been made to sustain, by a criticism of *ζωοποιέω*, the idea that Christ, in the present case, preached through Noah, "because,"

Τοῖς εν φυλακῇ πνεύμασι, *to the spirits in prison.* The remark of Calvin on πνεύμα here is just: "Peter says here that Christ came *to spirits*, by which name he signifies souls separated from bodies; for living men are never called spirits. He likewise repeats it in the same sense in chapter 4, and therefore these words properly refer to the dead." They were, of course, the spirits of men and not demons, v. 20.

(it is asserted,) "this word does not mean *to keep alive*, but to *give life*, to *reanimate.* (See Biblic. Repos. for Ap., 1845, p. 268.) Now the word is used but twelve times in the New Testament, and a professed critic ought not to appeal to lexicons, but to usage, to learn the meaning of terms. The very etymology of this word suggests something more than a mere isolated bestowment, and its usage is in strict accordance with that idea: for example, in 1 Tim. vi, 13, the phrase occurs, τοῦ Θεοῦ τοῦ ζωοποιοῦντος τὰ πάντα, translated "*God who quickeneth all things;*" but in the Hebrew mind precisely equivalent to the φέρων τὰ πάντα, "*bearing up of all things*," (Heb. i. 3,) or the τὰ πάντα ἐν αὐτῷ συνέστηκε, (Col. i, 17,) literally, "*all things stand together through him.*" I suppose that at the present time no intelligent man will question the truth of the great principle so patent to the whole Hebrew intellect, that *upholding or preserving in being is the same as a continually new creation of being;* and that "the giving of life to all things," as our critic would read 1 Tim. vi, 13, means nothing different from sustaining them in being, as in the other places referred to. In this case sustaining life is giving life.

So also in the other passages, giving and sustaining are both implied, though in some instances the one idea is foremost, and in others the other. Thus in John vi, 63: "It is the Spirit that quickeneth." 2 Cor. iii, 6: "The letter killeth, but the spirit giveth life." Gal. iii, 21: "A law which could have given life." Rom. iv, 17: "God who quickeneth the dead." Rom. viii, 11: "Quicken your mortal bodies by his Spirit." John v, 21: "The Father raiseth and sustaineth the dead; so also does the Son." 1 Cor. xv, 22: "In Christ shall all be restored to a life no longer mortal." V. 45: "The last Adam was a quickening spirit." And even in its application to the seed-corn in v. 36, the word retains its signification. "The existence of that which thou sowest is not continued, except it die." Its life could never be re-manifested in any other circumstances. The only other passage in which the word occurs is the one before us: "Christ being put to death in the flesh, but continued to exist in the spirit." To multiply words here were useless.

Another equally profound remark is made in the same connection, to wit: that if this verb here "refers not to Christ rising from the dead, then no mention of this event occurs at all in the passage." It would be pleasant to know how often this writer would have an event to be announced in the Scriptures. My impression is that there really is, in several other places, a mention made of the fact referred to.

The word *preached*, κηρύσσω, does not necessarily mean to preach good news, but simply to *announce, or proclaim openly*. What our Redeemer here announced or proclaimed we know not. We shall refer to this again. In respect to φυλακῇ, *prison*, Turretin (ii, 315) remarks that "it is never employed in the Scriptures to signify a place for happy spirits," and an examination of the passages in which it occurs will show this to be so. It is used nearly fifty times in the New Testament, to say nothing of the LXX. Still, as the word may mean a state or condition of "*reservation*," without regard to the design of such reservation, there is some ground for the remark of Horsley, that "the invisible mansion of departed spirits, though certainly not a place of penal confinement to the good, is nevertheless in some respects a prison. It is a place of seclusion from the external world, a place of unfinished happiness, consisting of rest, security, and hope, more than in enjoyment."* It is true the state of the unregenerate and impenitent is represented as one of bondage, chains, captivity, etc., but this bears not on the subject, for, 1. The passage refers to spirits, and not to men in the flesh; and, 2. The fetters and chains of sin and lust do not thus bind or imprison the good.

It should be likewise noticed that the particle ποτε, (verse 20,) rendered "*sometime*," has no such definite sense in such a connection. The idea which it conveys is "some time or other," or simply "*formerly*," in the general, unrestricted sense of that word.

Tittman, after Crellius, (Pol. Fratres iv, 328,) to whom, however, he expresses no acknowledgment, suggests that ὅτε, in the same verse, is put elliptically for ὡς ὅτε, (*as when*,) the ὡς being left out, as is often done in comparison. (Compare 2 Peter iii, 4; Psalm xi, 1.) The verse would then read: "In which also he proceeded and preached to the spirits in prison, which formerly were disobedient; *as when* once a long-suffering God waited in the days of

* See Müller on the Doctrine of Sin, ii, 333–337, and the quotation from President Edwards, in No. 10, above.

Noah," etc. And in fact Wakefield has so rendered ὅτε in his version: "In former times *as when* the patience of God continued waiting in the days of Noah." Glassius, also, justly observes that the term *once*, ἅπαξ, here declares the limit of the divine patience to those antediluvians. (Philol. Sacra, p. 969.) See also verse 18.

The participle πορευθεὶς (*went*) is the same as that employed in verse 22, where it is rendered "is gone," and means that Christ "*having gone* into heaven is at the right hand of God." In both places, therefore, it refers to a period subsequent to his death. And hence the import and proper connection of this word in verse 20, are sufficient to evince the absurdity of representing this preaching of Christ to have been through Noah, or previous to his incarnation. See also Acts i, 10, 11; John xiv, 2, 3, 12, 28; xvi, 7, 28; in all of which instances it refers to his own *personal* act, and not to anything performed through an agent, or by an instrument. And such alone can be its meaning here. Hence Winer, the accuracy of whose judgment in a question of grammatical construction or usage will scarcely be questioned, arranges the words as expressive of their true sense, as follows: τοῖς ἐν φυλακῇ πνεύμασι πορευθεὶς ἐκήρυξεν: "*Having proceeded to the spirits in prison, he preached*," etc. See Idioms of the New Testament, Append., sec. 67.

All the supposed difficulty in the passage, however, is embraced in the question, "Why should Jesus preach to the spirits of the damned? They have passed from probation to retribution, and cannot now be converted." But while we know not what our blessed Redeemer did announce to them, we do know that he preached neither repentance nor faith. (John ix, 4, with Eccles. ix, 10.) Flacius Illyricus, in his Clavis, pp. 457–462, has given a very extensive theological (not exegetical) exposition of the whole passage; and supposes that Jesus, while in Hades, announced to all the lost, rebellious spirits there, that his work, which they had slighted and disregarded, was now finished, and all the ancient promises fulfilled. His remarks are learned, able, and suggestive. Glassius, likewise, seems to favor that view. (Philo. Sac., lib. iii, tract. iii, can. 16.) Horsley, however, remarks, in accordance with his view above given, that the souls of those who, though they had perished in the deluge, repented during the forty days of rain, but who, though with the saved in paradise, felt still uneasy on account of their having perished under a divine judgment, were now assured by Jesus that their repentance had been accepted. These suppositions are of no actual importance to the argument itself, whatever weight may or may not be allowed them. And the remarks of J. D. Michaelis in this connection are worthy of consideration. See his Theol. Dog., c. viii, sec. 105; Goet., 1760; and also the note of Calvin *in loco.*

The application of the passage to the subject before us is, however, very plain and obvious, and in no way affected by our not being able to tell the purport of Christ's announcement to the spirits in prison; for the apostle expressly declares that he went thither and preached. The fact that we know not *what* he preached, will in no way justify us in refusing to believe the apostolic testimony that he did as there stated, or in attempting on such ground to turn the passage from its plain grammatical import, and to impose upon it another meaning.

The inferences therefore are plain, and apply directly to the subject in hand. The passage teaches the uninterrupted immortality of the human spirit of Christ, and by consequence that of his redeemed.

It teaches, likewise, the uninterrupted immortality of the spirits of wicked men, and of course that they do not cease to exist at death.

The disembodied spirit of Christ, and the disembodied spirits in prison, possessed and exercised active powers, and of course, therefore, death is not the extinction of the life of the whole man, nor does the soul sleep between death and the resurrection.

Our opponents have ventured to say but little respecting this passage. Priestley's remarks are below criticism. Blackburne (Int. State, pp. 262, 263) is not willing to have it teach anything, because he cannot understand why Christ should preach to the spirits of the lost.* W. 63 thinks it "a very unlikely interpretation" of the passage, to regard it as teaching "the conscious state of departed spirits," and that Christ "visited, in the interval between his death and resurrection, the souls of those who perished in Noah's flood." He finds the passage "extremely obscure," and has never met with any explanation of it that is "free from objection." He attempts in no way to reconcile it with his theory. H. 2, pp. 89, 90, finds it difficult, and says: "What its precise meaning is I do not pretend to say, and I shall only make a few remarks rather by way of pointing out some of its difficulties." He then, after repeating the inanities of Blackburne and Priestley, says that "the time when Christ preached was *not before* his incarnation, nor was it between his death and resurrection, but after his resurrection." "For my own part, I have not the least doubt that the phrase 'spirits in prison' refers not to *men*, but to certain *spiritual beings* who were disobedient in the days of Noah in some such way as to bring them within the reach of Christian redemption." And he refers to the "sons of God" and their progeny, mentioned in Gen. vi, in illustration of this notion. G. 22 says: "The spirit of Christ in Noah, preached to those who were in the grave when Peter wrote. 2 Peter ii, 5." F. 25–28 adopts the same idea, and in like manner J. T. 24 turns the *spirits* into human *carcasses*, and finds their prison in the grave. Such wretched stuff is not worth remarking upon. Mr. Dobney and the rest of the fraternity conveniently forget that there is any such passage in the word of God.

* See also the pretentious but inane criticism on the passage in the Biblical Repository for April, 1845, pp. 266, 267.

# CHAPTER IV.

## THE NEW TESTAMENT ARGUMENT CONTINUED.

### § 34. *Miscellaneous Passages considered.*

THE foregoing catalogue of Scripture passages from the Old and New Testaments is quite sufficient for extended critical remark on this subject, nor are we willing to tax further the reader's attention to such lengthened exegesis. It is, however, not necessary, since we have already treated what are regarded as the chief passages which bear upon the question. There are, nevertheless, many others which may justly claim to be adduced in the same connection, and to a few of which we shall now briefly refer; for as Knapp justly remarks: "It is most truly the constant and perpetual doctrine of Christ and the apostles, that all who confide in Christ are, immediately after death, (*statim post mortem*,) blessed, and associated with Christ. Nor is any one known to us who would dare so to limit the sense of the words ὅπου εἰμὶ εγὼ, καὶ ὑμεῖς ἔσεσθε, (*where I am, there ye shall be also*,) John xii, 26, and xvii, 24, and in interpreting restrict it into so narrow an import as to convey only the idea of that union with Christ which is expected after the return of the dead into life."* Of course, therefore, we cannot pretend to cite here all the passages which bear upon the topic, and our references must be mainly to those which are representative of classes.

In such places, for example, as Job xxxiv, 14, 15, an actual separation between soul and spirit is declared to take place at death: "If he set his heart upon man, if he

* Scripta Varii Arg. in Joan., xiv, 1-7, page 287.

gather unto himself his spirit and his breath, all flesh shall perish together, and man shall turn again into dust." (Comp. Eccles. xii, 7.) The *spirit* (not the mere *breath*, for here is a plain distinction made between the two) is *taken from man*, and he perishes. In C. F. 17 it is admitted that this fact is here stated. But how can the spirit be *taken from man* if it is only the result of organization, as is so roundly asserted in § 5, above? In Psalm civ, 29, God's providential agency in the death of animals is also described in language somewhat similar; but in this passage there is no distinction observed between spirit and breath, as in the other, which refers to man alone. Breath only is specified. Hence too the language of James ii, 26: "As *the body without the spirit is dead*, so faith without works is dead also." Now if the spirit is merely the result of corporeal organization, it is inseparable from the body while the body remains organized; but in these passages we are taught that the body is dead *only as separated from* the spirit. The apostle's employment of this expression as a figure of speech, and as a familiar illustration of faith, proves clearly what must have been the views entertained on the subject of death, as a severance between soul and body, by the first Christians; since, if they had held that the spirit was inseparable from the body, James would not have employed an illustrative phrase which implied the contrary; or, if he had, it is impossible that they should have understood him.

In like manner Paul, in Heb. xii, 9, contrasts in antithesis the fathers *of our flesh*, and the father *of our spirits*. He refers to our parents as the authors or propagators, instrumentally, of course, of our bodies, and to God as alone and directly the author of our spirits. We receive the one from our earthly parents, and the other from God. Of course, then, the spirit is not a result of material organization, but is separable from the body. On any other supposition the antithesis, and consequently the sense of the passage, is destroyed. Our opponents forget this passage also, or at least remain silent respecting it.

Another text evincing the same is 2 Peter i, 13–15: "Yea, I think it meet, as long as I am *in this tabernacle*, to stir you up by putting you in remembrance; knowing that shortly I *must put off this my tabernacle*, even as our Lord Jesus Christ hath showed me; moreover, I will endeavor that ye may be able, *after my decease*, to have these things always in remembrance;" that is, the things to which he calls their attention in the epistle itself.

Here then the apostle speaks, not *of a living tabernacle*, but of living in a tabernacle, and he employs the phrases *putting off this tabernacle*, and *my decease*, as meaning one and the same thing. Now it will not be denied that he employs the word *tabernacle* (σκήνωμα) here for his *body*, and in the true sense of a temporary residence of the spirit. (Comp. Acts vii, 46.) It has the sense of σκῆνος, as in Wisdom ix, 15; 2 Cor. v, 1, 4. It was a familiar term with the old Greek Pythagoreans, and is of course in this sense agreeable to classical usage, for in their sense of it the term could only mean the body. The Doric poets use it also in the same sense, and as equivalent to σκηνὴ, though their dialect spells it σκᾶνος.

*To lay aside this tabernacle*, therefore, can only mean to die—death, for any other sense would be not only inadmissible but absurd. The word for *laying aside* is properly employed to signify a putting off the garments, (see Acts vii, 58,) and hence its use in 1 Pet. iii, 21; and the sense is, "For I know that in a little while there will be a putting off of this my tabernacle." Paul, in 2 Tim. iv, 6, utters a similar prediction respecting himself, and no one can doubt that he too refers to death as his departure. And hence the import of *naked*, in 2 Cor. v, 3, is plain. It means the spirit that is unclothed by putting off the tabernacle or body. Hence too in the following verse Peter uses, as equivalent to the foregoing phrase, and in apposition with it, the word *departure*, ἔξοδος, (properly rendered *decease.*) And that the Greeks used this word to express the idea of *death*, or *departure from the present life*, will not be denied. In the same sense the Latins also employ its etymological equivalents *exitus* and also *excessus*. The idea too was perfectly familiar to the Jews. For as their exodus from Egypt was a deliverance, and the commencement of their liberty, so in their view the departure of a good man from this life was a deliverance from bondage, and an entrance into the happy life to come. (Luke ii, 29.) Hence too the first Christians regarded death in Christ (Rev. xiv, 13) as the way to glory, and loved to call death "the departure," or "exodus." This gave rise to the phraseology of Peter here, and of Paul in 2 Tim. iv, 6; Phil. i, 23, etc. Irenæus too, and Clement, and others, use the same word to express the same idea, as Grotius remarks on Luke ix, 31, where Jesus employs the term in respect to his own death. This passage, therefore, completely subverts the notion of the Materialists and Annihilationists; for in their sense death is not a laying aside of the tabernacle, but an utter blotting out of existence of both tabernacle and inhabitant.

F. 7, however, makes the tabernacle to be "the active service of God in the house of Christ—*the house of this tabernacle*—'for the dead praise not the Lord.'" The only other one of their writers, so far as I remember, who refers to the passage is C. 41, who is willing to admit that the tabernacle is "the human body," but he adds: "Observe, it is not the tabernacle which is about to die, but something *in* the tabernacle." That is, it is not the tabernacle which is about *to put itself off*, but something in it. Such is the amount of their criticism.

It is on the same basis of eternal truth that such expressions as that in Eph. iii, 15 are found: "The whole family in heaven and earth," (Comp. Phil. ii, 10. See also sub-sections 10, 13, of section 33, and Knapp's Scripta Var. Arg., p. 249,) and in which we are also assured that the already departed saints *do now inherit the promises.* Heb. vi, 12. The passage refers to the patriarchs among others, as the context shows. Of course, then, they were living in their departed or separate state, they being in the possession of a *present* inheritance. (See the Greek.)

H. 2, p. 88, is the only one of our Annihilation friends, if I remember rightly, who has ventured to grapple with this passage. He objects to the sense of it above given, on the ground that it is inconsistent with Heb. xi, 13: "'These all died in faith, *not having received the promises*,' that is, the fulfillment of them." He likewise quotes to the same effect verses 39, 40. These passages assert that the saints under previous dispensations *died* without having *during their life on earth* received the fulfillment of the promises, for Mr. Ham will not suppose that any other life than that on earth is here referred to. And this being so, how does that statement conflict with another statement, which assures us that *since their death* they do inherit them? But *aliquando bonus dormitat Homerus.*

Omitting other passages, however, we shall conclude this examination with a reference to a few in the Apocalypse. The first eighteen chapters confessedly refer to events which transpire before the resurrection of the body; and the allusions to man and his condition or state, must of course be to him as he is previous to that event. There is neither sense nor propriety in objecting that the import of the book is dark and uncertain, since it is by no means necessary that we should understand all that is in the book in order to understand and practically employ certain of its allusions and expressions. Do not our opponents thus make use of Ecclesiastes, the most difficult and obscure book of the Old Testament, and often deduce therefrom their conclusions and proof-texts?

The first passage is Rev. vi, 9–11: "And when he had opened the fifth seal, I saw under the altar the souls of them that were slain for the word of God, and for the testimony which they held: and they cried with a loud voice, saying, How long, O Lord, holy and true, dost thou not judge and avenge our blood on them that dwell on the earth? And white robes were given unto every one of them: and it was said unto them, that they should rest yet for a little season, until their fellow-servants also and their brethren, that should be killed as they were, should be fulfilled."

The prayer here is in the true Hebrew form, one which the spirit of God has prompted in many of the Psalms, and refers to events which must transpire before the end or blessing sought can be obtained. Christ must triumph over all his foes, and a prayer for his triumph, therefore, is a prayer, in effect, for their overthrow; that is, for the fulfillment of his own promises and threatenings so far as they relate to the matter. Sometimes the one idea is expressed and sometimes the other. So here these souls of the martyrs, knowing that Christ would accomplish the overthrow of his enemies and the renovation of earth, and raise his people from the grave to dwell with him forever, refer to the great event by a specification of the avenging judgments which must then occur. They are represented as looking forward to that day and waiting for it; and hence, in answer to their prayer, they are told to rest yet for a season, till their brethren, etc., are gathered home, and that then the happy day of their final triumph should occur; that is, the day of their resurrection.

Here, then, is the condition of the separate spirits or souls of the ransomed delineated, for that they were such is clear from the distinction referred to between themselves and "*those that dwell on the earth.*" They still look forward to the day of resurrection as the completion of their bliss. See also Rev. vii, 13–17. This passage, therefore, is destructive of soul-sleeping and Materialism.

But few of our opponents refer to this text, and even they say but little. S., App. 14, says that if such were the feelings of the martyrs *after* they left earth they were not happy; but this is nonsense, as above shown. C. 42, A. 91, G. 21, pretend that it is a parallel case to that of the *blood* of Abel crying *out of the ground.* And this is all they have to offer. The rest are silent. *Requiescant in pace.*

So too in Rev. xiv, 13, we have the following: "And I

heard a voice from heaven, saying unto me, Write, Blessed are the dead which die in the Lord from henceforth: Yea, saith the Spirit, that they may rest from their labors, and their works do follow them."

Griesbach rejects μοι (*unto me*) here as unauthorized in the text. Still, it is undoubtedly implied or understood; for the command to write was certainly to no other than the apostle. In our version, however, the words μετ' αὐτῶν have not their proper force. The idea is not merely that "their works do follow them," but "follow *with* them." And if they follow with the believer, they go *when* he goes, and not at some vast distance of time afterward. But he departs *at once* when he leaves his earthly tabernacle, and so do they. And then, moreover, the word *follow*, ἀκολουθεῖ, has here the import of *following with their reward.* As Bretschneider (*sub voce*) has exactly expressed it: "The blessings or benefits accompany them to God the Judge; that is, that they may immediately after death receive their rewards;" *statim post mortem accipient præmia sua.* This writer will not be suspected of partiality for evangelical doctrine. It needs no words to show how utterly repugnant to all this is the annihilation theory; for in what sense could these rewards be said "to *follow* with them" immediately, if they pass at death into utter extinction of being? It is equally repugnant to the soul-sleeping theory; for the believer cannot be said to receive his reward immediately after death, if he then pass into a state of unconscious existence. This reward supposes actual enjoyment. On the contrary, "they *rest* from their labors"—their toils and sufferings, and struggles against corruption, sin, and Satan. And the Holy Spirit here pronounces them to be blessed in that rest and by means of it. Now if they at death cease to feel or to exist, they are therein and thereby no more blessed than a block or a stone. And how absurd is the supposition that would make us believe that an utterance so deeply solemn and impressive as this might be given forth from heaven as an announcement of precious interest to man, that a stone or a clod was blessed in its repose. The word translated *from henceforth*, (ἀπάρτι, or ἀπ' ἄρτι, as Griesbach reads it,) whether it be referred in point of time to the period when John heard the utterance, or to the one immediately contemplated in that portion of the prophecy, clearly announces that this blessedness commences previous to the time of the resurrection. This text therefore furnishes a full refutation of the doctrine of our opponents.

The last passage to which we shall refer is Rev. xviii, 20: "Rejoice over her, thou heaven, and ye holy apostles and prophets, for God hath avenged you on her." The text as given by Bengel and Griesbach (and which is undoubtedly correct) differs from the Received Text as follows: *εὐφραίνου ἐπ' αὐτῇ οὐρανὲ καὶ οἱ ἅγιοι καὶ οἱ ἀπόστολοι καὶ οἱ προφῆται, ὅτι*, etc., "Rejoice over her, thou heaven, and ye saints, and apostles and prophets! for," etc. The context shows this to refer to scenes which transpire previous to the resurrection; for it calls upon those persons herein referred to, to rejoice over the fall of Babylon, which had just occurred. Who then are the persons thus called upon? Let us consider the language.

1. *Thou heaven.* This is not an unfrequent Hebraicism (at least in the plural) for angels; though it may here stand as simply including what are named in the following clauses: "Rejoice over her, thou heaven, even ye saints," etc.

2. And *ye saints.* This term may include the angels; but if so it also includes all the redeemed who are not specified in the verse. They are called saints, or *holy ones;* as in Heb. xii, 23, "*perfect.*" Of course their separate state is here asserted in every form. They are inhabitants of heaven, or are such at all events when the occurrence referred to takes place; and that occurrence does take place anterior to the resurrection.

3. *Ye apostles;* that is, their spirits, of course; for they, too, must have died previous to this event, and they were

not yet raised from the dead. See also chap. viii, 9, 10; xi, 15–18; xiv, 2–5; xv, 2–4. And that the names of men are given to them as spirits, see Luke xvi, 23.

4. *Ye prophets;* that is, those who had foretold these events, and were now departed from this life.

Such, then, is the import of this passage, and the reader will judge whether it is not sufficient of itself to explode the whole theory of the soul-sleepers and of the Annihilationists.

Our opponents do not trouble themselves by attempting to explain this text. But should it be said that these saints, prophets, etc., are called on to rejoice only in retrospection, this would be very absurd; for the call is to them to rejoice at the time of the occurrence, and over the effects resulting therefrom to the kingdom of Christ. And, moreover, the saints after the resurrection will not need to be *thus* apprised of the past triumph of our glorious Redeemer.

Before passing to the next great division of the subject, we must here pause a while in order to notice the objections of our opponents to the Scripture argument.

## § 35. *Assumptions of our Opponents.*

Their assumptions are numerous, and would be offensive were they not ludicrous. H. 2, p. 66, accuses us of not relying on the Bible, but on philosophy, in support of our views, and of following Plato rather than Christ, and (on p. 90) of "clinging tenaciously to ambiguous texts;" and as a climax, he adds on p. 91, that "the charge of our Lord is painfully applicable to every promulgator of the popular theory: 'Ye make void the law of God *through your traditions.*'"

Such unfounded accusations are perpetually brought by this whole school of writers, and have considerable effect upon the illiterate and thoughtless. The reader may however learn what to think of such a procedure by recurring to sect. 25, above, in which the parentage of their own theory is sufficiently demonstrated.

In all their exceptions to the Scripture argument they employ much equivocation in the application of terms. We need not here, however, dwell specifically upon this point. We shall be obliged in the following chapters to refer to it occasionally, but for the present sufficient has been said in relation to it in sect. 27.

They likewise abound in very positive denials and asseverations, which they employ in the place of argument. H. 2, p. 95, for example, says: "*It is beyond all reasonable contradiction* that the Bible nowhere teaches that deceased believers enter upon their reward, nor that deceased unbelievers experience their recompense, either in part or wholly as disembodied spirits." And then again on p. 66, in order that his own profound scientific attainments may bear with their full weight of influence in support of this idea, he says: "We are not acquainted with any species of organized being whose individuality survives disorganization." But did he never know that the vital principle even in the seed-corn survives that very disorganization which is called death? We commend to these writers the perusal of John xii, 24, and 1 Cor. xv, 36. They abound likewise in such statements as the following: "There is in the Bible no mention of disembodied felicity," (see H. 2, pp. 77, 79, 83;) that man is dependent on the resurrection for future existence, (G. 9, 10;) that body is necessary to thought, (R. 13–22; see also § 5, above,) and ask, "How can an immortal being die?" (H. 1, p. 120, and A. 38, a question which we shall answer in another chapter;) and assert "the evil tendency of the doctrine of innate immortality." C. 22–24. And in their usual style of perversion, it is asserted that "*the whole truth*" on the subject *is in Paul*, (Has., passim;) and that we will find it in the discourses of Christ, (D. 186.) The object of these representations, however, is sufficiently apparent. But we are willing to leave all these assumptions, asseverations, and denials to be considered in the light of the passages which we have cited and examined in sections 27–33 and this chapter. It is needless, however, to occupy more space with them here, and we shall now proceed to a specific consideration of those passages of Scripture which our opponents are in the practice of adducing in support of the views they advocate.

# CHAPTER V.

## OBJECTIONS ANSWERED.

### § 36. *Objections, founded on Texts from the Old Testament, answered.*

WITH respect to those texts, with the arguments founded upon them, which, in the subjoined catalogue, are taken from the Old Testament, we have already, to some extent, remarked upon them, as the reader may perceive in sec. 27, sub-sec. 4; and though we design to give them a thorough and critical examination, (for justice cannot be done to the Biblical argument without it,) it will not be amiss, in this connection, to cite the following passage from a late work of one of the more prominent of our opponents. We refer to Mr. Hudson, who, on page 262, thus adverts to the point: "The argument to prove unconsciousness is often based on the expressions 'the dead know not anything;' their love, and their hatred, and their envy, is now perished, and 'there is no work, nor device, nor knowledge, nor wisdom, in the grave whither thou goest.' Eccles. ix, 5, 6, 10. But these expressions are evidently (verses 2, 4) the conclusion of an Epicurian argument, including the denial of all future life, which the 'Preacher,' had taken up. And when Hezekiah says: 'The dead cannot praise thee,' (Isaiah xxxviii, 18,) the language is rather that of despair respecting *any future life.* (Verse 11.) The same may be said of the expressions in Job iii, 11, 16; xiv, 10, 14; Psalm vi, 5; xxx, 9; lxxxviii, 10–12; cxv, 17; with which compare 1 Cor. xv, 18, where the argument evidently shows that those who are fallen asleep in Christ are *not* perished, since Christ has risen." Still, as these passages are greatly insisted on by many of the writers opposed to us, we shall now proceed to their examination, after which we shall take up and consider those which they adduce from the New Testament, and also the other objections which they urge against the doctrine we are defending.

1. The first objection is from the following passages: Psalm xlix, 12, 14, 15: "Man being in honor abideth not; *he is like the beasts that perish.* Like sheep they are laid in the grave; death shall feed on them; and the upright shall have dominion over them in the morning," etc. On this C. 46, 47, remarks: "How do the beasts perish? does the whole beast perish, or only a part of him? If the whole beast perish, the whole sinner must." This, however, is based upon a misapprehension of the sense of the passage. The Psalmist is speaking of a rich fool, (see Luke xii, 20, for the word honor has reference to *wealth*, and means *price* or *value*,) and refers to his pride of station. The idea strictly is: "He shall not lodge therein; he has become like the brutes; they are *destroyed*, *silenced*, *hushed in death;* they mingle no more with men in this world." It requires some boldness of conception and execution to represent such passages as opposed to our views.

2. Psalm cxlvi, 4, is a passage of somewhat similar character: "His breath goeth forth, he returneth to his earth; *in that very day his thoughts* perish." They assert with great vehemence that this furnishes a full proof of their doctrine that man becomes extinct at death.* In fact they are never weary of repeating it. C. asks: "How can a thing be tormented that has no thoughts?" E. says that it teaches that "*all* which belongs to man, *as man*, must perish." And H. asks: "Will our antagonists explain how it can harmonize with their theory of a state of consciousness after death, that in the day of death a man's 'thoughts perish?'"

All this looks like being pressed rather hard to find

* See C. 49; A. 95; E. 109, 115; H. 2, pp. 70, 71.

matter of objection against the evangelical doctrine; for it would require no very deep reflection to perceive that in such a connection the word *thoughts* means simply *expectations or desires connected with the present life;* for in multitudes of cases this is the meaning of the word. Take, for example, Isaiah lv, 9: "Let the unrighteous man forsake *his thoughts.*" He could not, of course, be enjoined to forsake his thinking. The meaning is, let him forsake his purposes, designs, or expectations, and return to the Lord. So also in such passages as the following, in which we shall substitute the one word for the other: Psalm xlix, 11: "Their *desire* is that their houses shall continue forever." Isaiah xxvi, 3, (see margin:) "Keep him whose *expectation* is stayed on thee." Job xvii, 7, (margin:) "All my *expectations* are as a shadow." Acts viii, 22: "If the *desire* of thy heart may be forgiven thee." In fact, so common is this usage, that, as though to prevent its being misunderstood, we find the one term used as exegetical of the other, as in Job xvii, 11: "My purposes are broken off, even my thoughts." Now this meaning of the word, so plain and obvious to all, at once divests the passage referred to of even the shadow of antagonism to the doctrine of the uninterrupted immortality of the soul.

3. Another passage is the following: Eccles. ix, 5, 10: "For the living know that they shall die; but the dead know not anything, neither have they any more a reward, for the memory of them is forgotten." "Whatsoever thy hand findeth to do, do it with thy might; for there is no work, nor device, nor knowledge, nor wisdom, in the grave whither thou goest." This passage is likewise perpetually quoted and insisted on as justifying the views of our opponents; yet, though they often refer to it, they attempt no explanation of its phraseology. And perhaps this is the wiser plan.* The passage speaks, of course, of *all* the dead, without distinction of character; and with the same solemnity with which it announces that they "*know not*

* See C. 47; E. 116; A. 95; H. 2, pp. 70, 72.

*anything*," it likewise assures us that "neither have they *any more a reward.*" If, then, the words are to be taken literally, as our opponents insist, it is certain *that there is to be no future resurrection or retribution for mankind.* The one declaration is just as full and explicit as the other. Why then do these men thus trifle, and insist upon objections based on such a passage, when confessedly, and on their own principles of literal construction, it makes as much against their views as against our own? Is such a procedure honorable? But the passage has reference to the present world and life, (and not to the future,) and to things as they appear to the eye of sense; and in view of the fact that we must soon lose all our interest in relation to these things, it gives the solemn admonition to improve our probationary state while we may. And is not this wholly consistent with the doctrine of the soul's immortality?

That such is the import of the fifth verse, at least, is further manifest from verse 6, where the expressions, "their love and their hatred," etc., refer to the dispositions which they might have here indulged, and hence the writer adds: "Neither have they any more a portion forever in anything that is done *under the sun.*" Should it be thought, however, that the term translated *grave*, in verse 10, has reference to the future state of man, there is nothing in the verse which at all militates against the doctrine of immortality. "Do with thy might all that is required at thy hand, for *in the unseen world* (בִּשְׁאוֹל) whither thou art going, there is neither work, nor planning, nor knowledge, nor wisdom;" nothing to remedy the neglect of which men are here guilty; no *work* that can in such a case benefit thee; no *planning* or *contrivance* by which to escape thy doom; no *knowledge* of any help to be obtained, and no *wisdom* that can comfort and support thee in such circumstances. The very repetition of the idea, according to the genius of the Hebrew tongue, gives a fearful intensity to the meaning. See the excellent note on the passage in Clarke's Commentary.

4. Eccles. iii, 19–21, (which we have considered in sect. 30, sub-sect. 3,) likewise is perpetually quoted and insisted on by our adversaries: "For that which befalleth the sons of men befalleth beasts; even one thing befalleth them: as the one dieth, so dieth the other; yea, they have all one breath; so that a man hath no pre-eminence above a beast: for all is vanity. All go into one place; all are of the dust, and all turn to dust again. Who knoweth the spirit of man that goeth upward, and the spirit of the beast that goeth downward to the earth?"

Here, too, our opponents are quite unwilling to make a thorough application, at least to themselves, of a literal construction; for they do not believe that in strictness of speech "a man hath no pre-eminence above a beast." Yet should they insist on believing it, we must, with all due deference, insist on their believing it only in relation to themselves; for our Saviour certainly taught the contrary when he said, "How much then is a man *better than a sheep*." Matt. xii, 12. See also Matt. vi, 26, and Luke xii, 24. Judging from their comments on the passage,* we might suppose they had been studying in the school of the philosopher mentioned by Berkeley,† who made a threefold partition of *the human species* into birds, beasts, and fishes, being of opinion that the road of life lies upward, in a perpetual ascent through the scale of being. Their remarks on the passage are of no account whatever, being pedantic and illiterate. We pass them, therefore, and proceed to its explanation.

Le Clerc, *in loco*, remarks that "the very doubt to which the passage refers appears at least to intimate that certain wise men in the East were then teaching the doctrine of immortality, and that others would deny it." And that Solomon is here really referring to some notions which such discussions had developed in the minds of those men, is quite apparent upon the very face of the passage. The as-

* See E. 116, 117; J. T. 13, 27, 35; H. 2, p. 86.

† Minute Philosopher, Dial. V., sect. 33.

serted reason for the doubt or question here expressed, is stated as follows: "Both men and animals spring from the dust; they inhale the same vital breath רוּחַ; they die alike and go to the same place, the place from which they sprang, and to which they again return." Then, having thus spoken of their *bodies*, the questioner goes on to refer to the *vital principle* of each, and continues thus: "Who knoweth the spirit of man whether it ascendeth, and the spirit of beasts whether it descendeth to the earth?" This question, *so far as the spirit of man is concerned*, he proceeds to answer in due time by saying that "it shall at death return to God," Eccles. xii, 7, and annexing thereto the practical application in verses 13, 14; but *as to the spirit of the beast*, inasmuch as the question relating to it is of no real concern to mankind, he drops all further remark in relation thereto, and so leaves the inference to be naturally and reasonably drawn, that as the spirit of man *does* thus ascend to God and is judged, (v. 14,) and of course survives the dissolution of the body, the spirit of the beasts must of course descend to the earth, and, along with their bodies, return to dust. Compare Job xxxiii, 28–30, and xxxiv, 14, with Psa. civ, 29.* And it is obvious, therefore, that the asserted resemblance between man and beast refers only to that which is visible and strikes the eye of sense, since man equally with the brutes is deprived of that life by which the pleasures of sense are enjoyed. The passage thus clearly sustains the doctrine of man's immortality, though it does bear hard against that of beasts, since they are formed solely from the dust; and, of course, it bears equally hard against the immortality of those persons whose spirit is "merely the result of corporeal organization;" for our opponents affirm that there are such, and many of them profess even to be of the number. Surely they will not object to the *argumentum ex concessis*.

5. The next passage is Job xiv, 10–15: "But man dieth, and wasteth away: yea, man giveth up the ghost, and where is he? As the waters fail from the sea, and the flood de-

* See § 34.

cayeth and drieth up: so man lieth down, and riseth not: till the heavens be no more, they shall not awake, nor be raised out of their sleep. O that thou wouldst hide me in the grave, that thou wouldst keep me secret until thy wrath be past, that thou wouldst appoint me a set time, and remember me! If a man die, shall he live again? all the days of my appointed time will I wait, till my change come. Thou shalt call, and I will answer thee: thou wilt have a desire to the work of thine hands."

In their proof-texts our opponents perpetually forget the good old maxim in all sound reasoning, *Qui nimis probat, nihil probat.* In fact, in adducing their texts they seem to care nothing as to what becomes of other doctrines of the Bible, provided they are able to rid themselves of that thought, so terrible to the vicious and impenitent, that man, in respect to his spiritual nature, shall retain a conscious existence after death. There is not one passage in all God's word that even implies, much less announces, the idea of annihilation in respect to man, unless it be in respect to man *as man*, and not in respect to his constituent parts. As to those parts neither the body nor spirit is annihilated, although *man, viewed as a composite being*, ceases at death, and continues thus till the resurrection. Such a cessation as this we ever have asserted, for it is plainly announced by most of the passages urged against us by our adversaries. But this amounts to nothing; for it concedes nothing that is in dispute, and presents no issue on the question whether to man's spiritual nature there is a conscious survivance of the stroke of death. The body sinks under that stroke, and ceases to exist. There is no question therefore on that point. But does the spirit likewise cease to exist? This is the issue. And to pretend to decide that issue by bringing texts to prove that man, *as man*, ceases to exist in this world and shall be here no more, is only trifling with the subject.

Now if the phrase in v. 12, "till the heavens be no more," means, as many critics suppose, "forever," then if the assertion of our opponents be true, that the passage is to be literally interpreted, it follows that man is never to be raised from the dead; an idea which these men utterly repudiate. And equally apparent is the folly of endeavoring to reconcile the idea of "sleep" (v. 12) with that of extinction of being. How can that which has no existence sleep? And so too in v. 13, the patriarch prays that God "would keep him secret." Now how can that which has no actual existence be *kept* in any way, secret or otherwise? How can the "*me*" here mentioned *be annihilated* and yet be *kept?* When a person utterly destroys a thing, can he be said to keep it? The ideas of *keeping* and *annihilating* are in perfect antithesis to each other. The passage therefore is utterly subversive of their theory. Their critique upon it may be found in H. 2, pp. 66, 67, 70, and A. 93. It contains not one idea that is worthy of notice.

The import of the passage is obvious. Job, in considering the calamitous condition of our fallen nature, remarks that man, when he dies, (unlike a tree, whose root being left in the ground may still live and grow,) passes forever from this state of being, and is no more. He does not in reality exist, and never shall till the heavens pass away. For man, being compounded of body and spirit, as above remarked, is utterly dissolved when soul and body are separated. The spirit is not man any more than the body itself is man. Man is therefore dissolved into his constituent parts, as the question "Where is he?" plainly intimates. He can mingle no more with the sons of men. He has done with earth and the scenes of time.

Of his better and immortal part, however, the patriarch is not here unmindful, and in view of death he prays, "O that thou wouldst hide me in *sheol*, (בִּשְׁאוֹל, see on Eccles. ix, 10, above,) that thou wouldst keep me *in secret*, until thy wrath be past." He prays here for that relief from his sufferings which he should find with the happy spirits in the invisible world, who are there kept *in the secret place* of the Almighty, (Psalm xci, 1,) until that time when God's wrath shall cease to go forth in judgment upon earth, and that God would then remember him, and have a desire to the work of his hands. Then "thou shalt call," that is, by the voice of the archangel. (1 Thess. iv, 16,) "and I will answer thee." (Comp. chap. xix, 25–27.) Could Job have said this if he had expected then to be extinct? But according to the Annihilation theory, the patriarch did not expect to hear this call until after he had obeyed it and come forth.

Scultetus and other eminent expositors maintain that the phrase in verse 12, "*until the heavens be no more*, they shall not wake," is designed to intimate that when the heavens do pass away mankind shall be raised. (See Luke xxi, 33; 2 Peter iii, 10; Rev. xxi, 1.) Nor has any really sufficient reason been given for disregarding this conclusion, for the meaning of the phrase in its later usage proves nothing as to its earlier import with the patriarchs, for even the preaching of Enoch announced a universal judgment and resurrection of the dead.*

6. The same remarks substantially apply to such objections as our opponents derive from passages like Psalm xxxix, 13: "O spare me, that I may recover strength before I go hence, and be no more." (See also Jer. xxxi, 15.) The language is perfectly intelligible on the principle of the soul's uninterrupted existence, for in this case there is a real departure, a real "*going hence* and *being no more*" among the sons of men. But what *going* hence is there, according to the idea of the Annihilationists? since the soul is inseparable from the body and is extinguished at death. And then, further, do our opposers believe that man "will be no more" after he dies? They do not, for they hold that he will live again. Why then adduce this passage, and parade it, as though it refuted our views and sustained theirs? If it prove not that man will not live again at the resurrection, neither does it prove that he does not, in his spiritual nature, exist between death and the resurrection; but it does prove that, *as man*, living and acting in a probationary state, he shall be no more.

* See Bush on Gen. v, 21-24.

As an illustration of the manner in which our opponents employ such and similar passages, let us suppose that one of that school should undertake to prove the extinction of Enoch, (a not unlikely supposition,) and should, in proof of his notion, quote Gen. v, 24, "*He was not*, for God took him," we should have the same kind of proof that Enoch has ceased to exist, that we have of the annihilation of the spiritual nature of Rachel's children, (an instance often pleaded by our opponents in this connection,) or of the annihilation of the spirit of any good man whom *God takes away* from this world of sorrow, and suffering, and death.

7. It seems hardly necessary to criticise those other passages of the foregoing character, on which they so greatly insist; as, for example, Job vii, 9, 10: "He that goeth down to the grave *shall come up no more;*" (comp. Dan. xii, 2; and Obadiah 16;) or Psalm xc, 3: "Thou turnest man *to destruction;*"* for it is perfectly obvious that if such language prove a literal annihilation, then annihilation is not inconsistent with the continuance of existence, and if so it must be a very harmless matter after all. That this is so is plain from passages like Job xix, 10, where, speaking of God, the patriarch says: "He hath *destroyed me* on every side, and *I am gone.*" Now Job, when he used this language, was of course still *alive*, and he lived many years afterward; so that if *destroy* means annihilate, Job, while still living, was *destroyed*, *annihilated*, and *gone;* that is, after he ceased to exist he was yet alive. And why may it not be that the *annihilation* of all the dead has affected them in the same manner? Will our adversaries tell us?

8. There are, however, other classes of passages which are pertinaciously insisted on, and we ought not therefore to pass them without notice. See, for example, Psalm xxxvii, 10, 20: "Yet a little while and the wicked shall not be;" "they shall perish." Psalm cxlv, 20: "All the wicked shall he destroy."† They quote these and other

* See C. 49, A. 92, E. 124.

† See J. T. 64, C. 48, E. 124.

passages, which refer to God's treatment of the wicked in this world, and so grossly misapprehend their import as to refer them only to the world to come.

9. They employ likewise such passages as the following: Psalm lxxxviii, 10–12: "Wilt thou show wonders to the dead? *Shall the dead arise and praise thee?* Shall thy loving kindness be declared in the grave? or thy faithfulness in destruction?" etc. And Psalm xxx, 9: "What profit is there in my blood, when I go down to the pit? Shall the dust praise thee? Shall it declare thy truth?" Psalm cxv, 17: "The dead praise not the Lord, neither any that go down into silence." Isaiah xxxviii, 18, 19: "For the grave cannot praise thee, death cannot celebrate thee, they that go down into the pit *cannot hope for thy truth.* The living, the living, he shall praise thee, as I do this day." Psalm cxix, 175: "Let my soul live, and it shall praise thee." Psalm vi, 5: "For in death there is no remembrance of thee: in the grave who shall give thee thanks?" *

It is scarcely conceivable that, with the Bible open before them, men should so misconstrue the import of language like the foregoing, when the context indicates, in every instance, that the very expressions which our opponents here dwell upon as justifying their treatment of the doctrine of immortality, relate to a matter altogether the reverse of mere corporeal death. In the sense of the penalty of the Divine law, death is the displeasure of God, and the soul that suffers that penalty is cut off from the source of spiritual life and happiness; and if it remain under his displeasure during the term of its probation here, that same death must be its portion forever. The children of God in all ages have been fearful of incurring this death, knowing that if they received according to their personal deserts it must be their portion. This apprehension prompted many fears, and bitter tears, and earnest prayers, and the assurance of deliverance therefrom filled the heart with thanks-

* E. 114, 115, 120, 121; C. 47, 48; H. 2, pp. 68, 70; A. 94; S., App. 25.

giving and joy. And well might even Hezekiah apprehend that the sentence of corporeal death which had been uttered against him was evidential of a displeasure which might rest upon him forever.* Hence, therefore, it may well be said of death, (in the sense of Gen. ii, 17,) the true penalty of the law, "*In death* there is no remembrance of thee." Psalm vi, 5; Isaiah xxxviii, 18, 19. See too Job xxviii, 22, where, in this sense, *destruction and death* are associated. Even in spiritual death during the present life, God is not remembered, but forgotten and disregarded, and how much more shall it be so in the world to come! The Jews of course derived their idea of death, in its proper sense, from Gen. ii, 17. (Compare Psalm xxx, 9; lxxxviii, 10–12; cxv, 7.) The people of God, then, knowing their sin and frailty, perpetually feared that they might, in justice, be given over to death, the penalty of the law, and therefore pleaded with God to protect and deliver them from it, and in their supplications they refer to the fact that it is their heart's desire to serve and praise him, and that those only who live, that is, who are rescued from this penalty, can praise him.

It is strange that a careful reader of only the Old Testament should so egregiously misunderstand its import, but

* The remarks of Mr. Greenham on Psalm cxix, 175, refer to this subject. After adverting to Luke i, 46; Psalm ciii, 1; civ, 1; cxv, 17; vi, 5; and Isaiah xxxviii, 19, in illustration, he adds: "How grievous a thing it is now every man may judge, that a man should go out of this world, or ever he knew wherefore he came into the world, and this is that which maketh us so loth to die. This was it that made the saints of God, in former times, so unwilling to leave life; not that they wanted any hope of the life to come, or had not the joy of a blessed resurrection; but either they had some special sins heavily pressing their consciences, whereby they had dishonored God, or else they desired to live in greater measure to glorify God, either in entering into the way of repentance, or else growing in the same, after they had entered; because as yet they could not say in truth, *I have fought a good fight, I have run a good race, I have kept the faith, from henceforth a crown of glory is prepared for me.* For they knew that, whereof we are willingly ignorant, that we shall never incessantly praise God in heaven, unless we carefully serve God on earth; and we shall never praise God in the congregation of angels, which praise not God in the congregation of his saints." Works, page 689; *folio*, 1601.

much more remarkable is it that this should be the case with any one who has ever perused the New Testament.

The remark of S. 60–62, that "spiritual death cannot be the penalty of sin," is a mere equivocation. The penalty of the law, as we shall show more fully in a future chapter, is death—a severance from the source of spiritual life and happiness, a breaking up of all harmony between God and the creature. The soul that sins is thus at once severed from God, and consequently, on the very day and hour that Adam transgressed he died. The *consequence* of this was suffering, misery, and the incurring of spiritual death to himself and posterity, a death which Redeeming Love alone can prevent from being eternal, and from which Christ alone can arouse the children of men. Hence the unregenerate are properly called *dead*, and it is expressly declared that the voice of God alone can awaken them to life. (1 John iii, 14; 1 Tim. v, 6; John v, 25.) And in this last passage this death is carefully distinguished from death in the sense of corporeal dissolution, verse 28. See also Eph. v, 14. And hence the regenerate and justified, though they die corporeally, are said to have passed from death unto life. The connection between them and the source of life has been restored. (John iii, 5; i, 12, 13; Eph. ii, 5, 10; iv, 32. Compare also Rom. vii, 6; viii, 1, 2.) And this is in perfect accordance with the promise which follows the twofold repetition of the threatening in the Old Testament, (Ezek. xviii, 4, 20,) for immediately thereafter it is added that "if the wicked turn *he shall not die.*" Verse 21. These thoughts, obvious as they must be to the reflecting mind, evince the futility of the objections to immortality, based on such passages as the preceding.

10. These considerations will throw light upon another class of texts on which our opponents are in the habit of basing objections; for example, where the *soul* is spoken of as *suffering death.* But death, as we have shown already, does not infer extinction of existence. In this connection they quote Ezek. xviii, 4, 20: "The *soul* that sin-

neth, it shall die," which we have explained above. And also Psalm xvi, 10: "Thou wilt not leave my soul in hell," (*sheol*,) which passage refers to our blessed Redeemer, (Acts ii, 31,) and proves that he suffered the penalty of the law for his people; but to infer from it that his human spirit was annihilated between his death and the resurrection is an appalling idea. (C. 46, E. 115. See our remarks on 1 Peter iii, 18–20, in a preceding section.) C. 46 ludicrously quotes, in the same connection, "He spared not their soul from death, *but gave their life over to the pestilence*." E. 12, 43, 75, likewise makes a great effort to prove that *souls can be killed*, and that "*there are such things as dead souls*." He makes no attempt, however, to reconcile this with his materialistic notion that the soul is merely the result of physical organization, and *inseparable* from the body.

11. The only remaining passages alleged by them which call for notice are these: "The man that wandereth out of the way of understanding shall remain in the congregation of the dead," Prov. xxi, 16; and, "I will make them drunken, that they may rejoice, *and sleep a perpetual sleep, and not wake, saith the Lord*." Jer. li, 39. But surely we may again inquire here, What is to become of the *resurrection*, if they "are to remain in the congregation of the dead, and sleep a sleep which is perpetual, and knows no waking?" In the same connection, also, they quote Dan. xii, 2: "Many that *sleep* in the dust of the earth shall arise;"* by which it seems that this *perpetual* sleep is after all to have a waking. It seems like trifling with the reader's patience to dwell upon such exhibitions of logic, and we should not do it were we not aware that all these instances have been successful in the hands of our opponents in deceiving the unwary and illiterate. With a single remark or two, however, we shall dismiss the point.

The expression "*deep* or perpetual sleep," which occurs in the passage from Jeremiah, and refers to the doom of the

* See C. 49; H. 2, p. 70; S. 63; B. 74–76.

wicked Babylonian oppressors, had quite a familiar application among the Jews. A single instance will illustrate this. Asaph says, (Psa. lxxvi, 6,) "At thy rebuke, O God of Jacob, both the chariot and the horse are cast *into a deep sleep*." The expression was employed in relation to anything which, having had visible existence, had lost its form or activity, (as, for example, the horse and chariot when rushing into action,) and had been laid aside or become invisible to human observation.

By a familiar figure, common among all nations, death is referred to as a sleep. The soul may be still active, as in dreaming, but the exhibition of life, or vital power, has ceased to be apparent. In fact, so like in appearance are sleep and death, that the poets have spoken of them as brothers; an idea, I believe, first suggested by Homer.* Among the Jews, however, this figure of death as a sleep became transferred to that death which was known as the penalty of sin, and is spoken of in the New Testament as the *second death*, so that it too was called a *sleep*. A single instance will suffice for illustration. In Psa. xiii, 3, David prays, "Consider and hear me, O Lord my God; lighten mine eyes, lest I sleep the sleep of death." Now David expected not to escape corporeal death, and never prayed to be exempt from it. The remedy for the death against which he prays was spiritual illumination.† By that alone can any one escape, or be delivered from sleeping that sleep which knows no waking, and from which none ever arise to praise God. If they have spent their term of probation in sin, they arise to shame and endless infamy.

12. And now, in conclusion of this examination of the passages adduced from the Old Testament by our opponents, I have a brief remark or two to offer.

1.) It is obvious from the whole examination that *the principles which they adopt in interpreting the foregoing passages* make it perfectly plain that "God destroys both the perfect

* So too the aphorism: *οἱ δαρθάνοντες νεκροῖσιν ὅμοιοι εἰσὶν.*

† I am indebted for this to the Clavis of Flacius, *sub voce* DORMIRE.

and the wicked; that all flesh shall perish together; that the Babylonians are to sleep a perpetual sleep and not wake; that those who are in the grave God remembers no more; that the dead shall not arise and praise God, and that he that goeth down to the grave shall come up no more; that Job shall return no more, and shall see no more good. Or, in other words, we are thus taught that *death is an eternal sleep*,"* and therefore their principles of interpretation are false.

2.) I have remarked above that we were under the necessity of omitting many positive proofs from the Scriptures that the soul survives the stroke of death. But in concluding this list of passages adduced by our adversaries, I will briefly refer to one proof of the doctrine of future rewards and punishments, and of the soul's immortality, which learned Jews complain has been overlooked by Christian writers in treating the subject. God, speaking to the human race through Noah, says in Gen. ix, 5, 6, "And surely the blood of your lives will I require; at the hand of every *beast* will I require it, and at the hand of man," etc. The first clause contains the general announcement, and the others are explanatory of its import, which is a very common form of expression in the Hebrew tongue. In respect to the second clause, however, the word rendered *beast*, חַיָּה, cannot possibly have that import according to the genius of the language. For that word, as Rev. J. F. Denham remarks, is never applied to the brute creation unless in conjunction with that of *cattle*, *reptile*, or *bird;* or if none of these accompany it the expression is, either beasts *of the field*, or *forest*, or *of the earth*, or *wild beast;* and whenever, as in this instance, it stands without an adjunct, *it invariably relates to the soul of man.* The best Hebraists allow this rule, and that there is no exception to it in all the Scriptures, unless this is claimed to be one, in which our translation refers the word to the brute creation. But now let the rule hold good in this instance, for there is no sufficient reason

* See the little tract by Rev. N. D. George, pp. 14, 15.

why it should not, and the verses read as follows: "Surely your own life-blood will I require; of every soul will I require it; (that is, of every one who sheds his own blood, or perpetrates suicide,) and at the hand of man, yea, at the hand of every man, will I require the life of man his brother. Whoso sheddeth man's blood, by man shall his blood be shed, for in the image of God made he man." If this be so, then of course the meaning of the second clause must be "from the *soul* of the suicide will I require his blood;" and so we have in the Scriptures this early and perfect indication of a punishment to the soul after death, and, consequently, of its immortality.*

* See Kitto's Cyclopedia, under the word *Soul*, which contains also the references to the Jewish authors sustaining the above.

# CHAPTER VI.

## THE SUBJECT CONTINUED.

### § 37. *Objections derived from the New Testament.*

THE passages adduced in the form of objection from the New Testament are "few and far between," and our opponents have evidently been hard pressed to find anything therein which could be so construed as even to seem to favor their old epicurean notions and atheistic philosophy, as the subjoined examination will evince.

1. The first passage which we find them insisting on is Matt. xxvii, 52, 53: "And the graves were opened, and many bodies of the saints which slept arose, and came out of their graves after his resurrection," etc. And to this they annex also the following: "The hour is coming in the which all that are in the graves shall hear his voice, and shall come forth." John v, 28. These passages are cited by H. 2, p. 79, and S. 64, but as they do not favor us specifically with their object in adducing them in this connection, we must be left to conjecture. It is, however, perfectly idle to pretend that these passages in any way conflict with man's uninterrupted immortality, or favor the notion of our opponents. As respects the latter passage it is sufficient to observe that Jesus, just before uttering it, had said that the *spiritually dead* should hear his voice and live. And then, to distinguish the corporeally dead from them, he adds in this verse, that "all who *are in the graves* should hear his voice and come forth." By the phrase "all that are in the graves," therefore, he meant, (in accordance with the usage of the Jews, who held to the survivance of the soul,) all who

are corporeally dead. As respects the former passage, as I have shown, in referring to it in my work on the Resurrection, p. 263, the remarkable change of gender in the Greek evinces a reunion of soul and body. It is not said that the bodies (σώματα) were raised *and came forth*, but that the bodies being raised, the persons, the saints themselves, came forth, (ἐξελθόντες,) an idea wholly subversive of the notion of the Materialists that the soul is a result of corporeal organization.

2. The next passage is Acts ii, 34: "For David is not ascended into the heavens." The apostle had just stated (v. 29) that "David was both dead and buried," and in this passage he affirms that he had not ascended into the heavens. Of course then, say our opponents, David must have perished body and soul at death. Their *literature* on this point may be found in B. 40, C. 47, E. 115, and H. 2, pp. 70, 71. They certainly make the most of this argument, and we shall, therefore, listen to what they have to offer. C. says, David "was not so fortunate as some modern professors, who expect to ascend into heaven immediately at death, and give their souls no opportunity to be redeemed from the power of the grave." B. says, referring to those who believe that the soul is immortal: "These men say, 'David is *not dead*, and *has* ascended into heaven.'" E. is somewhat more full, and, after quoting the passage, says, "Yea, his *soul* has been *left* in (*sheol, hades*) the *state of death*, and has seen *corruption*, and therefore he can no longer praise God till he awakes in the likeness of the Saviour, and his 'corruption puts on incorruption,' and '*when* Christ, *who is our life*, shall appear, (in the clouds of heaven,) THEN shall he also appear in glory' with him." Col. iii, 4. H., however, is very full and emphatic, and has presented the strength of the argument both analytically and synthetically. Let us hear him, therefore.

In presenting his argument he shows most conclusively and satisfactorily that Peter could not have here intended to say that the *body* of David had not ascended into the heavens, and also that for the same reason he could not have meant to say that his soul had not thus ascended, for neither the *soul* nor the *body* of David could be regarded as *the man David.* And then further, that David in Psalm xvi (quoted here in the context) did not speak of himself, but of Christ, is conclusively proved by Peter, from the fact that David was not only dead and buried, *but that he had not ascended into the heavens.* Mr. Ham then concludes the argument as follows: "It is, I think, apparent, that Peter's argument requires us to understand that *David himself*, the '*Patriarch* David,' *not* simply his body, was 'dead and buried,' and that David in no sense had ascended into the heavens. Therefore, if the Patriarch David has no conscious life in the intermediate state, but is awaiting the manifestation of the life which is at present hidden in Christ, (Col. iii, 3, 4,) the life and the light of men, and which shall take place at the resurrection, when Christ shall come to be glorified in his saints; if this, we say, be the case of the sweet Psalmist of Israel, we may fairly presume that the case is the same with all others. Then *the Scriptures teach* that although *in the midst of life we are in death**—in the midst of death we are *not* in life."†

Now a very little reflection might have suggested to Mr. Ham and his brethren several things of importance in this connection: and, 1. That as Peter *does not say* that the soul of David had not ascended into the heavens, his language

* The italics here are our own; but it is sometimes really difficult to know what these writers mean by "*the Scriptures.*" We have found them, as shown on a former page, quoting as such, passages not in the Bible, and then reasoning from them as inspired testimony; and here Mr. Ham, *though a Congregationalist*, quotes an expression from the book of "*Common Prayer*" as "*the Scriptures.*" To say that they do these things from ignorance would be impolite. How is it, then? They certainly need another Bible to sustain their system, and perhaps they have one. But if so, why not bring it out frankly and openly, and not be quoting from it in this sly manner, as if incidentally only, and not designed? There is an unfairness about such a course, and we protest against all proceedings of that sort. See § 33, sub-sec. 5, above.

† Pp. 70, 71.

cannot be adduced to prove that the soul of that Patriarch had not so ascended; and, 2. That Moses was as perfectly "dead and buried" as David was, (Deut. xxxiv, 5, 6,) and had continued so according to the language of Christ (John vi, 49) and the asseverations of the Jews. (John viii, 52, 53.) Nor could he have been raised from the dead previous to the resurrection of Christ, for then Christ would not have been "the first-fruits of them that slept," and "the first-begotten from the dead." (1 Cor. xv, 20; Rev. i, 5. Compare Rom. vi, 9.) And yet, before the death of Christ, *Moses* appeared on Tabor along with Elijah. (Matt. xvii, 3.) (I say *Moses*, for, as already shown, it is the custom of the inspired writers to give to the spirit of man the name of man himself. Luke xvi, 23.) Of course, then, it was just as proper to say of Moses at this very time (and the words of Christ in John vi, 49, were spoken about the time of the occurrence recorded in Matt. xvii, 1–9,) as it was to say of David, that he was "dead and buried," and "had not ascended into the heavens," and this though his spirit still survived in a state of conscious blessedness; and, *vice versa*, it is just as correct to say of David as of Moses that, although he was "dead and buried," and had "not ascended into the heavens," his spirit still existed. These things are so obvious as to need no further illustration. Of course, then, the passage can in no sense be brought into antagonism with the doctrine we teach. And, finally, in support of this view, we here offer an authority which Mr. Ham and all our opponents must respect, and ought to regard as conclusive in the matter. We refer to Mr. Ham himself. In referring to and exposing the Pagan notion, that man is immortal as to the soul only, and not as to the body, he remarks as follows: "Where is this anomalous breaking up, so to *speak*, of the *unity* of man's nature to be found in the Bible? It is not a religious doctrine, but a philosophical refinement, which started into existence when Platonism meddled with the simplicity of the Scriptures. NEITHER THE BODY NOR THE SOUL SEPARATELY IS THE MAN, BUT THE UNION OF BOTH.

To borrow the illustration of a living writer, 'as the union of oxygen and hydrogen produces water, so the *union* of body and soul constitutes a man.'" (See H. I., p. 119.) Now all this is plain, and therefore the soul of David (though it might, as in the instances of Moses, Abraham, and others, be called by his name) was not David. And what Peter here asserts is that the *man* David, the constituent man, soul and body, had not ascended into the heavens, and that, therefore, he was not the promised Messiah referred to in Psa. 16. But Jesus had ascended, and therefore he is the Christ. We have in our *Reply to Professor Bush*, p. 279, criticized the original of this passage, and need not repeat the criticism here.

3. The next and only other passage presented by our opponents as containing a *direct* impeachment of the doctrine of the soul's uninterrupted immortality is 1 Cor. xv, 16–18: "For if the dead rise not, then is not Christ raised. And if Christ be not raised, your faith is vain, ye are yet in your sins. Then they also which are fallen asleep in Christ are perished." These verses contain the gist of their ground of objection, though the reader had better turn to the whole context in verses 12–32. The literature of the subject, as presented by our opponents, may be seen in D. 147–151; H. 2, pp. 81, 82; S., App. 20; M. 21, 22; C. 54; E. 124–131. Add also Priestley *in loco*. There is no passage either in the Old or New Testament on which they so much insist as this; though in reading them one is often reminded of the saying of old Scultetus, *Ut vacca vaccam, ita autor autorem sequitur.*

M. explains it thus: "'They also which are fallen asleep in Christ are perished;' THAT IS, ARE NOW TOTALLY EXTINCT." But how is this? Paul says that *if* Christ be not risen *then they are perished;* implying, of course, that since he has arisen they are *not perished.* And if they are not perished, how can they have become "*totally extinct?*" It is hardly doing justice to the reasoning powers of the apostle to make him say that whether Christ has risen or not, those that "are fallen asleep in him are perished." E. likewise explains *perish* here as *extinction;* but S. is very emphatic. He says: "How could Paul say, 'If the dead rise not, then they that have *fallen asleep* in Christ are *perished?*' if the saints go into a conscious state of blessedness the moment they die? If it be said, Paul means their bodies are perished, I reply, . . . It seems to me that Paul intended to teach that our entire future existence depends on a resurrection from the dead; and if there be no resurrection, then at death, man *ceases to have existence*, and will live no more forever." H. remarks that "the apostle, in his concise piece of reasoning, distinctly affirms that if there be no resurrection of the dead then there is no future life;" after which he asks: "Can the orthodox of the nineteenth century agree with Paul in his affirmation that if the dead rise not, Christians who have departed this life are *perished?* No, they say, 'if the dead rise not,' the *soul lives on*—its life does *not depend* upon the resumption of the body." H. is usually great at making a display, but on this text, however, he must yield the palm to D. He extends his criticism, and without offering a new idea, arranges the arguments in rank and file; and after speaking to the reader in the following modest and peculiarly distinctive style, announces the conclusion, which we subjoin likewise: "For my own part, I have not the presumption to disagree with an apostle, and always rest satisfied with either the argumentative processes, or the authoritative assertions of inspired men. [See Luke xviii, 11, 12.] And I therefore receive with implicit faith the apostolic doctrine contained in the conclusion: '*What advantageth it me, if the dead rise not?*'" "And this 'perishing' would have been as complete and final as that, had it been the prospect before him, Paul would himself have said, 'Let us eat and drink, for to-morrow we die.'" Such are the decisions of this *corpus criticorum* on the passage.

In order, however, to see the utter futility of all this, it is only necessary that the reader should examine the argument of the apostle.* It is briefly as follows: "I have testified to you, ye Christians of Corinth, that Christ *died for our sins*, was *buried*, and *rose again*, according to the Scriptures of the former economy; and moreover, that he was seen, after his resurrection, by multitudes of witnesses, who are still living, and lastly by myself. So we preach, and so ye believed. Here, then, is the evidence that he has arisen, and that he consequently is the promised Saviour; the Scriptures declare that it SHALL *be* so, and multitudes of still living witnesses testify that it *has been* so. But if Christ be preached that *he* rose from the dead, how say some among you that there is no resurrection of the dead? For if there is no resurrection, then Christ is not risen; *because*, as I have already shown to you, (v. 3,) he died, was buried, and rose again, *not for himself*, *but for us—for our sins*—according to the Scriptures. And therefore if he has arisen *we must arise*, and, on the contrary, if we rise not, then is he not risen; and consequently our preaching is false, and your faith in the Scriptures and in him is vain; and we who profess to have seen him after his resurrection are proved to be false witnesses, because we have testified that God raised up Christ, whom he raised not up; and consequently you are yet in your sins, (for, if he has not arisen, then he is not our Saviour from sin, ver. 3, 4;) and those too who have departed this life trusting in him as their Saviour have trusted in one who cannot save them, and have therefore perished, or failed of salvation." Such is the argument, lying upon the very surface of the language, and plain, one would think, to the capacity of a child. And it is really inconceivable how these men could so egregiously have mistaken it. The question of consciousness or unconsciousness after death is in no way here connected with or involved in the apostle's argument. The term *perished* has reference merely to the hypothesis that these persons on entering eternity

* If I may venture again to refer to my little work on the Resurrection, I would remark that the reader will there find, on pp. 188–244, a thorough analysis of the argument in 1 Cor. xv.

were found to be destitute of a Saviour from their sins. How preposterous is it, therefore, for our opponents thus to attempt to draw into the apostle's argument an element with which it cannot possibly have the slightest connection, and then to undertake to build up a theory on such a foundation.

And then, further, this egregious blunder of Mr. Dobney and his friends, whether intentional or not, is characteristically ludicrous. For, as above intimated, a moment's reflection would have shown them that if "*perish*" means extinction of conscious being, *not perishing* must mean a *continuance of conscious being.* Now the passage avers that those who are fallen asleep in Christ are perished *if he is not really the promised Saviour.* But since he *is* the promised Saviour, they, of course, have *not* thus perished, but continue to exist, our adversaries themselves being judges. All this is transparently obvious from the very ground assumed by Messrs. Ham, Dobney, and friends, in their objection founded on this passage.

I may here remark, in passing, that the import of the following verse (verse 19, which has perplexed many) is perfectly easy when considered in this, its proper connection. Paul there says that "if in this life only we have hope in Christ, we are of all men most miserable." That is, if we go into the world of spirits relying on Christ to save us from sin, and there find ourselves disappointed in respect to all the bright hopes and expectations which the Gospel has awakened within us, (as we must be if he is not the promised Messiah,) there are none of the damned who shall be so truly miserable as we, for none had such hopes and prospects as those which through life have cheered our hearts.

4. There are other objections urged by them, however, but which are presented less in a textual, and more in a doctrinal form. For example, they maintain that *the attainment of immortality by man is purely conditional;* in support of which they urge three points: first, That *God*

*alone* possesses immortality. (1 Tim. vi, 16; i, 17. On which passages see their views in D. 112; M. 13–15; Has. 34; E. 131–133; G. 16; C. 63.) They urge, secondly, that man is required to *seek* immortality, which could not be if it were inherent, and not conditional. On this point they plead Rom. ii, 7, where it is stated that they who *seek for immortality* shall have eternal life.* In support of the same idea they plead, thirdly, that immortality is affirmed to come only through Christ the Saviour, and is dependent solely on the resurrection.†

In maintaining it, however, our Annihilationists are not quite as careful in their statements as they ought to be. For instance, both S. 12 and C. 63, roundly assert that "the term *immortal* occurs but *once* in the Bible, namely, 1 Tim. i, 17, and is applied to God." Has. 34 likewise asserts that "Paul is the only writer in the whole Bible who makes use of the word *immortal* or *immortality*." These three men lay claim to pretty considerable knowledge; but how they will attempt to reconcile these statements with such claims, and with truth, the reader must be left to determine, in view of the following facts. The word *immortal*, (ἄφθαρτος,) besides being employed in 1 Tim. i, 17, is used in Rom. i, 23; 1 Cor. ix, 25; xv, 52; 1 Peter i, 4, 23; iii, 4. The word *immortality* (ἀφθαρσία) is employed, in addition to Rom. ii, 7, in the following places: 1 Cor. xv, 42, 50, 53, 54; Eph. vi, 24; Titus ii, 7; 2 Tim. i, 10. Compare also Dan. vi, 24; and in the Apocrypha see Wisdom xii, 1; xviii, 4. I refer to these instances not merely to correct the blundering of our opponents, but that the reader may have at hand the facts in the case.

In section 27, sub-sections 2 and 3, I have referred to, and briefly exposed, the equivocations of our opponents in

* See what they offer on this passage: D. 98; M. 13–15, 36, 37; C. 63; I. *passim;* Has. 34; H. 2, p. 92.

† See H. 1, pp. 128, 129, and H. 2, pp. 92, 93. They all take this ground. It was maintained likewise by Dr. Chauncey, "Universal Salvation," p. 132; Abner Kneeland, "Lectures," p. 48; Dr. Priestley, in his Notes on the New Testament; and by Taylor of Norwich, and others.

regard to these words, and I beg leave to refer the reader to those paragraphs. But we shall now proceed to consider their proofs that the attainment of immortality is conditional.

In their argument they employ the term immortality in the sense of *actual being*, or *existence*, in distinction from that of a *state* or *condition of existence*, and so infer that it does not mean merely a *state* of existence, either happy or miserable, but *existence itself.* They claim that those who obtain this immortality, or existence, will be, of course, ineffably happy, but that all others shall not only forfeit happiness, but be deprived of existence itself.

Their first proof, as above remarked, is 1 Tim. vi, 16: "God *only* hath immortality;" and they infer from it that man possesses no immortality, unless conferred through grace by Christ. But the absurdity of this inference is plain from the fact that in this passage the word means *underived and eternal existence*, and surely no one pretends that a *creature* can possess immortality in that sense; and I hardly believe that our opponents would maintain either that man should seek such an immortality, or that it can be conferred by grace, or in any other way. And then further, that such must be the meaning of the word here is apparent from the fact, that in the sense in which immortality is to be sought by man, and is conferred by Christ, it was already in possession of a considerable number of the race at the very time when the apostle declared that "God alone has immortality." Besides Enoch and Elijah, who had long been in possession of it, there were the "many saints" referred to in Matt. xxvii, 52, 53, and who were already in full possession of the same immortality which shall pertain to all true believers after the resurrection. Of course, then, Paul could never have employed the term in the sense in which our opponents pretend. A further reason may be stated if it should be deemed necessary, namely: in the sense wherein Paul here declares that "God alone has immortality," the statement will remain true to all eternity. But it will not, after the resurrection of the dead, be true of him in the sense in which our opponents apply the term; for, on their own admission, the resurrection will confer a final and everlasting title to immortality upon the saved. This text therefore proves nothing but what we have always emphatically maintained, that God alone possesses *inherent*, that is, *underived and eternal*, immortality. And yet no text is so often quoted by the Annihilationists as this, to prove that man has no *derived* immortal nature; a point to which it does not in the remotest way refer.*

It is obvious that in 1 Tim. vi, 16, and as related to God, the term *immortality* (ἀθανασία, from ἀθάνατος,† *immortal,*) is employed in a specific and restricted sense. In its general import, however, and as applied to the creature, it simply means that which is not obnoxious to corruption or decay. (See the word as applied in 1 Cor. xv, 53, 54. Compare the usage also in Wisdom iii, 4; viii, 14, 18; xv, 3.) In the *specific* sense God alone possesses it; in the *general* sense the creature may. The one refers to underived immortality, the other to that which is derived. In the other text, however, which they quote to sustain their objection, (1 Tim. i, 17,) the term, though different, is in usage equivalent. It is ἄφθαρτος, and, as employed in the above-cited instances, evinces what is the import of *both* in their general usage. In 1 Cor. ix, 25, it is used to express the idea that the crown which the believer shall receive at the last day is *incorruptible;* (compare 2 Tim. iv, 8;) and in 1 Cor. xv, 52, it is applied to the resurrection body, and in 1 Peter i, 4, 23, to the inheritance to which the believer is begotten by the grace of God; and finally, in 1 Peter iii, 4, to the regenerated nature of man

* The reader must pardon the particularity with which we dwell upon the points of this objection. It forms the very nucleus of the theory of our opponents, and whole volumes have been written in defense of its baseless assumptions.

† Ἀθάνατος is not employed in the New Testament.

in this world, that nature which is here pronounced immortal or incorruptible, (see also Rom. viii, 1,) but which our opponents thoughtlessly affirm is not so, inasmuch as it is to become extinct or annihilated when man dies. Such, then, are the usages of these terms. In the sense of the *everlasting inheritance*, and *crown of life and glory*, we always have maintained that immortality is conditional. But this of course refers not to *being* or to *simple existence*, in itself considered, as our opponents pretend, but to something the possession of which is offered to man, and which he may possess, and become thereby ineffably happy, but which he also may refuse, and so render his being unhappy through the wasteless ages of eternity.

As respects their *second* point, we admit, and always have affirmed, that the text which they employ to sustain it (Rom. ii, 7,) represents immortality as something to be sought by perishing man. The foregoing remarks, however, apply to this passage also. In fact the words referred to, and which are employed in this and the forecited passages, are equivalent in import, and as such are employed in 1 Cor. xv, as may be seen by referring to the instances of their use above given, wherein they refer to the resurrection body. Now there is a sense in which *the resurrection itself is to be sought*, (Phil. ii, 7–11,) and yet we are expressly assured that the resurrection will be universal, comprehending both the just and unjust. (John v, 28, 29; Acts xxiv, 15.) And so, too, there is a sense in which everlasting or immortal life is to be sought, and another sense in which all mankind are to possess it. In the one case it means mere existence, without reference to state or condition, and in this sense all possess it. In the other case it means a *happy* state or condition of existence; and in this sense none are to possess it who refuse the offer of Christ. The same word, moreover, is employed in Eph. vi, 24, to designate the true believer's love of Christ; and in Tit. ii, 7, to express an uncompromising adherence to the doctrines of Christ; and finally in 2 Tim. i, 10, for *immortal life;* for here ζωὴν καὶ ἀφθαρσίαν is plainly a hendiadys for *ζωὴν ἄφθαρτον*. This, too, is its meaning in the text referred to, (Rom. ii, 7,) a condition of perpetual or unceasing happiness, "a glorious and honorable immortality," as opposed to that state of sin and misery which must be the undying portion of those who do not seek happiness through Jesus Christ.

In their *third* point they likewise plead, in support of the objection, that immortality comes to man only through Christ, and therefore is neither natural nor inherent, but a gracious gift to those who accept Christ as their Saviour, and is dependent solely on the resurrection.*

In their reference to the *resurrection*, they do not, of course, mean to exclude from immortality Enoch and Elijah, and those other saints referred to by Paul, who are never to be raised from the dead, (see 1 Thess. iv, 15, 17,) and whose immortality, therefore, does not depend upon their resurrection; and yet, from the positive and wide-sweeping character of their statements, one might be led to suppose the contrary. What we have offered above, however, applies equally to this third point, for our opponents can scarcely believe that immortality, in the sense of underived and independent existence, is to come to any creature through Christ; and in the other sense of the term we, of course, maintain that it can come alone through him. As to the resurrection, we have always maintained that the immortality of all men who die must depend upon that event. Man, that is, as consisting of body and soul, is not immortal *as man*, when the body is severed from the spirit. His spirit is immortal, but the spirit is only a part of man. And *as man*, in the true and proper sense of the term, the immortality *of all who die* is dependent upon the resurrection of the body.

5. Their next objection, and one on which they labor considerably, is of the same character as the foregoing. It purports to be based on the prominence given to the resurrection in the word of God, and from which they infer that

* See H. 1, pp. 128, 29, and H. 2, pp. 92, 93. They all take this ground.

there can be no immortality for man without the resurrection. To this, however, as above remarked, we assent, so far as all who die are concerned. But the design of our opponents in urging the matter is to endeavor to deduce the inference that therefore there is no intermediate or self-conscious state for man's spiritual nature, no interval of conscious existence between his death and resurrection.* But until these men point out what possible or conceivable connection exists between their premises and conclusion, we shall not occupy either our own time or the reader's patience by dwelling upon a specimen of such egregious nonsense.† The doctrine to which this idea is thus attempted to be brought in antagonism gives to the resurrection equal prominence, as the reader may perceive by referring to our remarks on 2 Cor. v, 1–9, and Heb. xii, 22, 23, above, (section 33, subsections 10 and 13,) and we dismiss their objection therefore, with the following passage, quoted and adopted by Mr. Hudson, one of their own writers, from the work of Dr. Nevins, on the "*Mystical Presence*:" "The doctrine of immortality in the Bible, is such as to include always the idea of the resurrection. It is an *ἀνάστασις ἐκ τῶν νεκρῶν*. The whole argument in the 15th chapter of First Corinthians, as well as the representation in 1 Thess. iv, 13–18, proceeds in the assumption that the life of the *body*, as well as that of the soul, is indispensable to the perfect state of our nature as human. The soul, then, during the intermediate state,

* See D. 151–160; G. 10–16; H. 1, p. 28.

† It may be proper here, however, to add a brief paragraph from Edwards: "The reasonableness of the doctrine of the resurrection will appear, if we suppose that union with a body is the most rational state of perfection of the human soul, which may be argued from the consideration that this was the condition in which the human soul was created at first, and that its separation from the body is no improvement of its condition, being an alteration brought on by sin;" "from whence we must conclude that the former state of union to the body was a better state than disunion, which was threatened. It introduced that death that consists in the separation of body and soul. The state of innocency was embodied; the state of guilt was disembodied. Therefore, as Christ came to restore from all the calamities which came from sin, it is most reasonable to suppose that he will restore the union of soul and body." Vol. vii, p. 240.

cannot possibly constitute, in the Bible view, a complete man; and the case requires, besides, that we should conceive of its relation to the body as still in force; not absolutely destroyed, but only suspended. The whole condition is interimistic, and by no possibility of conception capable of being thought of as complete and final. When the resurrection body appears it will not be as a new frame abruptly created for the occasion, and brought to the soul in the way of outward addition and supplement. It will be found to hold in strict organic continuity with the body, as it existed before death, as the action of the same law of life, which implies that this law has not been annihilated, but suspended only, in the intermediate state."*

6. Another objection is, that the doctrine of immortality, as maintained by us, makes the dead to be judged twice once immediately after death, and then, a second time, at the general judgment of the great day. See H. 1, p. 140, and others. This would be plausible, to be sure, if the point we insisted on were merely hypothetical. But the reader will doubtless be inclined to do full justice to the exemplary modesty of our opponents in producing this objection. It has a peculiarly beautiful aspect, as coming from those who assert that the sinner is *literally* to suffer the penalty of the law twice. That penalty, they aver, is annihilation; it is inflicted upon the sinner once when he dies, and then, as they inform us, he is to be raised from the dead, not to continue in existence, but merely to be annihilated over again.

In reasoning, however, it is a fair maxim that *retorquere non est respondere;* nor do we design the foregoing remarks as a reply to the objection itself, which at best, however, is a mere equivocation on the word "*judged.*" The spirit, when it has departed from the body, must, in the very nature of the case, be either in a happy or a miserable condition, and take its position accordingly either among the happy or unhappy. Its very existence and moral nature itself, of course, involve such a necessity. And the attempt

* See "Debt and Grace," by Mr. Hudson, pp. 262, 263.

to confound this necessity of its nature with the formal judgment which must be passed upon all at the last day, in the presence of the assembled universe of angels, men, and devils, is the fatuity of inanity. But then again, if the doctrine of the uninterrupted immortality of the soul did actually infer a twofold judgment, this would furnish no valid objection against it in the view of any believer of the Bible; for, that man should be judged twice constitutes no more a valid reason against the continuity of his existence during the interval which elapses between those judgments, than it would form a valid reason against the uninterrupted existence of the fallen angels during a similar interval. Now we read expressly that when angels sinned they were immediately condemned and adjudged to hell; and not only this, but that they are *reserved* in everlasting chains of darkness *unto the judgment of the great day.* (See 2 Pet. ii, 4, and Jude 6.) Suppose then that the sinner is judged and condemned at the last day, (as all admit he will be,) and what reason does this furnish for denying that he is likewise condemned and adjudged to hell immediately after his death?

7. Another objection frequently repeated by them, and equally the result of ignorance or misconception, is, that the Romish purgatory is based upon the doctrine we are defending. But, even admitting the statement to be true, what would it prove? Is not transubstantiation built upon the expressions which our blessed Saviour used at the last supper? And are we, therefore, to throw aside those words, and never employ them in the communion service? Or, should we not rather retain them in use, and show that they have been perverted by the Romish priesthood? In another chapter, when we come to speak of the separate state of the soul, we shall, upon a historical basis, show that this objection is false both in its statement and conclusion.

8. The last objection which we find our opponents insisting on is, that annihilation is not necessarily an evil, and consequently that there is no actual necessity for supposing

that the conscious existence of the soul is continued between death and the resurrection.*

It is not very extraordinary that men who endeavor to maintain that the Apostle, in Phil. i, 21, meant to say that "annihilation *is gain*," should assert that it is no evil, for this is not really coming up to what they make Paul himself aver. Their statements on this subject, however, are so preposterous that we need here take up no time with them, as we shall in another chapter have occasion to treat fully the question of annihilation in its relation to the whole subject before us. Let it, therefore, suffice here to remark, that though they thus assert that annihilation is not necessarily an evil, they yet maintain in other parts of their writings that to the sinner it is a more terrible punishment than endless misery itself. They moreover maintain that annihilation is the veritable and proper penalty of the divine law, as enunciated in Gen. ii, 17, and Ezek. xviii, 4. And is not then the penalty of the divine law necessarily an evil to those who suffer it? But such nonsense may very well be passed without further remark.

### § 38. *Conclusion of the Scriptural Argument.*

In concluding our remarks on the catalogue of objections brought by our adversaries from the Old Testament, we adduced a single passage out of many which we had omitted, and offered an observation thereupon. We shall do the same here likewise after we have briefly noticed a clause in a passage applied to the subject in § 33. Jesus, in speaking of the deceased saints and of their condition anterior to the resurrection, says that they are *like unto the angels;* that is, their disembodied spirits are like them, for, when re-embodied in flesh, that likeness is not, of course, so apparent. And in the context, referring to the ancient patriarchs and others of the pious dead, he says they all live to or with God, for God is not a God of the dead, (since he could not

* See D. 242–244, and others.

be such to them, if, in the Sadducean sense, they had ceased to exist,) but of the living. Any man who will take his Greek Testament and read Luke xx, 34–38, (or Matt. xxii, 29–32,) will see that the grammatical construction imperatively requires this sense of the passage. Our Saviour's language there can allude only to the state of the saints referred to anterior to the resurrection. He names them expressly "sons of God," (in reference mainly to their prospective public adoption at the last day,) "*being sons of the resurrection*," τῆς ἀναστασεως υἱοὶ ὄντες. Thus, "sons of the kingdom" (Matt. viii, 12,) were those to whom the kingdom was appointed or destined; "son of death" (Psa. cii, 20,) was one who had been appointed to die; "*children of wrath*," (Eph. ii, 3,) namely, destined to wrath. (See also Psa. lxxix, 11, and Alexander's note.) And as the saints and patriarchs here referred to by Christ were destined to receive this public adoption by God, as his sons, at the last day, so they were, of course, appointed to be raised from the dead, and were sons of the resurrection. The Hebræism, or rather Orientalism, cannot be misunderstood. Hence, therefore, Jesus says *they are* (not *shall be*, but *are*) like the angels of God. It is impossible otherwise to construe the words, according to the rules of language and the fair principles of interpretation, and to make them refer to a period subsequent to the resurrection. Every term looks to that event as still future, and that the reader may at once perceive this. I quote here the two verses bearing directly on the point: "But they which *shall be accounted worthy to obtain that world, and the resurrection from the dead*, neither marry nor are given in marriage; neither can they die any more, for they *are equal unto the angels*, and *are the children of God, being the children of the resurrection*." Luke xx, 35, 36. I would not attach undue importance to any mere nicety of verbal criticism; this, however, is not such. For does not the phraseology, "they who are accounted worthy to obtain that world and the resurrection," include the pious dead of the past ages, as well as those of the future?* And does not the phraseology referred to clearly announce that those who had departed this life were yet to obtain the higher inheritance of heaven and the resurrection? In any other sense, according to the idiom, could they be "the sons of the resurrection?" In fact, in this whole dispute with the Sadducees, (the Annihilationists of his day,) Jesus deduces the doctrine of the future resurrection of the body from the present existence of the soul, (ver. 27–38,) as we have largely shown elsewhere.† And as the separate state is necessarily incomplete, and as the separate spirits of the ransomed dead look forward to the resurrection as the completion of their bliss, they are, by virtue of their union with Christ, through whom all are made alive, regarded in this sense as in the resurrection state; that is, they have safely passed through all their bitter sorrows and conflicts on earth, and a happy reunion with the body is now secured to them through atoning blood. That this is no new view of the passage quoted by Jesus, may be seen from the subjoined extract from Menassah Ben Israel: "When the Lord first appeared to Moses we read that he said, 'I am the God of thy fathers, the God of Abraham, the God of Isaac, the God of Jacob.' But God is not the God of the dead, who are not, but of the living, who do exist. Therefore it is a just conclusion therefrom that the souls of the patriarchs are even now living."‡

The other passage, however, to which I would call specific attention, and one to which we have not referred, is John viii, 56: "Your father Abraham rejoiced to see my day: and he saw it, and was glad."

* *Cudworth*, ii, 238, fully sustains this view. And *Calvin*, in his note on Luke xx, 27, says very forcibly: "Qui fit ut mortuos potius, quam vivos, respiciat Deus, nisi quia primum honoris gradum Patribus tribuit, apud quos fœdus suum deposuerat? Quomodo autem præcellerent, si morte essent extincti? Hoc etiam clare exprimit relatio; nam sicuti pater nullus esse potest absqve liberis, neque rex absque populo, sic proprie Dominus nisi vivorum vocari Deus non potest."

† In reply to the Anastasis of Professor Bush, pp. 253–259. See also section 33, sub-section 5, above.

‡ De Resurr. Mort., lib. x, cap. 6.

Franzius, De Interpret. Script. Orac. 67, (as quoted by Glassius,) speaking of this passage, says that no one can doubt that there was presented to Abraham, in a very clear Divine vision, the person and face of Jesus Christ, as he was born of a virgin of the seed of Abraham, and began the performance of his official labors, and was exalted through suffering to the right hand of the Father, etc. But Calvin suggests another interpretation as adopted by some, to wit: that Abraham, in his state of separation from the body, beheld the presence of Christ when he appeared on earth. He justifies the sentiment, but is not fully satisfied that it is taught here. Mosheim, however, in his "Meditatio de die Christi ab Abrahamo visa," (Hamburg, 1751,) has, as it appears to me, placed the matter beyond doubt, that Christ refers to the present existence of Abraham, and to the fact that he in heaven had witnessed the fulfillment of the promise made to him respecting the coming of the Messiah. See his paraphrase of the passage itself in sec. 10. of the work above referred to. J. D. Michaelis, in Theol. Dog., cap. xiv, sect. 157, gives it the same exposition, and says in view of it: "*Aliam (interpretationem) autem, quæ ferri possit, prodi ab interpretibus non video.*" And I am well satisfied that a thorough criticism of the passage would show this to be the only correct view: "You slight and reject me, O ye Jews, and profess to be sons of Abraham. But your father Abraham rejoiced to see my natal day; and he saw it and was glad."

Tholuck (*in loco*) remarks that "the narrative in Matt. xvii, 4, also leads to the assumption that the great men of the Old Covenant partook in the redemptive work of Christ." And Maldonatus thus reasons on the import of the passage before us: "When Christ says that Abraham *saw*, he doubtless means that he saw in that way in which he had declared that he so greatly desired by faith alone to see; for after he did believe, and when he had no knowledge of Christ, he could not desire to behold his day, but after he had that knowledge, he desired indeed, but not by faith alone, because he already did behold the day of Christ by faith. He therefore saw the day of Christ *actually and really* (*re ipsa*) as both he and all the fathers had desired to behold it." This conclusion is abundantly supported by the premise, and until it is fairly invalidated the passage must be regarded as containing a clear announcement of the doctrine that the soul in its state of separation from the body is in the full possession of its consciousness.

# CHAPTER VII.

## JEWISH AND PATRISTICAL TESTIMONY—OBJECTIONS ANSWERED.

As the argument derivable from the views entertained by the Jews and early Christians is not intrinsically of any strictly logical force, I should be willing to pass without remark the topic suggested in the heading of this chapter. The state of the controversy, however, in relation to the whole question of man's uninterrupted immortality, is, at present, such as would prevent the possibility of doing justice to the whole matter should this point be passed over in silence. Our opponents unite in making the most unwarrantable assertions in relation to it, and appear to copy indiscriminately, and even without remorse, the exploded "Corruptions" of the well-meaning, but (in this department of literature) superficial Dr. Priestley. We shall treat the subject as briefly, however, as is possible in doing it the justice which the state of the case requires.

### § 39. *Jewish Testimony.*

Our references to the Jewish testimony must of course be independent of the canonical Scriptures, since what relates to that point has been presented on the foregoing pages. (See sect. 30.) It may to a considerable extent, however, be learned from the Apocrypha. See particularly Ecclesiasticus xv, 18; xxxiii, 14, 15; li, 9; Wisdom iii, 1–11; ii, 23, 24; viii, 13; 2 Mac. vii, 9–38; xii, 43, 44. And also from Josephus, Antiquities, Book i, chap. i, section 2, and Book xviii, c. i, sections 3–5. In his work on the Jewish War likewise, B. ii, c. viii, sections 10, 11, 14. As these works are easily accessible by all, we shall not occupy space by citing their testimony.

The testimony of Philo is equally explicit. In his book on Rewards and Punishments he says: "For some indeed adopt the notion that death is the end of punishments, *πέρας τιμωριῶν εἶναι θάνατον*; but in the view of the divine Judge this is scarcely the beginning. Hence, therefore, when, for instance, a new crime has been perpetrated by any one, it is proper that a new punishment should be appointed for him. But what is that? Why that he should live a perpetually dying death, *ζῆν ἀποθνήσκοντα ἀεὶ*, [suggested perhaps by the מוֹת תָּמוּת of Gen. ii, 17, and which the LXX. express by *θανάτῳ ἀποθανεῖσθε*,] and sustain, as it were, a death that is interminable." He speaks of the soul, too, as a sacred *depositum* committed to the keeping of man by his Creator. For example, in his book respecting Abraham, he says: "No wise man will be displeased when any one calls for that which he has intrusted to him; why then should we be offended that God or nature requires what they have committed to our keeping?" The same term (*ἡ παρακαταθήκη*, *deposit*) is employed in the same sense by Josephus, in his De Bello Jud., lib. iii, cap. viii, sect. 5, in the following manner: "The immortal soul, which has its original from God, dwells in the body; now, if any one embezzles or evilly entreats that which is committed to him by man, he is regarded as wicked and perfidious. If, therefore, any one casts out of his body by self-murder the *depositum of God*, *τὴν παρακαταθήκην τοῦ Θεοῦ*, can he hope to conceal himself from him that is thus injured?" The survivance of the soul is here so plainly taught that it need not be dwelt upon. And on the question whether it be the conscious and acting personality of man, the Jewish testimony is uniform. Rabbi Simeon, for example, (in Berachot, fol. 10,) referring to the expression in Psalms ciii and civ, "Bless the Lord, O my soul," observes that "it refers to God and the soul. For as the blessed God fills this whole universe, so does the soul occupy the whole body. As God sees, and yet is himself invisible, so the soul sees, and is not seen. As God sustains or nourishes the universal world, so the soul nourishes the whole body." See Wagenseil, Sota, p. 1017; and also the story of Rabbi Meir, respecting the work which treated of "the seven (planetary) worlds and the seven heavens," the abodes of departed spirits of good men. Mantissa, p. 1163. Nor will it be questioned that they believed both in Gehenna and Paradise as the abodes of human souls between death and the resurrection of the body, which, they held, would take place at the coming of the Messiah. See Wegscheider's Dogmat., § 191, and Bretschneider's Handbuch, § 166, vol. ii, p. 378, *seq.*

The testimony of the Book of Enoch likewise ought not to be overlooked in this connection. Prof. Stuart (Biblic. Repos. for July, 1840) has given an interesting account of it, and of its testimony respecting future punishment. It was undoubtedly written during the first century of our era, and by a serious man for serious purposes, for his great theme is the reward of the righteous, and punishment of the wicked, in the future state. He moreover seems evidently to have been a Jew. Now he speaks in the clearest manner of the separate state of the soul or spirit, τὰ πνεύματα τῶν ψυχῶν τῶν ἀποθανόντων ἀνθρώπων. And speaking of the wicked he says: "Never shall they obtain mercy, saith the Lord of spirits." "Henceforth I will not have mercy upon them, saith the Lord of spirits." "Their evil deeds shall become their greatest torments, when their souls shall be made to descend to the receptacle of the dead."

Of their later writers who profess to give the earlier and traditional testimony, the following may suffice.

In the Tanchuma it is said: "Our *dead* (that is, those of Israel,) *are not dead;* as says the Psalmist, 'Let the saints be joyful in glory.'" In Jalkut Simeon: "There is no difference between the *living* and *dead* righteous; they differ only in name." In Synop. Sohar: "Jacob our father, and Moses our teacher, upon whom be peace, are *not dead;* and so of all who are in perfection, for upon this *true life* depends. And although it is written of them that they are *dead*, yet this is to be understood only in respect to us, and not in respect to them." And Menasseh Ben Israel, (in his De Resurrect. Mort.) speaking of Gen. xvii, 7, 8, says: "It is plain that Abraham and the rest of the patriarchs did not possess that land; it follows therefore that they must be raised in order to enjoy the promised good, as otherwise the promises of God would prove vain and false. Hence, therefore, is proved not only the immortality of the soul, but also the essential foundation of the law, the resurrection of the dead."

It is not necessary that we should multiply citations, for the fact alleged will scarcely be doubted. An endeavor has been made, however, to neutralize the force of this testimony by maintaining that the Jews obtained their ideas of immortality from intercourse with other nations after the Babylonian captivity. Le Clerc, I believe, originated this notion, and our opponents strenuously assert it *per fas, per nefas.* And even those who deny that those nations ever had any such knowledge, scruple not to solve the problem in this way, unless I err. In like manner they strenuously deny that the Scriptures teach the immortality of the soul, and yet defy us to show an instance of "any nation which had not some knowledge of revelation" entertaining that doctrine. One might see, if disposed to look, that if there be any truth in such representations, the difficulty must logically be, to find any nation, possessing a knowledge of revelation, which entertained the doctrine referred to. But as to the Jews deriving this knowledge from the Gentiles, the reply of the excellent C. E. Weissmann* is complete: "As to what he (Clericus) says, that after the Babylonian captivity this matter became more clear, we ask, Through whom was such knowledge communicated? Where are

* Institutiones Theologiæ, loc. xv, page 1082. Tubingæ, 1789.

those *prophets* who taught the Jews more clearly? Perhaps Clericus thinks that the Jews learned this truth more fully from the Babylonian mystics and the philosophers of the Gentiles. But in such notions there is not even *one particle of salt.*"

That subsequent to the captivity some of the later Jews became divided into sects, and in their disputes had recourse to pagan philosophy to solve the doubts engendered, is true. The little but opulent sect of the Sadducees adopted the Materialism of Epicurus, and maintained that it was not inconsistent with the only portion of the Scripture which they recognized—the Pentateuch. And that in meeting the statements of the Sadducees some of the Pharisees resorted to the Pythagorean notion of transmigration, is clear. From the same source arose also that diversity which is noticed in their writings respecting the resurrection of the dead. The Sadducees maintained that the soul was material, and died with the body. The rest of the nation disclaimed the idea. But in reasoning on the topic, some of the Pharisees and others entertained doubts whether there would be a resurrection of the Gentiles as well as of the Jews; and still further, whether all the Jews, both good and evil, were to be partakers of the resurrection. This brought up the question, likewise, whether the wicked, who were not partakers of the resurrection, were not destroyed? And here too there was a division; though Menasseh Ben Israel, in his treatise on the Resurrection, (cap. iv,) gives the caution that, in the sense in which they there use the word, "*destroy* does not mean a total annihilation, but only a ruin;" a caution which it would be well for such writers as Mr. Hudson and the Annihilationists to regard. And then further: by *immortality*, in multitudes of instances, those Jewish writers mean not *existence*, but perpetual happiness, and with such the loss or extinction of immortal life was simply the forfeiture of everlasting bliss.

In illustration of these statements we shall here offer a

few brief references and quotations. David Kimchi, in remarking on Psalm i and civ, says: "As regards the wicked, there shall not be to them a resurrection;" and that the soul is destroyed or perishes when the body dies. Rabbi Bechai says that "the resurrection pertains to the Jews only, and in no sense to the Gentiles," but that the Israelites who depart from the law shall be raised from the dead, and suffer eternal torment in both soul and body. But Rabbis Higgaion, Saadia, and Aben Ezra, say that all "the Israelites who are not raised from the dead to a state of glory, shall remain in a state of ignominy, which shall never have an end." Kimchi, in 1 Sam. xxv, 29, says that such likewise was the idea of Rabbi Eliezer. So that the wicked Jews and all the Gentiles, according to this notion, suffer the punishment of eternal ignominy in a state of separation from their bodies, since they are not partakers of the resurrection.* As Professor Bush, in his forcible and impressive style, remarks: "Though they continue to exist, yet having no participation in that principle of Divine life of which Christ is the sempiternal source, and the only bestower, their existence, though perpetual, is penal, and no deliverance ever reaches them from the fearful bondage of their doom."† And the Chaldee Targum on Dan. xii, 2, says expressly: "The *souls* of the wicked shall never die."

That some, however, in polite compliance with what they regarded as the reasonable claims of the Material and Epicurean philosophy of the Sadducees, did entertain the notion that the soul would finally die, may be, perhaps, conceded;

* Those learned Jews who so admirably defended the religion of their fathers against the cavils of Voltaire, say, in reference to this matter: "The Pharisees believed that the souls of good men went into a state of the highest happiness, from which they might return to this world and animate other human bodies. But at the same time they held for certain that the souls of the wicked were forever shut up in dark dungeons, where they suffered, to all eternity, punishments proportioned to their crimes. These ideas, if we are not mistaken, do not square well with the Metempsychosis, 'which was brought from the Indies by Pythagoras, and sung by Ovid.'" Letters of Certain Jews, etc., p. 212.

† Anastasis, p. 313.

(though our opponents, in treating upon the subject, have confounded all the forenamed distinctions;) but in those cases the notion had the same origin as the same conception now has—an unwarrantable desire, at the expense of eternal truth, to reconcile the holy utterances of God with those notions of "reason" which are claimed by a fallen, depraved, and, of course, selfish and prejudiced nature; the same which in its outgrowth has developed itself in Socinus, De Servatore; Bush on the Resurrection; Beecher's Conflict of Ages; Whately's Future State; Hudson's Debt and Grace; Tindal's Christianity as old as the Creation, and hosts of works of similar aim and tendency.

## § 40. *The Patristical Testimony.*

It is frankly admitted by our more learned opponents that the immortality of the soul, and its conscious existence between death and the resurrection, was believed by the first Christians and clearly taught by the early fathers; though many of them disclaim the idea that the soul goes immediately to the highest heaven at death, but hold that it remains in an intermediate state till after the resurrection of the body. See, for instance, Priestley's Notes on 2 Cor. xii, Phil. i, and 1 Pet. iii. True, these concessions are of small literary importance; but it is certainly proper to refer our opponents to their own authorities.

The idea of Hades, (ᾅδης, שְׁאוֹל,) known to both Hebrews and Greeks, was prominently developed by Christianity; and quite early in our era it was maintained that the *full* happiness and the *final* misery of the departed do not commence until after the general judgment and the resurrection of the body. This assumption seemed to involve the idea of an intermediate state, and the soul was regarded as tarrying in *Hades* from the moment of its departure from this world, until it should become fully qualified for the higher bliss of heaven itself through reunion with the body, which, though sown in corruption, must be raised incorruptible.

So strong, moreover, was this conception, that Justin Martyr and others not only utterly discarded the idea that souls went *immediately* to heaven, but they refused the name of Christians to those who entertained it, and regarded the idea as assimilating Christianity to Paganism on this point. (Compare Cicero's Tusculan Questions, lib. i, cap. 9, 10, 11, 12.) And the disputes existing in the Jewish schools, or between the sects, as referred to above, were to some extent likewise transferred to the Christian Church, and some of its theologians entertained doubts as to whether the soul itself were not corruptible. They did not deny its immortality, or entertain doubt as to the possibility of the thing. But such writers as Justin and Tatian suppose the soul to have no *inherent* immortality; while the more systematic and able theologian, Theophilus, of Antioch, states, in reply to the question, Was Adam created mortal or immortal? that "he was fitted for both, though neither mortal nor immortal." Adam contemplated as *man*, that is, compounded of spirit and matter, was of course in this condition; and therefore, *as man*, immortality as well as lasting happiness depended upon himself. This distinction is confounded in their speculations, and our modern German scholars, with all their attainments in literature, have, by their decisions, made the "confusion worse confounded," and seem unable to comprehend these plain distinctions. With great parade of learning they often talk upon the subject in the most undiscriminating manner, mistake one idea for another, and advance theories which are as unsubstantial as the figures formed by the curling smoke of their pipes. We love them, and are deeply indebted to their vast learning, unwearied patience, and *con amore* industry; but some of them seem to have forgotten that there is, after all, such a thing as logic in the world, and that there ought really to be some connection between the premise of an argument and the conclusion.

It cannot be doubted, however, that several of the fathers did entertain the idea (referred to by David Kimchi on

Psalms i and civ, as held by some of the Jews) that the soul was mortal in such a sense, that the wicked at death might perish soul and body forever. They made no attempt to elaborate the view systematically, and therefore it commanded but little attention comparatively. Clement of Alexandria, and Origen likewise, held the Oriental idea of a purifying fire; rather in sympathy, however, with our opponents than with ourselves, for this fire was not to perform its work in the intermediate state of the soul, but stood in some connection with the resurrection of the dead and the conflagration of the world. Their ideas on the subject are expressed in a very general and indefinite manner. Arnobius, (A. D. 300,) however, was the first to introduce into the Christian Church the positive doctrine (derived from the Jewish fables) that the wicked *would be* annihilated. And the efforts made to find traces of this doctrine in Justin and Irenæus, though ingenious, are not very flattering to the literary pretensions of their authors.* The idea of Arnobius, however, seemed rather designed as an antagonism to the notion which Athenagoras (A. D. 160–181) was first to introduce from the Pagan philosophy into the Christian Church; and his expressions ought to be considered from this standpoint. Athenagoras taught the *natural* immortality of the soul, by which he meant that it was *sempiternus*, (see § 21, above,) *eternal*, in the true sense—pre-existent and self-existent. This was purely a Pagan conception, as we have seen, and opposed to the whole theology of the Church. And here had our German cousins remembered that the question which was now started was in relation to the *traduction* of the soul,† and that the manner in which it was

* After referring to the views of Tatian, Justin, and Theophilus, Hagenbach remarks: "On the contrary, Tertullian and Origen, whose views differed on other subjects, agreed in this one point, that they, in accordance with their peculiar notions concerning the nature of the soul, looked upon its immortality as essential to it." See History of Doctrines, vol. i, § 58.

† See some of their reasonings on this point in Lactantius, De Opificio Dei, cap. xix; Theodoret, Sermon 4 and 5; Curat. Græc. Affect. Hilary, (Pictav.) De Trinit., lib. x; and Jerome, Epist. ad Pammachium.

decided by any one was regarded as determining his views of its *mortality* or *immortality*, (*θνητὸς* or *ἀθάνατος*,) they might have avoided much of the confusion into which they have fallen. All who held that it was not, along with the body, derived from the parents, were regarded as holding (in the philosophical sense) its *immortality*, while those who taught the contrary were deemed as holding it to be corruptible and mortal.* The former idea involved its pre-existence with many of them, and favored the notion of transmigration, (which, among the Pagans, was originally built upon it,) while the latter was of course antagonistic to such ideas; and the common ground taken against its innate immortality was, that it may be begotten, since, if immortal, *ἀθάνατος*, it is unbegotten. Hence you find that those who are thus con-

* It will be in place to furnish here for the general reader an illustration which will present the point referred to in a light that will render it perfectly apparent. In a work on Justification, by the Rev. Dr. George Junkin, President of Lafayette College, that learned and venerable theologian, in referring to man's condition of dependence upon God, employs the following language: "In reference to our bodies, we have no self-sustaining power. Is his hand withdrawn? We return to dust. *Equally dependent upon the sustaining power of God is the soul of man; its immortality is not a matter of physical but only of moral necessity; it can no more exist without God than the body can.* If any man ask *how* God keeps us in being, the answer must be, We know not. The fact only is known. Modes of existence are among the secret things that belong unto the Lord our God." (Chap. i, § 2, pp. 15, 16.) These sentiments, so excellently expressed, and which now are but an announcement of the feelings [illegible] convictions of every Christian mind untinctured by the gross superstition of pantheism, had become so perplexed by the disputes of the philosophers that for a long time they were with difficulty apprehended even by some of the early Christians. Thus the *ἀθάνατος* of the soul was its eternity; and hence Cicero remarks that Plato not only taught the eternity of souls, *animorum æternitas*, but was the first that proved it by bringing reasons for it. See his Tusculan Questions, lib. i, cap. xvii. The soul they held was *a parte ante* as well as *a parte post*, or *sempiternus.* The opposite sentiment, so justly expressed by Dr. Junkin, which only taught that all creatures are dependent for *their continued existence* upon God, was regarded as teaching that the soul was not *ἀθάνατος*, but *θνητὸς*; *not immortal*, but *mortal;* and with how much reason, the reader can now judge for himself. Yet this is the main foundation on which our adversaries rest their imputations against the theology of the early Church in this particular.

structively accused of teaching its mortality and dissolution along with the body, utterly disclaim the figment of its annihilation between death and the resurrection, while they hold as we do, that, (in the case of the unregenerate,) being severed wholly at death from the source of spiritual life, it sinks into a wretched, degraded state, to which, indeed, some of the fathers added the idea of unconsciousness until the resurrection; nor did this conflict with their idea that it was ἄφθαρτος, *incorruptible.* The advocates of this view, moreover, assert the resurrection of all the dead, both good and bad, from which standpoint not only the reunion of the soul with the body was maintained, but also the continued existence of the soul after death. Nor do they ever anywhere intimate such an idea as that the soul at the resurrection of the body is created anew. But a brief reference to the views of *Tatian*, (A. D. 150,) who in his turn of mind was quite speculative, will illustrate the point. He says that "originally man had immortality in himself, being created in the likeness and image of God, which image consisted in a close relation between the spiritual nature of man and the Spirit of God." Then, after refining on this idea, he adds: "The soul is not (now) in and of itself immortal, but is capable of dying, though it may never die. If it has not received the truth (as taught and exemplified by Christ) it will perish with the body; yet at the end of all things it will be raised again, and, along with the body, endure everlasting punishment. On the contrary, if it has attained the knowledge of God it will not die, even should it become unconscious for a time." Upon this theory was subsequently based the doctrine of the repose of the soul between death and the resurrection; but it is preposterous to attempt in any manner or form to identify it with the materialist notion of annihilation.

But dropping these philosophical subtleties, we shall proceed to adduce the well-nigh concurrent testimony of the earlier fathers respecting the condition of the soul subsequent to the death of the body, for this is the great practical point before us. I admit, as Uhleman (Bib. Repos., x, 411, to whom I am somewhat indebted here) remarks, that the religious opinions, especially of ancient writers, should be always viewed with their system and whole manner of thinking; but unless we should expand this chapter into a huge volume, we cannot pretend to follow out literally this excellent suggestion. We shall endeavor, however, to present such abstracts as cannot well be mistaken, in regard to their true sense, by the reader, and this of course is all we can do in the circumstances.

I shall not encumber the pages with references, except in the case of the more voluminous writers, for the quotations can be very easily verified. Occasional references will be found among them to the subject of future punishment, which cannot be regarded as out of place in their present connection.

*Polycarp*, when perishing in the flames, declared that he should that day stand in spirit before God. The attempt to divest this testimony of its force by asserting that it comes to us at *second hand*, is worthy of no consideration.

*Justin Martyr* in his "colloquy" with Trypho, and referring to our blessed Lord's dying words, ("Father, into thy hands I commit my spirit!") says: "Thus also may we, when we come to the end of life, entreat the same favor of God, who is able to turn away from us any malignant angel, lest he should seize upon our soul." (Compare Wisdom iii, 1–3.) And referring also to evil kings who were dead, he adds that "if death should lead to insensibility, it would be gain to such." He likewise asserts the eternity of future punishment, in express opposition to the doctrine of Plato, who taught that it would continue for only a limited term. In the same colloquies he maintains that the souls of the righteous take up their abodes in a better, and the souls of the wicked in a worse place than here; but denounces as heresy the doctrine that the soul, in its *separate state*, is at once admitted to the highest heaven, and to that bliss which it can only possess in the resurrection state. Hence he most pointedly denied that souls are admitted to heaven immediately at death, and held that they remained in paradise till the resurrection.

*Athenagoras*, taught the natural immortality of the soul, and that at the resurrection man's first body will receive the same soul which tabernacled in it here, since, says he, God is destitute of neither efficiency nor will to resuscitate the same body.

*Irenæus* (lib. v, cap. i) says: "There are three things of which man properly consists, the flesh, the soul, and the spirit; the one that is the spirit, which communicates form; the other the flesh, which receives form; that however which is between these two is the soul, (anima,) which sometimes following the spirit is thereby elevated, but sometimes consenting to the flesh it sinks into earthly concupiscences." In c. xxxvi, he makes a distinction between *οὐρανός*, *παράδεισος*, and *πόλις*, and endeavors, from Matt. xiii, 8, and John xiv, 2, to prove the existence of different mansions for the just. See also lib. ii, cap. lxii, "Plenissimè," etc.

*Tatian* says that after the consummation of the world, the souls of the wicked, together with their bodies, shall endure punishment that has no end. In fact most of the fathers, as Hagenbach (Hist., § 78) remarks, regard the punishment of sin as eternal.

*Tertullian* (De Resurrect., cap. xvii) says: "For even now souls, although naked, as we see from the reference to Lazarus, are in hades, and are tormented." In his De Anima, c. xxvii, he says: "*Death* is the disjunction of body and soul; *life*, their conjunction." In c. lv: "No one on leaving the body appears immediately before God, unless perhaps that privilege is allotted to martyrs." In the same chapter he mentions a treatise of his, not now extant, in which he asserts that he proved that every soul remains in hades until the day of judgment. In c. lviii, he utterly repudiates the notion *that the soul sleeps* in its intermediate state. See also the quotations from him in Bretschneider's Handbuch, ii, § 167.

*Minucius Felix* opposes most decidedly the Pagan objections to the Christian doctrine of the immortality of the soul and the resurrection. He likewise affirms that there is neither measure nor termination to the torment of the damned.

*Origen* held that spirits existed before the visible creation, but were mutable, and might either forfeit or retain the favor of God. Some obeyed and others disobeyed, and they were all treated accordingly. He says, moreover, that when Christ had departed from life, having put aside his body, he went in his disembodied spirit and held converse with disembodied spirits. (Cont. Cels., lib. ii.) In his De Princip., ii, he further says that the blessed dwell in the aerial regions, and that immediately after their departure from this earth they first go to paradise; as they grow in knowledge and piety, they proceed from paradise to still higher regions, etc. And as Eusebius informs us, (Hist., lib. vi, cap. xxxvii,) Origen was present in a synod assembled in Arabia, and in a discussion which occurred he prevailed with those to change their minds who had thought that "the human soul died and was dissolved with the body, and would be restored along with the body at the resurrection."

*Clement* of Alexandria denied utterly the traduction of the soul. He held that it was sent from heaven and infused into the body, which thereupon became conscious. At the same time, however, he utterly denies the philosophical notion that the soul is sempiternal, or a part of the Divine nature. In a fragment from his lost work on the soul, he says: "The souls of all, as they are breathed forth, have the faculty of life, and though separated from the body, they are found to possess a love for it." He held to something like a purgatorial fire, and when accused of adopting that notion from the Pagans, replied that the Pagans stole it from the Jews.

*Cyprian* often in his works expresses a hope that those who perish from the visitations of pestilence shall be admitted immediately to the presence of Christ. See especially his tractate De Mortalitate; and from which see also a long extract in Hagenbach, § 78, containing his views of the present happiness of the departed patriarchs, prophets, apostles, etc.

*Hilary*, on Psalm cxxxvii, says: "It is a human law of necessity that our bodies being buried, our souls should proceed into hades;" and on Psalm cxx, he says that "souls are detained there until the resurrection of the body, and cannot, previous to that event, proceed to celestial glory." See also on Psalm ii, *in fine*.

*Lactantius* also says that the souls of the martyrs are privileged to proceed at once to paradise.

*Jerome*, on Mark xiv, says: "Before Christ suffered on the cross, Abraham was in hades; after he had suffered, the thief was in paradise." See also on Isaiah lxv, 4.

*Peter the Martyr*, (A.D. 295–312,) in his first discourse on the soul, says: "It is not to be admitted that souls sinned in heaven before they had bodies, nor that they existed at all before their bodies, for this doctrine belongs to Grecian philosophy, and is foreign and contrary to those who would live godly in Christ." The title of this discourse is, "On the soul as not having previously existed, nor being placed in the body in a sinning state."

*Didymus*, (A.D. 340–395,) a fervent admirer of Origen, entertained some sort of idea that souls had pre-existed. He says that "the soul suffers from the body." He held that after death the souls of believers are conveyed to Abraham's bosom, which he supposed to be some lofty etherial region. He avers that the wicked shall be led away to endure everlasting torment, having no more any opportunity for repentance.

*Gregory Nazianzen* says: "When the souls of the righteous are freed from their bodies, they joyfully hasten to the Lord, and enjoy inconceivable pleasure in his presence."

*Augustine*. We need not bring this investigation below the period in which he lived. His views are very fully given in his Enchiridion: "During the interval which elapses between the death of man and the last resurrection, souls remain in their unseen receptacles, which are adapted either to repose or suffering, according to what they did in the flesh while alive." In his Tract. x, in Epistola Joannis, not far from the end, and also in his De Origine Animæ, (lib. ii, cap. iv,) he likewise remarks: "Were you then so unacquainted with this solid and most wholesome article of faith, that *souls are immediately judged upon their departure out of the body? and that, too, before they are brought to that other judgment whereat they must be judged when raised from the dead*, so that they are either tormented or gloriously rewarded in those very bodies wherein they lived? Who has, with such obstinacy of mind, been so deaf to the Gospel as not to hear, and upon hearing, not to believe, these things," etc. See also his De Civitate Dei, lib. xiii, cap. xvi, and references to him in section 33, sub-section 10, above. In exact accordance with this, Bernard held that the souls of the righteous are received into the society of angels as soon as they are separated from their bodies.

We here conclude this catalogue of patristical testimonies. And as we are perfectly aware of the manner in which our opponents will endeavor to set aside its force, by representing it as not in all points consistent, we desire to call their attention to the fact that on the real issue involved in this discussion—the separability of the soul from the body, and its conscious existence between death and the resurrection—the testimony is well nigh uniform. The men to which we have referred are, moreover, nearly all representative men; so that here we have the real sentiments of the Church of Christ on the questions involved in this issue, during the centuries in which they lived.*

* I append here the following passage from the industrious and truly learned Limborch: "Hæc sententia naturæ tum animæ separatæ, tum ultimi judicii, tum testimoniis S.S., in quibus hominum defunctorum, seu animæ separatæ mentio fit, maxime est consentanea: fuitque ea communis Patrum sententia, Irenæi, Tertulliani, Cypriani, Ambrosii, Augustini, aliorumque; quorum licet phrasiologia sit diversa dum alii animas

The reply offered by our opponents to this branch of the argument may be found in S. 46; A. 61–71; E. 73, 74; H. 1, pp. 118, 135; H. 2, p. 83. Mr. Ham has likewise written a tractate purporting to be "A History of the present Popular Opinions concerning the Doctrine of Human Immortality." It is republished in E. 287–309, from which let the following extracts suffice: "In the estimation of those early writers, [the apostolical fathers,] death was the absolute decease of the conscious being man." He copies implicitly from the worthless treatise of Blackburne, already referred to, and gives a most dishonest representation of the patristical theology, and of the views of Luther and the early Reformers.

The grounds of exception taken by all these writers are the following: 1. Some of the reputed patristical writings are spurious, though others of them quote from those very writings. This charge cannot, however, be brought with fairness, unless I greatly err, against any referred to or quoted in the foregoing catalogue. 2. Popish priests invented the doctrine. 3. The Church held no such doctrine respecting the immortality of the soul and the punishment of sin until the second or third century. These two grounds of exception are beneath notice, as the reader can see from the above summary and preceding remarks. 4. Justin Martyr and others said that those were not Christians who entertained this doctrine of immortality. This too has been sufficiently disposed of already. 5. Luther held the sleep of the soul. Suppose he did: I cannot see what this has to do with the issue. But as this is perpetually repeated by all our opponents, and has done injury to the cause of truth, we shall notice it before concluding the chapter. 6. Their last exception is, that this doctrine of the separate existence of

in cœlo collocant, alii in inferno in re ipsa summus est consensus: animas piorum esse in statu securo ac felici, ac proxima felicitatis promissæ contemplatione frui; non tamen plenè esse consummatas: sed in resurrectione plenam promissi præmii consecuturas consummationem." Theol. Christ., lib. vi, cap. x, sec. 8.

the soul, was obtained from Plato. This too is perpetually repeated, and we shall notice it presently.

These cavils are all easily disposed of, and the illiterate writers above referred to, who, without either learning or discrimination, assume to instruct the public, may be passed without remark, for to no truly well-informed mind can their works do any injury. There is, however, an author who, with pretensions to real learning, has recently come before the public, claiming to have gone over the whole ground *de novo*, and to announce reliable information respecting it. He repeats the most of these petty cavils, and endeavors also to sustain them, and hence we cannot pass on without a remark in relation to his extraordinary procedure. We refer to Mr. Hudson, (whose work has already been named in these pages,) who, on pp. 288–309, has assailed the patristical testimony on the subject before us in a way that should not be passed in silence.

To illustrate the egregious and criminal misrepresentations of this gentleman, the reader will notice that in the later schools of Grecian and Roman philosophy the terms *ἀθάνατος*, *æternus*, and *sempiternus*, were employed as equivalents to designate the immortality of the soul. Previous, however, to the time of Pherecydes and Thales, *ἀθάνατος* had never the sense of *sempiternus*, or eternal (in the strict import) attached to it when connected with *ψυχή*, and was therefore never employed to mean, when used in such connection, what the later schools meant by it, who held that the soul was immortal because it was a part of the Divine nature, and that it never began to exist, and therefore its existence never could end. It was "*sempiternus;*" "a particle of God's own being." Plato and Aristotle, to a considerable extent at least, entertained this view; and such was the idea they all in later times attached to the word connected with the term soul.*

* I have already remarked that the sacred writers never employ *ἀθάνατος* to designate the doctrine, as the Pagan philosophy had rendered the import of the term dubious in such connection.

Now the Christian Church never received this doctrine, at least not until long after the Alexandrian school of philosophico-theology was established, and then a few did adopt something that resembled it in appearance, though the resemblance was more apparent than real. If it were that doctrine it was in an extremely modified form. But the Church as such already repudiated the idea, and never in any sense of the word received it; and when any of the Pagans who had entertained it became Christians (as Justin, Arnobius, and others,) they abandoned it utterly, and when they refer to the matter speak of having done so. The Christian Church, therefore, never attached to the term *ἀθάνατος*, as applied to the human soul, and *to express their own views*, the sense which was attached to it in the later schools of the philosophers, though they did employ it as therein used when they spoke of the *Pagan* sentiment on the subject; hence there were two obviously distinct usages of the word, the one having a philosophical and the other a theological sense. When the fathers employed it to designate their own views as Christians, they used it in a sense entirely diverse from what they attached to it when employing it in the then popular sense to designate the views entertained by them while Pagans. There is nothing remarkable in this, for instances of similar usage may be found in all languages. And as there was no convenient substitute for the term *ἀθάνατος*, they could speak (without danger of being misapprehended) both of believing, and of having rejected the doctrine of the soul's immortality. They had rejected it in the Pagan sense, and had adopted it in the Christian sense. Hence, too, the term *θνητός* came into vogue; and though not expressive of their own theological idea as attached to the soul, it formed the only direct contrast to the pagan import of *ἀθάνατος* or *ἀφθαρσία*, and was sometimes adopted as expressing therefore the Christian idea.

In like manner you find them using the term *immortality* to convey the idea of *underived* existence, and the term *mortal* for that which is derived, and in which sense man, (both body and soul,) angels, and every created thing is mortal. Their very method of argument is an illustration of this usage, as where Justin says " the soul either *has life in itself*, or *derives it* from something else ;" or Tatian : "The soul, O ye Greeks, is not in its own nature *immortal*, but *mortal; yet it is able not to die.*" In many of their references to *man*, moreover, in this connection, when they refer to him as not endowed with immortality, they refer to his *composite nature*, and not to body or soul exclusively. They say that *as man* he was not created *immortal* (using this word in the theological sense,) but mortal, etc.

Another and very familiar use of the term then as now (see § 37, sub-section 4, supra) was to employ it as equivalent to *salvation ;* a man seeking to be *saved* was said to be *seeking immortality*. The Gospel offer of mercy to man was spoken of as the offer of *immortality ;* its rejection the *rejection of immortality ;* and those who did reject it were, in the same connection, assured that they should, to all eternity, *feel* the consequences of such rejection, by being made to endure misery without end.

Now is it conceivable that any reader should perpetually mistake the import of such expressions, provided he had knowledge enough to understand the words, and sense enough to consider them in their connection ? If the thing be in any supposed case conceivable, I must say that in the case of any really honest mind and heart, sincerely and earnestly endeavoring to know the truth and to make it known, it is utterly inconceivable. The idea of intelligence and honesty of purpose being associated with perversions of that sort, is not to be entertained. A series of such blunders must, in the nature of the case, impeach a man's intelligence or moral honesty. To illustrate : Mr. Hudson, in treating upon this subject, takes the word immortality, in its present popular import, to mean *continuance of being.* In reading the patristical writings, however, he meets the word *immortality* frequently occurring, one writer denouncing the doctrine expressed by this term, another maintaining it; one asserting that it was a Pagan notion, and that when he became a Christian he repudiated it utterly; and another that immortality is a gratuity, and that men are commanded to seek it through Christ. Mr. Hudson, I say, finds the term employed in this or similar phraseology; he attaches to the term itself a uniform sense, the sense in which he himself employs it, and then comes before the public with the prodigious and astounding discoveries which such an interpretation of that term cannot fail to develop in their pages. One man says he renounces *immortality*, referring to the old philosophical idea attached to that term, and meaning, I renounce the notion of man's eternal or underived being; but Mr. Hudson learns from the expression that he renounces the idea of uninterrupted continuance of being. Another says, I am seeking for immortality, meaning everlasting life, happiness, salvation. Mr. Hudson informs us that the man here avows his purpose of seeking an existence itself. I deny, says a third, that man is either in soul or body *immortal*, meaning to affirm his belief that neither body nor soul pre-existed from eternity, or was a part of the Divine nature; but Mr. Hudson learns from the expression that the man denies the doctrine of the uninterrupted conscious existence of our spiritual nature, and consequently holds that the soul has no conscious existence between death and the resurrection. And these perversions are steady and uniform, and in the very face of abundance of counter statements and representations in the very books which he professes to have consulted. It is hard, very hard, to believe that this man could purposely and designedly have thus perverted facts so patent and obvious to all; and yet, if it were not with intention or design that it was done, this writer is, by his own showing, and on the score of the grossest incompetency, disqualified from presenting any adequate discussion of the subject on which his book professes to treat, or to furnish any reliable information respecting it. He lays the highest claim to general literature, and to a thorough acquaintance with the specific literature of his subject, and his book is, so to speak, almost disfigured by the masses of ambitious references which crowd its pages. As respects literary execution it is written in an apparently frank and scholarly manner, and its style is quite a model for controversy. These things, when, as in this instance, associated with misrepresentations, either in fact or theory, reach and impress an order of minds wholly unapproachable by such writers as Messrs. Storrs, and Moncreiff, and Reid, and Ham, and therefore, in a case like that of Mr. Hudson, it is necessary that such perversions should be pointed out and thoroughly exposed.

There are two things which require to be noticed likewise in this connection, namely, the above-mentioned assertions respecting Luther and Plato. We shall briefly refer to each.

## § 41. *Luther and the Sleep of the Soul.*

The assertion that Luther entertained and taught the doctrine of the unconscious repose of the soul in its state of separation from the body, is made by these writers without restriction or qualification. (Hud. 258, 346–350; S., Pref. vi; A. 67, 68; and H. in the tractate mentioned above.) Hud. quotes with approbation the following passage from Feuardentius on the subject: "I call most Lutherans new Sadducees, who, when they read in Luther's comments that the dead so sleep as to know and feel nothing, . . . say that the soul of man dies with the body." A. represents him as denying the natural immortality of the soul; and H. says that he did not conceive of the soul as an immortal substance, and did not believe in its continued consciousness between death and the resurrection. He embraced and taught the doctrine of the *sleep of the soul, and continued in that belief to the close of his life.*' These men are mainly indebted for these representations to the anonymous work of Blackburne on the "Intermediate State."

The following passage from Bayle may be taken as a

sufficient corrective of a portion of these misrepresentations: "I was amazed to find that Cardinal du Perron durst say that Luther believed the mortality of the soul. Should Francis Garasse vent a thousand such calumnies I should not wonder at it; and if I had found it in Luther's life, published at Paris in 1577 by the monk Noel Talepied, or in Nicole Grenier's book, or in the books of such like writers, who have no reputation to lose, I should not have been surprised; but I could not but think it strange that a cardinal of so great a name should be guilty of so much rashness." Mr. Bayle also referred the matter to a Lutheran divine, who in reply states that "Luther never taught that the soul died with the body, and was to rise with the body. His works very clearly show that he believed the contrary. The origin of the calumny is in a letter he wrote to Amsdorf, in 1522, in which he appears much inclined to believe that the souls of the just sleep till the day of judgment without knowing where they are." "He rectified this opinion in process of time, and though in his later writings he seems to attribute rest to the souls of the predestinate, he does not mean thereby a rest which is a profound sleep, and deprives them of the vision and conversation of God and the angels." See Bayle's Dict., Art. Luther, and note DD.

My own copy of Luther's commentary was published at Wittenberg in 1544, only a little while, therefore, before his death, and contains his latest revisions. In his note on Gen. ii, 7, he says: "After infinite perils and afflictions, we are *removed by death* from animal to spiritual life." He explains the word paradise, as used in the New Testament, to mean a *condition* in which the soul is in full possession of peace, security, and all those blessings which are found where sin does not exist. "As Adam lived in paradise, secure from sin, death, and the curse, and yet lived in the hope of future and unending spiritual life, so *the bosom of Abraham* is employed in a like figure for that life which they possess who have died in faith. They have peace and rest, and in that rest they expect future life and glory."

(P. 25, col. 2.) On Gen. iv, 9, he says, referring to Abel: "Therefore God is the God of the dead; that is, *even the dead live*, and have God caring for and preserving them in another life, far different from this corporeal life, in which the saints suffer affliction." "*The dead Abel lives*, and by God himself is canonized in another life, a better and more true canonization than ever they received whom the pope has canonized. His death was indeed horrible, but it was a truly salutary death, since he now lives a better life than before. For in this his corporeal life he lived in a sinful state, and was obnoxious to death; but that life is immortal, and without any sorrows, corporeal or spiritual." (P. 72, col. 2.) So, too, in Gen. v, page 101: "But if the holy patriarchs so anxiously desired the life to come on account of Abel and Enoch, *whom they knew were living with God*, how much more does it become us," etc. So also in the next two paragraphs, and in chapters xxiii and xxv, and places without number. In his Table Talk, speaking of death, he says: "When Christians pray for a long life and for tranquillity, they do it not for their own sakes, for death to them is gain, but for the sake of posterity and the Church." When his little daughter Magdalene was dying, he said: "She is very dear to me; but, dear Lord, if it is thy will to take her hence, I shall know with joy that she is with thee." When she had expired in his arms, he said: "I have sent a saint to heaven; yes, a living saint." And to his sorrow-stricken wife he said: "Bethink thyself, my dear Kate, where she has gone; it is well with her." When he perceived himself to be dying, he said, just before he breathed his last: "Into thy hands I commend my spirit, O heavenly Father, although this body is breaking away from me. I am departing from this life; yet I certainly know that I shall be forever with thee, for no one can pluck me out of thy hands. O take my poor soul to thyself!"

No one who is aware of the use which our opponents endeavor to make of their perversions of the views of this great Reformer, will think that we have been too particular in laying the facts in the case before the reader. In all previous disputes on the point I know not that this has ever been done. That Luther or any of the Reformers believed in what has been called the natural immortality of the soul; that is, that God created the soul to live, as an angel, without the body, and to enjoy *in a separate state* the highest and most perfect bliss of the resurrection state, (a view which so favored the pernicious delusions of popery,) no man of sense believes, so far as I know. But that he and all his brethren held to its separability from the body, and to its separate and conscious, and happy or miserable state, between death and the resurrection, no man of reputation as a scholar will venture to deny.

As to the notion itself of the soul's sleep, the first that was known of it as openly advocated was in Arabia, as early, at least, as the time of Origen, who died at Tyre, A.D. 254, aged 69, and who, as Eusebius records, so satisfactorily refuted that notion in the presence of a synod convened in that country, that those who were entertaining the speculation abandoned it utterly. The doctrine, in its original form, was that the soul ceased to feel or to be conscious at death, and died, and was corrupted with the body, but that both soul and body will awake at the judgment day. This idea originated, of course, in the material philosophy of Epicurus; but as received and taught in Arabia, it is the origin of the notion now entertained by those Materialists who claim that the idea is consistent with the teachings of revelation. The doctrine truly and properly is, that the soul, as well as the body, is extinguished at death; but to call an *extinction* a *sleep* is certainly a preposterous abuse of terms. Taylor of Norwich, who, with Blackburne, endeavored to revive the notion, under the softer appellation of the "sleep of the soul," expressly adopts the material philosophy (so also does Archbishop Whately) as the basis of his reasoning in its defense. He denied, in fact, that the soul could exist independent of the body, and says: "All our present experience shows the contrary. The operations of the mind depend constantly and invariably upon the state of the body, of the brain in particular. If some dying persons have a lively use of their rational faculties to the very last, it is because death has invaded some other part, and the brain remains sound and vigorous." See also p. 5 of the supplement to his "Original Sin."

Warburton, to whom I am indebted for the foregoing quotation, after referring to these notions, concludes by saying: "But their *sleep of the soul* is mere cant, and this brings me to the last consideration, the sense and consistency of so ridiculous a notion. They go, as we observed, upon the Sadducean principle that the soul is a *quality* of body, not a substance of itself, and so dies with its substratum. Now *sleep* is a modification of existence, not of non-existence; so that the sleep of a *substance* hath a meaning; the sleep of a *quality* is nonsense. And if ever this soul of theirs re-exerts its faculties, it must be by means of a REPRODUCTION, not by a mere AWAKENING; and they may as well talk of the sleep of a mushroom turned again into the substance of the dunghill, from whence it arose, and from which not the same, but another mushroom shall in time arise. In a word, neither unbelievers nor believers will allow to these *middle men* that *a new existing soul, which is only a quality resulting from a glorified body, can be identically the same with an annihilated soul, which had resulted from an earthly body.* But perhaps, as Hudibras had discovered the receptacle of the *ghosts of defunct bodies,* so these gentlemen may have found out the yet subtler corner where the *ghosts of defunct qualities* repose."*

## § 42. *Plato's Connection with the Patristic Theology.*

The replies of our opponents to the argument from the patristical testimony, that the doctrine was derived from Plato, require a brief notice here, with which we shall conclude the chapter. They insist most emphatically upon the

* Divine Legation, Book V, sec. vi; Works, iii, p. 27.

connection of his philosophy with the early theology of the Church, (see the foregoing references to S., A., E., H., etc., in § 41;) and in fact there are but few of the so-called "corruptions of the Gospel doctrine" which have not been, at one time or another, fastened upon him; although Aristotle, who by these writers is claimed as a Materialist, has always had, beyond comparison, a higher authority in the Church when it had confessedly departed from the simplicity of the Gospel. How much influence Plato had, however, upon the earlier theology, may be learned by comparing the foregoing catalogue of patristic testimonies with the views which he affirms on the same points; a work which we should be happy to perform *in extenso*, but in the present connection it is impossible.

That the Pythagorean and Platonic notions respecting the soul's purification suggested and originated the doctrine of purgatory, subsequently incorporated with the papal theology, can scarcely be questioned; and that the Gnostics adopted substantially Plato's idea of purification, must be admitted, and also that to some extent several of the theologians of the Alexandrian school, as Clement and Origen, were tinctured with the same philosophy; but to say more than this is to make assertions without any historical basis to sustain them, unless I greatly err. And so far as these admissions go, they in no way affect the issue in question; for laying aside the testimony of Origen and Clement, etc., it could be more than replaced in power by that of Ambrose of Milan, and numerous others whom we have omitted to cite.* So that in no way whatever do the ex-

* See Ambrose comment, in Luc. vi, 20. Let the reader also turn to Quæst. et Resp. ad Orthodoxos, ad Quæst. 75, Μετὰ δὲ τὴν ἐκ τοῦ σώματος ἔξοδον, etc., a work of the second century, which, though strictly speaking anonymous, has ever been of high authority. See also Philastrius, (Brixiensis,) Catalogo Hæreseon, etc., Hæres., 73. Cassiodorus, (M. Aurel,) De Anima, cap. xix; Chrysostom, Homil. iii, de Lazaro, (circa medium,) and also in Homil. v, in Genesin. See also Tractatum De Rectitud. Cath. Conversat, (paulo antefinem,) published in tom. ix of the works of Augustine. The author is not known, though to him is likewise conceded high representative authority.

ceptions of our opponents either touch the true issue, or affect the argument.

Then further. It is a fact which no one acquainted with the subject will venture to deny, that the most eminent of the earlier fathers and others denounced pointedly and directly the doctrines of Plato on the very theme where, according to our opponents, their views became corrupted through the adoption of his philosophy; an example of which, pertinent to the very issue respecting the soul's separate existence, may be found in Augustine, De Civ. Dei, lib. xiii, cap. xvi. The matter, however, is not of sufficient importance (as the main facts in the case are already before the reader) to occupy in its present connection any more of either our space or time.

It is really, however, somewhat amusing to notice how, from Socinus downward, every errorist and his school who have assailed the fundamentals of the orthodox faith, begin by asserting that the doctrine to which they take specific exception, is an error which owes its origin and development to the philosophy of Plato. The Socinian and Arian assert that the Trinity thus became an article of faith. The Universalist and Restorationist find that future and endless punishment have had the same origin. The Anti-Satisfactionist finds in Plato the germ of the Church doctrine which he assails. And the Materialist and Annihilationist have discovered that the doctrine of the separate state of the soul, as taught by the evangelical Church, was derived from Plato. What will next be ascribed to him remains to be seen. But Plato was celebrated for his *broad shoulders*, and our opponents, doubtless from this circumstance, in the utter absence of evidence to sustain them, believe that he can bear up under all these imputations.

# PART III.

## ON DEATH AND PENALTY, CONSIDERED IN THEIR RELATIONS TO THE ARGUMENT.

---

## CHAPTER I.

### CONSTITUENT PARTS OF MAN—VARIOUS MEANINGS OF THE TERM DEATH—RELATION OF CORPOREAL DISSOLUTION TO THE PENALTY OF THE DIVINE LAW.

IN the remaining topics which require to be treated in this argument, and which may be represented briefly under the general heads of DEATH and PUNISHMENT, (each of which in this connection might easily be expanded into a bulky volume,) a more thoroughly metaphysical and philosophical form of discussion seems to be necessary, from the fact that they involve philosophical and metaphysical problems with which the mightiest intellects of every age have grappled, and which still in some respects demand solution in their own suggested relations to the subject. And then, too, there are other circumstances which clearly indicate the profound importance of the theme. Among these are the relation of death and punishment, in the past and present, to the whole doctrine of sin and redemption; their deep and soul-absorbing connection with eschatology, coming into view as they do in the very beginning of our race, and affecting its existence in one form or another through its whole course of probationary being; and the stupendous interests involved in their connection with our future, while the eternal ages shall roll onward. Rare qualifications are demanded of him who would venture to traverse this field, though his object might be to find merely its relation to the districts which lie on either side of it. He needs not only candor, and earnest heartfelt piety, and constant prayer to the Father of lights for wisdom and guidance, but a grasp of intellect, a pervading intelligence, accuracy of judgment, and depth of scholarship. He requires not only a knowledge of the specific literature and science mainly involved in the inquiries, but also a correct acquaintance with the principles of human knowledge generally. The contemplation of such requirements might well make the most athletic spirit shrink from the pressure of its responsibilities. The task, however, has been devolved upon myself, and I shall attempt its execution in the best way I can, though the bare idea of endeavoring to do justice to a subject of such far-extending relations to the theme before us, and that, too, within the compass of a few chapters at the conclusion of an argument, is really appalling. It is obvious, however, that what is offered in such circumstances (that is, if presented intelligently and in its true relations to the subject) must claim to be, in the main, only suggestive. But, even though in unfolding the relations existing between these topics and our theme, and *vice versa*, we are thus under the necessity of being brief, I trust that we shall not, with just reason, be regarded as either time-serving or obscure.

### § 43. *Man consists of Body, Soul, and Spirit.*

Agreeably to the inspired record, (1 Thess. v, 23,) man consists of *body*, *soul*, and *spirit*, *σῶμα*, *ψυχή*, *πνεῦμα*. This distinction is perfectly consistent with that in Matt. x, 28, where it is made according to the *visible* and *invisible*. And the whole dispute, therefore, whether man consists of two or three parts, is, so far as relates to Christians, a piece of absurdity, the one division being not really inconsistent with the other. The visible nature is the *σῶμα*, *body;* the invisible is the *ψυχή*, *soul*. The invisible may likewise be subdivided into *soul* and *spirit*, *πνεῦμα*.

The remark of Grotius, (who evidently paid no attention to this,) that *spirit* in 1 Thess. v, 23, means the Holy Spirit, is laughable, as a bare examination of ὁλόκληρος would show. That man consists of three *different parts*, τριμερὴς ὑπόστασεῖς, (an expression from the old Christian philosopher, Nemesius, which is quoted by Whitby on 1 Thess. v, 23,) was a doctrine so early known that it seems to have been communicated to man in that early revelation to which we have referred in sections 24, 26, and 28, above. It is wholly subversive of Materialism, and therefore the advocates of that theory hate and repudiate it; but it cannot be got rid of in this way. As illustrative of its early reception, I may remark that traces of it are found in the teachings of Zoroaster, and that Jamblichus (the pupil of Porphyry) declares expressly that Pythagoras received and taught it. That Plato did so no one will dispute. The same remark may be made in reference to the Stoics; and Antinonus states that the constituent parts of man are σῶμα, ψυχὴ, and νοῦς, *body*, *soul*, and *intellect*, or mind. Josephus and his school taught the same. See Antiq. i, cap. i, § 2, where he observes that God made for man *a body from the earth, and supplied it with a* ψυχὴ and πνεῦμα. (Compare Heb. iv, 13.) Justin, in his fragment on the Resurrection, and Irenæus, ii, 6, 2, and v, 9, 1, likewise taught it, and also Clement and Origen, though Tertullian's more practical mind was content with the simpler division made in Matt. x, 28.

The ψυχὴ is properly the connecting link between the σῶμα and πνεῦμα, and the fountain of our sensual appetites and desires, and hence perpetually associated with the σαρξ, *flesh*, and when it ceases to act *death* supervenes. The struggle between the higher aspirations which spring up within the spiritual nature, and those lower propensities and desires suggested by its connection with the ψυχὴ, is often mentioned in the references made to a religious life. See Rom. vii, 14–25; Gal. v, 16, 17; Rom. viii, 4–10. By following the low promptings of this sensual appetite the man is said to become ψυχικὸς, *animal*, and his body (and in fact the bodies of all men in a state of nature) is called *σῶμα ψυχικὸν*, a *mere animal body*, (1 Cor. xv, 44, 45 ;) but when brought fully under the dominion of the spirit it is called *σῶμα πνευματικόν*, a body adapted to the uses of the spirit. See 1 Cor. xv, 43, and note particularly ver. 44.

The same division, substantially, is observed in the Hebrew בָּשָׂר, נֶפֶשׁ, רוּחַ; *σάρξ*, *ψυχή*, *πνεῦμα* ; *carnis*, *anima*, *spiritus ; flesh*, *soul*, *spirit.* The Greek has two terms referable to the corporeal frame, *σῶμα* and *σάρξ*, the former referring to the *building* itself, the latter to the *material* of which it is built. The Hebrew has but one term, בָּשָׂר, and this is answerable to the term *σάρξ*. In Hebrew usage, however, it may be regarded as clearly suggesting the idea conveyed by *σῶμα*. See Psa. xvi, 9 ; Acts ii, 26, 27 ; Heb. x, 5. Originally these constituent parts of human nature were harmoniously united under the dominion of the high and noble *πνεῦμα*, or *spirit* in man. And in his perfect original state, man, having been created in the image of God, was, in respect to the three parts of his nature, immortal; but by the introduction of sin this bond of union was severed, and now the heterogeneous and conflicting parts of it are subject to various conditions, unless they are brought into a more exalted union under the dominion of the Holy Spirit. (See Biblic. Repos., vol. x, p. 413.)

I had designed to illustrate this topic more fully, but our subject will not permit it here, though we may recur to it briefly hereafter.

Such then are the constituent parts of man; nor does the fact that either of the terms referred to may be in a figure employed to designate the whole man, at all affect the question as to his constituent parts. They may be used metaphorically, as *σῶμα* in 1 Cor. xii, 14–27 ; Luke xvii, 37 ; Rom. vi, 6; and *σάρξ* in Rom. vii, 5, and vi, 6; or even interchangeably, as in Heb. x, 20; Phil. i, xxiv ; 1 Pet. iv, 1 ; Acts ii, 26 ; but an examination of such passages will lead to no perplexity as to the true meaning. Comp. John i, 14; Heb. ii, 14; x, 5, 10; Phil. iii, 21; Rom. i, 3;

Acts ii, 30. In treating upon the subject of this chapter, we shall not, however, attempt to keep up a metaphysical distinction between *soul* and *spirit*, but employ both terms indifferently, to express the idea of man's interior nature, as distinguished from the corporeal or visible.

### § 44.—*Import of the term Death.*

The term *death* is employed in various senses, both in the Scriptures and in popular usage; and here the nature of our subject requires that we explain those usages, and accurately define the meaning of the term as we propose to employ it, so that any application which we shall make of it may not be misunderstood.

1. That the term *death*, (*θάνατος*, מָוֶת, מוּת,) as applied to man in the Scriptures, ever means utter annihilation or extinction of conscious existence, is a mere assumption, and is entitled to no respect whatever, (see §§ 36, 37;) and yet upon this baseless assumption the entire theory of annihilationism is built; and the Annihilationists, against all reason, persist in attaching this meaning to the word.

2. In a very frequent use of the term it means the separation of the interior and incorporeal of our nature from that which is exterior and corporeal; though in strictness of speech, as Knapp remarks, death does not consist in the separation, but this separation is the consequence of death. As soon as the body loses feeling and motion, it is henceforth useless to the soul, which is therefore separated from it. In this sense, though not with strict theological propriety, it is called *natural death*, and the term in this sense is used in many places, as Jonah iv, 9; Matt. ii, 15; x, 21; Mark v, 23; Luke ii, 16; John xi, 4, 13; Phil. i, 20; Heb. vii, 23. Compare also Gen. ii, 7, and Eccles. xii, 7, with Gen. iii, 19, and v, 5. Hence, too, it is spoken of as a dissolution of this tabernacle, a departure from the body, an absence from the body. 2 Cor. v, 1–9; Phil. i, 20–23; 2 Tim. iv, 6; 2 Pet. i, 13, 14. See our remarks on these passages in section 33.

3. In another and very common use of this term it means a severance between the creature and Creator, as the source of true life or happiness. This is sometimes called spiritual death, because it is the antithesis of spiritual life; this *life*, however, is only another name for true happiness. It is not the life of the spirit of man in the sense of the existence of the spirit, but in the sense of a happy state or condition.

This severance is also spoken of as eternal or everlasting death. For though the word *eternal* is not mentioned in the law, or in the threatening, (Gen. ii, 17; Ezek. xviii, 4, 20,) it is simply because such mention was needless. For any one who will reflect a moment, can see that if a rational creature, by a direct act of choice, separate himself from God, the source of life, he never can, by his own strength or resources, reunite himself therewith, so that unless the infinite mercy of God interpose and prevent, that severance must continue forever. Hence there was not the slightest necessity for employing the word *everlasting* in the threatening, and none but a theologastrian would ever pretend that the word not being there furnished evidence in favor of Universalism.

It is important to the right understanding of the position which our opponents sustain in relation to our whole theme, that this sense of the term death should be fully illustrated, for their scheme utterly confounds these two senses of the word in their application to man's present state or condition. Now in such passages as the following the word is used in this sense: "The wages of sin is death." Rom. vi, 23. See also Rom. vii, 5, 8, 13; 2 Cor. iii, 7; 1 Cor. xv, 56. And so too in the language of James i, 15: "Sin when it is finished bringeth forth death."

It may be illustrated also by the fact that regeneration restores the aforesaid connection, which sin had interrupted and broken, between man and the source of life. (John, i, 12, 13; iii, 3–8; Eph. ii, 5, 10; iv, 32.) And hence they who are renewed, though they are not exempted from death in the second sense named above, are said to have *passed from death unto life*, and are assured that they *shall not come into condemnation*, and *shall never die*, (John v, 24; iii, 36; 1 John iii, 14; John vi, 50; viii, 51; xi, 26;) and yet they *do die* in *that very sense* which our opponents affirm to be the penalty of the law. In such passages too as the following death is employed in the sense of severance from the source of life. 1 Tim. v, 6; Eph. v, 14; John v, 25. "The unregenerate—the *dead*—hear his voice and live," or are renewed. In the context of the last passage too (see ver. 28) the same word is used for corporeal death: and in direct contrast with the sense of it in the other verse. Hence, too, the law is said to be *the minister of death*, not of the body, but of the man. The penalty is brought upon him, being a sinner, by its administration, (2 Cor. iii, 7,) and in contrast with it the Gospel is said to minister life, (ver. 8, 9.)

In the same meaning it is used very often in the Old Testament; and it would be strange indeed, as Edwards remarks,* if when the law of God was first given, and enforced by the threatening of a punishment, nothing at all had been mentioned of that *great punishment* ever spoken of under the name of *death*, (in the revelations which God has given to mankind from age to age,) as the proper punishment of the sin of mankind. And it would be no less strange if, when the punishment which was mentioned and threatened on that occasion was called by the same name, even death, yet we must not understand it to mean the same thing, but something infinitely diverse, and infinitely more inconsiderable.

Now by referring to the Old Testament Scriptures we find them speak of death, in this sense, as the proper end and recompense of sin. Ezek. iii, 18: "When I say unto the wicked man *thou shalt surely die*." (In the Hebrew the same expression as in Gen. ii, 17.) See also chapter xxxiii, 18. So too in Ezek. xviii, 4, 20: "The soul that sinneth *it shall die*." And that what is called corporeal death is not here meant, is clear from the fact that it is said of the

* Original Sin, Part II, chap. i, sect. 2.

righteous that they shall not thus die, and to the wicked also that if they turn they shall live and not die; (see chapter xviii, 9, 17, 19, 21, 22, and iii, 21;) and yet all of them *did die* corporeally. And Solomon also says: "In the way of righteousness is life, and in the pathway thereof is *no death.*" Prov. xii, 28. So too says Moses: "I have set before thee this day life and good, and death and evil;" "I call heaven and earth to record against you this day, that I have set before you life and death, blessing and cursing." Deut. xxx, 15, 19. He employs *life* here in the sense of eternal life, as in Levit. xviii, 5, with which compare Rom. x, 5; Gal. iii, 12.

And here too it may well be said of this death, (that is, in the sense of the penalty of the law, Gen. ii, 17,) that "in death there is no remembrance of thee," "no praise to thee," etc. See Psa. vi, 5; Isa. lviii, 18, 19; Job xxviii, 22; and so too in the sense of Gen. ii, 17, those passages which speak of *death* are to be understood, which our annihilation friends produce to show that the soul, or interior life of man, ceases to exist when the body dies. The Jews, of course, obtained their idea of death in its most true and proper sense from that passage. Comp. Psa. xxx, 9; lxxxviii, 10–12; cxv, 17. The saints then, (as we have already remarked,) well knowing their sin and frailty, perpetually feared that they might be given over to death, or the full and lasting penalty of the law, and so they prayed against it, though they knew they must die in the sense of losing their present earthly life. See Psa. cxviii, 17–19; 1 Sam. ii, 9.

Before concluding this point, it is important in the present connection to have a strictly accurate idea of what constitutes the penalty of the law, as denounced in Gen. ii, 17. On no point is there more of wretched shallow theologizing than on this. Instead of a careful discrimination, which, if needed anywhere, is needed here, there is the greatest conceivable lack of it. Augustine, in his De Civitate Dei, lib. xiii, cap. xii, has wholly confounded the penalty with its consequences, and *vice versa;* and no one since his time seems to think that there is any necessity for doing otherwise. His words are adopted as a text, and there the matter is left; * and the result of such a representation of the matter is seen in its obscuring effects through the whole science of Christian theology, and most sadly and lamentably in its bearings upon the doctrine of the atonement, and the whole work of our blessed Lord. But in its present connection I can offer only a few brief remarks upon the subject.

In the strict and proper sense of the term, by the *penalty of the law*, as denounced in Gen. ii, 17, is not to be understood anything that is merely a consequence of incurring it. Hence it is improper, in point of reason and fact, to say that remorse of conscience, or what is called corporeal death, is a part of the penalty, or even that eternal misery itself is such. The word *eternal*, as we have remarked already, is not in the law, and there was no necessity for its being there. The penalty is simply the *wrath*, *displeasure*, or *curse of God;* and this comprehends the whole idea. The voluntary perpetration of sin by our representative, Adam, brought the displeasure of God upon him, and at once severed him, and of course all who should descend from him by ordinary generation, from the source of life, and left him and them in an utterly ruined, condemned, and helpless condition; a condition in which they must have remained forever, (since neither Adam himself nor any creature could ever reunite him to the source of life and procure for him the forfeited favor of God,) unless the grace and mercy of God interpose to bring relief. The moment therefore that he sinned the penalty in its true sense overtook him, and he died; for such a severance was death in its most appalling form. Christ has brought and proffers to us relief from this condition; and all who accept the proffer are rescued, and restored to the favor of God. Those who refuse it must have the wrath of God continue to abide upon them,

* He speaks more intelligibly however in cap. xv.

and for that rejection (since God commands that we receive the deliverance which he has thus provided) will be doomed to everlasting fire prepared for the devil and his angels. It is not necessary therefore that, in order to speak of a sinner as damned, or under the penalty, we should regard him as having passed from the present life; for he is already under the curse and dead; and every one who sins suffers this penalty. The soul that sinneth dies, and none but Christ can awaken and restore him to life; and if Christ do not in this world, then the separation which sin has made between the soul and God must continue, with all its increasing consequence and horrors, through the wasteless ages of eternity. But this matter cannot be here further dwelt upon.

In concluding this point I remark, therefore, that in the *second* and *third* of the aforenamed senses, the term *death* is frequently applied to man in the word of God, but never, in a single instance, in the *first.*

## § 45. *Death in the Sense of Corporeal Dissolution.*

We shall now proceed to consider the subject of death, in the second of the foregoing senses, as meaning the loss of this present life, or the severance of the soul from the body, and the manner in which this is referred to in the Scriptures, and as relating to man's condition in the state between his departure from this world and the resurrection. A point, however, occurs here at the very outset which it is necessary to consider, and to it we must devote the following sub-section of the argument.

I. What relation has *death*, in this second sense of the term, to the penalty of the Divine law, as mentioned in Gen. ii, 17, and Ezek. xviii, 4, 20?

It is a very serious error, into which many theologians and critics have fallen, to explain the phrase מוֹת תָּמוּת, *thou shalt surely die*, or *dying thou shalt die*, in Gen. ii, 17, by the statement in Gen. iii, 19: "*Dust thou art, and unto* *dust thou shalt return*."* This has no real authority from reason, theology, or exegesis to support it. Symmachus, (A.D. 200, *circiter*,) who was but a semi-Christian, (or Ebionite,) and whose authority is of no account, undertook to depart from the LXX, (whose rendering is true to the Hebrew, θανάτῳ ἀποθανεῖσθε,) and to translate the phrase by the words θνητὸς ἔσῃ, *mortalis eris*, thou shalt be mortal. Theodoret† and *Jerome* likewise thoughtlessly favored the corruption, though the Latin Vulgate still retains the true idea, *morte morieris, thou shalt die the death.* Knapp, also, to speak of no others, favors the rendering of Symmachus, and in fact the whole exegesis of Gen. ii, 17, by Gen. iii, 19. I repeat it, however, that there is not the

* I dislike much to raise any exception to our English translation of the Bible, the very best translation, doubtless, that was ever made; but in rendering this verse (Gen. iii, 19) the translators have not observed an important idiom of the Hebrew language, and by a literal rendering of the words have failed to give the true shade of thought in כִּי־עָפָר אַתָּה וְאֶל־עָפָר תָּשׁוּב, *for dust thou art, and unto dust thou shalt return.* Were it not, however, for the use which Annihilationists attempt to make of the passage, it would scarcely be worth while to refer to it. The expression as given in our translation destroys all antithesis, for how can the fact that a thing *is dust* be given as a reason why it should *return to dust?* and how can it *return* unto a condition in which it already is? But with the Hebrews it is usual to omit the preposition מִן, *ex, of, out of*, in respect to the material of which a thing is being made, or has been made, (as Schmidt observes, Colleg. Biblic. i, 390.) Gen. ii, 7: "God formed man [out of] the dust of the earth." Exodus xxv, 19: "Thou shalt make the mercy seat [of, or out of] pure gold;" and verse 18: "Thou shalt make the two cherubims [of] gold." Exodus xxxvi, 30: "And there were eight boards whose bases were [of] silver." Exodus xxxvii, 22: "The whole of it was one beaten work [of] pure gold." So too in the passage above quoted: "For [of] dust thou art, and unto dust shalt thou return." And another in the context, verse 21: "The Lord God made for Adam and his wife coats [of] a skin, and clothed them;" a passage miserably mangled by Shuckford (Creation and Fall, chap. xii,) from not attending to this idiom. It is a metonomy of the material for the thing made.

† Theodoret thus paraphrases the rendering of Symmachus: "'*Thou shalt be mortal*, and every day shalt thou expect death,' which the Jews are accustomed to express by the words, *son of death*." Nothing can more clearly show the absurdity of the translation of Symmachus than this paraphrase.

shadow of any sufficient reason for trifling thus with the import of the passage. It is a mere unsupported, arbitrary assumption, and is therefore entitled to no serious regard. Pareus, (*in loco*,) after quoting the exposition, denounces it in these words: *Hæc Sadducæorum et Epicuræorum hominum est sententia.* The reader may find in *Glassius*, whose *theology* however is a little confused on the point, an excellent exegetical illustration of the import of the phrase, (Philol. Sacra., lib. iii, tract iii, canon 37,) though in canon 21, he adopts the rendering of Symmachus.

There is, moreover, a great inconsistency on the part of the critics who adopt this exegesis; for if Gen. iii, 19, refers to Gen. ii, 17, as its proper solution or explanation, why isolate and specify, as the threatened penalty, only the dissolution of our physical bodies, or their return to dust, and not all the particulars mentioned in the same connection? for example, all the sorrows of Eve, the unfruitfulness of the ground, the thorns and thistles which it brings forth, the toil and sweat of man, the eating of the herbs of the field, instead of the fruits of paradise. But this is not done for the obvious reason that these things are seen to be, not the threatened penalty itself, but the consequences or results, matters which ought not to be thus confounded together. And then the *theology* of many of these critics forbids such an idea, as they hold that such labor as is here specified is a blessing instead of a curse. But there is neither logic nor propriety in thus commingling causes and consequences. Toil and corporeal dissolution are not the threatened penalty, nor any part of it. They have, under the Divine arrangement, resulted from the introduction of sin into the world, and so far, and in this sense alone, can they be regarded as penal. I am aware how great authorities can be pleaded for the view that death, in the sense of corporeal dissolution, is threatened in Gen. ii, 17, and is actually a part of the penalty of the law; and the names of Calvin and Turretin, not to mention a host of others, would lead me to hesitate, could I willingly suffer myself to be influenced in Divine things by human authority. They are names which I love and venerate, and which every year become dearer to my heart. But I do know, and after the most careful examination I affirm, that they have in this matter confounded things which are radically different, and concerning which the word of God makes a radical distinction, and that the confusion into which this great subject has thus been brought has been most injurious in its effects upon the whole science of theology. I should not here, however, refer to it, were it not that the line of argument pursued by our opponents on the subject of immortality requires it. But I shall refer to it as briefly as possible, and defer the fuller consideration of the whole matter to another occasion.* I do not attempt to set up my *authority* in this matter against that of the great and venerable names above referred to, but merely ask the reader's attention to the reasons which I offer for coming to a different conclusion from theirs.

1. At the outset of the inquiry we are met with the objection that Paul avers that "*by man came death.*" 1 Cor. xv, 21. But a moment's reflection will evince that this presents no real issue. We freely admit the truth stated. It is again excepted that death is an *enemy*, and is so repre-

* Let any one, however, take Calvin, or Turretin, or good old Witsius, (whose confusion here is really ludicrous,) or the later theologians, such as Dwight, Dick, and Knapp, who sustain the foregoing exegesis of Gen. ii, 17, by Gen. iii, 19, and attempt to follow out their view into its remoter relations to their systems, and the effect will be a vagueness and indistinctness of perception in relation to some of the most important doctrines of theology in their deeper import. On the contrary, how admirably is all this avoided by our own excellent summary of Christian doctrine: "All mankind by their fall *lost* communion with God, *are under* his wrath and curse, *and so made liable to* all the miseries of this life, to death itself, and to the pains of hell forever." (Quest. 19 of Shorter Catechism.) In the Larger, Quest. 27, the same distinction is made: "The fall brought upon mankind the loss of communion with God, his displeasure and curse; so as we are by nature children of wrath, bond slaves to Satan, and *justly liable to* all punishment in this world and that which is to come." In another section, however, from strangely assuming that corporeal death is referred to in Rom. vi, 23, the aforesaid indistinctness and confusion of ideas on the subject are immediately apparent. See Quest. 84, 85.

sented in the Scriptures: "Death, the last enemy, shall be abolished or destroyed." 1 Cor. xv, 26. But if it be an enemy, (ἐχθρὸς,) how can its being let loose, so to speak, upon man be other than a penal infliction? I remark that it is an enemy, or penal infliction, as above stated, in the same sense that the other results of our having severed ourselves from God are enemies; the pains and sorrows of parturition, the toil, food to be gained by labor, and the return of our bodies to dust, are all in direct contrast to our paradisaical state, and so far are enemies to man regarded as in his primal state. In the same sense, too, death is called "the king of terrors," (Job xviii, 14,) and may be regarded as the enemy of God not less than of man, for it is represented as undoing his own work here on earth. The language, however, is merely popular; men *feel* death to be their enemy; and the Apostle refers to it in the language of men. It is to be abolished and wholly destroyed, however, along with spiritual and eternal death in the case of the elect of God, and this is what Paul directly refers to here. Turretin repeatedly avers that *death* to the pious is not penal, (vol. ii, 390, and iv, 557,) and both he and Calvin aver that after our blessed Lord had assumed our nature he was not mortal, and that there was no reason, aside from his own will, that he should suffer corporeal dissolution,* which is undoubtedly true, though in utter conflict with their exposition of Gen. ii, 17, by iii, 19. His corporeal death was truly necessary as a testimony to earth, that he had borne the full curse; but in strictness of speech the separation between soul and body is not necessary in order to endure that curse, for the impenitent are to be raised from the dead (their souls and bodies to become reunited) in order that they may endure the penalty in its true and lasting import. This death, therefore, though an enemy, is not penal in the sense of being threatened in Gen. ii, 17. For that penalty Jesus did strictly and *literally* endure,† and yet the necessity

* See Turretin, Opp. iv, 557, and Calvin's Note on Matt. xvii, 3.

† This point, I am persuaded, can be established beyond all controversy, and I hope hereafter to be able to give my reasons for thinking so.

which called for his endurance of this is confessedly not the same as that which called for his endurance of corporeal death.

2. Christ has satisfied the law, and endured its full penalty for his people, and thus saved them from the curse of the law. Of course, then, that from which he has not saved, and does not save them, is no part of the curse. But he does not save them from corporeal death, and therefore corporeal death is no part of the threatened penalty. In reply to this Turretin, (iv, 556, 557,) though he, in a manner most strange for him, confounds sanctification with justification, (an illustration of the forementioned vagueness resulting to theology from the above explanation of Gen. ii, 17, by Gen. iii, 19,) does admit corporeal death to be, so far as relates to believers, not really penal, but a blessing to them, an arrangement of divine compassion, and that it is not to them the punishment of sin. But what is it then? for they do die. And how can this death be a part of the threatened penalty? And further, what proof is there that it is the punishment of sin to any, except so far as it is a consequence of sin's entrance into the world?

3. Then, too, it is affirmed, in every form of expression, that the justified are freed from *all* condemnation, as remarked above. They *are passed* from death into life, and yet they physically die. In what sense then can corporeal dissolution be a part of the penalty or curse threatened in Gen. ii, 17? It cannot be unless it is a part of the condemnation of the law. But the just are so fully delivered from the threatened curse that to them "there is *no* condemnation." Rom. viii, 1.

4. We have already remarked that the penalty of the law, in its full import, and without any restriction, as threatened for sin, is most directly and pointedly distinguished from corporeal death. The sinner, though he must at all events *die in the physical sense*, and no repentance or anything he may do can prevent this, is yet threatened with death if he persist in sin; and a promise is moreover made

to him that he shall *not* die if he turn. (Ezek. iii, and xviii, and xxxiii.) Now this threatening is a threatening of the true penalty of the law, as is admitted by all. That penalty shall be inflicted beyond hope if he persist in impenitence, but it shall be remitted if he turn and repent. In what sense, then, can *that death which he must suffer, whether he repent or not*, be a part of this threatened penalty? In no sense whatever, for if it were a part of the threatened penalty how could the promise be fulfilled to him that he should not endure it if he would turn? The pretense of Turretin, that the promised deliverance contemplates the future resurrection, is an evasion unworthy of that illustrious theologian. The point in question relates to the endurance of temporal death. And does it prove that a man shall not die a temporal death because he is to be raised from the dead in the general resurrection? The question simply is, how temporal death is under these circumstances a part of the threatened penalty of the law.

5. Death is spoken of as the end of suffering to the good, a *passing* (μετάβασις) *to a better life*, (John v, 24;) a *departure from this world*, (2 Tim. iv, 6; and in this sense is Enoch said to have died, Heb. xi, 5, 13;) also a *sleep*, (Matt. x, 24; John xi, 11;) a *deliverance* from the body of death, (Rom. vii, 24;) a *desired dissolution*, (Phil, i, 23; Luke ii, 29;) *an entrance into rest from labor*, (Isa. lvii, 2; Rom. xiv, 13.) It is therefore to the believer not the penalty of the law, but a part of the remedy for the disease of sin. How then can it be a joy to the righteous, and yet *a curse?* as it must be, if truly and properly a part of the penalty.

6. The justified in heaven are surely delivered from all the threatened penalty of sin. Yet they are dead. Now can any one suppose that the spirits of the just made perfect in heaven are enduring the penalty of the law in any sense? That they are not in that perfect state in which they would be if united to a glorified body is admitted; but this is the result not of wrath, but of that redeeming mercy which has

ordained the separation between soul and body, in order to prepare in the best way the redeemed for their final triumph. It was the most appropriate way of terminating man's probationary state, after our blessed Lord undertook to secure for us a second probation.

7. Paul says, moreover, that *to die is gain*, (Phil. i, 21;) and desirable, (ver. 23; 2 Cor. v, 8.) Now can it be to any one gain, or desirable, to endure the curse of the law in himself and on his own account?

8. He says too that "*death passed upon all men*," (Rom. v, 12,) showing it to be as universal as sin. The death or curse here referred to, therefore, no more admits of any exception than sin, in respect to mankind. And yet corporeal death has exceptions. Enoch and Elijah, and the great multitude who are alive at Christ's final coming, shall never suffer the pains of this dissolution. And yet not one of them in any way escapes the death threatened in Gen. ii, 17; Ezek. xviii, 4; and to which Rom. v, 12 refers. This death has passed upon all of them who have yet lived, and shall pass upon the others when they shall live. They shall *die* in that sense; though mercy, through our Lord Jesus Christ, shall so arrest the curse in their case as to prevent its becoming final. The death threatened in the law, therefore, neither knows nor can know any exception among all the race of Adam. And yet not one of these persons shall suffer corporeal death. How then can this death be the penalty of sin?

9. Even to the wicked the separation of soul and body, or corporeal death, is not necessary in order to the endurance of the penalty. In fact it is rather a prevention, so far as the endurance of the full penalty is concerned. And hence the full endurance of it is reserved till soul and body are reunited at the resurrection. In what sense then can this arrangement be a part of the penalty for sin?*

* Dr. John Taylor, with his usual *profundity*, says, in his "Original Sin," that if the curse had been *at once* inflicted Adam and Eve would have had no posterity. This seems like claiming a "Key" not only to

10. Corporeal death therefore has been appointed by God, (Heb. ix, 27; Psa. xc, 3,) in consequence of the introduction of sin and disorder into this once happy creation. But if it were the penalty of the law, then the law would demand that the finally impenitent should never arise from the dead. Now the resurrection is of both the just and unjust, (1 Cor. xv, 21, 22; John v, 28,) and is through Jesus alone as Mediator. *All* shall hear his voice and come forth. But the resurrection is in no sense a salvation from the penalty, since all are raised; and the wicked are in no sense saved either thereby, or in any other way, from the penalty. Therefore the separation of soul and body, the antithesis of which is the resurrection, is no part of the penalty, but, as above remarked, an appointment or arrangement made in consequence of sin's introduction into the world, and of God's intention to redeem mankind.

11. In fact the separation of soul and body was an arrangement *subsequent* to man's incurrence of the penalty, and after the curse had come upon him. It pertains not to the covenant of works, but to the mediatorial intervention, (and hence *Messiah himself* announced it,) and was entered into after the promise of redemption was made, that the seed of the woman should crush the serpent's head. All things, all men, and all power, were at once committed into the hands of the second Adam, our Mediator, immediately when the first Adam proved unfaithful to his trust; and though

"Romans," but to the secret purposes of God. He bases the announcement, however, on the assumption that the death of the body is, at least, part of the penalty of the law. But why may not man have continued to suffer the real penalty without this separation of soul and body? The wicked must thus suffer it after the resurrection. And if Adam and Eve were to live on the earth, why not have posterity? God had said, "Be fruitful and multiply;" and the same injunction is assumed as continuing in force after the fall, (Gen. iii, 16;) and the death threatened *has* really *passed upon all men.* (Rom. v, 12.) Andrew Fuller expresses the true idea of the matter as follows: "The original constitution of things provided for the existence of every individual that has since been born into the world, and that whether man should stand or fall." Works, p. 350. London, 1848.

he does not deliver all from the curse, he does deliver them from corporeal death, by the reunion of soul and body at the resurrection; and so presents them to receive, on the original legal ground, their final reward, whether they have accepted him or not.

12. As respects the righteous, therefore, death, as above stated, is only a merciful contrivance of mediatorial love to prepare them for the thorough new creation which awaits them. The soul is renewed in the present life, and the body shall be at the resurrection. God could indeed renew both body and soul without this separation. But this would not comport with the altered condition of things in this sin-stricken world, wherein everything (and in a certain sense the heavens likewise, see Rom. viii, 16–21; Heb. i, 10–12; 2 Pet. iii, 10–13) has been rendered corruptible, and needs to be purified. This purification shall take place when Christ comes, and the living saints shall share in the result without suffering death. Hence, though God is said to turn man to destruction, (Psa. xc, 3,) the death of his servants is declared to be *precious* in his sight, which it could not be in any such sense if that death were the penalty or curse for sin. And they are said *to die in the Lord*, (Rev. xiv, 13;) and is not the bare idea of their thus enduring the curse or penalty of sin an absurdity? To the wicked, however, this arrangement must become a curse, as do all the other consequences specified in Gen. iii, 16–19, (and hence we read that even *their* cultivation of the soil is sin, Prov. xxi, 4;) and especially must it become a curse to them, because it ends their probation, and ushers them into the unchanging retributions of eternity. But surely all this proves not that it is the penalty of the law even to them, for it is an admitted truth that they so abuse all the provisions of mercy as to turn them into a curse.

13. Hence, too, when Adam sinned, he was debarred from the tree of life. We know nothing about this matter more than is revealed; but we are informed that the reason of this exclusion was, lest he should eat of it and live for-

ever; that is, live forever in his then fallen and ruined condition. But God had a better arrangement to make respecting him, to wit: the severance of the soul from the body, which would prepare the way for the renovation of the body through its return to the dust and subsequent resurrection, the soul having been renewed by regeneration. How then could this better arrangement be part of the curse of the law?

14. I repeat it, therefore, that corporeal death was an arrangement which grew out of redemption, and not in wrath but in mercy to man. Theophilus of Antioch, (A. D. 168–181,) in his Apology, addressed to Autolychus, (lib. ii, cap. xxiv,) referring to this matter, says: "Death was bestowed by God as a great blessing upon man, lest he should remain for all time in sin; but he banished him for his transgression from paradise, that, being in exile, he might through this punishment (his sin having been expiated) be reinstated therein." (Referring doubtless to Rev. ii, 7.) "It must break him into pieces, that he may be rebuilt in the resurrection and be restored to righteousness and immortality." And yet, as all the other results of the introduction of sin into the world, it is to be viewed in the light of a chastisement, and so far *penal* (if theologians insist upon using that term) as being a result of the introduction of sin. Nor is it, I repeat in this connection, necessary in order to the endurance of the penalty, since before the sinner can *fully* undergo that penalty, he must be raised from the dead. (See how the word *body* is used in this connection in such passages as 1 Cor. v, 10; Isa. lxvi, 24.) And the fact that this corporeal dissolution comes to be called death subsequently, proves nothing, even though the very expression, as in 1 Kings ii, 37, be employed for this purpose.*

* Edwards, referring to this point, says: "It is wholly without reason urged that death properly signifies only the loss of this present life, and that therefore nothing else was meant by that death which was threatened for eating the forbidden fruit." (Orig. Sin, Part ii, sec. 2, p. 423.) The whole section deserves a careful perusal in this connection. But the remarks of Gussetus (in his comment, Ling. Hæb., p. 463) on this subject

The Socinians argue that the plural terms in which God in the beginning of creation speaks of himself, do not prove a plurality in his nature, because kings who lived some thousands of years afterward employ the same style, and the argument and inference in the one case are as good as in the other. Adam had already incurred the penalty and had died, was severed from the only source of life, and had God's displeasure and curse resting upon him when the arrangement specified in Gen. iii, 19, was made respecting him. He died the very moment he sinned; and the same death must in the very nature of things rest, and does rest upon every one who is a partaker of his fallen nature. They are all severed from the source of life; and Ezek. xviii, 4, 20, is true of every soul of man, and is fulfilled in them, and must continue to be to all eternity unless where sovereign mercy interposes and rescues those who accept of salvation through Jesus Christ.

Witsius* is exceedingly confused on this point; and though so mighty elsewhere, he here talks at random and without point, denouncing the opposite view as heretical, and giving no reasons for regarding it as such; and in section 5 he ascribes to the Socinians the sentiment that the death of the body is not the penalty of sin, and undertakes its refutation; and then, in section 12, he quotes from "*their theology* as adopted by the Arminians," the statement that Adam was not threatened with eternal death, but only and directly

are so excellent that we must lay them before the reader: "Cæterum, מוּת. primario et ex vocis institutione, antiquissimoque usu, designat pœnas æternas totius hominis, constantis corpore et anima, eas scilicet, quas discimus aliunde sedem habere in abysso, nam sic Deus intelligebat in comminatione, Gen. ii, 17, ut patet ex parallello, (Rom. vi, 23,) utque satis annuit absoluta locutio. An vero potuerit Adam ita sumere, cur dubites? cum enim nullo usu nulloque exemplo, nôsset mortem corpoream magis, quam, illam absolutam, neutra ei in mentem venire ad hæc verba potuit, nisi eadem vi, qua ei, linguæ cognitio infusa est, at certe statuendum est, Deum ipsi illam infudisse juxta verum ejus intellectum, et ita, ut verba Dei eodem sensu intelligeret, ac Deus dicebat. In tamen hæc altera significatio synecdochica, et partem corpoream solum spectans, promanavit hæcque quia de rebus sensibus subjectis frequentius loquimur, frequentior fuit in usu."

* Œcon. Fœd., lib. i, cap. v, and ii, cap. vi.

with that which is corporeal, or a separation between soul and body, and pronounces it rank poison. His vehemence is imitated by Dr. Dick,* and also his absence of argument on the subject. They utterly confound causes and results, (as Dwight also, ser. 28,) and involve themselves in inextricable confusion. As an instance: Witsius weakly argues (and it is about the only fair attempt that he makes at argument on the point) that "it would be very unbecoming in a divinely just and good Being *to inflict anything on man by a sentence of condemnation, which had not been threatened previously as a punishment for sin.*" Hence he infers that as corporeal death is inflicted, it must have been threatened in Gen. ii, 17. But he here uses the words "*sentence of condemnation*" in a sense in which it is not used in the opposing argument. Neither the death of the body, nor any of the inconveniences resulting to man from the introduction of sin into the world, and as specified in Gen. iii, 16–19, are *sentences of condemnation* in that sense of the term as above shown. They are results of man's sin and departure from God.

In order to the infliction of the curse, it was in no way necessary that God should have any such intercourse with man as is there narrated. He might have left the race in that darkness and horror which at once came over our progenitors when they sinned, and which increased, impelling them to screen themselves from the presence of their Maker, and which would have gone on increasing amid blackness and darkness forever. The sinning angels were thus left in chains of darkness as the penalty for aspiring to get beyond their primal position, and so might man have been left. As Andrew Fuller remarks: "Had there been no provision of mercy through the promised seed, there could have been no more communion between God and man any more than between God and the fallen angels." (Works, 619.) This intercourse with him, therefore, after the fall, was a matter, not of strict justice, but of compassion, and to prepare the

* Lec. 46, vol. i, p. 466.

way for his redemption from the thrall into which he had been taken. It was therefore not of law but of grace, and this is the only proper way to view it. And let it be particularly noted, that *this whole arrangement* respecting the serpent, Eve, Adam, the ground, etc., was made *after* the promise had been given of a Saviour, and after the Saviour had commenced his work of redemption. And this being so, what idea would the opposite construction compel us to form of the Ruler of the Universe? He first promises redemption from the penalty, and grants a Saviour, and then goes back of this promise and inflicts the penalty itself! This cannot be, and therefore this whole matter is related to the covenant of grace and not of works.

And this is evident still further from the fact that the toil, labor, etc., here enumerated are all really blessings in a *sinful* world to all who are willing to serve God. How then can they constitute any part of the curse of the law? Is the curse of the law disciplinary, as this would infer? Why then object to universal restoration? If disciplinary, *in any instance*, where is the principle of limitation? There is none, if causes, results, and consequences are thus to be confounded together.

But not to dwell upon this point needlessly, let me here advert to an approved sentiment of all our best divines. It is expressed as follows by Andrew Fuller: "While its [the earth's] fruitfulness is withheld, this has a *merciful tendency to stop the progress of sin;* for if the whole earth were like the plains of Sodom in fruitfulness, which are compared with the garden of God, its inhabitants would be as Sodom and Gomorrah in wickedness. The necessity of hard labor, too, in obtaining a subsistence, which is the lot of the far greater part of mankind, *tends more than a little*, by separating men from each other, and depressing their spirits, *to restrain them from* the excesses of evil. *All the afflictions of the present life contain in them a motive to look upward for a better portion*, and death itself is a monitor to warn them to prepare to meet their God." (Works,

p. 354.) And hence, says *Isidore*, quoted by Bernard: "O mors, quam dulcis es miseris! quam suavis es amare viventibus! quam jucunda es tristibus, atque lugentibus!" And he adds: "It puts an end to all the evils of this life, and a period to all the miseries of time, removes every calamity, and ends all our troubles." Such language is common with all Christians. Why then claim that these provisions of mercy are the curse of the law? I repeat it, that such an idea may well lead the impenitent to hope that mercy will thus interpose in relation to the execution of the penalty also in the world to come. And I know not why such a hope may not be indulged, if disciplinary chastisement is to be thus made a part of the threatened penalty of the law.

15. In conclusion, therefore, I remark that theologians generally have perplexed this whole subject by insisting that the severance of body and soul is a part of the penalty in Gen. ii, 17, instead of permitting the matter to stand in the relation wherein God has placed it; that is, as not connected with the covenant of works, but with the work of the Mediator, Christ Jesus. To say that the results, or consequences, of the Divine arrangements which followed the introduction of sin into the world, are the threatened penalty of sin, is not to speak with logical precision, nor as the Scriptures themselves speak on the subject; for all that God has done in mercy for the world may be thus brought into the same category, as it is, in fact, substantially, by not a few who have written on the subject. Such speculations have, moreover, favored the Annihilationist scheme, and have involved in confusion the whole subject of the Divine penalty in its relation to the expiation of sin through our adorable Redeemer, till we now see men on precisely the same principle maintain the silly notion that remorse of conscience is part of the penalty, and on such preposterous grounds assert that Jesus did not endure the legal penalty for sin because he did not suffer remorse!

I shall conclude with a passage or two from Dr. Hopkins, who has evidently given much thought to the subject. "It farther follows," says he, "that separation of soul and body is *no part* of the punishment threatened. The death threatened was quite of a different kind, and not only does not include, but necessarily *excludes*, separation of soul and body. Had the punishments taken place and been executed without any mitigation, or had there been no reprieve and redemption for man, this separation of soul and body could not have taken place; because the punishment deserved, and therefore the punishment threatened, was evil to the *whole man*, or the man made up of soul and body. This creature, consisting of body and soul, which were essential constituent parts of the man, was threatened, and, if he sinned, was to be punished; and not one part only, while the other is taken down and annihilated. Therefore this could not take place consistent with the full execution of the threatening. It is not so great an evil for the mind only to suffer, as it is to be miserable, or to suffer evil, in body and soul. The man is capable of suffering unspeakable evil, or pain, in his body; therefore this suffering must be included in the threatening. And this proves that separation of soul and body could not be the subject of a *threatening*, that is, could not be *threatened;* for this would not have been an evil, in that case, but a negative good, which cannot be the subject of a *threatening*, but rather of a promise; for evil only can be threatened, and not good, negative or positive. Separation of body and soul would have been a mitigation of punishment, and would have rendered man not capable of suffering so much as in body and soul united; therefore it could not be threatened as a *punishment*, it being no part or kind of punishment, but the contrary. And under that constitution under which the threatening was made, there was no provision for a reunion, if a separation once took place; nor was it indeed possible there should be a reunion, if a separation was threatened as a punishment, and had the threatening been executed. Is it not hence evident to a certainty that separation of soul and body could not have taken place had man been punished for disobedience according to the true threatening; and therefore this was not included in the threatening, but on the contrary, was necessarily excluded?" "They therefore must have been greatly mistaken who have taught and asserted that this was all that was threatened (that is, corporeal death) in the Divine law, or as the penalty of eating the forbidden fruit; and they have made as real a mistake who have supposed that turning the body to dust is included in the threatening, or any part of it, since the contrary is evidently true, namely, that the threatening necessarily excludes it." See Hopkins's Divinity, vol. i, pp. 275, 276, 280.

II. There is another idea in this same connection which calls for remark before we pass on: it is the assertion frequently made, though the Annihilationists profess to dissent from it utterly, that corporeal death is natural to man; that is, that it is a *debt of nature*, and not a result of sin.

While the Socinians, and along with them the semi-Pelagians generally, maintained that corporeal death was the penalty of the law, they were strongly inclined to take under their protection that precious bantling of Pelagius that death is natural to man, and that God really created him mortal, that is, *sub necessitate moriendi;* a notion which some claiming to be evangelical assert at the present time. The logic by which these two ideas are divested of their mutual antagonism to each other, and brought into a peaceful and harmonious relation, has thus far remained concealed from the knowledge of the uninitiated, though from other abundant evidence that with the Socinian school logical consistency is not regarded as a jewel, we are led to infer the existence therein of a principle of doctrinal sympathy, or assimilation, which lies far back of all the acknowledged principles of ratiocination, at the same time that none have ever put forth higher claims to be guided by pure reason in all such matters than they.

Now if death is natural to man, that is, if man were created under the necessity of dying, it can need no words to convince any person of common sense that it can be neither the result nor the penalty of transgression; and *vice versa*, if it be the result of sin it can be in no sense regarded as natural. To dwell upon so obvious a truth seems quite unnecessary. Dr. Hodge, in his commentary on Romans, has, however, inconsiderately countenanced the inaccuracy by employing the phrase "*natural death*," a phrase which, unless I err, is never found in the Commentary of his great exemplar, Dr. Gomar.

When men permit themselves, however, to lose sight of the fact that all the proceedings of God in respect to this world are regulated by the consideration that we are fallen beings, having departed from our original position in the scale of moral intelligence, their speculations may well be expected to run into hallucination, and to develop many such preposterous notions as the aforesaid. A signal example of such extravagance is furnished by the well-intended treatise of Dr. Combe on *the* "Constitution of Man," which, while it enunciates with the air of a profound discoverer in philosophy facts and principles of which any intelligent school-boy would blush to be thought ignorant, its author undertakes to arraign, without giving himself the trouble to understand it, the principle asserted by the venerated Dr. Wardlaw, that the world in its present fallen and sin-cursed condition does not present a fair representation of the principles of its original constitution, a statement which, one might well suppose, could scarcely be objected to by an intelligent mind. And any attempt to account for the evils and miseries, and apparent disorders of this world, on principles which do not recognize as a starting point the depravity of man or his voluntary departure from God, must be not only futile and abortive, but in their logical sequence produce skepticism, and eventually the denial of God. The *fall of man* alone furnishes the key to the mysterious proceedings of Providence in relation to our world. The idea that in man's pristine state the natural elements were at war with him as now, is perfect folly. (See the note of Calvin on Gen. iii, 19.) To pursue this point would lead us from the immediate issue; but it may be proper to remark, that since the fall God's creative power even has been called into operation for man's chastisement as a consequence of sin, and produced "thorns and thistles," which previous to the entrance of sin had no existence in this then lovely universe. *Junilius* beautifully remarks: "Ex eo, quod Deus dixit: Ecce dedi vobis *omnem herbam*, patet quod *nihil noxium* terra protulit, et nullam herbam venenatam, et nullum arborem sterilem." And our best divines have ever affirmed that noxious plants, insects, reptiles, etc., were the result of sin's introduction here. It is needless to dwell upon the point, or to give numerous references. Let the reader consult *Basil*, in lib. de Paradiso; *Luther* in Gen. i; *Polanus*, Syntag. Theol., p. 975; and *Pareus* in Gen. i. and iii. They present not only their own, but the approved views of the Church of Christ in relation to the subject.

It would therefore be as proper to plead that these disorders, and all antagonisms to the pristine and happy condition of the earth, are in accordance with the original constitution of things, as that sickness and mortality are. And the objections of Socinus, Pye Smith, Sturm, and others, are of no weight, since they all illogically take for granted the baseless assumption that sin has produced no change in the nature of things. See some of the speculations of Socinus on this subject in Opp., tom. ii, pp. 305, 308. His opposition to the doctrine of *imputation* brought forth such utterances.

It is scarcely proper to omit noticing in this connection the mistaken views of that truly great and good man, the late Dr. Emmons, in relation to the same point. He has in his speculations partially ignored the effects of the fall, and the views to which he was logically led in consequence appear to me to be impious in a high degree. His language on the subject would better befit a real atheist than a Christian divine. (See, for instance, his sermon on Gen. xlv, 5.) His favorite argument to prove God the efficient author of sin was this: "Sin takes place according to the usual laws of nature; and as, according to Newton, the laws of nature are the established modes of the Divine operation, therefore God is the author of sin." And in exact accordance with this, he says: "When Moses called upon Pharoah to let the people go, God stood by him and moved him to refuse; when the people departed from his kingdom, God stood by him and moved him to pursue after them with increased malice and revenge." He thus utterly confounds the idea of *sustaining in existence* a voluntary agent, with the idea of *acting through the will* of that agent—a distinction which is perfectly obvious. But I refer here to this unintentional but intolerable blasphemy, as an illustration of the consequences which must flow from any attempt to reason from the present disordered state of the world, to its primitive condition; that is, to lose sight of the fall, and to regard the present condition of the earth and mankind as their original constitution. And I shall here add a few words showing the mistake which Dr. Emmons, and those who agree with him, have made in consequence of this assumption.

In the foregoing argument Dr. Emmons has included, without distinction, both physical and intellectual nature, and reasons from one to the other. This is correct on his principle, that sustaining in existence is not to be distinguished from actuating; a principle, however, which, if true of material nature, is by no means necessarily true of the intellectual and moral.

A distinction is therefore here made by others; and it is maintained that the laws of material nature are nothing more nor less than God operating, as when a stone is cast into the air the attraction of gravitation, called a law of nature, is only God drawing it down again. Such is the philosophical idea, and even Tholuck says: "The life in the universe cannot be regarded as absolutely distinct from the life of God. God continues and supports the world by a continual creation, for such in fact is preservation. The life of the world is the breath of Jehovah, its active powers the working of his omnipresence; the laws of nature are not therefore fixed once and forever." And he quotes Augustine as saying, "*Lex naturæ est voluntas Dei*," etc., and then adds: "The laws of nature are mere abstractions which men make from the usual operations of God. It can therefore by no means be said, that his usual operations, as in immediate revelation and miracles, are violations of the laws of nature. There is no essential difference between immediate and mediate operations; it is merely the difference between the unusual and usual."*

Such is a fair presentation of this philosophical theory as regards material nature; and while something in the representation may be properly admitted, the adoption of the whole involves, by fair consequence, an admission of the substantial truth of Pantheism.

But other theologians, as above remarked, have, with Dr. Emmons, advanced a step farther, and carried these speculations into the world of mind; and by thus assuming that man, acting agreeably to the existing laws of mind, is God acting, God is irresistibly made the author of all moral evil, and of all the disorders of this fallen universe, in the very worst and most offensive sense that can be attached to the terms.

I have remarked above, that to sustain or continue in existence a moral and intellectual being, does not by any means infer an authorship of the acts of that creature; and to affirm (for this whole argument is built on the assumption) that God cannot form an intelligent creature who shall be wholly dependent upon him for the endowment and continuance of all its powers and faculties, and for rendering them fit and apt for their most natural movements and operations, and yet who shall not be dependent upon him for its volitions, or for the manner in which it uses its powers,† is, to speak plainly, an assumption which is as nonsensical as it is arrogant. Who dare lay claim to knowledge sufficient to justify an asseveration so audacious?

* Princeton Essays, 1846, p. 606, 607.

† We shall refer to this more fully in another chapter.

Now in contemplating the matter in its relation to man, we are ever to bear in mind that God created him to endure, that is, endowed him with an immortality of existence. And while we despise and throw back upon its authors the pitiful imputation of "making God a machinist," we will suppose, for illustration, that a man were able to construct and give operation as well as rational powers to a complex piece of mechanism, which at all events he designs should exist and operate for a long period of time, say fifty years; but a portion of the work soon becomes disordered and produces confusion, yet, as by a specific arrangement he has formed it for continuance of action during the period of time above named, he continues to preserve it in existence. Now for all purposes which are actually involved in the issue, this analogy (though imperfect, as all analogies on such a subject must be) is precisely in point; and in view of it I ask, Will any man who can make a distinction, pretend that this inventor is the *cause* of the confusion referred to? Will any one pretend that he is the author of the continued confusion, simply because he fulfills his arrangement to keep the machine in being? It is obvious that such reasoning would be false, and not even touch the point of the question raised, because, when he gave existence to the machine, its continuance for fifty years was to be irrespective of the question whether it would for that time continue to move correctly or incorrectly. By hypothesis it is endowed with rationality, and with the power to move correctly. Should it choose to move otherwise this does not oblige the author to cease to supply it with sustaining power, nor does it infer that because he does not cease to do so, he is therefore the author and contriver of its evil operations.

So too with the universe. God originally created it "very good," and established good and supremely excellent laws in relation to its operation. None of these laws worked pain, or disease, or death, but they have become disordered now by the voluntary act of the creature, *and against the wish of the Creator*, (for this is Scripture and common sense, however metaphysical subtlety may labor to perplex the point,) and they do now work pain, and disease, and death; and therefore it is as sheer folly to say that the operation of those laws in this disordered state of things is God operating by his original constitution, as it would be, in the case supposed, to say that the confusion working in the aforesaid machine is the skill of the artist in operation, or that he is the author and contriver of all the ill-working of his design. While the work continued to move correctly, it is fair to say that its results were the operations of the artist; but when they ceased to operate thus, it is a shameful perversion and abuse of language to say that its ill-workings are the operation of its author. So too with respect to God; his primary plans, his unknown purposes and laws, have nothing to do with the question in its relation to us; and according to what is known and revealed, we affirm that while nature continued in its original constitution, that is, as he called it into being, it is fair to say that its operation was the operation of God; but to assert this, especially of mind now in its disordered condition, is the fatuity of imbecility.

The fall of man, therefore, and the voluntary perversion of his powers, and the consequent perversion of all the powers of nature in this world, are ever to be taken into the account in treating upon this subject.

To return to the point immediately at issue, therefore, I remark that corporeal death is not a debt of nature, but a result of sin.

The true idea on this subject is thus presented by *Paræus* (in Gen. ii, 17) in reply to the allegation of Socinus, that death is natural to man: "God did not create death; how then can it be natural to man? And how can death be called natural to man when it is, *per se*, the destruction of his nature? How shall that be natural which is against and not according to nature, and which is totally abhorrent from nature? and which, with such great sorrow and suffering, is conjoined to nature? and of which nature, previous to the fall, was free, and shall be also free after the final judgment? Death is therefore not natural because it destroys nature." And *Schmidt* (Colleg. Biblic., ii, p. 375,) with equal force remarks: "Certainly that which is congruous to nature, and which pertains to it in its integrity, cannot be called an *enemy* and *hostile*, as death is here expressly said to be by the apostle." 1 Cor. xv, 26. I make these quotations not as authoritative, but as carrying their own weight in the argument, and as representing also the views of the Church of Christ in the matter. And that they do this is further apparent from the following extract from a sermon ("On the State of Man before the Fall") by the learned *Bishop Bull:* "That Adam should not have died if he had not sinned, is so manifestly the doctrine of the Scriptures and of the Church of God, both before and since Christ our Saviour's appearance in the flesh, that Pelagius of old, and Socinus in this latter age, are justly to be esteemed the most impudent of mortals for daring to call it in question." And accordingly we find in the first four centuries of the Church an unbroken testimony on the subject. For example, *Gregory Nazianzen* (De Creat. Hom., c. xi,) says: "For if God had created man mortal from the beginning, he never would have condemned sin by death; for in no conceivable way could he condemn a mortal by inflicting upon him mortality." *Augustine*, too, (De Civ. Dei, lib. xiii, cap. xv,) says: "It is agreed upon among Christians who truly hold the catholic faith, that corporeal death is not by a law of nature, but deservedly inflicted on account of sin; because God, in avenging sin, said to the man in whom we all then were, (*in quo tunc omnes eramus*,) 'Dust thou art, and into dust thou shalt go.'" And accordingly, when the Pelagian notion called for particular attention in the fifth century, the Church uttered her voice in the following canon of the council at Milevia in Numidia, A. D 416: "Whoever shall say that the first man, Adam, was created mortal, so that whether he should sin or not sin, he would have died corporeally, not from desert of sin, but by a necessity.

of nature, *anathema sit.*" Cap. i. I trust that even theologastrians will not mistake my object in adducing these testimonies, as my intention is thereby to present a fair expression of the views of the Church of Christ on the subject.

III. We shall now proceed to consider death in the sense of a severance of soul and body, and also the manner in which it is referred to in the Scriptures; though, as we have been in the course of our argument already necessitated to refer to this matter so frequently, it will be needless here to go into any lengthened details respecting it.

The terms by which death, in the sense of a severance of soul and body, is designated in the Scriptures, evince the idea which the Spirit of God designed that man should attach to it. Some of those terms have been referred to above and explained. A brief enumeration of them is all that we shall here attempt:

1. It is spoken of as *a return to dust*, (Gen. iii, 19,) which of course imports a dissolution of that part of our nature which was originally derived from the earth, and of that only. See Gen. ii, 7; Eccles. xii, 7; Hag. ii, 23.

2. It is also a giving back of the spirit, (Gen. xlii, 13,) an idea which is sometimes expressed also by referring to the visible effect—a ceasing to breathe. (Psa. civ, 29.)

3. It is also a departure from the earthly body when that is destroyed. (2 Cor. v, 1.) Hence, too, it is called a going away. (Job. x, 21; Psa. xxxix; iv, 13.)

4. It is also named a sleep, (Psa. lxxvi, 7; John xi, 13,) and hence is also described by the term "lying down."

5. It is called a gathering to one's people, or a going to one's fathers. See sect. 29, sub-sect. 3, above.

6. It is an entrance into rest. (Rev. xiv, 13.)

This enumeration is sufficient for the argument, and we proceed to the subject of our next chapter.

# CHAPTER II.

## MAN'S CONSCIOUS EXISTENCE NOT INTERRUPTED BY DEATH—INFERENCES—CONCLUSION OF THE ARGUMENT.

The proof that man retains his conscious being after corporeal dissolution has been in general exhibited on the preceding pages. It is not our design, therefore, to present here a recapitulation of that proof, but to consider and illustrate the fact itself from various points of view, analogical and otherwise, in which it is not therein contemplated.

### § 46. *Separation of Soul and Body does not infer the loss of Consciousness.*

The severance of the interior of our nature from the exterior and visible in no sense infers either the extinction or unconsciousness of the former. To employ (without indors ing all the phraseology) the impressive language of a writer quoted in the little work of Professor Bush on the soul, "Into the spirit-world man enters at death. While in this lower world his spiritual body was within his natural body, giving it life, and power, and sense. It was always his spiritual eye which saw, his spiritual ear which heard, his spiritual sense which took cognizance of all things about him. But while he lived in the material body it was only through the material organs of that body that the eye of his spiritual body could see and its ear could hear; and for that purpose these natural organs were exquisitely fitted to the spiritual organs, which they served as instruments. But when these material organs or coverings fall off the spiritual eye, the true and living eye does not lose the power of seeing. It loses the power of seeing the material things for which it once possessed a material organ, and acquires the power of seeing the spiritual substances and forms which this material organ had vailed." P. 113.

In the soul, as is conceded by all, dwells the conscious personality, the principle which gives life and animation to the body. On what ground, therefore, is it to be inferred that the dissolution of a material organism infers also the dissolution of the power which employed that organism as the instrument of its perceptions? The man who should infer in respect to another person, that the faculty of vision was utterly extinguished in him, because he had lost or mislaid his spectacles, would support his position by as good reasoning as our antagonists herein support theirs.

1. That the soul may exist separately from the body is conceded even by many of our opponents who claim to be materialists. *Ab uno disce multos.* E. 85 says: "Some beings seem to live by the pure *ruah*, or spirit, without the intervention of the atmosphere; such are called spiritual beings." "Demons are called spirits, by which we understand spiritual beings, beings that live by means of the pure or unadulterated spirit, or principle of all life." According to this admission, then, the only question to settle is, whether man's interior life is spiritual. And that such is its nature, and that it can exist in a state of separation from the body, is evident from the fact that its conscious existence is not necessarily suspended by swoon, coma, drowning, etc.

The facts are so abundant which establish this point that it were idle to attempt to specify all, or to enlarge upon them. Let the reader refer to the well-known treatise of Rush on the Mind, or Abercrombie's "Inquiry into the Intellectual Powers," or Nelson's "Cause and Cure of Infidelity," especially chapter lvii, for facts on the subject. The well-attested case of Rev. William Tennent, of New Jersey, and also that of Thomas Say, are in point.* Dr. Adam Clarke

* See Life of T. Say, by Dr. Say, of Philadelphia. 1796.

also stated to Dr. Lettsom, of London, that during the period of his apparent death or unconsciousness from drowning he felt "indescribably happy, *and did not for a single moment lose his consciousness.*" Similar and equally well-attested facts have been abundant in all ages, evincing the separability of the soul from the body. The same is shown by the case of *Clazomenius*, mentioned by Pliny, Hist. Nat., lib. vii, cap. lii, and that of *Cornelius*, mentioned by A. Gellius, Noct. Attic., lib. xv, cap. 18, and the similar one of *Apollonius*, mentioned by Philostratus, lib. viii, cap. xxvi. See also section 14, *supra.*

The phenomena of *Mesmerism* may be likewise here referred to in illustration of the same point. We have nothing to do with any theory on the subject. We advert merely to the well-established facts, which may be found, for instance, in the work of I. P. F. Deleuze, or in the Psycodunamy, by Theodore Leger, (New York, Appleton & Co., 1846,) in which treatises there are many facts given, (whatever may be said or thought of the others,) the truth of which cannot be set aside except on principles which must, if applied, unsettle the basis of all history; facts, too, which are utterly subversive of the whole theory of materialism.

The favorite objection by which the Materialist endeavors to sustain his system against facts like those above referred to is, that *pressure on the brain produces unconsciousness.* By *unconsciousness* he means a total suspension of thought, or intellectual exercise. But this is a mere assumption. All that he is entitled to claim is, that in specific cases, pressure upon that organ has produced such an effect as prevents *the remembrance of our mental exercises* in the interval. And this we are willing to admit; nor does it at all conflict with the facts alleged above in the case of Tennent and others. (This point has likewise been considered in sect. 14, *supra.*) And in the same connection we may refer our Materialist friends to such facts as the following. In the fourth volume of the Memoirs of the Literary and Philosophical Society of Manchester, Dr. Ferriar has fully established the fact that every part of the brain has been injured without affecting the act of thought. The facts therein presented have shaken the whole theory of Materialism to its foundation; nor have its advocates attempted a reply.* The same may be said of the remarkable occurrence which took place at Cavendish, Vermont, September 13, 1848, and which has been fully reported by Dr. H. I. Bigelow, Professor of Surgery in Harvard University, and attested also by Drs. Harlow and Williams. By an accidental explosion of powder in blasting a rock, an iron bar, weighing thirteen and a quarter pounds, (three feet and seven inches in length, one inch and a quarter in diameter,) was projected directly upward, passing entirely through the head of Mr. Gage, (who was holding it,) and was picked up some rods distant from the place, besmeared with his brains and blood. There was no perceptible suspension of consciousness, or of thought, and he ultimately recovered his health. The testimony throughout is positive and complete, and is of such a character that no intelligent man would imperil his reputation for sense and candor by attempting to call in question the truth of any of the details respecting it. The theory of Materialism can no more sustain itself against the testimony of facts like these, than (to use a simile of Isaac Taylor) a citadel of rooks can sustain its integrity against a volley of musketry.

2. The subject may be illustrated likewise by the ancient ideas of the soul, as preserved by tradition. The idea of its *divine* origin is presented, for instance, by *Seneca*, Epist. xcii; *Epictetus*, Dissert. i, cap. xiv; *Cicero*, Tuscul. Quæst., lib. i; and De Divinatione, lib. i, not to name the other and earlier philosophers referred to in part i, chapter iii, above. But on these things it is unnecessary to enlarge.

In all languages there is a clear distinction made between the soul and body, and to the soul is attributed a separate name.† Now original terms, according to the unvarying

* See Wood on the Mosaic Creation, pp. 387, 388; and also Abercrombie's Inquiry, pp. 121, 122.

† See in Biblic. Repos. for Oct., 1850, an article on the "*Names of the*

laws of language, always indicate a distinct belief of some corresponding entity; for men do not *thus* invent words as original and distinguishing names, without such belief; and hence the mere fact that in all languages there are names for *soul* as distinct as those for *body*, evinces that man has always believed as much in the independent entity of the one as of the other.

In the Scriptures we find this idea exemplified in every form, and the terms נֶפֶשׁ, ψυχή, employed to designate the idea expressed by our English word *soul.* The origin of these terms (and in fact of all through which they are supposed to be derived) seems in some way to convey the idea of *air in motion*, as in *breathing* and *blowing.* The same may be said of the corresponding Latin terms, *animus*, *anima*, *spiritus.* And Grimm has traced our Saxon term *soul* to a similar origin so far as etymology is concerned. The word *ghost* likewise has the same origin.* There is, however, another term, often used interchangeably with *soul* in the Greek and Latin, and in modern European tongues, which has no such origin, the Greek νοῦς, from νώεω, *to know;* the Latin corresponding term is *mens*, and the English *mind.* Originally these terms signified that which *knows*, or understands, and they are derived from the root *mena*, *to know*, an etymon which, though now lost in the European languages, is preserved, like many of their common roots, in the Sanscrit.†

The former of these etymologies has been made the foundation of an objection by the Materialists to the separate existence of the soul, which should be here noticed. It is claimed that men originally could have had no other idea of the soul's existence than that it was evanescent, like the breath. But this appears to be a very frivolous objection; certainly

*Soul*," by Dr. Tayler Lewis. It displays his usual masterly ability, but is disfigured by his use of the term *immateriality*, and by a captious objection to the phrase "*man's interior life*," as applied to express the idea of the soul's existence within the body.

* Trench's explanation of this term is pedantic and unauthorized.

† See Bush on the Soul, p. 26.

it does not evince a very profound view of the subject. *Breathing*, as thus associated with their idea of the soul, referred not to the *act* of inhalation, but to the *thing* inhaled—to wit, the air. Now the body of man being visible, and his soul or inner life invisible, though active and powerful, they, in giving expression to this idea, chose that object in nature which to them seemed to express it most nearly. Hence the air, atmosphere, wind, was selected as being an invisible and yet active and powerful agent, and as giving, as near as could be, expression to their ideas. The objection, therefore, only confirms the position which it aims to subvert.

3. That the term *soul* in the Scriptures is employed in the sense of personal hypostasis no one can question. See נֶפֶשׁ, as used in such passages as the following: "*My soul* (that is, I myself) shall live because of thee." Gen. xii, 13. See also xix, 20; xxvii, 4; xix, 31; xl, 6. So too in Exod. xxx, 15: "To make an atonement for your souls;" also, xi, 43, 44; Deut. iv, 15; Judges v, 21; 16, 30; Esther iv, 13; Job vii, 15; and in other places. So too in Psa. iii, 2; vii, 5; xxxi, 7. But it is unnecessary to specify other instances. In the same manner also ψυχή is employed in the New Testament. (Luke i, 46; Rom. xiii, 1; 2 Cor. xii, 15; James v, 20; 2 Pet. ii, 14.)

It is proper to observe likewise in the same connection, that נֶפֶשׁ, רוּחַ, and ψυχή and πνεῦμα, are employed indifferently *in the sense of person or personal agent.* Let the following examples suffice: Gen. xiv, 21; xvii, 44; Exod. i, 5; Lev. xvii, 12, 15; xxiii, 30; Deut. ii, 30; Job xv, 13; Psa. xxxii, 2; Prov. xiv, 25; xvi, 32; Luke i, 46, 47; Acts ii, 41; vii, 14–27, 43; Rom. ii, 9. And let the reader compare this usage also with that which occurs in such passages as the following: 1 Sam. xvi, 14; 1 Kings xxii, 21, 22; Job iv, 15; Zech. xiii, 2; Matt. x, 1; Luke xxiv, 39; Heb. i, 14; xii, 22, 23.

To save space, I make these references merely instead of quoting the passages. Every reader can easily turn to them and verify the truth of the representation which we have made. The interior, living, acting principle of man is thus as fully recognized as a personal agent as angels or devils themselves. It is always recognized as the ultimate agent of thought and feeling in man; and it is scarcely necessary to add, this recognition comports entirely with human consciousness. What man ever felt that his body, or any part of it, is this ultimate agent or personality? And I may add, in conclusion of this point, that the Bible everywhere affirms that it is to this *soul*, or *spirit* in man, that all human thought, feeling, and consciousness should be and must be referred. See Psalm vi, 4; xxxiv, 18; li, 10; lxxvii, 6; Prov. xi, 13; xv, 13; Eccles. i, 14; vii, 8, 9; Ezek. xi, 5; Dan. ii, 1; Matt. v, 3; xxvi, 41; and other passages almost innumerable.

4. The diligent inquirer into the truth on the grand subject before us will here be led, doubtless, to ask, If these things are so, on what principle, either of Scripture, reason, or common sense, is it to be inferred that this conscious personality is to cease upon its being divested of a mere material instrument for holding intercourse with a material sphere? In nature itself there is no reason for such a supposition, and all analogy is against it. And the only ground which, with any degree of plausibility, has been pleaded from the Scriptures, is that death is therein sometimes spoken of as a sleep. And this we grant. The question, however, is, what is the import of this language?

It is a fact acknowledged in philosophy, that sleep does not necessarily suspend our intellectual operations; on the contrary, we are assured that God has often chosen this as the period to commune with the souls of his people. There is, however, one thought on the subject which it would be well for those to remember who, on such ground, hope for impunity after death. Sleep generally suspends only those intellectual operations which depend on volition, (though sometimes these are by no means suspended, as facts abundantly show,) and hence all such operations as depend not on the will may continue during sleep. Those which depend upon association, for instance, continue; and the soul may, and often does, suffer during them as much as during wakeful hours. Take then the idea in its literal import, and death, while it suspends the power of choice, leaves memory awake, and the soul must, by association, dwell upon the past, while conscience still prophecies of the future. For the sinner in hell, therefore, volition can accomplish nothing. (See Luke xvi, 23–31.) He will be, so to speak, beyond that; but memory, the power of association, conscience, will still live, and perform their terrible and effectual work. (Mark ix, 43–49.) If our opponents, therefore, claim that *death* is literally *sleep*, it will bring no relief to their theory.

But that the term sleep is often employed metaphorically none but a theologastrian will dispute, for what else can be made of it in such passages as Psalm xliv, 23: "*Awake*, why *sleepest thou*, O Lord?" (Compare Psalm cxxi, 3, 4.) See also Psalm lxxiii, 20, and lxxviii, 65. As applied, too, to the dead in sin, it implies no suspension of consciousness. See Eph. ii, 1, with v, 14. And as applied strictly to the corporeally dead, it is but a metaphorical euphemism which may be found in all languages, and (whatever may be the popular belief respecting death) is derived from the resemblance which a dead body bears to the body of a person asleep.* But to dwell upon such a matter here is needless, and I will merely add a remark or two evincing what has always been the view entertained of it by the Christian Church.

The excellent reformer *Andrew Hyperius*, in his commentary on 1 Thess. iv, 13, 14, after remarking that the word sleep does not mean, as some dream, that the *soul* will be unconscious until the day of judgment, or become extinct, adds: "The death of the righteous is truly nothing

* See section 27, sub-section 4, above; also the excellent remarks of Limborch, Theol., lib. vi, cap. x, sec. 8, and Flacius, Clavis, Art. Dormire, p. 258, and Campbell's Prelim. Dissert., vi, part ii, sec. 23.

else than a sweet repose, whence they shall be aroused at the coming of Christ to enjoy a far higher felicity." And *Calvin*, in his Psychopannychia, (as quoted by Henry, vol. i, p. 45,) says: "We would now say somewhat respecting the peace of pious souls separated from the body. Holy Scripture, by 'Abraham's bosom,' intends us to understand nothing more than the state of rest. In the first place, then, we call *rest* that which those masterly theologians call *sleep*; and by *rest* we understand, not a state of stupor, torpidity, or drunkenness, as they do, but a state of conscious, happy security and trust, which faith indeed already, in some degree, bestows upon us, but which cannot be perfected until after death." And *Augustine*, the Calvin of the early Church, says: (De Civit. Dei, xiii, cap. viii:) "For the souls of the righteous, being separated from the body, are at rest; but the souls of the wicked are punished until the time when the bodies of those shall be awakened to eternal life, and of these to eternal death, that death which is called the second death."

5. Nothing can be plainer, therefore, even from these considerations alone, (not to speak of the long catalogue of proofs in the foregoing part of this volume,) than that the soul continues its conscious existence when the body dies. There are, however, several points of illustration on which we might dwell; for example, its activity when the body is dying,* and the plain fact that extinction is inconsistent with

* What does Dr. Post mean by proposing to "dismiss all arguments from the phenomena of the soul at or near the death of the body?" (See New Englander, xiv, p. 115.) The expression, however explained, was wholly uncalled for, and the reasons offered to justify it are, to say the most that can be said for them, simply puerile, and evince that Dr. Post has no just appreciation of the facts in the case. In other branches of the argument he has evinced consummate ability; but as a chosen representative of the evangelical sentiment, (and as such he wrote,) he had no right, by a vapid attempt at rhetorical flourishing, which will not even bear analysis, to ignore the argument referred to. Butler, in the "Analogy," has stated it with his usual felicity and power, and it is illustrated by many facts of overpowering interest in that truly remark-

identity, which no reasonable person can deny. But omitting these, I shall briefly illustrate the point that separation does not involve extinction of consciousness or of vital power on the part of the soul. We cannot pretend to add anything to the force of the Divine testimony on the subject, but yet it may be perfectly proper to illustrate the point by analogies derived from nature; for, as Butler remarks, (Analogy, chap. i,) death removes the living creatures from our view. It destroys the *sensible* proof which we had before their death of their being possessed of living powers, but does not appear to afford the least reason to believe that they are then, or by that event, deprived of them.

I have remarked that all the analogies in nature are against the supposition that the disappearance, through death, of the manifestation of the living powers possessed by our fellow-creatures infers the extinction of those powers, however intimate we may conceive the relation to be which

able work of Dr. Nelson on "The Cause and Cure of Infidelity;" a work, *major omni non solum vituperatione, sed etiam laude.* Now what does Dr. Post mean by the assertion that "those phenomena are too various, and too much associated with doubtful or occult causes, to authorize any sure inferences from them?" It looks very much like taking a step in the direction of Dr. Whately. But he adds that "they [the phenomena] of necessity cease when the organ of their manifestation—the body—perishes;" a statement intended, doubtless, to correct the misapprehensions of such persons as may think that "the phenomena" do *not* then cease. He adds likewise that "the battle between the soul and the terrible foe which has conquered its material companion, now withdraws into an awful mystery, where mortal vision cannot follow it." And yet he insists that death is simply a severance between soul and body! The soul, then, has its *battle* with death after the body perishes? What does Dr. Post mean by this? It is quite a step toward the Annihilation theory, to bring death into battle with the soul after the soul has left the body. He ought to know that the human mind never has associated any such idea with physical death, and that it is as false in the light of reason as of revelation. But if Dr. Post intended only a rhetorical display, (and this is the most rational way to explain the egregious trifling,) he should look at the sentiment as well as the figures of his rhetoric, and select a topic of less importance to the eternal interests of man. Let his Pegasus fly, but there is no necessity why it should in its course brush out the stars.

may subsist between soul and body. Take for instance a piece of silver, and immerse it in diluted nitric acid, and the affinity of the acid and the metal will cause them to unite, a brisk action will ensue, and in a short time the silver will be entirely dissolved, and yet the liquid will remain *as limpid as before.* What then has become of the solid piece of silver? Its hardness, luster, tenacity, specific gravity, in a word, all the characteristics which distinguished it as a metal are gone, its very form has vanished, and the hard, splendid, opaque, ponderous metal that we saw existing but a few moments before is apparently annihilated. Shall we conclude then that the metal is really destroyed, because its presence is no longer appreciable by our senses? We must so conclude on the principles of our adversaries. But stay; place a piece of copper in the solution, to which it has a stronger affinity than to silver, and the latter will be disengaged and fall to the bottom in brilliant metallic crystals, and the quantity thus deposited will correspond exactly with the weight of the metal dissolved, and the particles may be melted and the piece reproduced in its original form.

We can scarcely conceive a greater change than that which takes place on the decomposition of water, and the conversion of its tasteless and salubrious liquid particles into an inflammable, invisible, and noxious gas, and into a solid body combined with iron. No annihilation could appear to be more complete than that of the water in this process, to those who are ignorant of the nature of the phenomenon, and yet when that is known it affords one of the strongest proofs of the indestructibility of matter. The changes that occur on death are not greater, nor do they present a more decided appearance of annihilation than the decomposition of this fluid.

When we find too that the active and intimately connected subtile agents, light and heat, can be separated, and that the balance of evidence warrants the supposition that they are really distinct essences or forms of matter, all objections to the separate existence of the soul from the body, founded upon their intimate connection with each other, appear futile; for in the instance before us we perceive two subtile essences, of whose nature or of the minuteness of whose particles we can form no conception, united so intimately as to appear one and the same, and yet capable of being severed, and of having separate existences. The union between the sentient principle and the human frame, it must be borne in mind, is a union of two principles that are manifestly distinct; and whether or not we admit that the mind can exist without the body, we must allow that no two conceivable things can exhibit greater dissimilarity than gross substantial matter and the subtile essence, or incorruptible principle, which directs and controls it. In the case of light and heat, however, the two subtile essences possess so close a resemblance that it becomes doubtful whether they are identical or not, and yet those closely connected properties of matter may be separated, and exist, apparently at least, in separate and independent states; and numerous experiments might be adduced to show that heat is never annihilated, and that, when it is brought from a latent into an active state, it is again diffused by radiation and by conduction to other bodies.

But it were endless to specify all the analogies which suggest themselves in view of this point, and it is time to think of drawing this chapter to a close. There is one illustration, however, which may be adduced as a complete offset to the reiterated asseverations of the Annihilationists, that the destruction of the corporeal structure through which the mind or soul manifests itself must necessarily infer the extinction of the soul itself.

If, for instance, a ray of the sun's light be admitted through a small hole in the shutter of a darkened room, and be permitted to fall upon a piece of black cloth, which reflects none of the light, the room will appear to be in darkness, notwithstanding the ray of light from the sun passes directly through it. If however an orange, or other bright object, be placed in the ray, the reflection of the light from its surface will not only render the object distinctly visible, but will diffuse light to all parts of the room. Now in this case no more light actually enters the room when the reflecting substance is placed in the ray, but, owing to the peculiar conformation of the surface of that body, it is enabled to decompose the light, and to absorb all the colored rays but the one which gives to it its peculiar color, and that ray it reflects with inconceivable velocity in every direction. If the reflecting substance be destroyed the room will again become dark, for there will no longer be any object to reflect the ray. But are we to suppose, in accordance with the theory of our Annihilationists, that with the destruction of the reflecting substance the light it emitted is also destroyed? The presence of light is indeed no longer apparent, nor is the substance that reflected it capable of re-exerting the same power, but nevertheless the light exists with equal force, and possesses the same properties, though the form of the object that caused the previous sensation of light and color is destroyed. That object was only the medium through which the presence of light was manifested to the senses, but the light still exists and streams onward, unseen, indeed, but possessing the same energy as when rendered sensible to the visual organs by the agency of a body competent to reflect it. Now if we were ignorant of the source whence the light is derived, would not the supposition that the light and color are still existing unaltered and undiminished, and that the substance we had beheld was not the cause of the light, but was merely endued with properties capable of rendering them apparent, be deemed utterly incredible? Assuming, therefore, that we were ignorant whence the light originated under such circumstances, it would be equally difficult to imagine the continued presence of light and color in the midst of darkness, as it is, in our admitted ignorance of the principle of life, to conceive that it should continue to exist after the dissolution of the body; and skeptics might raise even more weighty arguments against the former hypothesis than any they are able to raise against the continued and conscious existence of the soul.*

### § 47. *Inferences from the foregoing.*

Thus, then, by the united testimony of tradition, the light and analogies of nature, and the word of God, we are led to the stupendously important conclusions:

1. That the life after death is an immediate continuation of the present life. The soul is not altered in death, but takes along with it its dispositions, its habits, and whole tendency, into the future world. The life to come, taken in connection with the present, make together one whole, even as manhood is only the continuance of youth.

2. That our state in the life to come is to be regarded as the *consequence* of the present, since the consequences of all our present dispositions, inclinations, and actions continue here. Death determines the destiny of men in the future world. It is here that man lays the foundation either for his future happiness or misery; this is the state of probation, that of retribution.† (See Luke xvi, 25; Heb. ix, 27; Rom. ii, 5–12; 2 Cor. iv, 7; v, 10; Gal. vi, 7, 10; 1 Tim. iv, 18, 19.)

* See the foregoing, and many other illustrations and analogies, in "Natural Evidence of a Future Life," by F. C. Bakewell. London, 1835. I have made many efforts to procure a copy of this work, but in vain, and my acquaintance with it is only through an able review in the Quarterly Christian Spectator for 1836.

† See Knapp, Theol., sect. 148. In stating the foregoing inferences I have adopted the language of this calm and philosophical, but devotedly pious theologian. Let those words be seriously pondered by every reader. And I may be permitted also to refer to the impressive remarks of J. D. Michaelis, in Theol. Dog., sect. 157, De Statu Piorum, etc. With all his propensity to trifle and play the fool, his great intellect could not approach the contemplation of this theme without being manifestly aroused to deep and earnest reflection. In my little work entitled "Rabbah Taken," chap. iv, sect. 5, I have illustrated at large the proposition that the soul of man preserves its vital power unharmed through the whole process of corporeal dissolution.

## § 48. *Conclusion.*

In our preceding allusions to the subject we have mentioned the received doctrine that the souls of the pious do not at death enter upon the enjoyment of the highest bliss of which they shall be capable after reunion with the body. (See, for example, sect. 33, sub-sect. 10, above.) But let no one infer from hence that there will be any absence of heavenly felicity. It is only their imperfect state (a state in which they are not possessed of their full being as men) which necessitates this arrangement. At the resurrection their public adoption, as the sons of God, and their joy and happiness, will be complete. Hence the children of God on earth, and those in their disembodied state, look steadily forward in expectation of that glorious consummation. And I allude to the subject again here, in order to present a few brief extracts from eminent moderns, and also the explanation given of the whole matter by the early Church, whose views are so grossly perverted by our opponents.

1. *Lord Verulam*, referring to the subject, says: "I believe that the souls of such as die in the Lord are blessed, and rest from their labors, and enjoy the sight of God, yet so as they are in expectation of a farther revelation of their glory in the last day, at which time all flesh of man shall arise and be changed, and shall appear and receive from Jesus Christ his eternal judgment."* The great *Cudworth*† says: "The complete salvation of man consisteth in the perfection and happiness both of soul and body; for though our salvation consists chiefly in the former, in the victory over sin, and in the renovation of the mind, yet without the latter, which is the victory over death, and the immortalizing of our bodies, it would be a lame and imperfect thing." *Leland*, too,‡ says: "Man is, in his original constitution, an embodied spirit. Though the rational soul is the noblest part of our nature, yet it is not the whole of it. Nor could

* Works, i, 339. London. 1838. † Vol. ii, p. 607.

‡ Necessity of Revelation, part iii, chap. ix, vol. ii, p. 404.

the whole man be properly said to be made perfect in bliss, if the body, which was from the beginning a constituent part of his frame, in which he lived and acted during his abode on earth, were left utterly to perish in the grave. Eternal life, therefore, as it signifies the happiness of our entire nature, takes in not merely the immortality of the soul, when separated from the body, but the resurrection of the body too, and the immortal existence of the whole man, body and soul united, in a state of felicity and perfection."*

2. The misrepresentations which our opponents make of the sentiments of Justin Martyr and others of the early fathers, (referred to by us on a former page,) to the effect that the primitive Church held that in the intermediate state the souls of the pious did not enjoy the presence of God, may be seen in their true light by the following passages, which we shall quote without remark. *Polycarp*† says: "Paul and the rest of the apostles are in their appointed place *with the Lord*," παρὰ τῷ κυρίῳ. *Irenæus*‡ says: "Our Saviour shall be seen, not in heaven only, but in Paradise, by those who are worthy (ἄξιοι) to behold his face." And in the *Quæst. et Respons.*, 75, it is said that the "souls of the righteous go to Paradise, and there hold intercourse with Christ by vision." See also 85, in which the author speaks particularly of those saints mentioned in Matt. xxvii, 52, 53.

3. Hence is apparent the reason why the apostles do not so frequently and emphatically, as we might otherwise suppose they would, refer to *death* as the motive to diligence and faithfulness, but rather to the appearing of our Redeemer in the clouds of heaven. See some of the allusions to it in the following passages, which a careful and serious reader will be pleased to have the facility for considering in connection with the whole theme: Matt. xvi, 27; xxv, 13; Luke xii, 35, 37; Acts iii, 19, 20; 1 Cor. iv, 5; Phil. iii, 20, 21; iv, 5; Col. iii, 4, 5; 1 Thess. i, 4–7; iii, 13; v, 4–6;

* See likewise the excellent observations of Witsius, Œcon. Foed., lib. iii, cap. xiv, sections 33–41.

† Epist., § 9.

‡ Lib. v, cap. 36.

2 Tim. iv, 1, 2; Tit. ii, 11–13; Heb. ix, 28; James v, 7, 8; 1 Tim. vi, 13, 14; 1 Pet. i, 6, 7; iv, 12, 13; v, 1–4; 1 John ii, 28; iii, 2, 3; Rev. xvi, 15; xxii, 7.

4. As a severance from the body, therefore, does not in any way interfere with the conscious existence of the soul, the great practical question of course is, What is its *destiny* in this its next stage of being? That it is not disciplinary, is evident from the fact that at the day of judgment all sinners are found to sustain unaltered the same character which they possessed on earth. Nearly two thousand years ago Jesus said: "Whosoever is ashamed of me in *this* adulterous and sinful generation, of him shall the Son of Man be ashamed *when he cometh* in his glory," etc. Mark viii, 38. And, speaking of Sodom and Gomorrah, which were destroyed nearly two thousand years before his time, he avers that they shall appear with their original characters unchanged at the judgment. (Matt. x, 14, 15; xi, 21–24.) Of course, then, the separate state of the soul is not a state of discipline. And as the soul cannot at death pass out of being, it must live, and in the nature of the case be happy or miserable.

5. In treating of its ultimate destiny, however, and in order to join issue with our opponents, we shall omit further reference to its separate state, and consider the question formally at issue between us. *Shall the sinner after the resurrection be blotted out of being, or continue to suffer forever in conscious misery the penalty of the law?* Preliminary, however, to this discussion, it is important to consider the subject of *punishment* itself, and this shall be the theme of our next chapter.

# CHAPTER III.

## PENALTY, PUNISHMENT, AND UTILITARIANISM.

### § 49. *On the term Punishment—Definition of Plato—The Utilitarian Theory.*

1. The terms *penalty* and *punishment* have been employed with great vagueness and latitude of meaning, and in our own times very important practical inferences are attempted to be drawn from certain usages of them, which are altogether unauthorized. For, as Cudworth remarks, there have not been wanting pretended philosophers in all ages, who have asserted that naturally and immutably there is nothing just and unjust, good and evil.

2. The two leading ideas in the world on the subject of punishment are in entire antagonism to each other. The one pertains to immutable and eternal justice, and the other to utility or expediency. The former necessarily includes the element of retribution, though it does not necessarily exclude the idea of prevention and reformation, as being contemplated in the exercise or administration of the ruling power or authority; but the latter must logically and necessarily exclude the element of retribution, and is confined to prevention and reformation alone. In other words, the one principle contemplates *directly and mainly* the Creator, the other the fallen and depraved creature.

3. Previous to the time of that wonderful genius Plato, the world seems never to have entertained a doubt that punishment could be other than simply and strictly retributory in its primary sense and intention, or that anything else, (like prevention of crime, reformation of the criminal,

etc.,) which might become associated therewith, could be other than incidental and secondary. Though the illustration of the consequences of crime, which might be furnished by any given example of penal infliction, could be appealed to, and such references might be salutary in their effects, and operate to prevent the recurrence of transgression either in the individual himself or in others, yet the idea of inflicting punishment solely for this purpose was, unless I grievously mistake, unknown until the time of Plato,* who advanced, in relation to the matter, that utilitarian principle which underlies so much of the theology, morality, ethics, and philanthropic enterprise of the present day, and is, in fact, applied more or less to the settlement of every question in morals, jurisprudence, and in almost everything wherein the rights and conduct of men are concerned. Nor are even the teachings and proceedings of the eternal Jehovah exempted from this audacious application. Justice, for instance, is recognized as justice, only so far as its utility is discoverable, and right and principle are tested by the same alembic. And though a far-sighted heathen jurist (Cicero, De Leg. 1) had said, *Lex est ratio summa, insita in natura, quæ jubet ea quæ facienda sunt, prohibetque contraria*, Christian jurists and divines may be found, in no small number, who scruple not to resolve even virtue itself into utility or expediency.

4. The sentiment of Plato, to which we refer, and which is of frequent occurrence in his works, is that *no one should be punished because he has sinned, but lest he should sin,*

* By one of those unaccountable but ludicrous leave-takings of actually possessed and well-digested knowledge which sometimes, to the perplexity of mental philosophers, occur with the truly learned, (as when the celebrated advocate Erskine, in a most animated oration, eulogized Julian the apostate, as having been so zealous in favor of Christianity, as to have deservedly obtained the soubriquet of Julian *the apostle.*) Dr. Tayler Lewis, than whom few men are better acquainted with Plato, has, in the Biblical Repository for Jan. 1847, pp. 77, 82, assigned to this Platonic doctrine, and even to Plato's aphoristic utterance of it, *a much later date.* It occurs in one of Dr. Lewis's essays on "Human Justice," which will richly reward a thorough perusal.

*since we are not able to recall the past, but may prevent the future;* (or as the famous English judge expressed it to the horse-thief, "You are not punished for stealing horses, but in order that horses might not be stolen!") See the Protagoras of Plato, §§ 39, 118, 122, and also the 9th and 11th books of his Laws. *Seneca* translates and highly applauds the passage; (De Ira., lib. i, cap. xvi; ii, xxxi; and also in his De Clementia, i, xxii;) while *A. Gellius*, in his Noctes Atticæ, lib. vi, cap. xiv, has undertaken to set it off by a magnificent paraphrase. But the manner in which the early Christians regarded the sentiment may be learned from Augustine, De Doct. Christiana, lib. iii, cap. xiv.

5. I do not propose here however to enter the lists with Plato, (seeing he has already fared *so hardly* in the hands of the Annihilationists,) further than to protest against this principle utterly, and against every application of it. Whatever be his real meaning on the subject, (for he certainly is far from being consistent in his applications of the principle,) that must be a most shallow understanding which can fail to perceive that utility and expediency, in their true sense, require that retribution, or the punishment of crime for its own intrinsic demerit, must enter into the administration of law or justice.* Divest punishment of the retrospective moral element, and make it merely prospective, and what hold can it have upon the conscience of the criminal, or of others? Wherein can consist its true moral, warning, restraining, and reforming power? Expediency and utility may therefore, and properly enough, be consulted or considered in any actual relation they may have to a specific case, but never can they, in any sense, become the primary principle or rule of moral action, without throwing helplessly out at sea the whole superstructure as well as the foundations of all virtue and moral principle.

6. The utilitarian principle has been introduced by our opponents into the discussion relating to the punishment of sin under the Divine administration, and they have made it

* See this illustrated in the above mentioned Essay of Dr. Lewis.

to apply so as practically to neutralize and even to set aside the strongest declarations of God in his word, on the subject. Instead of inquiring, and endeavoring to ascertain what is right according to the express statements of Jehovah, the question is made to turn upon what is best in *our* view of the matter, and what is most in accordance with the character of a God of goodness and compassion; or, in other words, what *ought* the eternal Jehovah to do in the case in order that his character may not suffer in man's estimation? for it all comes to this. See the discussion as conducted by the whole mass of Socinians, Pelagians, Rationalists, Restorationists, Modern Universalists, and Annihilationists, (names which we use not invidiously, but only for distinguishing.) They seem to have adopted from Horace (sat. 1, 3, 98) the maxim, *Atque ipsa utilitas, justi propé mater et æqui.* And on this principle, moreover, questions intimately connected with the satisfaction of Christ, human ability and obligation, future punishment of sin, etc., are to be mainly adjusted and settled even by reputedly evangelical divines.

## § 50. *The true Sense of the Terms Penalty and Punishment.*

1. Some of the old philosophers spoke of three kinds of punishment, (indicated by as many distinct terms,) which appeared to them to comprehend every idea really embraced in the subject. They were, 1. Νουθεσίαν, (likewise designated as παραίνεσις,) consisting only in words, and to be employed where there is hope of amendment with respect to the offender. This we name *reprehension* or reproof. 2. Τιμωρία, (from τιμωρέω, *to aid, to avenge,*) which expressed the idea of penalty inflicted as a vindication of authority, or to support official dignity. The term and its usage clearly express the idea of *vengeance, vindication against the transgressor;* and hence the old phrase, *house of correction,* to designate what, in more modern parlance, we ridiculously express by the term *penitentiary,* (*pœnitentia-*

*rius,*) which originally had the twofold import, (1.) of a priest who imposes penance on an offender; and (2.) a place for hearing confessions. 3. Παράδειγμα, *an example,* a term by which they designate punishment when inflicted mainly with a view to its salutary effect.

2. *Pœna* (Fr. *peine*, Ger. *straffe*, Eng. *penalty* or *punishment*) is a Greek term, ποινή, (Doric, ποινά,) and comes from ποινάω, *to avenge*, *to obtain compensation for an injury*, whence ποινή (*pretium*) is a *price* with the Greeks, because murderers were delivered to death by their relatives and neighbors lest the guilt of the murder should be laid to their charge. (Comp. Deut. xxi, 1–9; Ezek. xxiv, 7, 8.) So Mausachus teaches out of Hesychius; and in the Laconics of Pausanius, ποινή is defined to be ἁμαρτήματος ἐκδίκησις, *the revenging of sin*, (without any reference to that *Platonic* definition, attributed however to Speusippus, "*a curing of the soul for an error committed;*") or as the Roman jurists say, *noxæ vindicta*, or *delictorum correctio.*

3. Punishment, then, in its true idea, and in all the proprieties of speech, is *suffering judicially inflicted as a satisfaction to justice;* a point which the reader may find further illustrated in Grotius, De Satisfactione, cap. iv, or in Howe's "Living Temple," part ii, chap. v, § 6.

4. Paul, the jurist, undertook to maintain in part the Platonic notion of punishment, *pœnæ constituantur in hominum emendationem.* But Grotius (in his De Jure Belli ac Pacis, lib. ii, cap. xxi, § 12) has thoroughly refuted the assumption;* and in fact it needs no words to show that this notion effectually resolves all virtue into mere expediency, and justifies doing evil that good may come. Instead of saying that a thing is right because it tends to utility, the true idea is, that it tends to utility because it is right.

5. Grotius not only directly opposes the Platonic figment, (De Jure, etc., ii, 20, 4, and as above,) but gives (in cap. xx, § 1) the following antagonistic definition of punishment: *Est pœna generali significatu malum passionis quod infli-*

* See also his reference to Carneades in the Prolegomena.

*gitur ob malum actionis:* "punishment, in the general sense of the word, is the evil of suffering which is inflicted on account of the evil of an action." In his De Jure Naturali et Gentium, lib. viii, cap. iii, § 4, Puffendorf fully sustains this: "Punishment in general may be thus defined: an evil of suffering inflicted for an evil doing, or some uneasy evil inflicted by authority in a compulsory way, upon view of antecedent transgression." Blackstone (iv, 7) sustains the same idea; and if we turn to the theologians we find Turretin, Owen, Ridgley, and in earlier times Augustine, and others without number, expressing the idea in substantially the same words.*

## § 51. *The Principles of Truth and Justice are immutable and eternal.*

1. The relation of the foregoing to the theme under discussion is sufficiently obvious; for the connection between the utilitarian theory and the future punishment of sin appears, as already remarked, in all the writings of our opponents. In fact it furnishes the whole staple of their argument, and renders imperative the necessity for examining it in this connection, though to attempt to do this fully, and in the whole range of the subject, and in its various relations to morals, jurisprudence, philanthropy, etc., would at once double the size of our volume. On no topic in the whole argument do

* It is sometimes edifying to see how heedlessness will undertake to confound the plainest matters of fact. The Rev. Mr. Barnes, for example, in his Defense, p. 283, asserts that Grotius, in his De Jure, uses the terms guilt and punishment in their obvious and proper sense; "*but when he had a controversy with Socinus, and a theory to defend, he labored to prove that the words were employed without reference to personal ill desert.*" Now, 1. Grotius never had a controversy with Socinus, who died in 1604, while the De Satisfactione was not written till 1616. 2. When Grotius wrote this work he had no theory to defend, unless a desire to defend the common faith of Christians could be so named. 3. He wrote his De Jure in 1625. 4. When he wrote this work he was committed to a specific theological theory, as may be seen by his correspondence with Crellius in 1631, so that the real facts of the case are *the very reverse* of the forementioned allegation. Such an attempt to neutralize the force of the above statements of this great jurist deserves to be reprehended severely.

we feel more severely the restraint which necessity has imposed upon us to be brief, and we have no alternative therefore but to abandon the higher and more philosophical form of discussion, and to consider the subject in those bearings mainly wherein our opponents have undertaken to associate it with the grand themes of eschatology; for nothing is more common in their writings than the assertion that eternal punishment is of no conceivable utility, and the broad inference from thence, that consequently there can be no such thing; that the existence of the wicked in misery through eternity is contrary to all our conceptions of God's goodness and compassion, and can answer no good end conceivable by us; and that if we are not willing to believe they are to be restored to his favor and to holiness, we are compelled to believe that they will be annihilated.

2. Thus at the very outset, laying aside all idea of the just demerit of sin as settled by the averments of Jehovah, they assume that utility (in their conception of it) is to be the measure of our faith; that is, (for it is folly to pretend to evade the logical sequence,) that we are not to believe anything to be true, just, good, right, or proper, unless so far as we can see it to be useful. Now as the human idea of utility is variable, often contradictory, and at best but relative, and confessedly has no ultimate standard, either for reference or appeal, it is the sheerest folly imaginable to attempt to settle on this principle any question, either in ethics, jurisprudence, theology, or even the simplest questions in natural history. Is it true that there are no such things as poisonous plants, noisome insects and reptiles, because we cannot see or understand the utility of such things? And would it be wisdom or insanity to assume the position of refusing to believe in their existence until we should be able to understand how they are useful? And are we, on the same ground, to ignore (as Universalists do) the existence of the devil, and of all fallen spirits, and finally of all moral evil, and conclude to deny that evil is evil? This notion has led many to

these lengths, and even farther, and by a fair and logical application of the principle. But the Annihilationists have hardly proceeded so far; they profess to have found a stopping place, (where all is vacancy,) and they admit that such things do really exist, but claim that they may be useful in ways unknown as yet to us or even to finite capacity. Exactly so, my good friends. And now please inform us what should hinder other things, yes, even the eternal misery of the damned, from being useful to the government of God in ways unknown to us? Your assertion is that it *cannot* be, and on this assumption you infer that it *will not* be. We meet you on your own ground, and ask you *why* it may not be? The question is every way fair and proper. It is but a request that you furnish the reasons why you ask our assent to such a statement; and to attempt to ignore or to evade it, or to treat it with levity, or as unworthy of notice, must evince, either that you have impertinently made such an assertion on this transcendently important theme, with no reason to sustain you, or that something aside from love for the truth is prompting your efforts.

3. There are innumerable admitted facts and truths, the reasons for which lie clearly beyond the range of our faculties in this stage of our being. And hence, let theologasters say what they please, we are required both by common sense and the Bible, and often by human testimony, to believe that things are true without being able to explain how they are true. And in relation to the fact of their existence, all we can do is to give the reasons for our faith. For over the *rationale* itself, the God of nature has thrown an impenetrable vail; and any attempt to explain the why and the wherefore in relation to their existence, is at once felt to be a departure from the known to the unknown, and involves all our speculations in confusion and uncertainty. The whole principle, therefore, upon which the aforesaid application of the utilitarian idea is based, must, in the very necessity of the case, (and it seems impossible to avoid seeing it,) un-

settle the basis of all actual knowledge, as well as of ethics, jurisprudence, etc., as Plato might have seen had he despised Aristotle's syllogism less. That he had no sympathy, however, with those notions of right and wrong, just and unjust, etc., which are at present so rife among utilitarians, is obvious from many portions of his writings; for in the *Minos* (which some "Amber Witch" critics in Germany and England deny to be his) he asserts that νόμος, *law*, is not δόγμα πόλεως, *a decree of state*, since there are unjust decrees, but that which is in its own nature absolutely and immutably just.* And in his tenth book on laws, cap. iv, he condemns those who maintain that nothing is naturally just, but is made so by human laws and conventionalities.

4. That there is an infinite, immutable, eternal mind, the intelligent first cause and source of all things, atheists alone will deny. And that the principles of his administration are based in eternal rectitude, will be freely conceded on both sides in this discussion. And hence it is, if strictly considered, all nonsense to talk, as many do, of the mere will of God being the standard of right and wrong; for either he can or may will things contrary to his nature, or he cannot. To maintain that he can, is to deny the immutability of his nature, and consequently his eternity; and if he cannot will what is opposed to his nature, then to pretend to make the aforesaid practical distinction between his will and nature is folly. The nature of God, therefore, furnishes the foundation for an immutable distinction between the right and the wrong, the just and the unjust, and this too without respect to any such things as expediency or utility, in the low sense now attached to those terms. His justice and righteousness in no way can depend upon such things; nor is his administration of government over his fallen creatures regulated in any way by their selfish conceptions of utility and expediency.

* See Cudworth's Tract on "Immutable Morality." The speculations of no man now on this subject are worthy of attention who pretends to discuss it without having thoroughly mastered the reasoning of that treatise.

5. Then, further, that there is such a thing recognized and known among men as certain, immutable, and eternal truth cannot be questioned. (See Locke, book iv, chap. xi, § 14.) I am not speaking of the distinction which philosophers pretend to make between what they call the different kinds of truth, but simply of the idea, and of men's recognition of that idea. If such distinctions must be made, and pompously discussed, they should be correctly made, for it is, in true philosophical speech, as inaccurate to "jumble together," in relation to this matter, man's moral and intellectual nature, as it is to "jumble together" mathematical and moral truths. And I affirm, without fear of contradiction by any sensible mind, that the moral nature of man is as fully adapted to certainty of actual knowledge in relation to moral truth, as his intellectual is in regard to mathematical.* But passing this, for it cannot be here dwelt upon, I prove that man has not only a conception but an actual knowledge of immutable and eternal truth, by a reference to geometrical theorems. For instance, that the three angles of any triangle are equal to two right angles is, and ever has been, and ever will be, true in this world and in every world. Nor can we conceive that an act of the Divine will can change it, without at the same time affecting also a corresponding change in nature itself, and in man's rational powers. And to assume the contrary, and that God may have created our faculties so that we shall clearly perceive and understand that to be true which is not true; or, in other words, to understand that which it is impossible to understand, is not only a contradiction and absurdity, but the consequence is, there can be no certainty of anything, since if things that are contradictory to each other may be likewise true, it is impossible to make an affirmation or denial respecting anything whatever. There is no doubt that the human faculties may become more or

* The obscuring influence resulting from his alienation from God, has more deeply affected his moral than his intellectual nature, and hence the apparent difference in perceptive power. But see what Locke says, Essay, book iv, chap. iii, § 18.

less disordered and obscured, but it is impossible that they should ever be made clearly to apprehend and know the true to be false and the false to be true.

6. And then, further, that from the earliest times mankind had a similar and universal conception of the eternal nature and immutability of moral truth (however they may have mistaken in regard to the thing itself) can be easily demonstrated. Let a single illustration suffice. All the early Pagan legislators found themselves under the necessity of respecting this impression of the people, and to favor it by assuming the divine origin of their laws. Zoroaster declared that the laws which he gave the Persians were obtained from Oromazes, Hermes (the Egyptian) ascribed his to Mercury, Minos to Jupiter, Draco to Minerva, Lycurgus to Apollo, Numa to Egeria, etc. So firm and universal was the conviction of antiquity, from the earliest ages even to the time of Plato, (who pretended that the laws which he gave to the Magnesians and Sicilians were obtained from Apollo and Jupiter,) that there was an eternal distinction between right and wrong, justice and injustice. And these things were so far from being dependent upon mere human enactment, that had those lawgivers pretended that the laws they promulged were derived from the nature of things, or from mere principles of utility and expediency, they would have brought themselves and their codes into contempt and disregard. The conviction impressed upon the whole human mind (and never to any serious extent impaired till Protagoras and his fellows perplexed it by their wild theories) was, that the principles of right and justice are divine and immutable, and could in this world of perplexity and confusion be derived from God alone.

7. It would be an interesting inquiry, how this idea that there is something naturally and immutably true and just, and that things are what they are, not by arbitrary will or institution, (*θέσει*,) but by nature, (*φύσει*,) should have been from the earliest ages so universal, on the supposition that the utilitarian theory of our opponents can be true?

Whence could this conviction of the immutability of the distinction between good and evil, right and wrong, have originated in a world of selfish creatures, who are proverbially prone to regard expediency and utility, rather than the immutable principles of justice and morality, in all their pursuits and avocations? Whence could the opposite conviction have originated, unless from the eternal and immutable Jehovah himself? and how, in such circumstances as the aforesaid, could it have been entertained, unless from a thorough and inherent conviction of its truth? There can be no other explanation of the fact. Nor do we find that legal enactments and commands ever run in this form—that any specific thing *shall become* just or unjust; but they simply require obedience, and announce the penalty for disobedience. So far is it from the truth that moral right and wrong are, or ever can be, constituted by mere will or arbitrary command.

8. Such being the fact, it follows, not that things are right merely because God wills and so appoints them, but that he wills and appoints them because they are right, and because they are the utterances of his own immutable and eternal nature. Still, if any one insists that the will of God is the standard of right and wrong, I should not dispute with him, if he mean, as many who employ such language do mean, that God's revealed will is the only true standard by which *we* are to know fully and clearly what is right and wrong. Or if it should be insisted that, as God cannot will anything contrary to his nature, which is eternally and immutably just and righteous, therefore the expression of his will shows what his nature is, and is in this sense a proper standard of right and wrong, no serious objection could be made to it; but the doctrine held by some of the schoolmen, that no act is morally evil except as it is forbidden by God, and that there is none which cannot be made morally good should God command it to be done, is not to be entertained by any intelligent Christian in this day. It is utterly repulsive to the feelings of any community where the Bible is

received as the word of God. Who can suppose that if God were to will (were such a thing conceivable) that twice two make seven, or that the three angles of a triangle are equal to the four angles of a parallelogram, the thing would necessarily be so, and that we should see it to be so? And if such a thing is impossible to be imagined in relation to material forms, can it be conceived in relation to moral truth, that should God will right to be wrong, and wrong to be right, the nature of things would be immediately changed, and along therewith his own eternal nature? Such a supposition would at once blot out all science and truth, and actual knowledge, for in such circumstances nothing could be either true or false; and therefore moral truth and justice depend not on the will of God, but upon his own eternal, immutable nature, and the nature of things. And this being so, it is obvious that all those speculations which assume that God, by a mere act of his will, can or may reverse the utterances of his law, (which is but the expression of his nature,) are in a high degree absurd and ridiculous.

### § 52. *Utilitarian Theory of Punishment and Legal Administration.*

1. And now, as respects the aforesaid Platonic idea of punishment, (though Plato obviously refers to human legislation alone,) and the utilitarian idea of legal administration, where, on such principles, shall be located or established the assurance of public safety for any member of the body politic? When, for instance, parents or masters, on leaving home for a season, have called up their children or servants, and administered to each a sound flagellation to insure good behavior during the interval, it has not been generally thought to evince the most refined and perfect imaginable type of moral administration. But certainly the idea is strictly utilitarian, and might, if those principles are true, be of advantage if generally adopted; for as, according to this idea, the design of punishment is not to recall the past but to prevent the future, surely a sound flagellation, under the

aforesaid circumstances, was but a fair practical development of the theory.

2. But since, on this theory, there neither is nor really can be any guilt or demerit attached to criminality, none at least deserving of retribution, why should the criminal be selected to exemplify, through inconvenience and suffering, the results of misdemeanor? Admit that the perpetration of crime may be *supposed* to indicate the proper subject to be selected for such a purpose, why should that supposition be heeded? and why may there not be, if utility is the object to be secured, some other principle of selection adopted than simply the vulgar one that he has "stolen the horse?" The fact that he has perpetrated the crime does not prove that his sufferings will be the most useful to the state, unless on the old "*exploded notion*" that crime for its own sake deserves retribution; an idea which plainly could not be adopted without at once surrendering the renowned maxim aforesaid, that the thief is punished, not for stealing the horse, but that horses may not be stolen. The difficulty of establishing an obvious connection between the crime and some other person who had no hand in it, could be easily obviated by some enactment like that of the old Dutch alderman in Southwark, Philadelphia, who made it a point to mulct the constable in the costs whenever he ventured to bring into his august presence an offender who could not pay them. This had the high advantage of securing the administration of the law from pecuniary loss, and also of making the constable peculiarly careful whom he ventured to apprehend. Or why not adopt it as a principle that when any useful, active citizen commits a trespass, some useless old "fogy" should be immediately apprehended, or some lazy, worthless vagabond, and by "making him smart for it," evince the consequences of committing offences against the state? In such a case the useful, active citizen would be still spared to labor on in his avocations, and all useless fellows, and mere encumbrances of the body politic, would in time be got rid of entirely. Or, still

further: why not adopt the principle, that when the laws are violated the wealthiest man in the community shall be taken and punished, and his wealth be either cast into the state treasury, or distributed among the poorer classes? Would not this be a much more useful appropriation of it than to have it lying unemployed in his coffers? Such an enactment must, moreover, have a strong tendency to make the rich doubly watchful that the laws be not infringed, for frequently they are known to be rather indifferent about such matters. At any rate, if these principles for selection be not adopted, why may not some others be fixed upon, instead of the merely arbitrary one which associates the offender with suffering merely because of his connection with the offense, seeing that the offense itself cannot possibly have any moral desert attached to it? For I do affirm that, on the utilitarian principle that "moral guilt is in no sense the ground of punishment," such things might be perfectly proper; for on this principle there is no more propriety nor justice in punishing the criminal than in punishing any one else whom a legal enactment may designate for the purpose. Dr. Cheever, in his work on Capital Punishment, has truly said, "If utility is the sole ground of punishment, then there may be cases in which it might be useful to punish the innocent as well as the guilty."*

3. But then again, what, according to this principle, are

* In fact this may be easily demonstrated; for it is conceded that the sinner may be properly punished, or made to suffer, for his own good, since it may restrain him from future sin. And for the same reason, as is obvious, and as utilitarians themselves concede, he may be thus made to suffer for the good of others, as it may restrain them from sin. But what is the *moral basis* of such a procedure? for it must have one. Is the good of the sinner himself and of others a sufficient reason *of itself* to inflict suffering? If so, then any one, and of course the innocent, may be thus afflicted or punished at any time. If they may *not be*, then the aforesaid reason *is not sufficient* to justify punishment; and of course guilt deserves, on its own account, punishment, irrespective of any such considerations whatever. Hence the utilitarian theory is utterly false, or the innocent may be made to suffer whenever and as often as it should be decided that such suffering may be useful either to themselves or others.

these so-called "consequences of crime," which are to be evidenced by the sufferings of somebody? What consequences result from crime, which suffering can illustrate, according to this principle? The offender is simply "*unfortunate;*" and how can his suffering or that of some other person show that men ought not to be *unfortunate?* These consequences cannot be shown through his sufferings on the ground that they are retributory for ill-desert, for this at once destroys the whole utilitarian theory. To punish a man for being "unfortunate" is not only idle but wicked. Suppose the law had required that Mr. Collins should be fined or hanged because his most estimable lady perished on board the Arctic? Would such an enactment have any tendency to prevent shipwrecks? Would it commend itself to our moral nature? What then, I demand, are these so-much-talked-of "consequences of crime," in the utilitarian sense of the word, which are developed by the sufferings and inconveniences of the *unfortunate?* There is no room for remorse, according to the principle, for a man cannot feel remorse on account of an unavoidable calamity. But it is needless to press the matter. On this theory repentance, and consequently reformation, becomes an impossibility, for the very idea of such a thing is sheer absurdity, when severed, as it is in this case, from the impression and conviction of ill-desert.

4. It is obvious therefore, upon every view of the matter, that the law is compelled to admit an idea back of and higher than any asserted utility, and from which the utility itself depends for support. To punish the innocent, as our utilitarians admit, would not be useful. Why? Simply because it would not deter from crime and could have no reformatory effect, for the reason that it would be recognized by man's moral nature universally as unjust. And the utilitarian himself says it would be unjust. Of course, then, the existence of a principle of immutable justice is thus recognized in the very effort to explode that idea by carrying out the utilitarian theory.

### § 53. *Punishment in its true sense is retributory.*

1. Upon the whole, then, it must be admitted that no man or set of men can have a right to call justice expediency, or benevolence justice, and *vice versa*. It must be admitted that intrinsic demerit, aside from inconvenience, does enter into the one unchanging idea of crime; that retribution, or the suffering for such intrinsic demerit, does enter into the one idea of punishment, so that whatever government, divine or human, employs it at all must either employ it with this inseparable idea, or substitute something radically different in its place. It is a fact that in all languages, invariably, the terms corresponding to our word punishment are formed upon the idea of suffering for the intrinsic demerit of crime, and that in none of them do the utilitarian ideas, as constituting the sole or highest ground of punishment, human or divine, have place.* *Right*, as Cudworth has fully demonstrated, (though Horne Tooke, in his shallow method of reasoning from language, has asserted the contrary,) *right* never came from a word signifying that which is ordered or commanded. For what code of laws ever attempted to enact that a specific thing shall or shall not become right or wrong.

2. Blackstone, (iv, 11, 252,) speaking of the end or final cause of punishments in human legislation, says that it "is not by way of atonement or expiation for the crime committed, for that must be left to the just determination of the supreme Being, but as a precaution against future offenses of the same kind." This, which the utilitarians seem unable rightly to understand, admits both the intrinsic demerit of the criminal and that punishment is retributory. But he does not assume that law is in its true and high sense (as

* I have here employed terms used in his essay aforesaid, by Dr. Lewis, who in that and a succeeding one (Repository for April, 1847) has made good the position, beyond the reach of anything hitherto advanced to the contrary.

utilitarians do) the creature of human legislation or enactment. The sole object of human legislators in declaring it, may be not so much retribution as prevention, and this may be mainly their object in executing it. But to pretend, as these utilitarians do, that because legislators have the right to declare and execute the conceded utterances of immutable and eternal law, they therefore have the right to substitute other principles in their stead, to ignore all moral distinctions, and to enact that good shall become evil, and evil good; or, which is the same thing, that utility shall be the measure of right and wrong, is to claim what men in their senses never will accord. For though a lower or a higher utility may enter into the idea of punishment when contemplated by human legislators, in declaring and administering law, yet to pretend that it is consequently the basis of the law itself is absurd, since the law itself, or the immutable moral distinction between right and wrong, exists, and, as demonstrated above, must exist, aside from the motives of all human legislation whatever.

3. The effort so often made to represent this view as being pharisaic, and as justifying revenge and vindictiveness, being based upon an ignorant misapprehension of the terms, is unworthy of notice; for the argument does not assume, either directly or by implication, that man in him self, and irrespective of divine sanction, has the least ground to punish at all. And let me in conclusion say, in reference to a subject perpetually on the lips of modern utilitarians and would-be reformers, that the true method of raising the fallen, and of recovering him from the degradation into which crime has brought him, is not by seeking to palliate or deny his guilt, but to lead him, by a correct view of that guilt, to feel, abhor, repent of, and forsake it. Such is the course ever pursued by the Father of our spirits in bringing back the sinner, through repentance, to salvation and to himself.

4. It must be conceded, therefore, that there is no way to avoid the inference that, in its strict and proper sense, *punishment is suffering judicially inflicted for ill-desert*, and that

its essential element is retribution, an idea irreconcilable with the theologastrian notion that it is merely *a preventive and reformatory discipline.* Such too is the representation of the whole word of God on the subject, and hence *desert* is everywhere therein declared to be the first ground of punishment. There are degrees of punishment, to be sure, and in its milder forms the infliction in this, our Mediator's world, is not designed to be destructive, for here justice is tempered with mercy. Still it is, in any and in every case wherein even this may be pleaded, disciplinary and reformatory only because it is retributory. It is the infliction of suffering for ill desert, and for nothing else, and hence may effect a reform, and a determination to avoid incurring such ill-desert in future. But to pretend that it is not retributory because it may have or does have this effect, is absurd in a high degree.

### § 54. *Application of the foregoing Principles to the Argument.*

I regret that the course pursued by our adversaries has rendered it necessary to occupy so much space with the foregoing discussion; but without referring to the matter thus fully, the whole of our remaining argument would be subject to idle cavils and senseless objections which would continue to have weight with some; we shall now, therefore, return to the discussion in its more direct relation to the Holy Scriptures and theological science.

1. With respect to the power or authority to punish crime, a single word, in addition to what has been already said, will be sufficient to place the subject in its proper light. Private persons in their individual capacity, and not otherwise authorized, are not permitted to avenge themselves upon the offender. Hence, says God, "Avenge not yourselves. Vengeance is mine, I will repay." Rom. xii, 19. The administration of his own law is either directly by Providence, or instrumentally by authorized human legislation. (Gen. ix,

5, 6; Prov. viii, 15, 16; Rom. xiii, 1–7.) The same is true also of a state, in itself considered, or of any number of individuals whatever. The right to punish crime, because it deserves to be punished, is from God our Creator alone.

2. The word of God everywhere regards the sinner not as unfortunate, but wicked. What then properly constitutes wickedness? On this point the statutes of enlightened Christian nations agree with the Divine code. And hence the old law maxims: *Actus non facit reum nisi mens sit rea: Actus me invito factus, non est meus actus.* "The essence of an offense," says Bishop, (Crim. Law, b. iii, chap. ix, section 227,) "is the wrongful intent, without which it cannot exist." And the Bible gives no other reason for punishing crime save that the criminals are wicked.

3. It will hardly be questioned that the man who voluntarily transgresses deserves to suffer all the natural evil which he effects by his sin, or which his sin tends to produce. I speak simply of personal desert. Nor can it be questioned that a man may incur more guilt, and of course deserve more punishment, than he really has capacity to atone for or endure. Suppose, for illustration, that he murders in cold blood thousands of persons, as Sylla murdered the six thousand in the Roman circus? his real desert would of course be death for every murdered victim; for to say that he deserved no more punishment for murdering thousands than for murdering one, would be plainly absurd. Now he deserves death for the murder of any one of the supposed six thousand, and of course by murdering the whole he deserves to suffer death six thousand times. But being incapable of suffering it more than once, it is plain that he may deserve a punishment immeasurably greater than he has capacity to endure. Compare also Matt. xviii, 23–35.

4. It is of course necessary that the laws of God have penalties annexed to them. A law without a penalty is merely advice, and it is absurd to name it law. And it is equally absurd to suppose that God in his eternal and infinite wisdom annexed penalties without designing to inflict them,

or threatened their infliction without any serious intention of executing his threatenings. A supposition like this must necessarily divest him of all the moral attributes of divinity. Or should it be supposed that, after he had announced the penalty, he, on further reflection, concluded not to inflict it, though he at first fully intended to do so, this would divest him at once of all the natural attributes necessary to Godhead.* All such conceptions of God necessarily revolt the feelings of every refined and well-balanced mind. It is admitted that the threatened penalty should not be more nor less than the crime deserves. But this must be left solely with God, whose word announces the truth on the subject. This is conceded by all who believe the Bible.

5. Our opponents in their vague dissertations on the subject, confound the object of the threatening with what they are pleased to call *the object of the law itself.* Now the law is eternal, and is based in the nature of things, and in the very nature of God himself; and the original object of proclaiming it was that all rational creatures may abide in a state of conformity to his moral character. The object of the threatening is to announce the penalty of departing therefrom. The object of this, therefore, is to deter, by evincing how great an evil transgression is, what is the desert of sin and rebellion against the law, as well as to make known how infinite is God's abhorrence of all moral evil. Such being the fact, therefore, we may expect to learn through these announcements the true nature of sin, its just demerits and its certain consequences, as settled upon the eternal and immutable principles of justice, wisdom, and goodness. Those announcements, however they may appear to our depraved, selfish creature conceptions, can really contain nothing contrary to the justice, goodness, and wisdom of God; and therefore it is obviously preposterous to array against his plain utterances on the subject any of our

* It is not necessary here to refute that wretched Socinian notion that God may possess the attribute of foreknowledge and not choose to exercise it.

own conceptions (for they at best are but the conceptions of sinful, selfish creatures) which may be in conflict therewith. He alone is competent to know and to declare what is really true on the subject; and whatever he has declared is, and must obviously be, perfectly consistent with justice, wisdom, and goodness, whether we are able to perceive it so or not. Nor is our failure to see it to be so, or to reconcile it with our ideas of the fitness of things, any argument that it is not so, since God does not require that we should see or perceive it to be so, but simply that we believe his declaration on the subject. He requires of us no blind, unintelligent faith, for it is not a blind, unintelligent faith to believe what eternal justice, truth, and goodness declare to be true. Hence the only question to be settled in the matter by those who receive his testimony is, *What has he said in relation to it?* It is not, (as some of our opponents seem to think,) What *ought* he to have said? or, Is what he has said consistent with our notions of justice or with our feelings? God has nowhere required that in this stage of our being it should be, and it is therefore very impertinent so to introduce such matters into the discussion as to constitute them the reasons of our faith, irrespective of what God has actually said. And it is equally preposterous to conclude that because we cannot see how a declaration of God can be true, we must therefore attach some other meaning to the words containing it; for instance: to say that because we cannot see how eternal suffering is consistent with goodness, therefore God never intended to say that the wicked shall be thus punished, but must have meant something else.

6. It is likewise obvious that in all moral administration the penalty of the law must be as much regarded as the precept. The penalty is of course essential to the law, in order to its support and enforcement, and the maintenance of its authority. This will be conceded as true. And therefore it is just as conceivable that God should dispense with the precept of the law as with its penalty. The precept requires

that we love him supremely, and our neighbor as ourselves. God cannot uphold his moral government and require of rational creatures less than this, and he does not require more. Now it is obvious that to neglect to enforce the penalty when incurred, is equivalent to the abrogation of the precept, (which ceases thereon to be preceptive, and becomes only advisory,) which is equivalent to an abandonment of the throne of the universe. Hence, whenever the penalty is incurred it must be executed in its true sense, as we shall have occasion to show more fully in the sequel.

7. It is, moreover, obvious that whatever forgiveness consists in, and however and whenever it is exercised, it cannot in any sense consist in the abrogation of the law. This cannot be supposed without gross absurdity, for it would be equivalent to saying that God may require less of some of his rational creatures than that they should love him with all the heart, and their fellow-creatures as themselves, which would be the same as to maintain that he may be indifferent as to whether his requirements are regarded or not; for to suppose any case of such forgiveness exercised, the persons forgiven will be required afterward either to obey or not. If they are not required to obey, then, of course, as above stated, God is indifferent in respect to their moral character and conduct; but if they are required to obey, and again offend, then we must suppose that forgiveness is again extended, and so on indefinitely; or that the penalty shall overtake them at last. If forgiveness is extended indefinitely, and whenever they transgress, then this is equivalent to his being indifferent as to their moral character and actions, which is both absurd and blasphemous to suppose. But if the penalty at last overtakes them, then the same objections will apply against its infliction, on the score of goodness, compassion, etc., as the objector urges against it now; so that after all he gains nothing to his argument by supposing the exercise of such forgiveness. And hence we may see why the Bible so fully declares that nothing but forgiveness through atonement or satisfaction can bind the heart

with supreme love to God so as effectually to lead it to hate and avoid all iniquity.

8. The necessity of having the law fulfilled to the utmost is very fully announced by our blessed Redeemer in Matt. v, 18, and Luke xvi, 17. Nothing is more fully conceded by all our opponents, especially the utilitarians, than the importance of God's maintaining steady and inviolable the laws of the natural world. (See Edwards, vii, 552.) And much more then is it important that he should strictly uphold and maintain those of his moral administration; for there cannot be a greater conceivable absurdity than that the law, either natural or moral, should give place to the transgressor of it. Such a principle would be regarded as insanely absurd in human legislation and jurisprudence; and yet many of our opponents substantially maintain that it ought to take place under the Divine administration. Now dispensing with the penalty of the law, as we have above shown, is the same thing as abolishing the law itself. It would be the same thing, Edwards remarks, (vii, 516–529,) as to have inserted in the law the expression, that if it should be violated the penalty should, nevertheless, not be executed. The law was promulgated that the subject might regulate himself by it, and not that it should be regulated by the subject. But to say that the law ought to give place to the subject, because he saw proper to violate it, is the same as to say that sin should annul and abrogate the law, than which nothing more preposterous can be imagined.

9. The same conclusion is apparent from the assumption that repentance alone is a sufficient atonement for transgression; for there is nothing in repentance that is compensatory, or that balances the desert of guilt, or in any way tends to its diminishing. It has no tendency to heal a fatal wound, or to recover to life the murdered. And then, moreover, if God can pardon on repentance, seeing there is nothing of compensation therein, and nothing that can relieve the soul from guilt, (unless it be evangelical repentance, which is efficacious only through the atonement of Christ,) why may

he not pardon without repentance? Repentance bears no proportion to the injury which sin may have done; and if sin can be pardoned with it, why not without it? But, for the argument's sake, admitting that both in this life and in the life to come it may secure forgiveness, the question still recurs, Shall it be deemed sufficient in all cases, and as often as offense is committed? If it is, then what effectual security is there against continued rebellion and transgression? None whatever, which it is absurd to suppose. But if it is not to be perpetual, then, as already remarked in respect to forgiveness, the penalty in all its fullness must at last overtake the sinner, so that our opponents gain nothing by this assertion except to shift the question a step backward.

10. Then, further, none will deny that some transgressors, on account of their egregious crimes, merit the full penalty of the law, whatever it may be that God in his infinite goodness and wisdom has announced to be such. Origen himself, in his book against Celsus, says that those who are found to be incurably wicked shall be punished without end. And even Celsus (as quoted by Origen, lib. viii) says there can be no doubt that the good will be everlastingly happy, and that the wicked shall be miserable forever. The sentiments of Plato may be seen in Gorgias, §§ 71–79. The same, too, is fully admitted by our opponents, though they make the penalty to be extinction of existence rather than suffering. See Hud. 371–373, 390–392; D. 244–251; M. 9–12; and even Abner Kneeland, Lectures, p. 47. They all admit, therefore, that sin deserves eternal punishment. Now this admission being based upon what God has said, its truth cannot be made to depend upon any explanation which a person may give of the word penalty; for, according to these admissions, that penalty, whatever it may be, is conceded to be just; and to admit, therefore, that sin deserves eternal punishment, is the same as to say that it is both fit and proper that it receive such punishment. And if it be fit and proper, then, whatever the penalty may be, it is absurd to object to its infliction as inconsistent with goodness and strict

justice. Others of them claim that God is not bound to execute his threatenings, but we have already shown that this is inadmissible and absurd. And then, further, if he is not bound to execute his threatenings, he may omit to do so in every case, and so punish no crime; which is the same as for him to resign the throne of the universe, and to proclaim impunity for sin and immunity to the transgressor. See Edwards, vii, 541.

11. It is confessedly necessary to a Divine moral government that *all* sin should be *forbidden* under the sanction of a penalty, for God is of purer eyes than to behold iniquity. (Hab. i, 13.) And for the same reason it is necessary that the penalty should be universally executed, unless, as before remarked, we would accuse God of uttering threatenings without intending to execute them.

12. There is but one more thought that need be mentioned in this connection. As all sin may be strictly resolved into hatred of God and our neighbor, (for between the love required and its absence there can be no medium,) it follows that it is justly and properly the subject of God's displeasure, since hatred of God, or a refusal to love him, is of course a rejection of his government.

## § 55.—*Objections considered.*

I shall now, in concluding the chapter, attend to some questions and objections.

1. The question whether eternal punishment is not inconsistent with infinite goodness, has been substantially disposed of above. Our opponents here make a distinction, and while they admit that eternal *punishment* is consistent with infinite goodness, they deny that eternal *suffering* is. They assert that punishment and actual or conscious suffering are separable. See M. 9–12; E. 234; H. 1, pp. 136, 137; A. 105; Has. 39, 40; J. T. 32. S. 83 affirms it, and on p. 39 appears to deny it.

This must be conceded to be a somewhat adroit method

of evading a point. The question simply is, *Shall the sinner* BE *happy or miserable to eternity?* Now what answer is it to a question like this to reply, as these men substantially do, by saying, *The sinner will not exist through eternity, and therefore he will be punished to all eternity.* Then, further, they make this actual *eternal* punishment of the sinner to be endured by him in a very short time, and mainly *by anticipation*, which I take to be the bestowing upon the creature a clear and absolute conception of eternity; so that the great problem which has so long puzzled the philosophical world, as to whether the finite is capable of conceiving of the infinite, must be regarded as now settled by Messrs. Hudson, Dobney, *et id genus omne;* for it is perfectly obvious that the sinner, in order to endure eternal suffering or punishment *by anticipation*, must have a very clear idea of eternity itself. This is one of the great advantages which accrue from having such men investigate topics like the one before us; and after having read their works with great diligence, I can testify that nothing which occurs in the way of their investigations, however difficult it may appear to others, seems to perplex them in the least. The most puzzling problems of the most recondite philosophy they solve with a promptness and readiness which would have made even Crichton stare.

This, then, is their answer to the question, a man may *be* miserable through all eternity by anticipation. Locke (b. ii, c. i, § 11) had the vulgar idea on the subject. He says: "For to be happy or miserable without being conscious of it, seems to me utterly inconsistent and impossible."

And then, further, if the wicked can suffer eternal punishment in this manner, why may not the good enjoy the happiness of heaven in the same way? If we can suffer punishment without being conscious of it, why surely we can enjoy happiness also unconsciously. And as this will not be denied, the conclusion to which we shall without difficulty arrive is, that the *idealism* of Berkeley is the natural outgrowth of *Materialism*, (a thing never suspected before,) and that Hume has given the most perfect definition of the *genus homo* which has ever been given—that he is *an impression or idea.* And thus all the hitherto discordant schools of philosophy are brought into harmony, and likewise shown to be, through the aid of annihilationism, perfectly consistent with revelation itself.

I am sorry, however, to be under the necessity of interfering a little with some of the proportions of this magnificent conception; for those to whom we are indebted for it, and who maintain that annihilation is inflicted as the just penalty of the law, aver also that neither men nor beasts have any natural title to live forever. Of course, then, extinction of being is only the natural course of things, and the bestowment of immortal existence is purely an act of favor, so that when God created man, and before man had sinned, they were all destined to everlasting punishment, irrespective of all personal desert, unless grace prevent. But it is unnecessary to pursue the subject here, as it must come up for consideration in another chapter.

2. Others of our opponents take the ground of the ultimate restoration of the wicked, (and the same idea is often alluded to even by Annihilationists, for they refuse to be trammeled by either logic or consistency,) urging that eternal unhappiness is too long a punishment for the sins committed in this brief life. The same argument must likewise prove that either annihilation is not the penalty of the law, or, if it be, it is too long a punishment to inflict for sins committed in time. For if sinners may, in this short life, deserve to be forever annihilated for their sins, (and even Dr. Priestley admits that they do,) then how idle is it for those who hold this view to object that eternal punishment is too much to be inflicted for sins committed in this life? But not to dwell upon this matter, I would, with all seriousness, ask our opponents how long a time is required to refuse an offer which is made to us, and pressed upon our immediate acceptance? The offer made to our sinful race is eternal happiness, glory, joy. The very constitution of man's

intellectual and moral nature requires that he should accept or reject an overture which comes to him as this does. He may of course refuse it persistently and finally, and having done so what is left but the opposite? He cannot take a middle position, and neither accept nor refuse. If he refuse eternal happiness, therefore, he chooses the opposite. And what is that opposite? To pretend that that also is eternal happiness, is to make the Gospel offer a farce.

### § 56. *Future Punishment and "Natural Laws." How Sin is an "infinite" evil.*

Is future punishment a direct and positive infliction of suffering for sins committed in this life, or is it merely the natural result of transgression, and depending for its continuance upon the future continuance of sin? This question, which presents two points, was wrought into the discussion some years ago; and from the manner in which it has been thoughtlessly decided by some of our divines, the truth has seriously suffered, and many have been led into grievous error. We cannot here discuss it, however, except very briefly.

1. The doctrine of the Scriptures has never been considered doubtful in reference to the doctrine of punishment in the world to come *for the sins done in the body* or in this life. See Heb. ix, 27; Rom. xiv, 12; 2 Cor. v, 10; Matt. xii, 36, 37; xxv, 31–46; Rom. ii, 5, 6; Prov. i, 24–28; Luke xiii, 23–27; 2 Thess. i, 7–9. In all these, and in multitudes of other passages, there is a clear retrospective reference to sin perpetrated here as the sole ground of the judicial decision and succeeding punishment; but the huge outcries of Universalists some years since, at what they called this "diabolical aspect of the doctrine," induced some good men, who were never created to be improvers of theology, to attempt to modify the representation, and make it less repulsive to the carnal heart of the impenitent and ungodly; a course of procedure which never can in any instance be justified, except on the assumption that our

blessed Redeemer was not so mindful of the interests of men as those are who make these attempts. A few references will suffice to bring the subject sufficiently before the reader to expose the glaring impropriety of such efforts.

In the earlier series of the tracts issued by the American Tract Society* we have the following: "Sinners will deserve to be punished as long as they continue in sin. If they sin during the whole of life, they will be exposed to suffering during life; if for a thousand years after death, they will deserve to suffer during that time; if eternally, their punishment will have no end. To disprove the justice of future endless punishment, then, it must be shown either that sinners will cease to sin," &c. Dr. Dwight likewise (in tract number 181, p. 7, and Theology, sermon clxvii) says: "God may justly punish sin so long as it exists, and it may exist forever. . . That while we continue to sin, God may justly punish us, if he can justly punish us at all, is equally evident." Dr. Lyman Beecher and others likewise assume the same ground; but further quotation is needless.

Now while it is undoubtedly true that those who perish in their impenitence will continue to sin forever, and that they are still held accountable for all the sin they perpetrate in this or in any other world, it is a grievous error to make their eternal severance from the source of life and light and salvation to depend in any way upon sin that is not committed in this their probationary state. What is this but to concede substantially that the sins of this life do not deserve eternal punishment? What is it but a substantial concession that if the sinner can be supposed to refrain from further transgression in the future world, he may expiate his former sin by suffering, (since it would be wrong to punish him any further,) and so be saved even without the intervention of Christ? Is it not something like a concession to the Papists and Restorationists that their so long-claimed principle of the purifying tendency of suffering may be

* No. 224, pp. 44, 45, I think, though I have not the tract now at hand.

reasonable? It is, in fact, placing the issue of the whole controversy upon the question whether future suffering may not have a tendency to lead the soul to hate and forsake sin. And it is plainly impertinent in any man to undertake thus to change the issue of a question of this character, relating so intimately to the dearest interests of the race. Let it be but conceded that this is really the issue, and how soon, in the hands of a learned and adroit disputant, may the whole power of the Gospel appeals to sinners on this subject be neutralized? In fact, the amount of this attempted modification is a surrender of the doctrine that sin deserves eternal death, since man is not punished in the life to come except as he shall there continue to sin, so that after all it is not necessary to suppose that he will be punished forever for the sins done "in the body," that is, in this life.

It is no reply to this to say that the sins of this life bring the sinner under the necessity of continuing to sin. This is not the point. The question is, Does future and eternal punishment depend on or result from sins perpetrated here? If it do not, then we must cease to insist upon the truth of the doctrine from such passages as those referred to above. And if it does, then this most uncalled for and unadvised attempt to modify the teachings of God on the subject should be abandoned.

2. As to the idea, so rife at the present time, that in the future world the sinner shall suffer only the *natural* results of sin, and nothing positive, it is contrary to the whole Scripture representation. That he does really and fully reap what he has sown, is true, and nothing is more frequently or more directly asserted in the word of God; but that these expressions relate alone to natural consequences, as they are called, is false. The Jews, "whose carcasses fell in the wilderness," and Achan, and Jezebel, and Uzzah, and Ananias and his wife, all reaped what they had sown by venturing to disobey God; and did they therefore suffer only the natural consequences of sin? Did the rich man in hell, being in torments, reap only the natural conse-

quences of his sins? The principle, therefore, is plainly false in respect to the government of God in this world; and that it is equally false in respect to the world to come, is plain from the fact that the same language is employed in reference to the future rewards of the righteous, and which are also declared to be far superior to any mere natural results. It is false, too, from the fact that the penalty of the law is retributory; and it is idle to make mere natural consequences the penalty of moral law. It is false, moreover, from the fact that it renders the pardon and expiation of sin an utter impossibility, and furnishes encouragement to the thoughtless and impenitent to persist in sin. They do so here in despite of all natural consequences, and of the penalties imposed by human legislation; and how then shall they be deterred through apprehension of mere natural consequences in the life to come?*

3. A great deal is also said at the present time about the absurdity of sin being an "*infinite* evil." See D. 249, and all the rest of the Annihilation school, not excepting Dr. Whately. They either use the phrase without understanding it, or else they willfully attach to it a meaning which is not attached to it by their opponents. A single instance will show this. The younger Edwards, in his Reply to Chauncey, uses the phrase frequently; but in repeated instances throughout his book (see pp. 22, 129, 131, etc.) he carefully defines it in some such connection as the following: "The expression *infinite evil of sin* seems to be very offensive to some gentlemen." Their "idea of the infinite evil of sin is very different from that which is entertained by those who hold that sin is an infinite evil. *All they mean is, that sin is in such a sense an infinite evil that it may be justly followed by an endless punishment.*" Now as the Annihilationists hold it to be in

* See Bellamy's True Relig. Delin., Disc. i, sect. 5, and a truly excellent essay by Rev. Samuel D. Cochran in the Bibliotheca Sacra for April, 1854. It is deformed, however, by a careless misprint of the word *elements* for *emotions* three times in the first paragraph.

this same sense an infinite evil, their objection to us for holding the same idea is absurd. The expression, moreover, was originally derived from the Bible—Job xxii, 5.

### § 57. *Future Punishment as a Motive.*

There is one more objection often insisted on by these gentlemen, which demands a brief notice. They perpetually asseverate that eternal suffering in prospect has no tendency to lessen crime. See C. 60, 62; D. 252–262; H. 1, p. 134, note, and 142, 143. Dr. Chauncey, pp. 340–357, asserts the same. But,

1. Neither has annihilation any such tendency, as we have abundantly shown in the notes to §§ 15 and 19, above. The facts there stated evince that it has a tendency the very opposite; and that Materialism always had the effect of discouraging virtue and encouraging vice, I could easily prove even by the testimony of the old philosophers, if it were necessary.

2. But even infidels, though, like the Annihilationists, they deny and ridicule the doctrine, are compelled to admit its restraining power. Bayle, referring to the libertines, says: "Nothing can more effectually reclaim those men than to convince them of the immortality of the soul," etc.; and again: "The two handles by which man is moved are the fear of punishment and the desire of reward." (See Crit. Dict., iv, 719, and v, 812.) Shaftesbury (Charact. i, pp. 18, 19, and iii, 315, 316) expressly affirms the restraining power of this doctrine. Hume, (in his Essays, pp. 244, 245,) referring to the Epicurean philosophy, says: "In fact men do not reason after that manner; they draw many consequences from the belief of a Divine existence, and suppose the Deity will inflict punishment on vice, and bestow rewards on virtue, beyond what appears in the ordinary course of nature. Whether this reasoning of theirs be just or not is no matter, its influence on their life and conduct must still be the same; and those who attempt to disabuse

them of those prejudices may, for aught I know, be good reasoners; but I cannot allow them to be good citizens and politicians, since they free men from one restraint upon their passions, and make the infringement of the laws of equity and society in one respect more easy and secure."

Bolingbroke makes substantially the same concession. He says: "The doctrine of rewards and punishments in a future state has so great a tendency to enforce the civil laws, and to restrain the vices of men, that reason, which cannot decide for it on principles of natural theology, will not decide against it on principles of good policy." (Works, iv, 227.) So also in vol. iii, 220: "The doctrine of future rewards and punishments, which suppose the immortality of the soul, is no doubt a great restraint to men." At the same time that he affirms all this, he caricatures and ridicules the Gospel account of the matter. I could add the testimony also of Lord Herbert, Chubb, and Blount to the same effect, if necessary, but the foregoing is a sufficient refutation of the cavils of the Annihilationists. And that mankind from the earliest ages entertained the belief of the perpetuity of future rewards and punishments, is sufficiently plain from the testimonies adduced in part i, chap. iii, above. Locke, who also believed in their perpetuity, says: "The rewards and punishments of another life, which the Almighty has established as the enforcements of his law, are of weight enough to determine the choice, against whatever pleasure or pain this life can show." See also Essay, B. ii, chap. xxviii, §§ 8, 12.

The patristical view has been sufficiently presented in § 40, and we shall conclude the chapter with the following quotation from Dr. Cheever's review of the Life and Writings of John Foster, in the Biblical Repos. for Jan., 1847: "The truth of eternal retribution is a citadel defended by many batteries. So fast as, to the vision of an enemy, one seems to be demolished, another rises. In the Scriptures, in human reason, from analogy, from the nature of things, from the character of God, from the character of man, the evidence is solemn and overwhelming. You may play your game of escape, if the laws of evidence be disregarded; but with one who holds you to logical conclusions, in every possible move you are checkmated. You cannot put the various doctrines of the Bible in any relative array but they lead to this; you cannot exclude this from any possible combination; and any one of the elements of the Scriptural problem given may lead you through the whole circle of truth. Given, the atonement, to find the character of man and its relation to the element of retribution; that would do it. Or, given, the character of man and the character of God, to find the element of retribution, that would do it. Or, given, the necessity of Divine grace to fit the soul for heaven, the atonement being the sole condition of that grace, to find the element of retribution; that would do it. Or, given, the existence and agency of fallen spirits, to find *man's* retribution; that would do it. Or, given, the bare offer of eternal life; that would do it. Or, given, the benevolence of God, the axiom of the universe, GOD IS LOVE; that would do it. For all retribution is invested with the atmosphere of love, and had not God been love, he might have let the guilty go unpunished. But justice only does the work of love, and love works by justice for the purity and blessedness of the universe. Where there is sin, love without wrath, without retribution, would only be connivance with iniquity. There is no such thing as love without justice, or justice without penalty, or penalty without execution, or execution *with* end, so long as there is sin."

# CHAPTER IV.

## FUTURE RETRIBUTION—THEORIES OF UNIVERSALISTS AND DESTRUCTIONISTS.

### § 58. *The Point to which the Discussion is brought.*

I HAVE now brought this long and really laborious investigation to the great point on which all the human interest pertaining to it is made by our opponents to revolve, and I trust it is scarcely necessary to say with what deep and overwhelming feelings of solemnity I approach it.

With my natural sympathies on the side of the creature, and conscious that through my native depravity, as well as actual sin, I am unfitted, in the very nature of the case, to form an unprejudiced and unbiased *à priori* judgment in matters wherein my own deepest interests are involved—matters too which intimately concern the infinite holiness, justice, truth, and goodness of the eternal God, and also the interests of the whole universe, so long as the throne of Deity shall endure—I cannot even venture to introduce my own speculations herein. All I propose to do therefore, and all that I can even hope to perform intelligently, is to employ the faculties which God has given me in the endeavor to understand the import of his message to man on the subject, as delivered in his written word, and as illustrated by his works of creation, providence, and grace.

Through the gentlemanly attention of the Rev. Thomas Whittemore, of Boston, Mass., I was enabled some years since to collect a large number of the ablest and most approved treatises of modern Universalist writers; for it was then my intention to furnish a very full and thorough discussion of the whole subject of future retribution. My studies, however, were interrupted, and my plans frustrated, and now, although it cannot be even attempted on the few pages of our volume which remain to be occupied, it yet is necessary to consider the question in its relation both to Universalism and Annihilationism; for though these may appear to some to present points of direct antagonism, every one acquainted with the history of the controversy in past ages knows that it is not so; and that although the Restorationists and Annihilationists quote the same passages, in innumerable instances, to support their views, and of course draw diametrically opposite conclusions from the same words, yet the Restorationists have always kept the theory of destructionism as a *corps de reserve*, in case they found themselves unable to be saved by their favorite doctrine. It is necessary therefore to take a little broader range in treating the subject than we should do if the works of our opponents evinced either consistency or precision of argument. The principles upon which they and the Universalists assail the doctrine of eternal retribution are the same, and this requires that an eye should be had to each in the argument.

### § 59. *False Issues pointed out and considered.*

Our argument hitherto has conducted us to the conclusion that man is immortal, that his conscious existence is uninterrupted by death, and that he was originally placed by his Creator under the eternal and immutable principles of moral law, by which he was to be governed. It is moreover conceded by ourselves and our opponents, that he freely and voluntarily violated the precepts of that law by disregarding an express prohibition of God, and that by so doing he incurred its penalty. It is in like manner mutually conceded that Christ Jesus came into the world to provide, through his labors and sufferings, a way of deliverance for man from the ultimate execution of that penalty upon him, and that he offers this his intervention freely to all. The question then arises: What shall be the final condition of those who, by rejecting this proffered intervention, (which rejection itself greatly enhances their guilt,) still remain under the penalty of the moral law?

1. This, I repeat it, is the only point now at issue; and the attempt to implicate that issue with other questions which have no real relation to it, so far as we are concerned, (a course pursued by all our opponents perpetually,) will scarcely be regarded as either proper or honest by any serious inquirer after truth. What propriety is there, for instance, in endeavoring to drag into the issue the question as to what will become of the nations to which the Gospel has not been promulgated? since it is freely conceded by all that God will treat them in perfect consistency with his justice, goodness and truth; and since the Annihilationists, moreover, are obliged to confess that they must either suffer the penalty of the law and become annihilated, or else escape it and live forever. If they escape it, then they do so without formally accepting of the intervention of Christ; but if they do not escape it, then why pretend to object to our theology, that the same conclusion might be deduced from it? All such issues therefore are to be thrown aside, as tending only to obscure the point really in question, since that point relates only to the final condition of those who reject the proffered salvation through Christ. Shall *they* be restored through suffering, or be annihilated, or live forever in conscious misery? This question thoroughly disposed of and settled, it will be time enough to go into inquiries as to what will become of others. And if our opponents have any real information to communicate on that subject, I, for one, will receive it thankfully; but at present it is not needed, since we have all the information that is required in order to settle the issue actually before us.

2. There are other false issues which they endeavor to raise in connection with the question, and by which they

have succeeded in perplexing it to many minds. For instance, they perpetually persist to reason from man to God, by inferring that as a tender parent would not punish his children forever, therefore God would surely never do so in respect to his creatures. This, however, cannot be urged by the Annihilationists without absurdity, since no tender parent would consent to annihilate his children forever, any more than he would consent to punish them forever, unless on the supposition that annihilation is a less fearful punishment than to live forever in alienation from God, and suffering the consequences of sin, which, however many of them explicitly deny. But at all events, what is the amount of this foolish attempt to reason from man to God? If carried out it must lead to Atheism. Since God does many things which no tender parent would do, (for what parent would have drowned his children in a flood, or have burned them, as in Sodom and Gomorrah, or would destroy them by pestilence, storm, and shipwreck?) we must conclude, if this reasoning have any foundation, that God has less compassion than man, and is therefore, in reality, no God at all.

3. Our opponents dwell upon the fact that some persons are very much impressed with horror and anguish at the idea of eternal suffering. Mr. Hudson, for example, rings the changes *ad nauseam* on this point, and Dr. Chauncey declared that he could find no way in which to make it sit easy upon the mind; and we are informed also by Mr. Hudson (353–355) that the celebrated German scholars of the present time have abandoned the idea. These things are frequently urged, and have great weight with some; but admitting the whole of the representation, what does it amount to in respect to the real issue before us? Nothing whatever, unless the principle be assumed that we are not to believe any announcement of God to be true, which some men are perplexed with, or have a difficulty in receiving. Great and learned men have been puzzled and much perplexed by the doctrines of the Trinity, Providence, Grace, Atonement, Incarnation, Resurrection, and everything relat-

ing to God's administration in the unseen and eternal world; and are we thence to conclude that nothing is to be believed by us in relation to these matters? The idea is absurd. Why then endeavor to perplex the issue in this manner? The statement, however, in reference to the German theologians is false, (as the articles of faith adopted by the Evangelical Alliance would of themselves evince,) and so far are they from having abandoned the idea, their renewed and thorough investigation of the subject has only confirmed them more fully in its truth.

4. Another matter which these men perpetually endeavor to drag into the discussion is stated by them in the often repeated assertion, that, according to the views which we inculcate, the greater part of mankind must perish forever. But if such a thing could be justly and logically inferred from the theological system which we adopt, what would it have to do with the plain simple question as to the final condition of those who voluntarily reject the Gospel offer of salvation? This question is to be settled by an appeal to the word of God, and not to any theological system. Why then attempt to drag any such system into the issue? Suppose that *as systems* they are all rejected, this question would still remain to be settled on its own intrinsic merits. I would remark however that the assertion on which this cavil is based is false. Our theologians do not teach that the great majority of mankind will perish forever. The constant statement of our best divines is that the number of the lost will bear no more proportion to that of the saved, when the final judgment shall forever settle the destinies of our race, than the convicts in a prison bear to all the inhabitants of the state.

5. Others make equally preposterous attempts to introduce into this issue their unfounded theories as to the final cause of God in creation. But what do they know of that final cause, except so far as God himself has seen proper to reveal it? Dr. T. Southwood Smith and Petitpierre assume, for example, that God, being benevolent, could have had no

other object than the happiness of every one of his creatures, and thence infer that all men shall be saved at last. But where in the whole Bible do we find that God's only design or object in creation thus terminates upon the creature? The redeemed in heaven and all the angelic host sing, "Thou art worthy, O Lord, to receive glory, and honor, and power, *for thou hast created all things, and for thy pleasure they are, and were created.*" Rev. iv, 11.* The testimony of the whole Scripture is uniform on the subject, and directly in conflict with the foregoing assumption. "The Lord hath created all things for himself." Prov. xvi, 4. "All things were created by him and for him." Col. i, xvi. See also Heb. ii, 10; Rom. xi, 36. And in the same manner he declares himself to be the end of his works. "I am the Alpha and the Omega, the Beginning and the Ending," etc. Rev. i, 8, 11, 17, and xxii, 13, with Isa. xliv, 6, and xlviii, 12. And that he constantly makes himself his end in his providential government and dispensations is plain from such passages as Isa. xlvii, 11: "For my own sake, even for my own sake, will I do it." Isa. xliii, 7: "For my glory I have formed him." See also Isa. xlix, 3; lx, 21; lxi, 3; Eph. i, 5. And that it is not for the sake of man, but "for his own sake," that he extends mercy to them. (Ezek. xxxvi, 22, 32.) And hence mankind are required to glorify him as the great end of their creation. (2 Thess. i, 10–12; Phil. i, 10, 11; ii, 11; Matt. v. 16; 1 Pet. ii, 12; 1 Cor. vi, 20; x, 30.) And Jesus likewise sought the glory of God as his highest end. (John vii, 18, and xii, 27, 28. See Edwards on the Last End of God in Creation, for an admirable view of this whole subject.)

Such is God's own testimony on the subject, and what right

* Professor Stuart translates the passage thus: "*For thou hast created all things, and by thy will they came into existence and were created,*" making it a mere inane repetition. And, unsupported by any authority whatever, he arbitrarily assumes "an *instrumental* sense," which he had not the shadow of a right to do, and thus most unexegetically confounds δτά before the accusative, with διά before the genitive. A more uncalled for and unsupported criticism never proceeded from his pen.

has any presumptuous mortal to assume, as these men do, that the contrary is the fact? But gross as is such impertinence, it sinks into insignificance, compared with the presumption which would lead the sinner to hazard his eternal well-being upon such an idle dream! That God's object in creation was both wise and benevolent no one will question. But how can it be inferred from this that it so terminates upon rebellious and sinful creatures as to lead him, for their sakes, to set aside his law by abrogating its penalty, and thus render all his admonitions and threatenings a farce? Is such an unfounded assumption sufficient to justify a rejection of God's own statements on the subject? If not, then the question still returns, What has he said shall be the final condition of the lost? For whatever he has said on the subject he will accomplish; and whatever that may be, it is certain to be perfectly consistent with infinite benevolence and truth, whether we, in this stage of our existence, can see it to be so or not.

The following illustration, for which I am indebted to Saurin, is in point here, and will set this whole matter in its true light. Suppose that previous to the creation of man God had communicated to certain holy intelligences his intention of calling our world into being, and that thereupon several of them had begun to speculate upon what kind of world it would be; what may we suppose (for the supposition is perfectly proper) would have been the views entertained by such beings on the subject, who knew God to be perfectly holy, wise, and almighty? But suppose that one of the number, during the deliberation, should have advanced, as probable, the idea that the world which was to be created should prove to be a universe of sin, disease, misery, and death; how may we suppose that such a theory would have been regarded by them? May we not well conclude that it would have been at once pronounced to be infinitely absurd and preposterous? And on the supposition that our opponents themselves could have formed a part of that assembly, and before experience had made them acquainted with the facts, would not they, in all probability, have been the loudest in denouncing the idea as not only absurd, but even allied to blasphemy? Such would doubtless have been their own feelings, and the feelings of the whole assembly; and yet how wide of the truth would such conclusions have been? For we find that, in the inscrutable counsels of a wise, holy, and righteous God, just such a world has been brought into being. And if present sin and misery are not incompatible with infinite goodness and benevolence, how audacious is the assumption that there ever will arrive a period when they shall become incompatible therewith? If their introduction and existence now are consistent with a perfectly wise and holy administration, who has fathomed the counsels of the Eternal sufficiently to warrant the assertion that they will not continue to be consistent therewith? And what impertinence is it to make such an assertion without the slightest knowledge whatever of the matter?

6. Of the same character is that kindred assumption, that moral evil is the positive appointment of God as a necessary means for promoting the greatest ultimate good of all his creatures. There is not the slightest proof to sustain such a hypothesis, and it is a puerile attempt to evade the true issue before us, since the only way in which we can possibly know anything of God's design in permitting the existence of evil, and of its ultimate results upon the creature, is from what he himself has announced respecting it. The question then returns, What has he said on the subject? And then, as to this hypothesis itself, it is directly contrary to all the Scripture representations of the manner in which God regards sin and treats the sinner. It makes God himself the author of sin, and man a mere machine, since he can feel and act only as the Sovereign of the world efficiently appoints. It utterly destroys conscience, and excludes all remorse for sin; annihilates the distinction between right and wrong, or moral good and evil, and turns the threatenings and admonitions of God into idle words. All these things can be easily demonstrated whenever occasion may require.

7. How impertinent then is it for Rev. Messrs. Whately, Dobney, Hudson, Ham, etc., to pretend to feel so very anxious about the character of God, lest it should suffer in the estimation of themselves and others, and on this ground to presume to modify his own awfully solemn teachings respecting those matters which pertain to our best and eternal interests. Well may such tamperers with eternal truth expect to hear him demand of them, "Who hath required this at your hand?" We commend to their sober and serious consideration the remark of Beza: "We cannot speak improperly of God, while we speak of him as he speaks of himself." *Qui sequitur Deum, emendate sane loquitur.* And that also of the wise and judicious Hooker: "*Whatever is spoken of God, or things pertaining to God, otherwise than as the truth is, though it seem an honor, it is an injury.*"

## § 60. *The Atonement cannot benefit the Lost. Their Resurrection.*

What, then, shall be the final condition of the lost? In answering this awfully solemn and momentous inquiry I remark:

1. It is obvious that the atonement cannot help them. Our blessed Mediator, through his labors and sufferings, opened the way for our return to the favor of God, and there is no other way by which man can be recovered from sin to holiness. He, moreover, has offered his intervention to all, and announces his willingness to save to the uttermost all who come unto God by him. But this offer is voluntarily rejected by those to whom the question in issue pertains; and that rejection is of course a voluntary renunciation on their part of all the proffered blessings of redeeming love. How then can they be benefited and saved by that which is left to their own choice, and which they freely refuse? It is obvious, therefore, that as the acceptance of the offer must bring salvation, so its rejection must preclude the possibility of being thus saved, since the effects of such refusal must

necessarily be as direct, and marked, and lasting as those resulting form the acceptance of the offer. The atonement, therefore, cannot save those who reject it, and they must consequently remain under the penalty of the law forever. And in exact accordance with this we find it stated that Christ, when all his enemies are prostrate and overthrown, resigns the mediatorial kingdom which he had received, thus leaving those enemies to the unending consequences of their impenitence and guilt. (1 Cor. xv, 24–28.)

The attempt of Universalists to extend the efficacy of the atonement over the whole human race, irrespective of man's treatment of the offered salvation, and whether he repent and accept it or not, is in every view absurd, as is shown in sect. 59; and then further, to pretend to offer to man's *free* acceptance or rejection what he *must* at all events accept, whether he will or not, is to charge God foolishly. It makes the atonement also a nullity; since, as is perfectly obvious, if God could thus save men without repentance, he could save them without an atonement.

2. In reference to the question, *What is their connection with the resurrection? Do they, or do they not arise from the dead?* I remark,

(1.) That the views of a few of our opponents on this matter, as may be seen from section 5, sub-sections 5 and 6, are somewhat undecided; so also is Mr. Hudson, in his book, pp. 263, 264, 299–308, 399, 400. The majority, however, emphatically affirm that the wicked shall arise; and that this is the truth is plain from many express declarations of Scripture: Dan. xii, 2; Matt. v, 29, 30; x, 28; Mark ix, 42–50; John v, 28, 29; Acts xxiv, 14, 15; 1 Cor. v, 10, and a multitude of other places. And the severance of soul and body being no part of the proper penalty of the law, they must of course be reunited body and soul in order fully to endure that penalty. See section 45, above.

(2.) The idea of their being thus raised merely to be annihilated over again, is not only contrary to the whole Scripture representation, but one of the most repulsive ideas that can be conceived by the human mind. (See sect. 19, sub-sect. 3.) Without the clearest inspired affirmation of its truth it should not be entertained for a moment; and much more should it be utterly repudiated, when it is based, as it truly is, upon a mere idle assumption. But as the question whether the wicked are to be annihilated is brought forward irrespective of the question as to their resurrection, we shall give it a thorough consideration in the sequel.

### § 61. *The Punishment of the Lost is not disciplinary.*

1. That it is not, according to the annihilation theory, is admitted by all its advocates. They who admit the resurrection of the wicked, admit that the process of annihilation may continue amid the most unutterable torments for a vast and indefinite period, until it is consummated. Of course, therefore, there can be nothing disciplinary therein, and it is simply retributory.

2. That the sufferings of the wicked during the interval between death and the resurrection are not disciplinary, is sufficiently apparent from the considerations presented in sect. 48, sub-sect. 4, and this point needs not to be further dwelt upon.

### § 62. *The Restoration Theory inconsistent with Scripture and Reason.*

That the sufferings of the wicked subsequent to the resurrection are not disciplinary is evident from many considerations:

1. The presumption (asserted by the Restorationists) that it may be, is fairly disposed of by the undoubted fact that the punishments inflicted by the government of God in this world are not necessarily of that character, but often are, indisputably, the very reverse. In order to place this beyond cavil, it is only necessary to refer to the Deluge, the destruction of Sodom and Gomorrah, the case of Pharaoh, of Nadab

and Abihu, of Achan and the house of Eli, of Saul, etc. There is, therefore, no correct principle upon which it may be presumed that the punishments inflicted in the world to come are of an opposite character.

2. If future punishment be reformatory and purifying, it must lead its subjects to repentance through suffering. This, in relation to moral agents, implies, of course, a state of trial and probation; for a state of discipline which is not of that character is an absurdity. They must, therefore, be in the possession of all the freedom necessary to constitute them moral agents, for to deprive them of this would be to make them render a forced or compulsory obedience, which, in such a matter, is really no obedience at all; and a compulsory purification, therefore, would be no purification in the true sense of the word. But if they possess their freedom, how is it to be presumed that this asserted discipline will prove effectual? If, after all the torments employed to bring them to repentance, their obedience and reformation still remain a contingent event, how is any one to know that their purification will certainly follow? It is a mere assumption, and to base upon it *certainty* of knowledge is therefore ridiculous.

3. Then, further, it is conceded by the Restorationists that this discipline must continue during a longer or shorter period, according as the moral state of the wicked may require; and that though it is natural to suppose it must necessarily require a longer time to reclaim the most hardened and obdurate than it would those of a less degree of wickedness, yet the torment shall in no case continue longer than is necessary to secure its end, which is the repentance and reformation of the sinner; and any further infliction would be inconsistent with that end, and therefore not to be supposed. These things being so, it is plain that during the infliction of these torments, the offer or promise is constantly held forth to the sinner, that if he will only repent and reform his sufferings shall cease. Now the very presentation of this offer to them shows that they retain the

liberty either to accept or refuse it; and we are assured, moreover, by the Restorationists, that many will continue to refuse it for a long time, and so be in continual torments for ages of ages. But here the question occurs, Is their resistance to this discipline sinful, or is it not? Is their continued refusal to yield and repent wrong or right? No one will contend that it is right; for it would be obviously wrong, in the same sense that the sinner's resistance in this world is wrong, and sinful, and wicked, as God has declared it to be. If then it is wrong, it of course cannot go unpunished; so that if the refusal to repent during some fifty or sixty years in this world may require a discipline of millions of ages, as some of them say, how long a discipline would a refusal continued through a million of years or ages require? And then, as Edwards remarks, (vii, 382,) it is plain that by persisting in impenitence and stubbornness, wickedness in the heart will be vastly established and increased; for it may be laid down as an axiom, that the longer men continue willfully in the perpetration of wickedness, the more is the habit of sin established and the more will the heart become hardened in it. So that after the lost have continued thus in sin and rebellion for ages of ages, and have arrived to that desperate hardness of heart and strength of habitual wickedness which must ensue, they will be, as respects every moral aspect of their case, in an infinitely worse and more hopeless condition than when at first cast into hell. And if in that state the torment should be lengthened out indefinitely, they must still continue to sin, and of course all hope of repentance and reform becomes simply an absurdity. But then we are not left to metaphysical reasoning on the subject; for a state of probation after the close of the present life is plainly contrary to the whole Bible. See, for example, Gen. vi, 6; Eccles. ix, 10; Matt. xii, 31, 32; Luke vi, 24; xvi, 25–31; John ix, 4; Heb. vi, 4–6.

4. That it is not disciplinary is further evident from the fact that such an idea must necessarily compel the belief

that the curse or penalty of the law is the greatest possible blessing which can be possessed by the sinner, which would be very absurd even to imagine. Christ failed to save them by his Gospel, and thus they were brought into a fearful state of wickedness and danger; but they are now taken and put into the midst of hell-fire, according to the threatening against rejecters of the Gospel; and this fire does for them what Christ could not do—it raises them to heaven and the joys of eternal life. Hell-fire, therefore, is to such persons, according to this principle, a greater blessing than Christ, and the penalty of the law more precious to them than the promise of mercy; for the promise failed, but the penalty was effectual. Now such persons could never unite with the blood-washed throng, and sing praises to Him who washed and redeemed them in his own blood; the objects of their praise and laudation must be hell-fire, and the curse of the law; and how perfectly preposterous this would be, every one can see for himself.

5. The very same conclusion is arrived at in another way; for it is plain that future punishment is either the infliction of the threatened curse or penalty of the law upon sinners, or it is not. If it is not the curse of the law against sinners, then what is it? and when and where is that curse inflicted? and on what ground? It is, however, admitted to be the curse by all who hold the doctrine of future punishment. But if it be the curse of the law, and yet disciplinary, that is, designed to lead sinners to repentance and salvation, then the curse of the law is the greatest of all blessings, and, as above remarked, a greater blessing than Christ; so that those who are thus disciplined into repentance and heaven, are not saved by the atonement of Christ, unless it be supposed that he died to procure the execution of the curse, instead of removing it from our race. This inference is logical and direct; and according to this view, therefore, the curse of the law is the greatest blessing that a sinner can receive. And how great the power of such a doctrine is to restrain or encourage sin, the reader will decide.

6. It is obvious, moreover, that according to this view salvation does not consist in forgiveness through mercy, or in being *saved* from anything, strictly speaking, but simply in doing justice to the sinner. He is made to eat the fruit of his own doings, and so soon as he has eaten it, he is thoroughly and eternally cured. Now this of course turns into nonsense all that the Bible says of sinners being saved by mercy, grace, etc.

7. That future punishment is not disciplinary or reformatory, is plain from all those passages which speak of its retributory nature. Such, for instance, as Deut. xxxii, 41: "I will render *vengeance* to my enemies, and will reward them that hate me." Rom. iii, 5: "Is God unrighteous, who *taketh vengeance.*" Rom. xii, 19: "*Vengeance is* mine; I will repay." 2 Thess. i, 8: "In flaming fire taking *vengeance* on them." Jude 7: "Suffering the *vengeance* of eternal fire." Heb. x, 27: "A certain fearful looking for of judgment, and *fiery indignation*, which shall devour the adversaries." See also Rev. xiv, 10. I include purposely here passages which refer also to God's administration in the present world; since, if in this probationary state of mercy vengeance often overtakes the sinner, and a retribution which it is impossible to regard as reformatory, what may the sinner not look for in the world to come?

8. Our opponents endeavor to perplex this point by confounding the retributions which overtake the sinner here, with the chastisement suffered by the righteous. There is no sense in this, however, as a comparison of the language referring to the two will at once show. God addresses men in such language as the following: "The curse of the Lord is in the house of the wicked, but he blesseth the habitation of the just." Prov. iii, 33. "Behold I set before you this day a blessing and a *curse.* A blessing if ye will obey," etc. Deut. xi, 26–29. "Thou hast rebuked the proud, that are *accursed.*" Psa. cxix, 21. "Their portion is *cursed* in the earth." Job xxiv, 18. "They that be *cursed* of him shall be cut off." Psa. xxxvii, 22. Also Jer. xi, 3; xvii, 5,

etc. And in the New Testament they are spoken of as "*cursed children*." 2 Pet. ii, 14. Now even allowing all these expressions to refer to men in this life, it is plain that some here are *cursed of God*. And a curse is certainly a punishment which does not promote the good of the subject. (See Edwards against Chauncey, pp. 76, 77.) But on the contrary the chastisements of the true child of God are all said to be in love: "Whom the Lord loveth he chasteneth, and scourgeth every son whom he receiveth." "If ye be without chastisement whereof all are partakers, then are ye bastards and not sons." Heb. xii, 5, 11. "For unto you *it is given* in the behalf of Christ, not only to believe on him, but also to suffer for his sake." Phil. i, 29. See also Psa. lxxxix, 30–34; ciii, 13, 14; cxvi, 15. There is as much difference, therefore, between the two as between a curse and a blessing; for to the one the infliction is in *vengeance, fury, wrath, and fiery indignation*, while to the other it is in *compassion, tenderness, and love*. To pretend, therefore, that these things are similar, and of the same import, is gross ignorance.

9. The idea which underlies all such representations is contained in the often repeated statement, that sin is only the necessary means by which God purifies a moral universe. It is repeated by T. Southwood Smith, and the Restorationists generally; but to me it seems that the mind of man could not conceive a more preposterous idea. What purification did the moral universe need before sin entered it? Of course it needed none. How then could it be purified by the admission of sin? Could the pure sweet waters of a beautiful pellucid lake be purified by turning into it a turbid stream redolent with the foul washings of kennels and sewers? But even should we grant the assumption, our adversaries would gain nothing to their argument, since a continuance of the same means which were thus originally necessary in order to purify the universe, may be likewise necessary in order to keep it pure.

§ 63. *Subject continued—Future Punishment eternal.*

That the sufferings of the lost are not disciplinary and reformatory is further evident from the fact that they are plainly declared to be eternal.* I merely refer to the fact here in a general way, and as it relates simply to the issue with the Restorationists. It will be necessary however, in the sequel, to consider it in its relation to the stand-point assumed by the Annihilationists.

1. That the future punishment of the sinner will be endless is clearly implied by innumerable declarations of the Scriptures. For example, it is distinctly stated that no mercy shall be extended to them in hell, which is obvious, moreover, also from the fact fully proved above, that their punishment is not reformatory. Now that strict justice will be awarded to the impenitent in hell, is clear from such passages as Job xxxiv, 2; Psa. lxxii, 12; Jer. xvii, 10; xxxii, 17; Matt. v, 25, 26; xvi, 27; Rom. ii, 6; 2 Cor. v, 10; Jas. ii, 13; Rev. xiv, 10; xxii, 12; and if God, even in this world, where mercy is displayed, often visits with retributory justice, much more will he in the world where mercy ceases to be offered. The same is likewise implied by the existence and misery of Satan, who is never to be restored. Toward him and his angels the word of God holds out no hope, but plainly the reverse. (Heb. ii, 14–16.) Dr. Chauncey (p. 225) assumes, directly in the face of the plainest statements to the contrary, (Matt. xxv, 41; Rev. xx, 10,) that they will be annihilated; but such assumptions are unworthy of notice.

2. The same words, as Mosheim remarks, (Gedanken, sect. 3, sub-sect. 2,) are employed by the Holy Scriptures, and in the same latitude of import, to describe the eternal sufferings of the damned, as are used to describe the

* On this whole subject let the reader consult the "Observations" of President Edwards in vol. vii, of his works, and the reply of the younger Edwards to Dr. Chauncey. Also the Gedanken of Mosheim upon the doctrine of Future Punishment.

eternal blessedness of the righteous. In Matt. xxv, 46, for instance, the same term (αἰώνιος,) is applied to both. So also are the words translated *for ever and ever;* for εἰς τοὺς αἰῶνας τῶν αἰώνων, and עוֹלְמֵי עוֹלָמִים (and עוֹלָם) mean an endless duration. This phrase is employed eighteen times in the New Testament, and in fifteen of these it is used to designate the continuance and perpetuity of the glory, perfections, government, and praises of God. In these instances the import of the phrase cannot be questioned. As to the other three, in one of them it is said of the devil, the beast, and the false prophet, that they should be tormented day and night, "forever and ever." In the second, it is said of the impenitent, that the smoke of their torment ascendeth *for ever and ever*, and in the other instance it is said of the righteous that they shall reign *for ever and ever.*

The objection which all our adversaries so insist upon, and which Messrs. Le Clerc, Chauncey, Kneeland, and others now bring forward with such pedantic display, that *the idea of time* is contained in all these terms, and therefore, however long a period we may suppose to be designated, it must come to an end, is not evincive of a reflection much more profound than their objections usually exhibit; since, if the fact that the idea of *time*, or *temporal duration* being contained in them, proves that the thing referred to must have an end, then of course the happiness of the righteous must have an end, and so must the glory, and praises, and government of God. But the pedantic utterance itself, however, is set in its true light in the following passage from Noah Webster: "It will be easily seen that as the human mind cannot comprehend *eternity* in duration any more than it can infinite space, no word which men could form would express the whole idea. All that men can do, in this case, is to express their ideas by a word of *indefinite meaning;* and what better mode can men take to convey their *limited* ideas of what is *unlimited*, than to use a word which expresses *enlargement* or *extension?* Eternity, then, is *unlim-*

*ited extent in duration;* and that the Greek word above mentioned (αἰὼν) is often used in that sense, is a fact which no critic can disprove, and no rational critic can deny." *

3. Future punishment is positively affirmed to be endless. Psa. xvii, 14; Matt. vi, 15; xii, 31, 32; Mark iii, 19; Luke xii, 10; xviii, 8; xxiii, 34; xxvi, 24; Mark xiv, 21; Mark ix, 43–49; Luke vi, 24; xvi, 25, 26; John iii, 36; 2 Thess. i, 7–9; Heb. vi, 4–6; x, 26, 27; 2 Pet. ii, 17; 1 John v, 16; Jude 13; Rev. xiv, 10, 11, and in many other places. Such language, too, as the following cannot possibly convey any other idea; and it is impossible to conceive that it should be employed if the damned, after many ages, are to be received into an eternity of bliss: "Woe to you that are rich, *for you have received your consolation!*" An expression which, if its import could be regarded as at all doubtful, is fully explained by such language as the following: "*Thou in thy life time receivedst thy good things.*" "Men of the world, *who have their portion in this life.*" Luke vi, 24; xvi, 25; Psa. xvii, 14. No language can possible express the idea of an endless deprivation of bliss if this do not, and consequently it asserts that the punishment of the wicked shall be eternal.

4. The same may be said also of Mark xiv, 21: "Woe to that man by whom the Son of man is betrayed. *Good were it for that man if he had never been born!*" The impossibility of reconciling these words with the idea that this man, after he had suffered any supposable length of time, should enjoy a whole eternity of bliss, is too apparent to require remark. (See also John xvii, 12.) And hence Judas was never to obtain such happiness. The remark that the expression is a proverb, is idle, as regards this issue. Suppose it were, and does this show that it may not have been literally applied to Judas by our Lord? Is language employed in proverbs never employed in its literal import? Are proverbs, in the necessity of the case, literally inapplicable to the subject concerning which they are spoken? But then

* Christian Spectator for 1836, p. 318.

there is not the slightest evidence that Christ used the expression as a proverb. All that Dr. A. Clarke, or any one else, has attempted to bring with such parade in support of the assertion, will, if conceded to be accurately presented, only go to show that the phrase had passed into a proverb some two or three centuries after the death of Christ, a time of sufficient length to turn consecutively any twenty expressions originally of an aphoristic form from their literal usage into proverbial. The exception therefore is nothing to the purpose.

5. The same truth is apparent, likewise, from such expressions as that of John the Baptist: "He that believeth not the Son *shall not see life.*" John iii, 36. The word *life* in the Bible has two meanings: 1. Mere existence; and 2. Eternal happiness. (See sect. 27, sub-sect. 2.) The first sense cannot, of course, be its meaning here, as the persons referred to do or shall possess existence, so that here it can only refer to future and eternal happiness. And it is impossible, therefore, to express in stronger terms the doctrine that the wicked are not to be restored to the possession of eternal life, however long their sufferings may be supposed to continue.

6. And, finally, the same truth is evident from the representations constantly made in the Scriptures respecting the manner in which God regards and treats the persistently impenitent. They are *lost*, *rejected*, *cast away*, *perish*, *destroyed*, etc. "Gathered the good into vessels, but *cast the bad away.*" Matt. xiii, 48. "They shall *utterly perish* in their own corruption." 2 Pet. ii, 13. "But we are not of them that *draw back unto perdition*, but of them that believe *unto the saving of the soul.*" Heb. x, 39. "The day of judgment, and perdition of ungodly men." 2 Pet. iii, 7. "Fear him who is able to *destroy both soul and body in hell.*" Matt. x, 28. "Who shall be punished with *everlasting destruction* from the presence of the Lord." 2 Thess. i, 9. Now if the damned were under only a salutary discipline, such language could no more be applied to their state than

it could to that of Christians who are under such discipline in the present life; and they are equally removed from that state or condition to which such terms as *destruction*, *lost*, *perish*, etc., are applicable in the strict and proper sense in which they are employed in the foregoing passages. Hence in no proper sense can they be regarded as *lost*, *cast away*, *rejected*, *destroyed*, on the supposition that they are merely being trained for the bliss of heaven, through the reformatory and "*salutary discipline*" of hell. The application of these terms, therefore, in this their strict and literal sense, to their state, evinces that they are under no such discipline, but that their sufferings are retributory and their condition final.

# CHAPTER V.

## ANNIHILATION IS NOT THE PUNISHMENT OF THE WICKED.

### § 64. *Position of the Annihilationists stated and disproved.*

All our opponents who are not Universalists maintain, and, as the reader has doubtless observed, greatly insist, that the wicked are to be annihilated, and that this is an eternal punishment. But that this is not to be their punishment is evident from the whole word of God. And,

1. Annihilation is not the penalty of the law. It is nowhere said to be such; and to take it for granted, as is done by D. 271, 272, and others, is inadmissible and absurd.

It is asserted with one voice by our opponents that man has no actual title to immortality or endless existence. They affirm that by Christ alone, man, since the fall, has been placed in circumstances in which it is at all attainable; and that this is the only foundation upon which he can become capable of immortality. They maintain, further, that he was originally created mortal. How, then, can the law threaten that if he sin he shall be mortal, and be deprived of that which does not in any way belong to him? According to their doctrine it belongs to man no more than to beasts, naturally, and yet they do not hold that beasts are sinners, and that when they die they are punished everlastingly, and suffer the penalty of the law. They are obliged to hold, moreover, that even had our first parents persisted in their integrity, and not sinned, as they were created mortal, God could have left them to the natural course of things without doing them any injustice, or depriving them of any native right whatever. They had no claim upon God for a continuance of life beyond the supposed period; and there could be no injustice therefore in not granting it, and in permitting them to pass into nothingness. An innocent being, therefore, according to this view, may suffer annihilation without the slightest injustice; and if so, annihilation is, strictly speaking, no punishment at all, and therefore cannot be the penalty of the law.

The theology of our opponents on this point is more remarkable than theological. At one time they claim that annihilation is the severest and most terrible of all punishments, worse even than eternal suffering; and then again, in their expositions of texts, they make out that it is no punishment to suffer it between death and the resurrection, but really "*gain*."* Now if it be no punishment in such a case, how can it be in any other case? Will a man who is annihilated forever *feel* it more than one who is annihilated only for a few thousand years? And do the wicked who are annihilated between death and the resurrection feel it more than the righteous who are also then annihilated? And if the annihilation of the righteous during this interval is not the penalty of the law, how can the annihilation of the wicked be?

It cannot, therefore, be the penalty of the law, even on their own principles, because it is inflicted upon the righteous, and may without injustice be inflicted upon the innocent, and all who have no claim to continued existence. A punishment is an actual evil brought upon any one as a testimony that his conduct is disapproved; but the non-granting of a favor to which there is no title is no testimony of disapproval and displeasure, though the refusal of a *promised* favor may be, for promise bestows a title to it, which is not the fact in the case supposed. To confound, therefore, the

* C. 40; S., App. 9, 21, 22; H. 2, pp. 68, 78; A. 90, etc.; E. 136, 137; G. 20; F. 11–14; W. 84, 88, 89; Hud. 256, 257.

non-bestowment of a positive and unmerited favor, or boon, with the execution of the fearful and threatened penalty of the Divine law, is absurd, unless it can be supposed that a right may both exist and not exist at the same time.

2. It is plain also that it cannot be the penalty, since, according to our opponents, it is really and fully executed twice: first, at death, and then after the resurrection. And here I may remark that it would be well if our opponents would favor us with some explanation in regard to their notion of the resurrection of the wicked. It is either an act of grace or of penalty. It cannot be on their principles an act of penalty, since while dead the wicked already are fully, and as much as they ever can be, under the penalty. Nor can it be of grace, for it is no grace to give a creature life merely for the purpose of torturing him to death.

3. Why, then, should the wicked be annihilated? The views of our opponents are greatly inconsistent and contradictory here. They say, first, that it is the just desert of their sins, and that God has threatened it, and will be sure to execute it. And at the same time they say that it would be more in accordance with infinite goodness and compassion to do this, rather than to preserve the wicked in existence forever in misery; that is, it would be more in accordance with goodness to deliver them thus from the just consequences of their sin. But it is proper to ask here, Would this be an act of mercy, or of justice? for it can hardly be both. And to suppose that they can have any claim to mercy, and that God is bound by goodness, or by anything else, to show them his favor, is to suppose that he is obliged to save them from the consequences which they have voluntarily brought upon themselves by rejecting his proffered mercy. In other words, because they have rendered themselves the fit objects of his displeasure, by despising his calls and admonitions, and the provisions of his mercy, he is bound still to relieve them from the consequences of so doing, though he had assured them they should "have judgment

without mercy." James ii, 13. What can be the effect of such a doctrine, except to encourage the wicked in sin?

Then, moreover, the idea that annihilation is an act of grace destroys at once and utterly the whole theory that it is the penalty of the law and just desert of sin, as maintained by our opponents, since it is hardly possible to conceive, on any other principle than that of suffering *everlasting misery by anticipation*, (see sect. 55, sub-sect. 1,) that the penalty of the law can be inflicted in mercy, and that mercy itself toward the sinner should require its infliction upon him.

4. But, as we have fully shown in sects. 53, 54, God's method of procedure, in his treatment of rational creatures, is not of this character. The justice of the law may be properly executed upon those who violate its precepts, as no man can rationally dispute. And, as Annihilationists are compelled to admit, the terrible anguish inflicted upon the lost, and which issues in the extinction of their being, is not for their personal good, but for the good of others, as a salu tary example of the consequences of sin; so, according to their own principles, if an unending continuance of their suffering would in the same manner be useful, it would be consistent with both justice and propriety to continue it forever. In such a case even Utilitarians, if consistent with their principles, must concede that it would be proper. (See sect. 52.) And even the aforesaid celebrated definition of punishment by Plato would justify it. (See sect. 49.) Let us then briefly contemplate the subject from this stand-point.

(1.) The attempt which many writers now make to throw this whole matter aside, by a sort of general caveat, and so take for granted that there is something back of all reason which will justify their refusal to believe it, however clearly its truth may be justified in the view of both conscience and the reason, is utterly irrational, and contrary to the principles of common sense. Is it so that we are at liberty, on the ground of the most unfounded assumptions, thus to ignore the clear announcements of revelation, and the deductions which reason cannot but draw therefrom? What is this but claiming the right to ignore the rational and moral nature which God has given us? But let those who thus trifle remember that however untrue we, by pursuing such a course, may prove to be to that nature, God is bound to recognize it, and to prove true to it in all his dealings with us. He can recognize no such conduct to be justifiable in any rational creature. "There is a way which seemeth right unto a man: but the end thereof are the ways of death." If sin and suffering were inconsistent with infinite goodness and mercy, God would not permit them here to exist. And we are entirely too little acquainted with the future state to determine that they will not be necessary there. Who durst say that when we are better acquainted with that state we shall not find that suffering, as connected with guilt, is even more necessary there than in this world?

(2.) It is impossible to conceive how God should deal with rational and moral creatures by any other arrangement than is here recognized. He finds them in a sinful and miserable state, and offers them deliverance. They refuse it, and thus practically prefer to remain as they are. What then should hinder his permitting them to continue to furnish to all holy beings forever an illustration of the consequences of sin and rebellion against his authority? Such is his government in the moral and natural world now. A man, disregarding the laws of life, wantonly severs an artery. Is God under obligation to arrest the tide of death, and heal the wound, that the man may be saved from the consequences of his act? No one will pretend such a thing. The man is left to suffer the penalty, and by that suffering to evince to others the consequences of such an act. The same principle is true also in God's moral administration; and though triflers have dared to ridicule the idea of God glorifying his justice, their trifling is rebuked by facts of constant occurrence under both his natural and moral administration which should make them tremble. Men must regard natural laws, or suffer the consequences; all concede this. And the necessity is equally imperative to regard moral law. We have referred to the Deluge, and the destruction of Sodom, and to other instances of the consequences of disregarding moral obligation under his administration; let us now briefly contemplate the Scripture doctrine of examples touching this subject.

(3.) The apostle, after enumerating a catalogue of such punishments for moral obliquity, expressly declares (1 Cor. x, 6, 11,) that "These things *were our examples*, to the intent we should not lust after evil things, as they also lusted. *All these things* happened unto them for ensamples, *and they are written for our admonition*." (Compare 2 Tim. iii, 16.) And then in the following verse he applies the instruction furnished by those examples: "Wherefore let him that thinketh he standeth take heed lest he fall;" thus plainly declaring and repeating the doctrine, that under the government of God the vices and punishments of men are employed for purposes of warning and instruction. The same, too, is declared in the case of Pharaoh. (Rom. ix, 27.) And let the reader consult what the Spirit of God has recorded in relation to the *effects* of that fearful example of disobedience and consequent wrath. See the reference to it by Jethro, (Exod. xviii, 10, 11;) and also that most instructive one in 1 Sam. vi, 6, three hundred and fifty years after Pharaoh was destroyed. The same idea is presented also in 1 Sam. iv, 7, 8; Neh. ix, 10; Hos. xi, 8; Deut. xxix, 21–29; Psa. lxiv, 2–6; lxxxiii, 14–18; cxxxv, 3–13; Ezek. vi, 2, 3, 7–14, and in places without number. See also in the New Testament, besides the passages already quoted, Heb. iv, 11, and 2 Pet. ii, 6.

(4.) Thus it is God's pleasure that the persistently wicked should be treated, without the slightest regard to their personal welfare. And I repeat the question, Why should God, in the world to come, cease to administer his government on this principle? From what he declares by the prophet (Isa. ix, 7: "Of the *increase* of his government *and peace*, there shall be no end,") it is plain that the number of his subjects shall still increase, by new creations of moral existence, through eternity; and who shall say that the collaterally continuing "*peace*" shall not be the result of these fearful examples of the consequences of transgression? (Compare Isa. lxvi, 24.) The existence of those present abiding examples (Psa. lix, 11,) must be forever salutary in evincing how terrible are the consequences of disobedience. And thus, therefore, even on principles claimed by the Utilitarian and Annihilationist, the propriety of the eternal sufferings of the damned is clearly apparent. And though God does not thus punish them *merely* for the sake of example, (for they receive only the just award of their guilt,) he does employ their sufferings as a salutary example to the rest of his rational creation forever.

(5.) It is therefore the very height of Atheistic folly and impiety to pretend that God is regardless of the actions of his rational creatures, (as the whole objection logically assumes,) for this is in effect to say with the atheist, that there is no God. To deny that God is the ruler of his creatures is practically to deny his existence altogether. And hence Epicurus and his followers, who did not deny that God existed, but only asserted that he did not concern himself with the actions of men, have ever been, by wise and reflecting minds, among Pagans, Jews, and Christians, ranked with atheists; for if God concerns not himself with the actions of his rational creatures, it must be either from want of power or want of will; and on either supposition, so far as all practical purposes are concerned, there is no God. This has ever been seen and admitted, and hence reflecting infidels, like Lord Herbert, of Cherbury, and even such as Jefferson and Paine, have strenuously asserted the doctrine of a particular providence. But if God concerns himself with the actions of his intelligent creatures, then, on principles of reason and common sense, it is plain that he holds them responsible, and must ultimately, at least, reward the obedient and punish the disobedient. And as the nature of those retributions is clearly announced by him in his word, what madness is it for rational and sinful creatures to attempt, in the aforesaid manner, to ignore the whole subject, and to exclude it from all proper consideration!

(6.) I will dismiss this point with a brief notice of an assumption which to many appears to give some degree of plausibility to the aforesaid method of treating the subject. It is assumed, and much insisted on by some of these writers, that the saints cannot be happy in heaven with the knowledge that sinners are thus suffering in hell. The principle upon which this assumption is based, is that such suffering must awaken the sympathy, and so far interfere with the happiness of the redeemed.

That undeserved suffering may thus excite sympathy is plain; but will any one pretend to say that deserved retribution has the same effect? What is the testimony of facts? In the word of God we find the souls under the altar (Rev. vi, 9–12) praying that the time of the Divine vengeance upon the ungodly may be hastened. We repeatedly find, moreover, that the execution of God's vengeance upon such is a subject of holy praise, (see Psalm cxlix, 6–9,) and that he is extolled for it as furnishing evidence "that his mercy endureth forever," (Psalm cxxxvi, 17–21; lxiii, 12; Rev. xix, 11–16;) and especial thanks in heaven are given to him on this ground. Rev. xi, 14–18; xii, 10–12; xv, 1–4; xvi, 5–7. And it is expressly stated that when the inhabitants of heaven shall witness the execution of the final judgment upon the enemies of Christ, they shall say "*Alleluiah*" as they see "the smoke of their torment ascending up for ever and ever." And to undertake to deride such representations, as our opponents, and especially the Universalists, do, and at the same time to profess to believe in the Divine origin and authority of the volume which contains them, is a most glaring instance of the strangest inconsistency and insincerity.

And then, further, what are the facts as connected with the present life? Are even our opponents themselves always unhappy on account of the sufferings of those condemned to the penitentiary, or devoted to capital execution? There is no evidence that their enjoyments are thus interfered with any more than those of other men. And we find that mankind do not the less enjoy the fruits of temperance and virtue, because the intemperate and the vicious suffer.

God has not thus placed the happiness of his faithful servants in the hands of the ungodly and disobedient, as this objection supposes, and the idea itself is a perfect absurdity. Are angels unhappy because the devils (once their beloved companions in glory) are suffering deserved torment and misery? Were Abraham and Lazarus unhappy because they beheld Dives suffering the torments of the damned? On what principle, then, is it to be supposed that the saints in glory will be unhappy on account of the just retribution which they suffer who, on account of their hostility to God and holiness, are confined in the prison of despair?

The urging of this objection by the Annihilationists is very absurd; but it is like their other theological inconsistencies. How is it that the happiness of the saved is not marred, while the wicked are undergoing the terrible agonies which, according to these men, are to issue in their extinction? Or how is it that their happiness is not marred on witnessing or knowing of the almost interminable ages of ages of torment and agony spoken of by the Restorationists? Suffering is suffering while it exists; and if its present existence awakens no such sympathy as is referred to, why should its continuance? A knowledge that it is just and proper relieves the mind in the one instance, and such knowledge must forever relieve it in view of all the family of God.

As corporeal death is the severance of all merely natural ties, so will the second death be the severance of all ties which once bound the unhappy and impenitent to the friends of Christ. The ties of earthly relationship, while they shall be remembered in all their controlling power by the lost, (as with Dives, who might well dread to see his brothers in hell, to which his own vile example tended to lead them,) shall, in the case of the redeemed, have no influence in view of the revelations of the eternal world. When they see, in the light of that world, the horrible position which they who have lived and died impenitent, assume against the holy government of God, and the merits and proffered salvation of the blessed Jesus, their sympathy shall be reversed. It is sympathy with the rebellious creature in this world of sin, rather than with the infinitely holy and glorious Creator, which lies at the foundation of this whole objection. But such sympathy will have no place among the redeemed. Higher thoughts and higher affections shall then take possession of their souls, and they will so fully sympathize with God in all he does, that the strength of an earthly affection for such as are his enemies will be utterly and eternally forgotten. Let not the rebellious and impenitent therefore be comforted with the idea that they are to have the holy sympathy of heaven on their side amid the retributions which they have defied. Such is not the fact. They have trifled with the sufferings and sympathy of Jesus, and must pass away to their doom with no sympathizing friend among all the redeemed.

An incident occurred some years ago, at the launching of a ship in Philadelphia, which may serve, in some respects, as an illustration of the point. As the vessel was one of the noblest that had ever been built in our country, an immense concourse of people assembled to see the launch. They thronged the wharves and surrounding buildings till every spot which could afford a view was occupied, while even the river for a great distance was covered with boats filled with men, women, and children, to enjoy the scene. By and by the appointed moment approaches, and every eye is turned toward the magnificent structure on the stocks, and the multitude, with breathless expectation, await the signal which is to dismiss her into her element. And now the loud booming of cannon gives the signal, and the cry, "*She is coming!*" bursts from the surrounding multitude. Just at that instant a man at the outer extremity of the long wharf misses his foothold and falls into the water. But the attention of the multitude is so intensely occupied by the grand pageant before them, that no one seems to notice the sufferer. He struggles and shrieks for help, and is within reach of hundreds, both in boats and upon the shore, but no one seems to hear him, and there he struggles, and sinks, and perishes, surrounded by those who could have rescued him, but whose minds are too intently occupied to witness his distress or hear his cries. Such is the all-absorbing power of a strong emotion; and when the redeemed are assembled before the throne in heaven, and behold before them the object of their most intense love and sympathy, and whom on earth they loved infinitely more than life itself, can any one suppose that they will be willing also to share their sympathies with those who have renounced his authority, despised his proffered love, "trampled under foot his blood," and derided his agonies, and thus intimate that they think he has treated these his enemies too severely? It may comfort the impenitently wicked and ungodly in this world to be assured that here they shall, at all events, secure this tender compassion and regard; but let them remember, Eternal Truth declares that, if after the present probationary state they are found among the enemies of God, they will meet with no sympathy from any inhabitant of heaven.

5. But to return. It is further assumed that annihilation must be the punishment of the damned, because it is not to be supposed, say our opponents, that Divine wisdom and goodness would have created a being that could be eternally miserable, and that hence we must suppose that those who would become so if they continued to exist will be annihilated. This objection is so nearly like the foregoing, that were it not that our opponents, and such *philosophers* as "Thorndale," appear to think it different, we should pass it unnoticed. And surely they might have seen that the same mode of reasoning which is here resorted to would, if

applied, prove with equal conclusiveness that Divine wisdom and goodness would hardly have created a being whom it would be necessary to annihilate. And then, moreover, to say that God would not create a being that could be eternally miserable, is equivalent to saying that he could not create one that was capable of vice or virtue, praise or blame, reward or punishment, as would appear if this objection were metaphysically followed out to its fair results. This is needless, however, for the question between us and our opponents is one of pure exegesis; and the folly of the idea of depriving a rational creature of existence, that he may escape the just award of his guilt, has been sufficiently exploded already.

6. That the wicked are not annihilated is further evident from the absurdity of supposing that they are raised out of extinction merely to be annihilated over again.* Their personal identity is of course utterly destroyed by the first extinction; † the chain is broken, and it is a new creation which is then called into being, (and which in no possible sense can become conscious of an identity that has no existence,) and which must then be annihilated merely to show the consequences of guilt with which it was in no way connected. If, however, our opponents reply that all this may be justified on the principle of imputation, we (though we hold to no such imputation as that) are content that they should say so. But they will of course remember that they cannot *justify* it on that principle without admitting the justice of the principle itself, and its logical sequences, a principle which, if admitted into their theology, would straighten it out considerably.

7. The same truth is evident, also, from the fact that the devil and his angels are not to be annihilated, and wicked men are to partake with them their punishment. (Matt. xxv, 41.) According to such writers as Hudson, Dobney, and Storrs, the object of the annihilation of the wicked is to banish all evil from the universe. Hence, if the devil is not

* See remarks on this point in sect. 19, above. † See sect. 18.

annihilated this object fails, and consequently his continued existence in torment (as our opponents must admit) will infer the continued existence of wicked men, so far as all their objections are concerned.

That the fallen angels are not yet annihilated is conceded by our opponents, (see sect. 5, sub-sect. 10;) and that they are not to be annihilated is plain from their apprehensions of future *torment.* "Art thou come to *torment* us before the time," said they to Christ. It is *torment*, and not extinction, that they are to suffer. Hence, they "*believe and tremble.*" See 2 Pet. ii, 4; also Rev. xx, 10: "They shall be *tormented* day and night, for ever and ever."

8. The annihilation theory, so far as the Bible is concerned, is built entirely upon a false application of the terms, *life*, *death*, *perish*, *consume*, *destroy*, *destruction*, etc.; and that this may be fully manifest to any who may choose to prosecute the inquiry, I will here subjoin a few references to the writings of its advocates.

(1.) On *Death* and *Life.* See S. 12, 19, 20–30, 52, 60; App. 1–8; G. 7–9; C. 46; Has. 14–20; D. 121, 129, 135, 152, 196, 197; E. 64, 256; B. 11, 12; H. 1, pp. 119, 126–129; H. 2, pp. 69, 70, 85; M. 31–33, 36, 37.

On *Perish*, *Perdition*, *Consume*, *Devour.* See C. 46–58; B. 14–22; S. 17, 49–56, 80, 82; H. 1, p. 142; A. 121, 122; E. 235–244; D. 168, 169.

On *Destruction*, *Destroy*, etc. See B. 12–14; E. 239–243; M. 52; A. 118–121; H. 1, p. 142; D. 85, 86; S. 47–56; Has. 20–28; C. 48–58. These few references are abundantly sufficient.

(2.) In respect to their inappropriate use of the terms *life* and *death*, sufficient has been said in section 27, and throughout the Bible argument. Their use and application of the other terms, however, is pure nonsense; for example, they confound *perish* with annihilate. But that it has no such meaning, in the sense attached to annihilation by our opponents, a few examples will evince; and if the reader will substitute *annihilate* for *perish* in these passages, he will at once perceive the folly of pretending to regard the words as interchangeable. "That the land *perish* not through famine." Gen. xxxi, 36. "The valley also shall *perish* and the plain be destroyed." Jer. xlviii, 8. "The law shall *perish* from the priest." Ezek. vii, 26. "Truth is *perished.*" Jer. vii, 28. "The good man is *perished.*" Mic. vii, 2. "The righteous *perisheth*, and no man layeth it to heart." Isa. lvii, 1. "There is a just man that *perisheth* in his righteousness." Eccles. vii, 15. "It must not be that a prophet *perish* out of Jerusalem." Luke xiii, 33. "The world being overflowed with water, *perished.*" 2 Pet. iii, 6.

(3.) It is equally absurd to pretend to confound the terms *consume* or *devour* with annihilate, as an attempt to interchange them in such passages as the following would show: "The famine shall *consume* the land." Gen. xli, 30. "They shall *consume;* into smoke shall they consume away." Psa. xxxvii, 20. "The sword is drawn: for the slaughter it is furbished, to *consume.*" Ezek. xxi, 28. "He shall *devour* the whole earth." Dan. vii, 23. "Your land, strangers *devour* it in your presence." Isa. i, 7. See Zach. ix, 15; Deut. xxxii, 42. "Fight against them till they be *consumed.*" 1 Sam. xv, 18. "I am *consumed* by the blow of thy hand." Psa. xxxix, 10. "Ye *devour* widows' houses." Matt. xxiii, 14. "For ye suffer, if a man *devour* you." 2 Cor. xi, 20. See also Gal. v, 15; 1 Pet. v, 8.

(4.) Equally absurd is their application of the terms *destroy*, *destruction*, etc., as may be evinced by such passages as the following: "The King of Babylon shall *destroy* this land." Jer. xxxvi, 29. "Knowest thou not that Egypt is *destroyed.*" Exod. x, 7. "He sent frogs among them which *destroyed* them." Psa. lxxviii, 45. See also Ezek. xxv, 16; Hosea xiii, 9. Even the expression "*utterly destroyed*," does not mean annihilated in the sense attached to that term by our opponents. See 1 Chr. iv, 41. 2 Chr. xxxi, 1; xxxii, 14; Isa. xxxiv, 2. And then such an interpretation would turn many passages into the sheerest absurdity. As for example: "God shall destroy them with a double destruction." Jer. xvii, 18. It is easy to understand what a double destruction is; but the phrase double annihilation can only be understood by some such method as our opponents have contrived for suffering *eternal* punishment. It is needless however to quote other passages; the Bible is full of them. Let the reader refer to Job v, 21, 22; ix, 22; xxviii, 22; Isa. xlix, 19; xiv, 20; Lam. ii, 11; iii, 17; iv, 10; Psa. xxxiii, 17; cvii, 20; Obad. 12; 1 Cor. v, 5. All arguments and inferences, therefore, which are based upon any such confounding of terms, are false and delusive; and it is amusing to reflect that Dr. Chauncey (pp. 224, 272–292) argues from the same words that the wicked shall *live forever*, after their purification, and that the fires of hell shall be put out.

(5.) And then, further, all the texts alleged by our adversaries to prove that the wicked are to be hereafter *destroyed*, *consumed*, *devoured*, or, in their vocabulary, annihilated, are met just as fully on the supposition that annihilation is to take place *at once*, as well as after, or in consequence of long-continued and terrible suffering; for not even the Restorationists insist more that the torments in the future world will be dreadful beyond description, and it is not to be supposed that the wicked are to be raised from the dead again merely to pass quietly out of existence. But as all this suffering is needless, unless as an example, (for, as above remarked, the texts alleged say nothing of any long-continued suffering which is to precede their destruction or "annihilation,") so, if needed for an example, it is obvious that it may be needed forever as such; for since the wicked are to be raised from the dead in order to be made an example of suffering, (and this is admitted to be the only object of their resurrection,) so it is plain that their sufferings may continue as long as there is occasion for any such example. And as we are nowhere informed that there will be no such occasion in the future state, there is no sufficient reason to say or believe that there will not be, as we have no means of knowing anything on the subject farther than what God has declared respecting it. And as he has not said there will be no such occasion, but, on the contrary, has affirmed many things which clearly declare and infer the very opposite, it is the height of impertinence for any one to say or assume that there will be no occasion for the continued existence and sufferings of the wicked.

(6.) The exposition of these words by our opponents is likewise destructive of their whole theory; for they affirm that *consume*, *devour*, *destroy*, etc., in the texts which they quote, mean the sufferings and torments which are, according to them, to issue in annihilation. Now if the words mean suffering and torment, they do not of course mean non-existence or annihilation, nor can they in any sense be regarded as proving annihilation; and it is a mere unsupported inference, therefore, that this *devouring*, *destroying*, etc., will issue in annihilation. If the words mean simply annihilation, they do not mean misery, (for the two things are not reconcilable;) but if they mean misery, as our opponents allege, it is perfectly gratuitous and impertinent to tack to their import the idea of annihilation also, since the texts alleged give not the slightest intimation of any such idea. They speak of destroying, consuming, etc., and as this confessedly means suffering and misery, no one has any right to say that it is misery which will result in extinction of being, since it is obvious, on the very admissions and expositions of our opponents, that to perish forever may be to suffer forever. They must therefore, in the very necessity of the case, deny their own perpetually repeated affirmation that the words mean suffering, or they must admit that they furnish no proof that the wicked are to be annihilated.

9. That annihilation is not the penalty of the law is evident further from the clear announcements in the word of God that there are to be degrees of punishment; that is, not in duration, for that would be impossible, but in extent or severity. All the finally impenitent shall be punished forever, but not all with equal severity.

The idea, though our adversaries endeavor to mystify it, is sufficiently plain even to a child's apprehension, and it is the basis of our Saviour's remark in Matt. v, 22. And accordingly we read that the servant that knows not his master's will, and commits things worthy of stripes, shall be beaten with few stripes, while he who knows his master's will, and transgresses, shall be beaten with many stripes. (Luke xii, 47, 48.) And the whole context shows that this has reference to the future state. (See verses 31–48.) And some shall receive greater damnation than others. (Matt. xxiii, 14.) And, referring to future retribution, our Saviour declares that it shall be more tolerable for Sodom, and Tyre, and Sidon, than for Chorazin, Capernaum, etc. (See Matt. xi, 21–24.) Now as there cannot be different degrees of annihilation, so annihilation is not the punishment of the damned. The reply to this, that the degrees may refer to the sufferings which result in annihilation, and that the suffering of some therein will be greater than that of others, is simply absurd; for if the sufferings which *precede* annihilation be here referred to, then the penalty of the law does not consist in annihilation, which is simply extinction of being, and requires no sufferings to precede it. And if these "many stripes" which precede annihilation are the penalty of the law, then annihilation is not the penalty of the law, and consequently it is a mere gratuitous inference that the damned are to be annihilated. And as they are to suffer according to their works, that is, endure different degrees of punishment, it is plain that annihilation is not the punishment of sin.

10. The falseness of the whole system is apparent too from the fact that it makes the righteous, not less than the wicked, suffer the full penalty of the law between death and the resurrection. But that they are not annihilated at death is proved by the whole of our preceding argument; and that they do not suffer the full penalty of the law at any time, is evident from the fact that they are members of Christ, (1 Cor. vi, 13, 15; Eph. v, 30,) and that they are redeemed by the blood of Christ (1 Cor. vi, 20) from all condemna-

tion, (Rom. viii, 1,) as we have already fully shown. Hence the theory which requires that they should suffer the penalty of the law after their union with Christ, is false; and therefore our opponents must give up either the assumption that death is the extinction of being, or that annihilation is the penalty of the law. And if it is not the penalty of the law, then it is sheer folly to say that the wicked are to be annihilated.

11. We omit other arguments, and conclude with the following: The future annihilation of the wicked is, according to this theory, in no sense the penalty of the law, but results from the intervention or mediation of Christ, which is a gross absurdity. This is plain from the fact that our opponents teach that the penalty of the law is death, or deprivation of existence. This, of course, therefore, all would have suffered without any reference to Christ whatever; but by or through his intervention the wicked are raised from this state of extinction, (in which they otherwise must have continued,) and, after untold ages of intolerable torment, are annihilated over again. And as all this comes purely through the intervention of Christ, according to the theory of our opponents, and would never have been inflicted were it not for that intervention, so it is the sheerest absurdity to pretend that the future annihilation of the wicked is the penalty of the law. And as it is not the penalty of the law, the assumption that it will ever be inflicted as such is simply ridiculous.

12. In respect to the issue, however, it is a matter worthy of most serious reflection that impenitence, or a refusal to accept of the salvation offered by Christ, if persisted in through the present stage of our being, must be followed either by eternal sorrow and despair, or by eternal extinction of being. The idea of extinction may bring relief to the minds of the incorrigibly wicked, as has been shown in a former section; but who can, without deep emotion, contemplate the alternative which awaits such, whichever way the issue presented in the discussion before us is decided

or the certainty, thus presented, that neglect of the Gospel must eventuate in utter and final exclusion from happiness and heaven? "It is well understood," as Mr. Hudson truly remarks, (p. 392,) "that the common doctrine of universal salvation offers in fact no salvation; for no one can be said to be saved from that to which he was never liable, nor from that which he actually suffers." And the theory of restoration to holiness and happiness through future torment is involved in so many insuperable difficulties, as well as inextricable contradictions, being based upon assumptions which are not only absurd and inadmissible, but destructive of each other, (as already shown in §§ 59–63,) that no well-balanced mind which views the subject intelligently and dispassionately can entertain it. Hence it has been, in modern times, generally abandoned, on the one side for the later form of Universalism, and on the other for Annihilationism; and therefore the great issue now is on the question, Shall the existence of the sinner be extinguished, or be perpetuated? We have in the present section considered the question in one of these aspects, and shall now proceed to consider it in the other.

# CHAPTER VI.

## THE ETERNAL SUFFERING OF THE WICKED CONSIDERED.

### § 65. *Future State of the Impenitent.*

Thus far we have closely followed the statements and reasonings of our antagonists in support of their theory that annihilation is the punishment of the damned. We have carefully analyzed their system, as exhibited in their multifarious productions, and in the course of this volume have fully and fairly presented every leading point in which it comes into conflict with our own; and have patiently considered and shown the inaccuracy of all their statements, professedly derived (in support of their theory) from reason, revelation, philosophy, ecclesiastical tradition, and the principles of law and justice; and along therewith have given also a tolerably full abstract of the direct and positive argument in support of the views which we entertain, and at the same time have pointed out the irrelevancy of the objections against them; and moreover, in our last sections we have met the great issue which their theory presents, and have shown that annihilation is not the punishment of the damned. We might, therefore, here rest the argument, as the inference is both fair and legitimate that the wicked are to live, and suffer forever the consequences of sin; but as we are not willing that the truth on this subject should seem to be a matter of inference, when there are so many inspired declarations to sustain it, and as the theme from this stand-point affords an opportunity to expose further the subterfuges of infidelity which are resorted to by Universalists and others in relation to the matter, we shall proceed to show that eternal suffering is the necessary consequence of sin. The charges of "cruelty," etc., brought against us for entertaining these views by Universalists *et id genus omne*, are deserving only of contempt, until they show that we *prefer* to advocate them, irrespective of all consideration of their truth or falseness. And we aver "that if a man would know what is now most fitting in the relations between man and his Maker and between man and man, he must learn these things mainly from the Bible; and that only as his feelings shall be in harmony with revealed ethics is he likely to be a believer in revealed theology."*

The reader is perhaps aware how all our opponents of every grade, from the Deist to the Annihilationist, (though a few of this latter class do aim to be more consistent,) endeavor to perplex this whole question by insisting on mere side issues respecting liberty and necessity. The true freedom of the will is logically and wholly subverted by T. Southwood Smith, Dr. Chauncey, Dr. John Taylor, Sir George Stonehouse, and by all the Universalists of the Ballou and Whittemore school—and in fact by all who maintain that omnipotence, associated with infinite goodness, furnishes a sufficient guaranty for believing that all men will be saved—just as effectually as it is by the materialistic theory adopted by most of the Annihilationists, which makes the soul of man a mere result of corporeal organization, in order to secure its extinction between death and the resurrection. But the bearing of the question upon the theme before us is a practical one, and relates to those expectations indulged by many, that God will in some way secure their ultimate salvation and happiness "in spite of themselves," and whether they regard the Gospel offer or not. A few remarks, however, will show that this effort to throw off responsibility in relation to our future well-being is irrational and ruinous.

* From the British Quarterly, republished in the Eclectic for January 1858, p. 3.

In order to understand the principle of moral obligation, it is not necessary that we also understand *how* the will can be free, for this, as Sir William Hamilton justly remarks, "under the present limitation of our faculties, must remain wholly incomprehensible;"* a statement supported, too, by the remark of Reid, that "to conceive *a free act* is to conceive an act which, being a *cause*, is not itself an *effect;* in other words, to conceive an absolute commencement. But is such by us conceivable?" *How*, therefore, moral liberty is possible in man or God, we are utterly unable speculatively to understand; but practically, the *fact* that we are free is given to us in the consciousness of an uncompromising law of duty, in the consciousness of our moral accountability. And this fact of liberty cannot be redargued on the ground that it is incomprehensible, for the philosophy of the conditioned proves, against the Necessitarian, that things there are which *may*, nay, *must* be true, of which the understanding is wholly unable to construe to itself the possibility.† In fact neither liberty nor necessity is in theory comprehensible. But no man is *conscious of necessity*, while for the fact of liberty we have the evidence of consciousness, and of its practical recognition in all human intercourse, by every man, woman, and child. And, as Dr. E. S. Ely (whose attainments in the philosophy of mental science are entitled to high consideration) has well remarked: "All of man's actions, of every kind, are as truly his own as they could be were there no God that minds the affairs of men."‡ Every man is conscious of being the author of his own volitions; and Edwards has clearly shown, (in his work on the Will, p. 56,) that "the activity of the soul may enable it to be the cause of its own volitions." Hence Dwight, in his Theology, (for we wish our opponents to understand that the view we present is not "got up" for the occasion,) says: "By the term *moral agent*, I wish it to be understood that I intend a real agent, a being whose thoughts, affections, and actions

* See his "Philosophy of the Conditioned," chap. ii.

† Ibid.

‡ Theol. Review, ii. p. 6.

are his own." And again: "It is as easy to conceive, to evince, and to admit that man is an agent as that God is an agent. No difficulty attends the former case which does not in an equal degree attend the latter. If man is an agent, then there is no necessity of tracing his actions beyond himself." Ser. 8 and 27. (See also Howe, 216, 217.) And that such has ever been the view entertained and recognized by man, aside from mere metaphysical speculation, will not be seriously called in question. With his usual trueness to nature, Homer (Odys., lib. i, 32) denounces the opposite sentiment thus:

> Perverse mankind, whose will created free,
> Charge all their woes on absolute decree;
> They to the dooming gods their guilt translate,
> And follies are miscall'd the crimes of fate.—BROOME.

And Hummel, one of the ablest and most decided fatalists, says: "I have a feeling of liberty, even at the very moment when I am writing against liberty upon grounds which I regard as incontrovertible. Zeno was a fatalist only in theory; in practice he did not act in conformity to that conviction."* This universal and conceded consciousness of liberty, therefore, a consciousness practically conceded and exhibited by man in all his actions and intercourse, and in all ethics and jurisprudence, sufficiently settles the question as to his moral obligations and responsibility to the Creator of all things. It settles the question that he is a moral and accountable agent, and of course the entire propriety of his being treated by God in accordance with this his nature. He alone is responsible for his actions, and God as his moral governor must take cognizance of them, and treat him accordingly. To suppose that God will not do this, or that he may neglect to do it, is to suppose that he is not a moral governor, which brings us at once into Epicurianism, and practically, into atheism.

Every man, moreover, who pretends to the least degree

* Quoted by the editor of Hamilton's Philos., p. 510.

of intelligence or discernment, must admit that in regard to God and his proceedings there is a vast and illimitable unknown, so far as the faculties and knowledge of mankind are concerned. To deny this is to assert that there are no limitations of thought and knowledge to man in this world. But it is needless to dwell upon the topic here, for Sir William Hamilton, in the essay aforesaid, has settled the principle so as to shut the mouth of even cavil itself. And he remarks, in view of it, that "humility thus becomes the cardinal virtue, not only of revelation but of reason. This scheme proves, moreover, that no difficulty emerges in theology which had not previously emerged in philosophy; that, in fact, if the divine do not transcend what it has pleased the Deity to reveal, and willfully identify the doctrine of God's word with some arrogant extreme of human speculation, philosophy will be found the most useful auxiliary of theology. For a world of false, and pestilent, and presumptuous reasoning, by which philosophy and theology are now equally discredited, would be at once abolished in the recognition of this rule of prudent nescience."

In reference to the subject of moral agency, however, it is usual with Restorationists, to throw themselves back upon a sort of heterogeneous notion combined of their vague imaginings respecting the omnipotence and goodness of God, and to say that whatever moral agency may consist in, it must be admitted that God can perform all his pleasure, secure the accomplishment of his purposes, and influence men to act in any given manner without at all impairing that agency, as is seen by his securing the conversion of souls in this world, and all his purposes announced in his word respecting human affairs, and that therefore it is a fair inference that he can in the future world secure any such results without impairing the moral agency of the creature.

It is conceded on all hands, and must be conceded, that for God to coerce and so impair the moral agency of a rational creature is, to all intents and purposes, to annihilate his moral nature; and there is no proposition which, in all its bearings and relations, is susceptible of a clearer moral demonstration than this. And that God will secure any purposed result in any world, without impairing the moral agency of any creature, is true; but to infer from this that he is bound to secure any and every result which *we* suppose infinite wisdom and goodness ought to accomplish, is indeed to draw an inference with "a cart-rope." Let it be shown that God has purposed the recovery of the damned to holiness and heaven, and we shall not object to the doctrine because we cannot understand *how* it is to be effected. The *how* relates to the unknown and secret things of God, and there, under any such circumstances, we are always willing to leave it. But it alters the case prodigiously to assume, without a just and sufficient foundation, that God is bound to perform a specific act, and then to ignore all attempts to consider the assumption itself in the light of reason alone.

There are, however, important matters relating to this assumption of what God is able to effect without impairing man's moral agency, which these men never take into the account, and which, notwithstanding, affect the very vitals of the question. That God does so arrange causations as to result in the final salvation of all foreknown faithful believers, without in any way arresting the free exercise of their choice or impairing their moral agency, is most true, and cannot be intelligently called in question. And that in this world he could so plan events as to result in the salvation of all men, need not be denied by the most careful defenders of man's free agency and God's impartiality. But *why* he does not so arrange causes, belongs to the province of the inaccessible and unknown, so far as relates to man in this stage of his being; a province into which no sensible man will attempt to penetrate. Doubtless the reasons are drawn from the best good of the universe as a whole; and to an eye grasping the entire, would be approved as accordant with the highest goodness and wisdom. In this world, however, which was given into the hands of the second Adam immediately after our first progenitor, by proving unfaithful to his trust, plunged it into ruin and death, and which is therefore Messiah's world, and which furnishes to man a state of probation in relation to a free offer of deliverance from the curse and pollution of sin, God secures the forenamed results by an influence whose operation is a part of redemption's contemplated work, and which therefore can pertain only to a state of probation or trial, and to the means of grace. These means and this influence pertain therefore to the present state alone, and are so associated with this world and the present life that they cannot follow or accompany us beyond it, (Eccl. ix, 10; John ix, 4,) for they can have no existence in a state of retribution, where we receive according to the deeds done in the body. And as they are associated with the mediatorial kingdom, altogether and entirely so, it is obvious that they must cease to operate, at farthest, when the Mediator surrenders that kingdom to the Father, which he will do while all his enemies are under his feet. Such, then, is the mode in which God effects his ends in full view of and without impairing their moral agency, and every instance of such effect, of which we have any knowledge whatever, is associated with the means; but to assume that because God can secure this result by these means he can therefore secure it *without them*, is practically to deny the necessity of redemption, and to make the work and sufferings of our blessed and adorable Redeemer a mere unmeaning pageant. It is equivalent to saying that because God created the universe by his omnipotence, therefore he could have created it by his omniscience; and consequently, as the means of grace by which God may, in their state of probation, and in the mediatorial kingdom, secure the conversion of sinners, confessedly cannot exist in a state of retribution and without a mediatorial kingdom, it is simply idle to assume either that he can secure the same result without these means, or that the employment of the coercion of retribution and torment to secure the same result, would not be (even if it were possible thus to secure it) a violation of the creature's moral agency. We know (as Mr. Caird in his Sermons remarks) that "nature and character are spontaneous. They will not take any form, or utter themselves through any exact and inflexible mode of expression which may be furnished *from without;* for who can love by rule, manifest sorrow by stereotyped gestures, indicate gratitude or admiration by adopting looks and postures authoritatively prescribed? *Try* to make a man do so, and instead of helping you will cramp and vitiate his feelings, and by the effort to force consciousness into one special mold or shape, kill the life you mean to cultivate. In attempting to work up feeling into another's forms, a man would end by ceasing to feel, or by becoming a hypocrite and formalist." Such is the fact, known and admitted by all who have ever considered the moral and intellectual nature of man; so that to insist that the coercion of torment and of inflicted suffering will secure, either mediately or immediately, the results secured by the Spirit's influence and the means of grace in the mediatorial kingdom, is to insist upon a proposition into whose very texture is inwrought the most revolting blasphemy, by a fair and logical deduction. To insist upon it, moreover, in the absence of anything like revelation to sustain it, is quite bad enough, but to urge it in direct contradiction to the Divine averments is still worse. It is fraught with the folly of attempting to make the inaccessible, the unknown, and unrevealed the foundation of moral obligation, and to set up notions thus originating in direct antagonism to the expressed truth of God.

It seems impossible to think that it can be so, and yet nothing is more obvious than that nearly every objection against the doctrine maintained in this chapter is based upon the merest assumptions in relation to that which is absolutely unknown, and unrevealed to us. We have made this manifest in many instances already, in this and preceding chapters, and it will be in place here to refer to an effort of like character in a recent English work, written in the "namby-pamby" style of a would-be philosopher of the modern utilitarian school, and who, without professing to have any views of his own, seeks, in the most discreditable methods, to unsettle public confidence in the averments of revelation.* But let us hear what he has to offer on the subject. He represents Cyril (one of his characters) as saying, in reference to a remark of Dr. Chalmers in his Bridgewater Treatise: "I believe it! It is most true that so far as our spiritual life is concerned we are here in a sort of fetal condition. The analogy is permissible. But, good heaven! am I also to believe what Dr. Chalmers and his Church will proceed to tell me—that the conduct of this *spiritual fetus* is to determine forever the condition of that higher being who is to be born into some higher world! I have a greater reverence for Dr. Chalmers than for any living man; but how am I to reconcile the argument in his book with what he and all his Church teach in the pulpit? He argues here for our immortality on the ground that we have faculties for a higher and more spiritual life than can be here fully developed; I admit the fact; I constantly maintain it; of nothing am I more thoroughly persuaded. O! what to me would be this earthly existence if I did not believe that it would usher me into another, where the knowledge, and worship, and love of God shall fill my whole soul! But how can I, or any man, use this argument for our immortality, and at the same time maintain that *this life*, where our spiritual powers are thus scantily developed, shall be the only trial-scene for determining the eternal condition of that *other life*, where our powers will be thus exalted? Is the *status* of a man in the eternal life to be wholly and irredeemably determined by his conduct in this mortal life, in which it is confessed that the very faculties peculiarly appropriate to that eternal

* See "Thorndale; or, The Conflict of Opinions." By William Smith. Edinburgh and London. 1857.

life are but imperfectly developed, and cannot be fully exercised?

"We say, indeed, with truth, that the man grows out of the boy, and each subsequent stage of existence must be influenced by its predecessor. But on the other hand, if the subsequent stage brings with it new powers, it cannot be wholly determined by the state that preceded. The man does in fact recover from the faults of the boy. And most certainly you would not judicially determine that the conduct of the boy should forever decide the condition of the man. In like manner, how can any one assert that the *immortal* is to suffer eternally, without possibility of recovering himself, from the conduct of the *mortal?* Are higher faculties to be given for no other purpose than to feel greater pain, and anguish, and remorse than the sinner could have done in the state in which he sinned? I cannot be wrong!" he exclaimed; "it is as clear as any demon stration in Euclid." Pp. 220, 221.

The author then proceeds to detail the subsequent speculations of Cyril on the subject, and his final resolve on suicide; a legitimate result of such speculation. And if the reader would see a striking practical illustration of the tendency of infidelity of this sort, he may turn to the account, given in the New York Tribune for July 16, 1858, of the "Suicide of a Berlin Heights Free Lover." His letter to his friends, as there given, and the determination which it announces, are a perfect transcript of this *experience* of Cyril, beginning, continuing, and ending alike; for that suicide is justifiable on those principles cannot be intelligently doubted.

But the style of reasoning in the foregoing extract is that which is adopted by our opponents generally, and by all Universalists and Deists in common. This of itself, however, proves nothing in relation to its conclusiveness, or the contrary; nor do I refer to the fact invidiously. But that its basis is laid in an utter ignoring of the testimony of Divine revelation will not admit of a serious doubt;

for if the argument be based in truth, (and it assumes to be as clear as the demonstrations of Euclid,) it is obvious that the whole representation of the Scriptures on the subject is false; and the men who assume it are bound, in all consistency and common honesty, to come forth from their lurking-places among professed believers of the Bible, and take the comparatively manly position of antagonism to its announcements. It is high time that such glaring dishonesty was met by the strong and avowed disapproval of every man of intelligence and moral principle.

The argument itself, however, proceeds with confounding a distinction, perfectly obvious to every mind on a moment's reflection, and recognized in all practical human intercourse, between the moral and purely intellectual. Man, in his present state, has as clear a perception of the distinction between moral right and wrong, good and evil, obedience and disobedience, as he can ever hope to have; and that he has powers adequate to the full appreciation of this distinction in all its relations to asserted consequences, in this and in all other worlds, is sufficiently clear even from the construction of the foregoing objection itself. His powers are fully adequate to the just and proper consideration of all the information which God has imparted on the subject. Had God imparted no information in relation to it, the reasoning might appear to be plausible; but since he has imparted all needed information, and has, withal, provided the means for our securing a happy immortality, it is idle to pretend that we are at liberty to disregard it, and to act on the assumption that we are left in darkness on the subject. Every objection brought by our opponents against a future state of retribution is a full proof that man is thoroughly able to appreciate that consideration as a motive to action; and we need look no farther for evidence to prove the shallowness of all such reasoning as the above. Nor does the fact that man's intellectual powers shall continue to expand as his stores of knowledge increase, bear at all upon the issue, since an increase of intellectual power and perception in no way infers a necessary increase of moral discernment. *That* may continue to increase forever, but *this* is here as clear and plain as is necessary for a probationary state.

It will be observed too that this train of thought *wholly ignores all idea of a probation for rational creatures;* for the same reasoning which would prove our earthly life too brief for such probation, would prove that any period, however extended, would be too brief in view of the eternity which shall succeed.

And here let me ask, Is it true, can it be true, on any principle recognized by man's moral nature, that a rational creature in this or in any other state may trifle with all his own convictions of moral good and evil, obedience and disobedience, right and wrong, truth and falsehood, on the plea that he is in an irresponsible state of existence, and may therefore disregard all such considerations any farther than respects the consequences of his actions in the present life? If this be not so, then this whole mode of reasoning is a convicted lie; for if our present life (call it "fetal" or anything else) has no such relation to the life to come as is claimed for it in the word of God, then it is obvious that man is irresponsible for his conduct here any farther than pertains to present consequences, or consequences related to the present life. This is the broad basis upon which all such reasoning ultimately rests, and the tangible *practical* difference between it and Atheism I leave to others to define. I can see none.

Of the same character is that inane and silly twaddle so often heard from this class of writers, to the effect that man, in the exercise of his rational powers, cannot believe without evidence; a statement which they employ for justifying the contemptuous disregard with which they treat the proffered evidence itself. The infidel, for example, who has never examined a thousandth part of the evidence in favor of the Divine origin and inspiration of the Scriptures, does not hesitate to ignore the whole inquiry on this pretended plea.

And in the same manner is the awful theme of future and endless retribution often treated by our opponents. Now all these men are perfectly aware that no one more than the intelligent Christian maintains the principle that God never requires faith without sufficient evidence. But what has this to do with the point? The question is not whether faith can exist without evidence, but whether these men have investigated the proffered evidence itself? And that they have not, is apparent from the ignorance of the subject which is patent in all their lucubrations. If a man may possess himself of all the evidence in a matter of deep interest to himself, and on which he is required to act, and yet through negligence or indifference fail to procure it, and consequently comes to a wrong decision, can he justify his decision on the plea that "man cannot believe without evidence?" Who would justify a jury which, through gross inattention to the material points of the evidence elicited, had rendered a wrong verdict, (even though the verdict were based upon other and immaterial points of the evidence to which they did attend,) on the plea that they had to decide according to evidence? It is true that, from the evidence which they did consider, they could come to no other verdict; but who will doubt that they were guilty, and deserved severe punishment for bringing in such a verdict, since, through gross and culpable indifference and inattention, they neglected to consider that portion of the evidence which must infallibly have led them to a different decision, and of which, upon subsequent inquiry, you find them utterly ignorant, although it had been brought out fully before them? Their attempt to justify themselves on the plea that intelligent belief cannot exist without evidence, would only enhance their criminality; since it would render apparent the fact that they were aware of the value of evidence and knew how to appreciate it, and yet permitted themselves to come to a false conclusion, in a most important matter, through a heedless disregard of the fullest and most conclusive evidence, which had been carefully brought within reach of their minds and spread out before them. I need occupy no space in *applying* the illustration.

I repeat therefore, that it is not inconsistent with wisdom and goodness to treat rational creatures as responsible, and to hold them answerable for their actions in this or in any world where they may enjoy a state of probation; and that God will do this cannot be intelligently questioned. And that moral agents must furnish an approved test of an obedient disposition is equally plain; which of course infers the existence of a probationary state for all such, and of course a termination of such state, (since it would be absurd to suppose that a state of *trial* is not to terminate,) and by consequence an approval or disapproval of their conduct while it continued. The existence of such a state, moreover, plainly infers the free and unconstrained use of all the powers constituting moral agency, for without this the idea of trial and responsibility is an absurdity; and consequently Divine goodness, in furnishing such opportunity for fair and full probation, cannot, without absurdity, be supposed to do more than to see that opportunity and means are afforded which, if improved and not neglected or perverted, shall secure the final happiness of him who is the subject of the trial. To dispute either of these positions, and at the same time pretend to assert the existence of moral agency, is idle. Nor is it for us to say what are the just limits of a probationary condition for moral agents; the Creator alone may determine that, so that all such speculations as the foregoing from "Thorndale" are mere inanities when tested by reason or common sense. Life (as Horsley remarks in one of his sermons) is to be esteemed long or short, not from any proportion it may bear to eternity, (which would be equally none at all, though protracted to ten thousand times its ordinary length,) but according as the space of it may be more or less than is sufficient for the purposes of probation. There must be a certain length of time, the measure of which God only may know, within which the promises and the threatenings of the Gospel, joined with the experience which every man's life affords of God's power and providence, may be adequately appreciated, and within which, if at all, this state of experience, joined with future hopes and fears, must produce certain degrees of improvement in moral wisdom and in virtuous habit. If, in all that time, no effect is wrought, the impediment can have arisen only from incorrigible self-will and obstinacy. The fact that God terminates the probation of any such moral agent at a given time is evidence of this. And the infidel assumption, therefore, that some of the impenitent die before they are incorrigible, is both arrogant and preposterous, (though many doubtless are, for wise purposes, permitted to live long after they become so,) since it assumes a knowledge of God's secret views and operations which no man in his senses can pretend to possess; for no man can, with the slightest degree of reason, pretend to know how long a moral agent must live in sin in order to arrive at the condition referred to, and therefore no man has a right to say that any sinners die before God as perfectly knows them to be incorrigible as if they had lived in sin a thousand years.* Nor is there any reason to believe that had they continued to live ever so long there would have been any change in their moral condition. "Qualities," as Horsley remarks, "are not to be measured by duration; they bear no more relation to it than they do to space. The hatefulness of sin is seated in itself—in its own internal quality of evil; by that its ill-deservings are to be measured, not by the narrowness of the limits, either of time or place, within which the good providence of God hath confined its power of doing mischief."

If a moral agent, therefore, become truly incorrigible in any state of probation assigned to him by God, it is plain that the retribution preannounced by God as the consequence of disobedience is his just desert; and it is plainly

* See on this point Edwards against Chauncey, chap. viii; a little work which Universalism has never even attempted to answer, though originally published in 1789.

impertinent to pretend that God, who knows all things from the beginning, and of course knew them all at the time on which he announced those consequences, is either not bound to inflict them, or that goodness should lead him to furnish a second probation. What assurance is there that another probation would secure results which the Gospel and its means of grace failed to secure? And how are the sins of his previous probation to be disposed of? (a point on which Beecher's "Conflict of Ages" is very weak.)* And how is such a second probation to be brought about so as to be certain in its results? Are infinite goodness and omnipotence to be called to the rescue? But, not to insist on what is above said respecting moral agency, I would ask, if such interposition be needed to secure that result, why was it not made so as to prevent man from coming into such a condition at all? If God's sole aim is to secure the happiness of every one of his creatures, it is manifest that this interposition could far better have been made at the outset; and in the utter absence of any principle, either in reason or revelation, to sustain the foregoing assumption, I affirm this to be so. In the same manner that God could operate after the close of this our present life, so as to secure by his Almighty power the future salvation of the lost, he could have prevented the introduction of sin and misery into the universe. And if he can, and therefore ought to renew

* Kant, (Religionslehre, sec. 78,) in referring to this matter, shows the folly of expecting salvation on the ground of our own works. He says: "Whatever may have been the circumstances under which the *sinner* began his course of piety, and however uniformly correct his deportment may be, still, previously to his change, he lived in sin, and the guilt then contracted he cannot possibly ever wash away. The fact that he, after his change of heart, contracts no new debts, will never pay off the old ones. Nor can he, however holy his walk, ever do more than he is bound to do, for he is under constant obligation to exert himself to the utmost of his ability in the service of his God." (Cited in Storr and Flatt's Theology, sec. 90.) Kant should have credited this argument to Bunyan's Pilgrim's Progress. It is perfectly conclusive, however, and should be most seriously considered by those who hope for salvation, and at the same time reject the offer made to them through the vicarious atonement and sacrifice of our Lord Jesus Christ.

men through the torments of hell, it is proper to say, in the absence of any inspired declaration to the contrary, that he can renew them at once and directly, yea, without even the discipline of suffering at all; for if it is to be effected, as this theory assumes, by pure almighty power or omnipotence, and irrespective of mediatorial intervention, it is plain, as omnipotence is not restricted to the use of instrumentalities, it can accomplish its end immediately and without them. And if this renewal is to be thus effected, (that is, by pure omnipotence, and by *ab extra* operation,) God can accomplish such a result at any time, either with or without an instrument. Why then does he permit his creatures to suffer as they do in this world? The question is perfectly proper in respect to a theory which professes to be founded on the reason and the nature of things. If the fact that he is good and almighty proves that he will prevent the continuance of misery hereafter, since, on the ground that he *can* then prevent it, it is alleged to be unnecessary, it is equally plain that he can prevent it now, and that therefore it is now unnecessary. Goodness and omnipotence, therefore, are confessedly not inconsistent with the existence of the misery they can prevent, and therefore to draw any such inference in relation to the prevention of misery in the future state is absurd. (See H. 1, p. 134; S. 65, 69; D. 87, 88, 122, 276–278; M. 29–39; Kneeland's Lectures, 227.) Essential goodness is defined to be the love of virtue for its own sake. Whether this is or is not a full and sufficient definition is, however, of no consequence here, for it is sufficient for the purpose. We know, as Horsley has remarked, that as virtue and vice are opposites, so love and hate are opposites. A consistent character, therefore, must bear opposite affections toward opposite things. To love virtue for its own sake, and to hate vice for its own sake, may therefore belong equally to the character of essential goodness. And thus, as virtue, in itself, and for its own sake, must be the object of God's love and favor, so incorrigible vice, in itself, and for its own sake, must be the object of his hatred and displeasure, and of course, therefore, it is in no way inconsistent with essential goodness to visit it with unending retribution; I say endless retribution, since from the very nature of sin it cannot be otherwise; for any creature, by knowingly and voluntarily perpetrating it, at once places himself beyond the power of undoing what he has done, or of recovering his standing as a pure and holy being with God his Creator. Hence, unless God interpose and save him, he is manifestly lost and helpless forever. Much more then must this be his condition when God, having freely offered to save him from sin, and to bestow upon him eternal life, he refuses the offer; and therefore we find it clearly announced that the refusal of the offer of eternal life necessarily involves eternal death as the consequence. (John iii, 36; Rom. vi, 23.) And as the wrath of God is to abide or remain (*μένει*) upon such, it is obvious that they are to sustain and realize that loss and its consequences; not by ceasing to exist, for it would be ridiculous to suppose that the wrath of God could abide upon a nonentity. Thus the guilt of those who die impenitent must be, in the very nature of things, perpetual, and of a twofold character, being derived both from transgressing the law and refusing the deliverance offered in the Gospel; and it is equally obvious that where guilt exists under the government of God, there also must misery exist likewise.

As the foregoing speculation is the stronghold of all who deny the eternal punishment of sin, it is very important to consider it in all those points of view in which they present it, and to give it a thorough refutation; and it is the more important from the incautious and culpable representations made on the subject by some divines. Nothing is more absurd than to say that because God may, on the sinner's acceptance of proffered mercy in a probationary state, remit a threatened punishment, he therefore is not bound to execute his threatenings when the sinner has, in his impenitence, passed into a state of retribution. And the contrary intimation, by some reputedly orthodox divines, has tended no little to relieve the minds of the impenitent and vicious, and to encourage such blasphemous assertions as that of Whiston, that "this doctrine supposes God to delight in cruelty;" and that "if certainly true, the justice of God must inevitably be given up, and much more his mercy;" and that also of Dr. Chauncey, who says: "It is high time that some generally received doctrines should be renounced, and others embraced in their room that are more honorable to the Father of mercies, and comfortable to the creatures which his hands have made." The same is countenanced too by such writers as Whately, Ham, Storrs, Hudson, Dobney, T. S. Smith, etc.

The remark of Archbishop Tillotson, that God may reserve to himself the right to inflict or not to inflict the threatened penalty of sin in a state of retribution, has already accomplished vastly more of evil to the souls of men than all the labors and influence of that most amiable and exemplary prelate have ever done good. Since his own time it has been reiterated by all the despisers of God's admonitions and threatenings, and multitudes have made it a plea to justify their casting off all practical recognition of moral obligation. God has said nothing like this in his word; and what right had Dr. Tillotson to theorize thus in respect to a practical matter of the most transcendent interest to human welfare? God has, moreover, not only said nothing to justify such an intimation, but all his utterances, as we shall see, are directly against the supposition. And what right, therefore, had any minister of Christ thus to interfere with those motives which God had furnished for practical human life and conduct, and to neutralize them thus by mere inferences from the absolutely unknown and inaccessible? Dr. Tillotson had no such right, nor has any other man; and those, therefore, who practically venture to build their hopes for the future on any such idle and baseless expectation, do it not only without reason, but at the imminent peril of making eternal shipwreck of their future well-being.

If to threaten is not inconsistent with infinite goodness, and mercy, and wisdom, on what principle is it inconsistent therewith to execute the threatening? We may admit that, in strictness of speech, God may not be obliged to execute simply because he has threatened, (as Edwards, vii, 527, remarks,) but yet he was under no obligation to threaten if he knew at the same time that he would not execute, for this would have been plainly inconsistent with truth. The necessity of the connection between the execution and the threatening, arises from the obligation which He who knows all things was under to threaten at all; and from this arises the obligation to conform his absolute threatening to the future execution, so that the truth of God forms an inviolable connection between absolute threatening and execution; for to suppose that he threatened in relation to a state of pure retribution, contrary to what he knew would come to pass, is to suppose that he threatened contrary to what he knew to be the truth. If absolute threatenings are significations of anything, they are significations of the futurity of the thing threatened. They are in one sense predictions; and the same argument which would prove that he could thus falsify them, and retain his character as a God of truth, would equally prove that he could falsify his predictions and still retain that character, which is plainly absurd.*

* A statement to the following effect is often made by infidels and Universalists for the purpose of ignoring all argument in favor of Christianity and the future punishment of sin: to wit, that if they believed these things they would not rest satisfied with the little efforts which are made for human salvation by those who profess to believe them, but would give their friends no rest till they had secured their salvation, and that they "would go out, and as it were, compel them to go to church, read the Bible," etc., from all of which they also deduce the inference that Christians do not really believe what they profess. And this silly rhapsody is regarded by them as sufficiently justifying the disregard and contempt with which they treat the whole subject of religious obligation. But while I would in no way attempt to palliate the most culpable indifference of many professors of religion on the subject, I would remark, in reference to the individuals aforesaid, that supposing they believed in future retribution, they *would not*, unless wholly ignorant of human nature, pursue any such course as they describe, since every man of sense can see that such a procedure, instead of securing the attention and salvation of men, must infallibly awaken their contempt and

No one supposes that the infliction of penal evil, as such, and in itself, is desirable to God, for no one believes that it is of itself a pleasure for God to destroy his own work. (Job x, 3; Ezek. xxxiii, 11; 2 Pet. iii, 9.) But what then? Are we to suppose that nothing can render it desirable to God that penal evil should be inflicted? This is the inference drawn by many of our opponents; but what means such language as that in Jer. ix, 29? "Shall not *my soul be avenged* on such a nation as this?" And Hos. x, 10: "It is *in my desire* that I should chastise them." Deut xxviii, 36: "The Lord *will rejoice over you to destroy you.*" Isa. i, 24: "I will ease me of my adversaries: I will *avenge me* of my enemies." No pretended metaphor or anthropology can divest this language of its awful import, or hinder its pointed application to the case in hand; for we know that God *has* thus *avenged* himself by the ruin and destruction of his enemies in multitudes of instances; and the reason is simply because he must do this or compromise his hatred of iniquity, the utterances of his nature, and, in the view of all his intelligent creation, set light by his word, (see Psa. cxxxviii, 2,) and hence the holy inhabitants of heaven witness, with the highest applause, the execution of his threatenings, (Rev. xi, 17, 18; xvi, 5–7,) as already shown above. There is none of the mawkish sentimentalism among them which is exhibited in such books as those of Dobney, T. S. Smith, Hudson, Whately, and in "Thorndale," wherein all possible sympathy finds utterance on behalf of the wicked, and rebellious, and impenitent creature, and none whatever on behalf of the holy and righteous Creator and moral Governor of the universe. Sin, and

disgust, as all such interference with man's right to think and act for himself must do; and for a man thus to prove himself destitute of wisdom, is not the way to do much good in this world. And then, moreover, neither Christ nor his apostles, nor the prophets, notwithstanding all their terrific announcements on the subject, ever sought to save men in this way. The objection is merely an attempt to lull a disquiet conscience, and those who are thus influenced are only planting thorns in their bed of death.

wickedness, and disregard of moral obligation are the common center of this sympathy, and holiness, and righteousness, and equity are ignored, and their claims cannot be even asserted without awakening repeated accusations of cruelty, want of mercy, etc., and similar utterances of false philanthropy and ambitious imbecility. It might be useful for our opponents to ponder a little upon Job xxxiii, 12, 13, and Isa. lv, 8, 9.

But set the rule aside that God is thus under obligation to fulfill his threatenings against the finally impenitent, and where shall be placed the limit of departure from his most solemn obtestations? If he may do it once, why not twice, or twice ten thousand times? But this is absurd, since the very object of these open and absolute averments is that his creatures may notice and rely on them, and act accordingly. Were probation and the mediatorship continued after the final judgment, (if such an absurdity were at all supposable,) then there might be some plausibility in refusing to regard threatenings as absolute. But we have abundantly shown that this idea of probation and mediatorial intervention cannot be entertained except at the sacrifice of Scripture and common sense; and therefore, if God has reserved to himself the liberty to depart from this rule, with no previous announcement, and no reason given to determine what his pleasure shall be, how may it be known that he will not, in any given instance whatever, depart from it? And on this ground what becomes of certainty in respect to the fulfillment of his word in any case? Thus, by a fair and logical sequence, along with certainty in respect to his threatenings, must depart also certainty in respect to his promises and predictions, (since, on the same principle, he must reserve the right either to fulfill them or not,) and thus the promised bliss of heaven becomes as much a matter of uncertainty as the threatened torments of hell.

The evasion that these threatenings do not announce what God will do, but only what the sinner deserves to suffer, can be entertained by no serious mind who will carefully consider the threatenings themselves. See, for example, Matt. xxv, 41, 46; 2 Thess. i, 7–9; Matt. xii, 32; xviii, 8, 9; Rev. xiv, 10, 11; xx, 10. The evasion, however, really amounts to nothing; for, not to speak of its being alike applicable to all Divine admonitions and announcements, and therefore self-refuted, it concedes that the threatenings themselves contain God's expressed announcements of the *true demerit of sin.* Sin therefore truly deserves all that these threatenings express.

Upon the whole, then, to adopt the language of Dr. Whitby in his discourse on the endless misery of the Wicked, "Either God may in justice inflict upon the wicked those punishments which he has threatened, or else it is unjust in God to execute upon them the judgment written, that is, the punishment which he hath threatened to them in the word of truth. If it be said, It is unjust in God to execute them on the sinner dying in his impenitence, either we cannot be obliged to believe that word in which these threats are contained, or else an obligation must lie upon us to believe that God will act unjustly."

Now it is conceded freely, and either directly or indirectly, by nearly all our opponents, that the sinner deserves eternal punishment. See, for example, M. 9–11; H. 2, p. 65; D. 51, 66–72, 164, 244–251; Kneeland, p. 47. And so, too, the Restorationists, Socinians, etc. But on what principle does he *deserve* to be thus treated? And further, on what principle is it unjust or improper to inflict upon him what he deserves? The absurd talk about *summum jus summa injuria*, of which the writings of Messrs. Dobney, and Hudson, and Kneeland, and Dr. Chauncey are so full, has no application here. The maxim may sometimes be true in the necessarily imperfect jurisprudence of men; but to reason thus from an imperfect human administration to the infinitely perfect and divine, is to proclaim one's self to be "not o'erfraught with sense;" and to venture upon any such hope is a fearful experiment. And if I may again refer to an idea already suggested, a fair and logical application of the utilitarian principles of our opponents will justify the continuance of this punishment forever. The employment of such penal execution as a salutary example is clearly brought to view in Isaiah lxvi, 24, (a passage which, in its relation to eternity, is strongly applied by our Saviour,) and its use is there also exhibited. The idea that because the *Sabbath* and *new moon* are referred to in the context, the passage must refer to a period antecedent to the general judgment, is absurd, and cannot mislead a child, unless that child should entertain a notion that the pristine condition of earth is incompatible with endless duration.

We have the assurance of the Holy Scriptures that the redeemed of Christ, after being gathered home to heaven, shall never fall, and that there shall be no violation of the peace of that government in which Christ shall still reign as Prince of Peace after he has resigned the mediatorial kingdom, or ceased from all mediatorial intervention on behalf of sinners, and no limit to its increase. Holiness, and righteousness, and peace, shall remain forever. And that the redeemed and all the future subjects of his kingdom are to be preserved from sin and fall by the influence of moral motives, will hardly be questioned by any who hold the moral agency of man. And who dare venture to say, therefore, that any specific order of motives may be dispensed with in securing this result? The man who should venture to say of any order of means employed by God in the matter, or which he announces shall be so employed, that it is *unnecessary* or *superfluous*, would by so doing convict himself of playing the fool in an important matter respecting which he knew nothing. Good ends are confessedly answered by punishment in this world; and when God assures us that punishment shall exist in the world to come, how impious is it to reply to him by saying that it is unnecessary because we can see no use in it? The text referred to in Isaiah lxvi, presents a view of this motive in its operation, and the salutary effect of such a spectacle is easily understood by the mind. And if the continued sufferings of those who have rebelled against God and renounced his authority shall be thus salutary, and if the salvation of the righteous, and the preservation of other beings who may be at any time created and pass through a probationary state, should call for this perpetual example of punishment, why should God spare the wicked and rebellious, and cease to inflict upon them their just deserts? I put the question to those who have dared to say that "perpetual punishment is needless, for no good can come out of it;" and that "it is so great an evil that it cannot be compensated by any good." Why, therefore, should God spare the wicked, and not fulfil against them his threatenings? Perpetual suffering is truly an infinite evil to those who suffer it; but in the same sense, as remarked already, the good arising from it is an infinite good to innumerably greater multitudes.

Before leaving this topic, it may be proper to refer in conclusion to the sentiments entertained on the subject by those learned and profound scholars and critics, the Polish Socinians. They represent the utmost limits to which "liberal principles" can venture in consistency with a profession of Christianity, and this, together with their uncompromising antagonism to the whole evangelical system of doctrine, renders their views on this topic a matter of importance; for men who venture beyond those limits are bound in all moral honesty to renounce the Christian name. Dr. Jared Sparks (late President of Harvard University) affirms that the Churches of Poland and Transylvania believed the doctrine of "the eternity of future punishment," and that it was taught by the Racovian Catechism, which was the approved expression of the faith of all those Churches, and was drawn up by Socinus, Smalcius, and others "among the most learned theologians of the fraternity." (Inquiry, p. 348.) B. Wissowatius, in a note on the passage in which this sentiment is affirmed, says that "it has been always the opinion of the

Church that the wicked will be doomed to punishment, and cast into the fire prepared for the devil and his angels," and that the eminent writers of the Unitarian faith "constantly maintained that there will be a resurrection both of the just and of the unjust, and that the latter shall be consigned to everlasting punishment, but the fomer admitted to everlasting life."

And accordingly Crellius, the leading and most profound genius of that school, in his discourse on Matt. iii, 11, 12, (Pol. Frat., iv, 3–9,) says that "*Ignis inextinctus* est imprimis ille futurus, qui ita consumet omnia, ut ad meliorem statum nullus sit reditus, et exitium plane æternum afferet." And in his exposition of Heb. x, 26–32, (pp. 285–300,) after largely insisting on the same truth, he adds the following, (well worthy of being pondered by all our adversaries:) "Ex his autem patet, *misericordiam non esse proprietatem in Deo naturaliter ac proprie residentem. Nam quædam sunt actiones Dei, in quibus nulla utitur misericordia, sed ejus contrario*, nimirum, ira et severitate." See also his note and paraphrase in Heb. x, 27. (tom. iii, 165, 263,) and on 2 Thess. i, 9, (p. 554;) also Slichtingius on John v, 29. (Tom. v, 43.) Wolzogenius also, though with some of his brethren a little inclined to favor the doctrine of the ultimate annihilation of the wicked, says on Matt. iii, 12: "*Igni inextinguibili.* Hoc igne significatur æterna damnatio è qua impii nulla nunquam tempore emergent aut liberabuntur." (Tom. vi, in loco.) And on Matt. x, 28, in a passage already referred to, he says: "Since Christ here names the place, even Gehenna, where God shall destroy the soul as well as the body, it appears that he by the word *destroy* did not understand simply *kill*, or *reduce to nothing—in nihilum redigere*, (for God can do this immediately while the soul is separated from the body,) but torment and torture, *sed torquere ac cruciare.* See his powerful note also on John v, 29.

Even the later Socinians of the Swiss and French Churches entertain the same view. Their "Geneva Catechism," says of the wicked that "they will be tormented with remorse and abandoned to despair, *because they have lost eternal happiness* by their own misconduct;" and to sustain this, Mark ix, 43; Matt. xxiii, 13, are cited. The "Christian Disciple," also, for March and April 1819, conducted by the late Prof. A. Norton, and other learned Unitarians of Boston and vicinity, (and which Dr. Sparks says "may be supposed to declare the prevailing sentiments of the Unitarians of this country,") thus speaks: "We cannot but wonder and lament that any should so far pervert the oracles of God as to persuade men to believe that there is no punishment hereafter; an error, we repeat, most dangerous to the interests of society; it breaks down the barriers of conscience, and removes those salutary restraints, without which neither virtue, nor reputation, nor property are secure." And President Sparks himself, in reviewing the matter, says: "The true state of the case is, then, that Unitarians, *as a body*, *universally* believe in the future punishment of the wicked. By a very large number this punishment has been considered *eternal*; by others it is supposed to be limited in duration, but to be severe and dreadful," etc.*

I have introduced these testimonies simply as an offset to those false representations of Mr. Hudson, and others, respecting the views of the divines of Germany, and to expose the folly of certain individuals who are ever evincing a morbid unwillingness that God should regulate the affairs of his own administration, and do what he himself esteems right and best, unless their own puny intellects are admitted into his counsels, and made to understand the whole matter. But while we appreciate and realise the overwhelming importance of being, in this probationary state, truly mindful of our eternal interests, we have no sympathy with any doctrine which either neutralizes or ignores the most solemn and impressive counsels and admonitions of the God of truth.

* Inquiry, p. 350.

# CHAPTER VII.

## THE ETERNALLY MISERABLE EXISTENCE OF THE WICKED IS FULLY ANNOUNCED IN THE WORD OF GOD.

### § 66. *Ultimate Condition of the Lost.*

WE return, then, to the question, What is eternal punishment? We have seen that it is not annihilation, and of course it cannot consist in happiness, so that there is no way to avoid the consequence that it is a state of endless retribution and irrecoverable misery. That God has afforded us (for, being a practical matter, it is better that in this business we confine our attention mainly to ourselves) a fair and full opportunity to obtain eternal life, will not be questioned; and that the terms on which this deliverance from sin and its penalty are offered are perfectly reasonable, will be admitted; and that many among us willfully refuse the offer, and even all proper consideraton of it, none can deny; nor will it be denied that they do this in utter defiance and disregard of all the expostulations, admonitions, and threatenings of God. And now, my reader, be candid with your own soul, and answer to your conscience and to God the question, Where is the impropriety or injustice of withholding the proffered boon from those who have deliberately refused it, treated the offer with disdain, and spent their opportunities for securing it in such pursuits and indulgences as must, in the very necessity of the case, render them in every way disqualified for the worship of God, and for the holy society of heaven? Eternal life was fully within their reach; they could have secured it, and become qualified for its enjoyment, and for companionship with the good and the excellent of all ages who have been gathered around the throne, but they refused it. And as it would be ridiculous to pretend that such a choice or refusal of a moral agent is the same in the long run as if he had chosen the opposite, so there is nothing that can remain to such but that they should have their choice; and that as they chose to be separate from the holy and redeemed family of God, they should be associated with his enemies in both their character and doom. An utter severance, therefore, from Jesus and his redeemed, and an abode and association with evil angels, are the necessary consequences which they have willfully brought upon themselves, and such is the eternal misery of the damned. There is for them no other alternative. The evidence is abundantly sufficient to convince any one who will seriously examine it, that man is a sinner, and alienated from God; that his moral nature needs renewal before he can be either holy or happy; that God freely offers to deliver and save him through Jesus Christ, and pleads with him tenderly and earnestly to accept the offer; and therefore either to hope or plead for impunity on the ground that these things *are not believed* by the exceptant, is as vain and hopeless as it is trifling and arrogant. This doom, therefore, is privation of eternal life, (John iii, 16; v, 29;) endurance of God's displeasure, (1 Thess. v, 3; Gal. vi, 8; John viii, 51; 2 Thess. i, 9;) and is called the *second death*, (Rev. xx, 14; xxi, 8;) and is an utter rejection from the society of Jesus and the blessed. (Matt. xiii, 48–50; xxv, 41, 46; Luke xvi, 26; Rev. xxii, 14.) And the spirit of God in describing it employs the following terms of fearful import: *ὄλεθρος*, *destruction*, (from *ὄλλυμι*, *to destroy;*) *κόλασις*, *a cutting off;* *ἀπώλεια*, *perdition;* *ὀργὴ τοῦ Θεοῦ*, *wrath of God;* *κρίμα*, *judgment;* *κρίσις*, (also from *κρίνω*, *to separate,*) *separation;* *θάνατος δεύτερος*, *second death;* *σκώληξ*, (*undying,*) *worm;* *φθορά*, *corruption;* *πῦρ αἰώνιον*, *eternal fire;* and *βάσανοι*, *torments.*

There is, moreover, the clearest announcement, made in every form that language will admit, that there shall be a direct contrast between the condition of the good and evil in their future existence. See Psa. xvii, 14, 15; Prov. x, 28; xiv, 32; Dan. xii, 2; Matt. iii, 11, 12; vii, 13, 14, 21; viii, 11, 12; xiii, 30, 40–43; xxv, 23, 30–46; Mark xvi, 16; Luke vi, 23, 24; John iii, 10; v, 29; Rom. xi, 21–23; 2 Tim. ii, 19, 20; Gal. vi, 7, 8; Heb. vi, 8, 9, etc., etc. And as the state of the righteous, here referred to, is of course final, it is obvious that the state of the wicked is final also.

God will accomplish this separation, (and hence the difference between the two states is described as *a great gulf*, *χάσμα μέγα*, *fixed*, Luke xvi, 26,) for he shall cast the wicked out of his kingdom. (Luke xiii, 28.) He shall sever the wicked from among the just, and send his angels to collect all that do evil, and cast them into a furnace of fire. (Matt. xiii, 40–43, 48, 50.) He shall separate the good and evil, one from the other. (Matt. xxv, 32–34, 41.) Compare also Rev. xx, 15, 20; xxi, 8; xxii, 14, 15.

The place appointed for the wicked of both men and angels is named *hell*, *γέεννα*, (from גֵּיא הִנּוֹם; see 2 Kings xxiii, 10,) Matt. v, 22, 29; x, 20; Mark ix, 45, 47, also *τόπος τῆς βάσανου*, *place of torment;* Luke xvi, 23, 28, *ἡ γέεννα τοῦ πυρός*, *the hell of fire;* also *σκότος ἐξώτερον*, *outer darkness;* *ζόφος τοῦ σκότους*, *blackness of darkness;* Matt. viii, 12; xxii, 13; Jude 13. See also Matt. xiii, 50, 52; Mark ix, 43–48; Rev. xiv, 10, 11; xix, 20; xx, 14. And here they receive every one *κατὰ τὰ ἔργα αὐτοῦ*, *according to his works*, (Rom. ii, 6;) or *according as he has sown*, (Gal. vi, 7;) *according to the deeds done in the body*, (2 Cor. v, 10;) *according to the wrong he hath done*, (Col. iii, 25;) for as this is their abode it is of course the place of their retribution.

We have, in the course of this volume, repeatedly adverted to the fact that it is neither unphilosophical nor unreasonable to conclude that as the present stage of our being is but the introduction to and preparation for the next, there are things recorded in the Scriptures which are designed to show the connection which really exists between the visible and invisible world. In this category is doubtless to be placed the fact of demoniacal possession; a fact which is patent upon the very face of the whole Gospel record, and which no ingenuity can set aside, as is conceded substantially by our adversaries themselves, in their adoption of the language of Mr. Mole, quoted and approved by his friend Dr. Lardner: "This affair of the possessions is an embarrassment which one would be glad to be fairly rid of." But there is no getting rid of it, whatever embarrassments it may place in the way of the mere rationalizing theologue; and as the appearance of Moses and Elias in glory foreshowed to man the future state of the redeemed, so, according to all Scriptural representations, the fearful spectacle of a human being possessed by evil spirits foreshows, by a terrible representation, the future condition of the damned. The demoniac, for instance, mentioned in Matt. viii, knew Christ, yet avoided and hated him. "An outcast from the intellectual and religious world, he grieved over his lot, yet he could not repent. In the deepest misery and distress he heightened his own agony by self-inflicted torments. The light of heaven, which occasionally broke in upon his melancholy dwelling among the tombs, served only to make more visible the darkness of his wretchedness, and embittered every anguish and suffering by the torturing remembrance of what he *was* and what he *might* have been." And such is the awful warning addressed to the wicked and impenitent among men to accept the Gospel offer of deliverance, lest they likewise come into the same state of condemnation.*

The question whether the term "*fire*," in its relation to this subject, is to be understood metaphorically or literally, presents every evidence of having been suggested by the devil himself, and in fact there is no possiblity of mistaking

* See Townsend's N. T., Notes, pp. 76, 77.

his hand in the matter; for, 1. We have no means of solving the question; 2. If solved it could answer no practical purpose; and, 3. In the attempt to solve it many errors have been run into; a vast deal of time and energy have been wasted; many souls have been led away from the practical into the merely theoretical, and their attention has been diverted from the important considerations calling upon them to secure their own salvation without delay. Men had infinitely better concern themselves with the inquiry how to escape the damnation of hell, instead of attempting to pry into the unrevealed and unknown; for we may fairly conclude that God has employed no expression or figure, in speaking on the subject, which conveys an idea stronger than the reality must prove to be. The Annihilationists, however, for obvious reasons, insist that all the more terrific expressions in reference to the doom of the wicked are to be taken in their literal sense; for they hope thus to establish their notion of the ultimate and utter extermination of the wicked; but as well might they insist that the metaphorical representations of the future happiness of the blessed are to be literally understood. On the one side *outer darkness*, *the undying worm*, *furnace of fire*, *lake of fire and brimstone, which is the second death*, etc., are mentioned; and on the other, *the bosom of Abraham*, *Paradise*, *sitting down with the patriarchs*, *tree of life*, *festal scenes*, *treasures*, *crowns*, and the like; and whatever the unvailed future may show to be the full import of these terms, the ideas which the human mind spontaneously attaches to them in their proper connection in the word of God, are sufficiently distinct and impressive to constitute motives to action in view of the life to come.

In the present and preceding sections the arguments establishing the doctrine of the eternal suffering of the damned have been so fully brought to view in their various relations to our whole theme, that, instead of attempting a recapitulation of them here, we shall conclude the whole argument by a brief consideration of some passages of Scripture which plainly and clearly teach this doctrine, but which our opponents have labored to divest of their significant application to the subject.

1. The first is Dan. xii, 2: "And many of them that sleep in the dust of the earth shall awake, some to everlasting life, and some to shame and everlasting contempt." The meaning of the latter clause of the verse may be seen by referring to Prov. i, 24–31.

The idea of some of the ancient Rabbins, that because the word here employed is *many* instead of *all*, therefore the wicked are not to be raised, is absurd; for the passage says expressly that of those who are raised, some shall arise to shame and everlasting contempt. But that it is in accordance with Scripture usage to employ such partitives often in a general sense, and terms of collective or universal import in a restricted sense, no reader of the Bible can seriously question. See Psa. xcvii, 1, (Heb.;) Isa. lii, 15; liii, 12. Comp. v. 6, and 2 Cor. v, 15; Rom. v, 15, 19; xii, 5, (Greek;) viii, 29; Matt. xx, 16, 28; Exod. ix, 6. Comp. v. 3 and Exod. xxxii, 3. Comp. v. 16, Matt. iii, 5, and many other places. See the principle illustrated in Glassius, Philol. Sacra, lib. v, Tract. i, c. 14, 15. The passage, therefore, expresses the same idea which is taught in John v, 28, 29; Acts xxiv, 14, 15; Rev. xx; and the sense is that "*the many* who sleep in the dust shall arise." And it contains a silent antithetical reference to those who do not thus sleep, but who shall be living at the time when the event occurs. (See 1 Thess. iv, 13–17.) And as the wicked, therefore, are to experience a sense of shame and everlasting contempt, they of course must continue to exist.

On this passage S. 63 remarks that "the text does not say that they awake to *everlasting* shame. It says they awake to *shame*—mark that—'some to *shame*' and everlasting contempt." "I affirm the text does not say the shame shall be everlasting, but only that they shall awake to shame; and surely they must feel overwhelmed with shame when God shall call them from their graves, and when they shall be condemned to death, as too vile to have a place anywhere in the universe of God," etc. See also M. 74–76.

Such ignorance is as near an approach to non-existence of knowledge as can well be imagined. Without referring to the Hebrew, these men could have seen, from the English translation alone, that "*and*" forms no part of the original; and the idea simply is, "some to shame, to infamy everlasting." *Endless*, or *everlasting*, is the attribute of both terms, as is plain from the construction, and from its being placed at the end of the clause. The sense is cumulative, and the repetition of the idea of shame in the second term, which not only includes it, but expresses that idea much more strongly, is intensive, according to Hebrew usage, as no one acquainted with the subject can fail to perceive. Hence the LXX render it *εἰς ὀνειδισμὸν καὶ αἰσχύνην αἰώνιον*, *to ignominy and shame eternal;* or, omitting *καὶ*, (to which there is no answering particle in the original,) *to ignominy, to shame eternal.* The phrase is לַחֲרָפוֹת לְדִרְאוֹן עוֹלָם, and needs no further criticism to show that while eternal shame shall be the portion of the ungodly, a consciousness on their part that they are a loathsome spectacle to all holy beings, (see דֵּרָאוֹן, as used in Isa. lxvi, 24,) shall cover them with eternal confusion.

2. The next passage is Matt. xii, 31, 32, (Mark iii, 29,) in which it is declared that the sin against the Holy Ghost shall never be forgiven.

The phrase "neither in this world, neither in the world to come," is explained in Mark to mean "hath never forgiveness." See also Luke xii, 10. And I can see no reason to suppose that our Saviour refers to actual pardon in this world, and the declaration of it in the future world on the day of judgment. The phrase was of frequent use among the Jews, and in the sense simply of *forever.* Dr. Chauncey concedes that "it was not our Saviour's intention here to suggest that any sins might be forgiven in the future world, which were not forgiven in this." (Universal Salv., p. 339.) The same idea is of course entertained by our opponents.

The idiom is well illustrated by Kuinoel, *in loco*, (who refers also to 2 Mac. vi, 26, which see,) as expressing simply the idea of forever. Glassius sustains the same view, and has established its accuracy beyond all reasonable doubt. (Phil. Sac., pp. 803, 2111.) The guilt of this sin, therefore, is forever to rest upon him who perpetrates it. There is no hope of his ever obtaining forgiveness. And as such language cannot, of course, be predicated of a nonentity, it is obvious that they to whom it refers must continue to exist forever.

3. Matt. iii, 10–12, which asserts that "every tree which bringeth not forth good fruit is hewn down, and cast into the fire," and that Christ "will burn up the chaff with unquenchable fire," is admitted to refer to the final destiny of the wicked; and from it D. 235–237, and H. 1, p. 138, argue their extinction. H. avers that the perpetuity "pertains not to the objects upon which the fire acts, but to the fire itself." D. sustains the same idea, and refers for illustration to Isa. xxxiv, 8–10, in which it is said that "the land shall become burning pitch, that shall not be quenched night nor day, the smoke thereof shall go up forever;" and also to Jude 7. "Sodom and Gomorrah, and the cities about them, are set forth for an example, suffering the vengeance of eternal fire;" and by *cities* he understands not the inhabitants, but the houses, walls, etc., constituting the *material* cities, (as though these "*had gone after strange flesh*,") which, says he, were "never again to be rebuilt." But the attempt, even on the ground of such an exposition, to obtain the idea of utter annihilation from these passages, is sheer nonsense; for the land of Edom still exists, and all the component parts of Sodom and the other cities, notwithstanding this fearful application of fire, burning pitch, and brimstone. These have produced their effect, and brought utter desolation upon the places specified; but annihilation and desolation are hardly the same; and so will the *fire* referred to in the text bring utter desolation upon the wicked.

The word *chaff*, ἄχυρον, (Matt. iii, 12,) here refers to the *straw* broken up by treading out the grain, and which the Jews were accustomed to cut up and burn to heat their ovens. See Matt. vi, 30; Mal. iv, 1. The terms *flame* and *fire* are often used in the Scriptures to signify Divine wrath, displeasure, etc. And the same terms are employed in popular language to express the idea of human anger; for example, as when the Latins say, *incandescere*, *inflammari*, *accendi ira*. Thus God is said to be a consuming fire. Deut. iv, 24. See also Deut. xxxii, 22; Isa. lxvi, 15, 16; Psa. lxxxix, 47; Ezek. xxi, 31. And as in our text the phrase, he shall "gather his wheat into the garner, but he will burn up the chaff with unquenchable fire," is admitted to be exegetical of the phrase, "He shall baptize you with the Holy Ghost and with fire," (see D. 236,) the idea of utter extinction by baptism of the person baptized is not only inadmissible, but ridiculous, and the folly of attempting to join the ideas is apparent. Baptism with the Holy Ghost (as also with water) is expressive of character in its subject, and so too baptism with fire. It settles the subsequent character and moral position of those who receive it; but to make it destructive of the existence of the recipient is as complete a piece of inanity as can well be imagined.

The figure of the chaff being utterly consumed is relied on as justifying the inference that the wicked are to be annihilated, but with how much reason a moment's reflection will determine. The Jews cast their chaff into the fire, which, having consumed it, was of course quenched. And John, to guard them against the idea which some of them entertained, (see § 39, above,) that the sufferings of the wicked would terminate, refers to the figure of the chaff, but adds, that those whom it represents are to be burned up with *unquenchable fire*; and of course as the fire is *unquenchable*, that which feeds it must continue to exist forever. And yet, from this self-same precautionary admonition of John, our adversaries would infer that the error which he thus refutes is, after all, the truth! But, on the supposition that the wicked are to be utterly annihilated by the fire, where is the propriety of calling it unquenchable? To say that it is unquenchable so long as the wicked are being extinguished by it, is saying nothing to the purpose, for the fire in which the Jews burned their chaff was unquenchable in precisely the same sense, and John is here, as above stated, distinguishing between the two; and as such an idea of unquenchable destroys the distinction, it of course is a mere evasion of the point. The evasion referred to above, that "the perpetuity refers to the fire, and not to the objects cast into it," renders the threatening itself simply ludicrous. For, *first*, as *fire* here refers to the wrath or displeasure of God, it would be absurd to say that it continues after the objects of it have ceased utterly to exist; and then, further, how could it add to the force of a threatening to say, You shall be burned up and extinguished in a fire that shall afterward continue to burn forever? Suppose that some man in Rome were now condemned to be burned at the stake, and that the judge should say to him, "You shall, for your great wickedness, be burned in a fire which the government has ordered to be kept burning for fifty years after you are consumed;" and who can suppose that the man could be influenced by that consideration, or that he would care how long the fire might burn after it had ceased to torment him? Such an idea, of course, cannot be entertained, and hence it is obvious that the wicked must suffer forever under the wrath or displeasure of God; let not the impenitent, therefore, entertain the hope that their existence is to terminate.

4. In Matt. xvi, 25, 26, (and Mark viii, 35–37,) Jesus says: "For whosoever will save his life, shall lose it, and whosoever will lose his life for my sake, shall find it. For what is a man profited, if he shall gain the whole world, and lose his own soul? or what shall a man give in exchange for his soul?"

D. 234, 235, undertakes to divest this passage of its impressive bearing upon our theme, by the puerile criticism, already noticed in section 33, above, that the word ψυχὴ is employed in both verses, and should be *uniformly* rendered *life*, instead of *life* in verse 25, and *soul* in verse 26. Dr. Campbell, in his loose, rambling translation, gives it the uniform rendering of *life*, though he at the same time affirms, " That our Lord has a principal eye to the loss of the soul, or of eternal life, there can be no doubt." But how does the fact that it is the same word in both these verses prove that it should be translated in both alike by the same English term? Every school-boy who has ever studied a language knows that this would be a most preposterous rule to follow. Our blessed Redeemer, in conversing with Nicodemus, after remarking that, " Except a man be born of water and of the Spirit, he cannot enter into the kingdom of God," and that " that which is born of the flesh is flesh, and that which is born of the Spirit is spirit," adds these words: " The wind bloweth where it listeth, and thou hearest the sound thereof, but canst not tell whence it cometh, or whither it goeth: so is every one that is born of the Spirit." John iii, 8. And it is the same word, πνεῦμα, which, in this one verse, is translated by both *wind* and *Spirit.* And even Dr. Campbell does not venture to apply here the aforesaid rule of uniformity. The objection of Mr. Dobney to the translation is therefore puerile, and of no weight whatever.

That Jesus refers in this passage directly to the future judgment is plain from the context. And the expression, " What shall a man give in exchange for his soul," alludes to the condition of the soul after it is rejected by the final decision of the Judge. Of course, then, continuance of being is clearly implied; for, independent of the fact that the loss of a thing in no way supposes its annihilation, if the sentence of the Judge was a condemnation to extinction of being, all idea of exchange would be absurd. It would be equivalent to saying, " What shall a man give in exchange for his nonentity? for himself when he has no existence!" Of course this is inadmissible. And the doctrine of the passage therefore is, that after the final sentence of the Judge, the condemned can give nothing by which to recover their forfeited happiness; and since, therefore, their existence after receiving this sentence is thus clearly declared, the sentence itself cannot be annihilation.

5. Matt. xxv, 41, 46: "Depart from me, ye cursed, into everlasting fire, prepared for the devil and his angels. And these shall go away into everlasting punishment; but the righteous into life eternal."

D. 212, and S. 25, 26, here remark that, "before this text can be fairly adduced as proving the sinner will exist forever in misery, an opponent must prove the sinner to be immortal." This issue we cheerfully accept, and appeal to the whole of the preceding argument, derived from the Scriptures, as settling the question of the soul's immortality. The passage before us, moreover, clearly supposes the future and interminable existence of both the righteous and the wicked. The one enters into reward, the other into punishment, and that reward and that punishment are both eternal. The idea of cessation of existence is in no way intimated, either directly or by implication, in either case; and it is just as reasonable to infer that the greatness of the rewards of heaven will extinguish the existence of the righteous, as that the greatness of the punishment of hell will extinguish the existence of the wicked. But if the immortal nature with which the righteous shall arise from the dead shall be such as to adapt them to the otherwise overpowering glories of heaven, (see Dan. viii, 27; x, 8, 9; Rev. i, 17,) the immortal nature with which the wicked shall arise shall be such as to adapt them to the otherwise overpowering sufferings of hell. The antithesis is obvious throughout in relation to the condition of the two; and consequently, as the righteous are confessedly appointed to happiness, the wicked are appointed to its opposite. Unhappiness or misery is the antithesis of happiness, and such therefore is the final condition of the wicked. It is simply silly to say that non-existence is the antithesis of happiness, as a child can see with a moment's reflection;

for in strictness of speech it is as much the antithesis of misery itself as it is of happiness. And then, further, eternal life here, by the admission of our opponents, means eternal happiness. But we have shown that *death* in no sense infers extinction of conscious being. (See sec. 27, sub-sec. 1.) Of course, then, eternal death infers no such extinction, and hence the final state of the lost is here designated by the singularly appropriate term κόλασις; punishment by *rejection*, or *cutting off from*, or by *depriving of*, that happiness which the saved enjoy. And they are said to go away *into* this everlasting punishment, as the righteous are said to go *into* their eternal reward. The reward, therefore, eternally finds the righteous in possession of it, and the punishment eternally finds the guilty and condemned in possession of it. Such is the obvious and unforced import of the passage.

Our opponents, in their efforts to evade this testimony, pretend that its force is invalidated by the exposition of the passage given by Dr. Duffield in his work on "Prophecy," and by Dr. Lord, (Theol. Rev. for 1850, p. 411,) who refer it not to the general judgment, but to that which will take place at the introduction of the millennium. The same view was substantially held by Curcellæus (Opp. p. 921) and Turretin, (Opp. iv, p. 750.) But admitting this criticism, it in no way affects the point in question, for it leaves wholly untouched the subject of the final condition of men, as brought to view in the passage itself.

6. Another passage is Mark ix, 43–49: "And if thy hand offend thee, cut it off: it is better for thee to enter into life maimed, than having two hands to go into hell, into *that fire* that never shall be quenched; where their worm dieth not, and the fire is not quenched." These are the words of our Saviour, and, after repeating them in relation to the foot and eye, he, in showing why the worm should not die and the fire never be quenched, uses those deeply impressive words: "For every one [that is, of those who come into this condemnation] *shall be salted with* FIRE."

The very element which, in the literal valley of Hinnom, consumed the dead body, and the worms which feasted on it, shall in hell preserve the body and the worm in being. They shall be *salted*, that is, preserved by it in existence. And hence the clear distinction which he observes between the fire in the vale of Hinnom, which was quenched, and the fire to which he refers: ἀπελθεῖν εἰς τὴν γέενναν, εἰς τὸ πῦρ τὸ ἄσβεστον, "*to enter into the hell, into that fire which never shall be quenched;*" thus distinguishing between the type and antitype, for the Jews regarded Gehenna as a type of hell. In the type the worm died, and the fire was quenched; but in the antitype the worm shall not die, and the fire shall not be quenched.

The utter hopelessness of the advocates of the opposing theories, in view of this awful testimony, may be seen by the false and flimsy comments by which they would persuade the reader to believe that our blessed Redeemer referred only to the vale of Hinnom, on the south-east of Jerusalem, and thus representing him as forewarning his followers of being cast into a valley into which none of them ever had been or ever would be cast, and which had no connection with the religion they were now appointed to teach, and in fact whose fires were extinguished before that religion was established. It would be well if such triflers would remember his admonition respecting the utterance of "idle words;" and if those also of them who blasphemously ridicule the images here employed by our Saviour, would remember that those who "are ashamed of his words," and who blaspheme the utterances of his Spirit, shall have no part in his kingdom.*

That the passage refers to the future and final state of the wicked, is further evident from the parallel expression in Isa. lxvi, 24. And too little is here known of that state to justify the arrogant assumption of Universalists and others,

* That the Jews were accustomed to describe the future punishment of the damned by the figure of *fire* and *worms*, is fully proved by quotations from the LXX, and Josephus, cited in Kuinoel on Mark ix, 44-46.

that certain specific representations which God has given of it, are inconsistent with such a state; as when, for example, Whittemore, (on the Parables, p. 65,) speaking of Isa. lxvi, 24, says: "This passage cannot be considered as having reference to a future state of punishment, because it is said to be fulfilled where time is denoted by *new moons and Sabbaths.*" That is, in other words, God cannot mean to say what his words announce, because we cannot see how those announcements can agree with our ideas of a future state. Such a rule of interpretation is unworthy of my friend Whittemore, and is purely theologastrian. Had the earth remained in the state in which it was created, and continued to be the abode of holy beings, would *new moons and Sabbaths* have had no connection with endless existence? And why then should they not have in connection with the earth's renovation? Our opponents speak much also of the term "carcass" in this passage, and endeavor from it to prove that as a carcass is a body bereft of life, the scene referred to must precede and not succeed the final resurrection and judgment; but carcass is referred to as the *visible* part of man, and is equivalent to *body*. It is simply nonsense to pretend that פֶּגֶר necessarily implies a body deprived of vitality, as the term מֵת, *dead*, applied to it, plainly evinces. See 2 Kings xix, 35; Isa. xxxvii, 36; and hence the expression, "*Your carcasses* shall fall in the wilderness." Numbers xiv, 28. Their carcasses were of course not *dead bodies* when thus referred to. Our opponents insist upon it, moreover, that "a *living* soul infers that there is such a thing as a *dead* soul;" (see, for example, C. 14–23; E. 31–49, 233,) and, of course, if this be so, a *dead* carcass must suppose such a thing as a living carcass.

Those who are here referred to, therefore, by Isaiah, are the wicked who had died the second death, and hence the term carcass is applied to them, intimating that they had thus died. Their visible part, their bodies, thus prostrate by the second death, are a loathsome spectacle to all the redeemed, as illustrating the fearful consequences of rebellion against God. And Jesus assures us *that the fire and worm shall never consume them*, an idea perfectly familiar to the ancient Jews, as may be seen by Isa. xxxiii, 14: "Who among us shall *dwell* with the devouring fire; who among us shall *dwell* with everlasting burnings." Compare Eccles. vii, 19; viii, 10; ix, 15; x, 11; Judith xvi, 21; also Matt. v, 22; xiii, 42. Philo, too, as quoted by Whitby, (in Mark ix, 43, 44,) states that the punishment of the wicked shall be "*to live forever dying;*" "to be forever in pains and griefs, and calamities that never cease."

The literature of our opponents on this passage may be seen in D. 204–9; S. 22–24; H. 1, p. 139; A. 103; M. 41–43; F. 29, 30; Hud. 197–206; Chauncey, 310–324; Balfour, 175–179.

7. There are many other passages which evince with equal clearness that the future punishment of sin is not extinction of being, but conscious and unending misery; but our limits forbid us to dwell at length upon them; for example, (Mark xiv, 31,) where Christ said of Judas, "Good were it for that man if he never had been born." This of course declares that the future condition of Judas would be worse than non-existence. Now as he did not exist previous to his entrance into this world, so, if after leaving this world he should at any period, however distant, pass out of existence, he would be in precisely the same condition as previous to his birth. How then could it be *good* for him *if he had never been born?*

8. In John v, 28, 29, Jesus, speaking of the resurrection, says that "they who have done good shall come forth to the resurrection of life, and they that have done evil to the resurrection of damnation." *Life* and *damnation* are here in antithesis. Now both the evil and good are raised to life or actual existence. Why then are they put in possession of existence by a reunion of soul and body? Plainly that they may be rewarded according to their works. The word *life*, therefore, expresses the reward of the righteous; and the word *damnation*, or *condemnation*, the reward of the

unrighteous. The one refers to a happy existence, the other to an existence which is the reverse of this—a miserable, unhappy existence. The term κρίσις, here rendered *damnation*, is employed nearly fifty times in the New Testament, and in not one of them does it import extinction of being, annihilation, or anything that even infers a deprivation of actual existence. And in the passage before us the phrase ἐκπορεύσονται εἰς ἀνάστασιν κρίσεως shows the utter incompatibility of that idea; for as the righteous shall come forth into a renewal of life, (the union of soul and body, interrupted by death,) which shall be a life of happiness, so *the wicked shall come forth into a renewal of life, a life of condemnation or unhappiness.* Such is the idea obvious upon the very surface itself of the language. The idea of renewal of life is clearly expressed by ἀνάστασις, (used nearly as often as κρίσις in the New Testament, and always in such a sense,) and the bare attempt to join the two terms, as they are connected in the text, and seriously to attach to κρίσις the idea of extinction or annihilation, would be worse than nonsense, for it would be turning into ridicule the words of Christ, and would be making him say, "They shall come forth to the renewal of life, a life of non-existence, or annihilation." The verb, therefore, expresses the idea of their *coming forth* out of their graves, ἀνάστασις, the *life* to which they shall return, and κρίσις, the *condition* or *state* of that life itself.

9. The same idea is clear also from John iii, 36: "He that believeth on the Son hath everlasting life;" has it now, is already passed from death into life which shall continue forever; "and he that believeth not the Son shall not see life, but the wrath of God abideth, (μένει *remaineth*) on him." That "everlasting life" here refers to *salvation*, and not to mere existence, is obvious from the fact that the believer even in this world is said to possess it. Comp. also Rom. viii, 1, 6; 1 John iii, 14; v, 12; John v, 24; viii, 51; xi, 36. And that *life* in the latter part of the text does not mean mere existence, is evident from the fact that the unbeliever in this

world does possess this, and shall repossess it at the resurrection. He both does and shall see life, therefore, in the sense of actual existence; but he does not, and never shall see it in the sense of salvation. The condition of the life which he shall possess is clear also from the last clause of the passage: "The wrath of God remaineth on him." And as it is impossible that this wrath should rest upon that which has no existence, so it is clear that the wicked must continue to exist: and that as long as they who believe the Son shall enjoy salvation, so long shall they who believe him not have the wrath of God abiding on them.

10. In Rom. ii, 4–10, the same contrast is presented, (as well as in many other places which need not be specified.) They who, by patiently continuing in well-doing, seek for *glory, and honor, and immortality*,* shall secure eternal life; while they "who obey not the truth, but obey unrighteousness, shall secure indignation and wrath, tribulation and anguish;" that is, a state or condition of being utterly irreconcilable with annihilation. The continued existence of both classes is therefore clearly indicated. The one is to inherit an eternal life of glory, and the other an eternal death (the antithesis of eternal life) of tribulation and anguish; and the idea that this eternal death is to terminate in annihilation, is as unfounded as the idea that the eternal life spoken of shall so terminate. Excessive joy and excessive grief may, either of them, produce asphyxia, but there is no more tendency in the one than in the other to produce extinction of being. In this passage, moreover, the penalty of the law and the effects of its infliction are clearly defined. The penalty is Divine "indignation and wrath," and its effects are "tribulation and anguish." And to attempt to connect extinction of existence with this tribulation and anguish, is simply impertinent; for if indignation and wrath, which produce tribulation and anguish, be, as is here asserted, the penalty of the law, then indignation and wrath, which produce

* A Hebraism for "a glorious and honorable immortality," as illustrated in section 37, sub-section 4, above.

the very opposite effect, is not the penalty. Extinction of being is, of course, the cessation of tribulation and anguish, and to say that *both* are the penalty of the law is nonsense. The infliction of the penalty produces suffering, and suffering, therefore, is the endless portion of the ungodly.

11. In exact accordance with this, the apostle, in 2 Thess. i, 6–9, declares that Christ shall come with his mighty angels in flaming fire to *award tribulation* to those who have troubled and persecuted his people; and this tribulation he declares to be "everlasting destruction from the presence of the Lord, and from the glory of his power." (Comp. Isa. ii, 19, 21.) The word here rendered *destruction* (ὄλεθρος) is used but four times in the New Testament, (1 Cor. v, 5; 1 Thess. v, 3; 1 Tim. vi, 9,) and in no instance means annihilation. Eternal, or everlasting destruction, therefore, is consistent with the everlasting endurance of tribulation or suffering, and of course everlasting tribulation infers everlasting continuance of existence. And then, moreover, the attempt to substitute *annihilation* for *destruction* in the passage would show the absurdity of the whole idea of our adversaries: "Who shall be punished with everlasting *annihilation* from the presence of the Lord, and from the glory of his power." It is not difficult to understand how overwhelming ruin and destruction should produce the tribulation referred to, but it would take an Annihilationist to tell how annihilation could produce it. The infliction of the penalty of the law, however, does produce trouble or tribulation in those who are suffering it, and therefore annihilation is not the penalty.

12. The continued existence of the finally impenitent is likewise clearly announced in Jude 6, 7, and 2 Pet. ii, 4–6, where the state of the sinning angels is referred to as furnishing an illustration of the consequences of transgression; and then the illustration is applied to the final condition of impenitent men. The angels, when they sinned, at once incurred the penalty of the divine law, which is death,

and were cast down to hell. They were deprived of happiness, but their conscious existence was not interrupted, and the infliction of that penalty, therefore, infers no such extinction in the case of a rational creature. And hence the wicked men referred to in these passages are not extinct, but are held forth as an example, suffering the vengeance of eternal fire.

But H. 1, p. 138, after denying that hell is now in existence, (a direct denial of what Peter and Jude here affirm respecting the evil angels and their doom,) asks, "Why did our Lord speak of their (the people of Sodom, etc.) punishment as yet future (Matt. x, 15) if they were already in hell." *Answer*: He speaks of that portion of it which was still future, as future, simply because it was future. See Prov. xxvi, 5. Mr. Balfour, (Inquiry, p. 93,) though he utterly denies the separability of the soul from the body, says that he is of opinion that Korah and his company are the angels here referred to, and (p. 99) that as the judgment of the great day means the destruction of Jerusalem, Korah and his company were reserved till that time. See Prov. xxvi, 4.

S. 26, 27, gives a characteristic perversion of the passage, and says that the inhabitants of Sodom and Gomorrah are here "expressly said to be *reserved*" for punishment. He doubtless quoted this from that other Bible, referred to above in the note to section 36, sub-sect. 2, for there is nothing like it in either our Greek or English Scriptures. D. 237 makes the phrase, "Sodom and Gomorrah, and the cities about them," refer to the *material*—the houses, walls, etc., and of course, then, these houses and walls "had given themselves over to fornication, and gone after strange flesh." But the material philosophy may logically admit of this, if we except the locomotion, or "*going* after," since, if matter of itself may think, all matter may think: so that, after all, the houses and walls may have been sinful, and may have been punished. Hud. 204 says: "It is here worthy of note that the adjective 'suffering' (ὑπέχουσαι) in Jude verse 7, refers to the cities rather than to the inhabitants;" so that the *cities*, as distinguished from their inhabitants, went after the strange flesh, and committed fornication. And thus too we are taught that Chorazin and Capernaum, (Matt. xi, 20–24,) *and not their inhabitants*, were upbraided by our Saviour, and are to be brought down to hell. The remarks of B. 63, 87, 88, are equally absurd. Dr. Priestley, *in loco*, says that the term "angels" here probably refers to those called "the sons of God," in the antediluvian world, who perished in the deluge. H. 2, p. 90, ventures upon a criticism of the original, and would fain supply a word to our English translation. He says: "The word τούτοις (to those) is left untranslated in our English version, and which, being in the masculine gender, agrees with the ἀγγέλους of verse 6." And he renders the passage as follows: "*Even as* Sodom and Gomorrah, and the cities about them, in like manner *to these* [angels] *giving themselves over to fornication and going after strange* [margin, other] *flesh*, are set forth for an example." This, I suppose, is the Annihilationist doctrine of angelology, and its resemblance to Christian angelology may be seen in Matt. xxii, 30, where being "like the angels" is given as a reason why, in the future life, the saved neither marry nor are given in marriage. The Greek word on which this folly is attempted to be based, is very properly left untranslated in our excellent version, because the English idiom fully expresses the sense without it. The inhabitants of Sodom and Gomorrah, and of the neighboring cities, are referred to, and those of the latter cities, following the example of the former, ran into their sin, and incurred their condemnation. This is the full idea, as expressed in the Greek, and our own version renders it with equal force and precision.* C. 45, F. 30, J. T. 36, say that Jude's lan-

* Dr. Bushnell has in his late work essayed a criticism upon the foregoing passage, and offers Faber as authority, aiming to show that it has no reference to *angels*, but only to the "Sethites," and attempts to drag Josephus into his support; but with what reason may be seen by referring to Antiq.,

guage does not imply that the people of Sodom, etc., "are *now* suffering, but that they are *now* an example of suffering." But of what suffering are they *now* an example? To say that they are now an example of what they had suffered would be announcing nothing but what everybody knew. The answer of Jude therefore is the only true one: "They are now an example, suffering the vengeance of eternal fire." Compare Luke xvi, 23, 24.

This notion of C., etc., has been thoughtlessly favored by some who ought to have known better than thus to trifle. The τὸ δεῖγμα, *example*, is the *fact* here announced; and to pretend that it refers to a visible, palpable example, is nonsense, for the material cities themselves have long ceased to be such; their precise locality even is unknown; and as the historical statement of their destruction is sufficient to present them to us as an *example* of the retributive justice of God on earth, and that too without any visible and palpable representation, shall not the emphatic announcement of the Spirit of God suffice to set them forth as an example of suffering the vengeance of eternal fire? Shall it be regarded as less veracious than the formal historic statement? This shallow attempt therefore to restrict the application of δεῖγμα to palpable objects, is not only ridiculous, but, if carried out, must divest the term of all present application to the material cities themselves.

book i, chap. iii, sec. 1. He moreover professes to be so well acquainted with the angelic state, as to know that the word οἰκητήριον (see Jude 6, and 2 Cor. v, 2; also οἰκία, as employed in John xiv, 2) is "entirely malapropos, when referred to celestial beings." See his "Nature and the Supernatural," pp. 130, 131. How this extraordinary attainment in the knowledge of the "supernatural" was made he has not informed the world, though perhaps he designs it should be inferred from the fourteenth chapter of his book, the title of which is, "Miracles and Spiritual Gifts are not discontinued." No man has a higher respect than I for Dr. Bushnell's great and transcendent powers, when exercised within their proper sphere; but the province of critical exposition lies not within that sphere. And in his whole book there is not one formal attempt at the exegesis of Scripture which would not be unworthy of the merest tyro.

I have here exhibited a full view of the imbecile and hopeless struggles of our opponents with the obvious import of this and other passages, (and had my limits permitted, should have done so in every instance,) to illustrate the folly of attempting to build up mere human theories in antagonism to the truth of God. But I must conclude these criticisms with a brief notice of two or three passages in Revelation.

13. In Rev. xiv, 9–11, and xix, 20, the sentence of those who worship the beast and his image, and the sentence also of the devil, and beast, and false prophet, is declared to be unceasing and endless torment: *εἰς τοὺς αἰῶνας τῶν αἰώνων*: literally, *through the eternity of eternities.* That this phrase is employed to designate an absolute eternity no one can reasonably doubt. See Gal. i, 5; Phil. iv, 20; 2 Tim. iv, 18; Heb. xiii, 21; 1 Peter iv, 11; v, 11; Rev. i, 6, 18; v, 13; vii, 13.

The criticism of our opponents on the expression has been noticed already in sect. 63. We can have no idea of eternity except as an endless succession of ages; and common sense, not less than the strictest philosophy, justifies the phraseology as applied to designate it. The attempt therefore to prove that *αἰὼν* may mean *an age*, and *οἱ αἰώνας τῶν αἰώνων*, no more than a limited duration, is simply puerile, as is evident from the fact that the phrase is employed to designate the perpetuity of the glory and government of God, and the happiness of the redeemed, in which any such sense is clearly inadmissible. It is employed but eighteen times in the New Testament, in sixteen of which it is applied to the former, and in one of the other two to the latter. Then as respects *αἰὼν*, whenever (whether in the singular or plural) it is governed by *εἰς*, it invariably in the New Testament signifies endless duration. In this construction it is therein employed sixty-one times, in fifty-five of which no one can doubt that it has this sense, and in the other six it is applied to future punishment. How idle then to question its import in these instances, or to undertake to prove that because αἰὼν may be employed to signify a temporary duration, it may therefore have this sense in the construction aforesaid, when every fact is against the supposition?

The adjective αἰώνιος may likewise claim a passing notice in this connection. It is used *seventy-one* times in the New Testament, in *five* of which the Restorationists themselves admit that it is applied to future punishment. In *fifty* other instances it is applied to the future happiness and glory of the redeemed, and of course means unending duration or perpetuity; in *four* others to God and his perfections; *once* to the consolation of true believers, which of course will never fail, (2 Thess. ii, 16;) *once* to things unseen, in contrast with the visible, (2 Cor. iv, 18;) *once* to the redemption of Christ, (Heb. ix, 12;) *once* to the covenant of grace, (Heb. xiii, 20;) *once* in Jude 7, (explained above;) *once* to that *evangelion* to be announced by the angel, (Rev. xiv, 6;) *once* to past eternity, (Rom. xvi, 25;) *once* to the indissoluble relation constituted by Christian brotherhood, (Philemon 15;) and *once* to the judgment, which decides the endless destiny of men. (Heb. vi, 2.) Besides these instances, which number *sixty-nine*, it is twice employed as follows: πρὸ χρόνων αἰωνίων, (2 Tim. i, 9, and Titus i, 2,) and means *before the endless ages*. It is common to divide eternity into *past* and *future*, since there is a point at which, so to speak, the endless existence of man begins.* And it is equally proper to designate the time previous to the occurrence of those transactions recorded in Gen. iii, 9–21, as *before the endless ages*, or specific dispensations referred to in Heb. xi, 3, and which so pre-eminently concern the eternal destiny of the sinner. Such metonomy frequently occurs in the Scriptures. See also conclusion of part i, chap. iii.

The instance of its application to the kingdom of Christ (2 Peter i, 11) has been pleaded as signifying a temporary

* See this illustrated, with his usual felicity, by Augustine, De Civit. Dei, lib. xii, cap. xv.

duration, but without reason; for although Jesus surrenders to the Father the mediatorial kingdom, (1 Cor. xv, 24–28,) can any one suppose that his relation to the redeemed will ever cease? They shall receive a crown *that fadeth not away*, (1 Peter v, 4; 1 Cor. ix, 25,) and *a kingdom that cannot be* moved, (Heb. xii, 28,) and *shall reign* forever and ever, (Rev. xxii, 5;) he shall dwell among them, and *his throne* be in their midst, (Rev. vii, 14–17;) and *the throne of God and the Lamb* shall continue as such forever, (Rev. xxii, 1, 3;) and therefore, although he gives up his *mediatorial* kingdom and offices, so far as the sinner is concerned, he shall, *as the Lamb once slain*, rule over *his redeemed* through eternity.

Thus full and clear is the evidence derived from all these terms and expressions, that the misery of the wicked shall have no end; and in relation to the passages we are considering, therefore, Prof. Stuart, on verse 10, makes the obvious remark that "the idea of the writer is that they [the wicked referred to] shall remain in the condition to which they are doomed, that is, they are still to remain living." And the expression, "the smoke of their torment ascendeth up forever and ever," evinces the true import, as given by the Holy Spirit himself, of such passages as Matt. iii, 12; Mark ix, 43, etc.

The manner in which our opponents trifle with these expressions is anything but creditable to them. B. 89–103 evinces his usual illiteracy, and though he draws largely from others, does not succeed in quoting anything really bearing on the issue. M. 49 says the *torment* here referred to is inflicted in *this* world; A. 104, S. 30–35, C. 41, 42, D. 224–229, H. 1, p. 138, say the same, and draw the sage conclusion, that because the wrath here mentioned overtakes the wicked while they are in this world, it therefore must end in this world. As well might it be said that because the righteous pass from death unto life in this world, that therefore their salvation shall end in this world. The inhabitants of Sodom and Gomorrah were overwhelmed with Divine vengeance in this world, and yet they suffer the vengeance of eternal fire. And what would be said of the man who should insist upon it that, because Divine wrath overtook the sinning angels, and cast them out of heaven, therefore their sufferings terminated in heaven? It is a fair application of the argument, and the logic is the same. F. 31 refers the language, however, to the future world and final judgment, but maintains from it that "the wicked shall be burned up, and consume away into smoke, which smoke shall ascend up." But how can this be according to the statements of the passage? After they are utterly consumed, how can the smoke of their torment ascend up? However distant that event may be supposed, there will yet an eternity succeed it, during which no smoke can of course ascend. But further, by what authority do F. and S. and D., and all these writers, make the wicked to be so long burning up? A lake of fire and brimstone would consume a man in an hour, or even less. True, God can preserve men alive in the greatest fires. (See Dan. iii, 25, 27.) But this idea is, of course, not to be brought in here, for our opponents insist that the penalty of the law is annihilation, and that the wicked suffer these torments in undergoing the process of extinction. For what, then, are they kept burning during the long period asserted by these men? They could be easily consumed in an hour, or less. Our opponents can give no reason for their opinion, except that God, for wise purposes, preserves them in being so long. And of course, therefore, all those arguments upon which they so much insist, about "the natural effects of fire upon human bodies," etc., are only trifling with the subject, and do not bear upon the question at all. It will not be doubted that he who can make a human body endure fire for a century, can continue its existence in fire forever; and if he find reason to continue its existence for a century, he may find reason likewise to continue it "day and night forever and ever."

14. The last passage to which we shall refer is Rev. xx, 9–15, which describes the events just previous to the usher-

ing in of the final judgment, and the judgment itself and its issues. The devil is cast into the lake of fire, where the beast and false prophet are; and then after mankind are judged, it is said in ver. 15, that whosoever of them were not found written in the book of life were also cast therein, and of course made partakers of his own doom, according to Matt. xxv, 41. Now so long as any one is tormented, he *lives in torment*, as must be obvious to all; and this torment is here said to be forever and ever. And as this is after the final disposal of man by his Creator, the terms forever and ever can relate only to an absolute eternity, even if in other connections they might sometimes express a limited duration. It is therefore the final condition, not of a nonentity, but of the wicked; a condition of torment. Nothing is to come after; no *æons* to close up in the sad experience of such; their condition is absolute and eternal; it is the second death, and can be followed by no resurrection; and the Mediator, when they are consigned to this doom, gives up his mediatorial offices, as no more of Adam's race are now to be reconciled to God. He ceases to act as mediator between God and sinful men, and thus the wicked are left hopeless and unredeemed forever.

The efforts of our opponents to divest this passage of its awful import, are of the same character with those referred to in our examination of the former passage. Some of them endeavor to symbolize the devil, but their remarks are beneath criticism. D. 229–234 is the only one among them who seriously and soberly endeavors to set aside the proof here furnished of the unending misery of the lost. He admits that the devil may, as here stated, be really tormented forever and ever; but denies that any proof is thereby furnished that wicked men shall be tormented in the same manner. And of course he denies that "the lake of fire," mentioned in ver. 10, is the same as that mentioned in ver. 14, 15; the one referring to the doom of the devil, and the other to that of wicked men. And further, that even admitting the lake to be the same, it is unfair to conclude that men are to live in torment as long as the devil shall. These are his exceptions.

(1.) As to Mr. Dobney's denial that the lake of ver. 10 and that of ver. 14, 15 are the same, it is simply contemptible. The devil is declared to be cast into "*the* lake of fire;" and then, a few verses afterward, and with not the slightest reference to the possible existence of any other lake of the kind, the wicked are said to be cast into "*the* lake of fire." But if even there could be room for a rational doubt on the subject, their identity is declared in the clearest possible manner in Rev. xxi, 8, where the phrase, "*the lake which burneth with fire and brimstone*," identifies the lake there mentioned with that of Rev. xx, 10; and the phrase "*which is the second death*," identifies it with that of ver. 14, 15 of the same chapter. And to deny their identity, therefore, is as utterly absurd and ridiculous as it would be to deny that "things which are equal to the same thing are equal to one another." We have therefore full proof here that the existence of hell is not, as our adversaries (who deny a *present hell*) affirm, consequent upon the issues of the judgment day, since they themselves maintain that the hell mentioned in Rev. xx, 10, is to be referred to a period antecedent to the judgment. And as this hell is the same with that which is to succeed the judgment, it becomes at once identified with that mentioned in Luke xvi, 23, 24; Mark ix, 43–49; Matt. xxiii, 33; Jude 6, 7, and other places. There is, therefore, a hell now in existence; and it is to continue forever.

(2.) Mr. Dobney denies, also, that because the devil is to be tormented forever and ever, it will follow that wicked men must be who partake his doom. But what is the ground of such denial? If it be the mere exigencies of an idle theory, it surely is entitled to no deference whatever. Have the Scriptures anywhere intimated a difference? The exception is a mere captious cavil, unless some sufficient reason can be given to justify or sustain it. The word *βασανισθήσονται*, *shall be tormented*, is plural; and all to whom it refers "shall be tormented forever and ever." And that all the wicked are to partake this doom is distinctly affirmed in ver. 15, and chap. xxi, 8. The *torment* is said to continue through eternity, and of course those tormented must continue to exist through eternity. The assertion which Mr. Dobney makes and insists upon, that this would infer an equal *degree* of suffering to all, is utterly groundless, for God has said that the wicked shall receive according to their deeds. He will not violate his words, even though Mr. Dobney and others cannot see how he can possibly verify them. When Mr. Dobney proves, therefore, that it is important to the subject that he and his friends should know exactly *how* Jehovah shall make his statements good, this argument will be worthy of consideration.

(3.) Mr. Dobney further states that, since Death and Hades are represented as being annihilated by being cast into the lake of fire, (ver. 14,) it is therefore reasonable to infer that wicked men will be likewise annihilated by the same process. Mr. Hudson also takes the same ground. But where is it said that *Thanatos* (Death) and *Hades* are to be annihilated? I am aware that some expositors have inconsiderately conceded this, but without the slightest reason whatever. There is no ground for any such concession. *Thanatos* and *Hades* are to be confined to the lake of fire, no more to blight or to harass, by their doleful influence and the terrors they excite, the fair creation of God. Their power and their terrors are to exist thenceforth only with the subjects of "the second death." They are *cast into* (*βάλλειν εἰς*) *that lake*, and are to return no more.

*Thanatos* and *Hades* are here, as in other places, personified. (Rev. vi, 8; comp. Rev. i, 18; Hos. xiii, 14; 1 Cor. xv, 55.) And *Thanatos* again in Rom. v, 14. (Sin also in Rom. vi, 14.) Satan is, moreover, spoken of as possessing the kingdom or dominion of *Thanatos*, Heb. ii, 14. (Greek.) *Hades* also expresses his power and operations, Matt. xvi, 18; (and in classical language it is both the name and dominion of Pluto). שְׁאוֹל, too, has an equivalent import, and hence the frequent antithesis between heaven and hades. (Matt. xi, 23; Luke x, 15; comp. Ezek. xxxi, 16–18; Amos ix, 2; Sirach, li, 7.) But Christ has conquered both *Thanatos* and *Hades*, and holds them in subjection. (Rev. i, 18; 1 Cor. xv, 55; Hos. xiii, 14.) They are now said to exist, and, in a sense, are said to rule in this probationary state of fallen man. But He who holds the power over them, (and all his enemies,) shall, when his mediatorial work is completed and man's probation ended, sweep them forever from the holy and happy universe of God, and confine them to the lake of fire, and to those who are associated with the second death. Such is the idea here conveyed. Instead of being annihilated, they shall, whatever other forms they may assume, still exist in more fearful shapes and with infinitely more hideous terrors in the world of woe. Such is the terrific and most awful picture here held forth by the Spirit of Eternal Truth.*

But even if Thanatos and Hades were said to be utterly annihilated, how preposterous would it be to infer, as do Messrs. Dobney, Hudson, and others of that class, that because a personification should cease to exist, therefore the thing personified must cease likewise to exist. The utmost that the passage can be made to convey is, that Thanatos and Hades shall cease to exist as regards the redeemed; but will this prove that they shall cease also in respect to the unredeemed? And will any sober man pretend this with the announcement in these very passages staring him in the face, that *deuteros thanatos* (the second death) shall still exist after Thanatos and Hades are cast into the lake of fire? The lake of fire is not itself the second death;† but to have a portion therein constitutes that death. Mr. Dobney and his coadjutors also quote 1 Cor. xv, 26: "Death, the last enemy,

* I am gratified to find that Dr. Post sustains the same view. See New Englander, xiv, 204–206.

† The ignorance, or something worse, of Mr. Hudson, in his attempted criticism of this phrase, is of a piece with what we have already exposed of his glaring perversions of fact.

shall be destroyed." But this passage refers to its abolishment in relation to the redeemed of Christ, as verses 54–57 evince, and of course it has nothing to do with the subject before us. Believers shall not be hurt by the second death, (Rev. ii, 11,) though the wicked shall be. But we must draw our work to a close.

# CHAPTER VIII.

## CONCLUSION.

A FEARFUL responsibility rests upon the man who, professing to be an expositor of the word of God, will trifle with those impressive warnings and admonitions which the ineffable love of Him who died to redeem us has given, in order that our guilty and perishing race may be led to accept of his proffered deliverance by being brought to see what are the certain consequences of rejecting it. It is hard to be compelled to believe that our opponents would voluntarily incur this responsibility; but to what are we to ascribe the perpetually distorted representations of truth and fact which characterize nearly all their publications on the subject? They iterate and reiterate their purity of purpose and honesty of intention; but how are such professions to be reconciled with their open denial and perversion of Divine truth, their misrepresentation of facts, and their ridicule and caricature of those overwhelmingly affecting counsels and admonitions in relation to our future welfare, given by the kindest, sincerest, and most affectionate friend that ever dwelt in human flesh, and who overpoweringly proved the extent and intensity of his love by dying the accursed death that sinful man might be furnished with the opportunity to flee from the wrath to come, and to escape from that fire which never shall be quenched? It is hard to think that even Mr. Dobney, in the face of his unceasing professions of piety and purity of intention, should willingly be guilty of this crime; but no serious and reflecting mind can read his work intelligently, and notice its adoption of the Universalist verbiage and sophistry, without wondering at such professions. And yet he *beseeches* his fellow-Christians not to represent God as punishing sin forever, and associating wicked men with the devil in punishment, unless upon a *renewed investigation* of the subject they should *be certain* that such is the fact. D. 223. In accordance with the same spirit, he charges the Edwardses and others with "*almost reveling* in descriptions of never-ending torment;" but says, at the same time, that he does not use the expression "in any offensive sense," (p. 255,) which is about as becoming as it would be for one to say, "Mr. Dobney delights in making excuses to encourage the impenitent in sin, and in countenancing the wicked in their reckless disregard of futurity; but I do not wish to be understood in any offensive sense." But let Mr. Dobney point out, in the works of either Edwards or of Mr. Melville, any passage half as obnoxious to such a charge as the declarations of our blessed Redeemer in Matt. xiii, Mark ix, or those in Rev. xx, or else let him retract this most unjust accusation. This is a common charge of our opponents, and as unfounded as it is common. They attempt to ignore all those admonitions of the word of God, and when we insist upon their truth and importance, they charge us with taking delight and "reveling" in the discharge of what we ever feel to be a most painful and soul-harrowing duty. But instead of dwelling upon the point, I will here add a word from the admirable essay of Rev. Mr. Campbell,* in which, referring to the general subject, he says: "*Whatever reasons, then, justified our Saviour in holding forth 'a fire unquenchable,' 'a worm undying,' 'a punishment everlasting,' will justify every other preacher in arraying the same awful issue of Gospel despising before the mind of every impenitent sinner.*"

The open and iniquitous trifling of such writers as S., H., C., Hud., B., M., E., and Balfour in relation to this whole matter almost surpasses belief. I call it iniquitous, for I

* "Life and Death," by President Campbell, of Bethany College, Va. See Mill. Harb., extra, for Dec. 1844.

most heartily accord with Dr. Johnson's remark: "I know of no crime so great that a man could contrive to commit, as poisoning the sources of eternal truth."* The pretense of wishing "to relieve the character of God" is sheer impertinence. (See sect. 59, sub-sect. 7, above.) Infidels have ever offered the same plea to justify their rejection of the Bible. But when did God ever put the keeping of his character in the hands of these men, or authorize them or any others to defend him by denying or misrepresenting his truth?

The assumption of this whole class of writers, and one on which they are perpetually ringing the changes, is, that "endless rejection from God into a condition of hopeless and final misery, being presented as a motive, serves only to harden men in sin and unbelief." It is a well-known fact that two or three wolves in a forest, or on the mountains, can so fill the woods with the echoes of their ever-varying howl, that an inexperienced observer would be led to suppose there must be scores of them in company. And in like manner Mr. Dobney, and writers like him, by their unwarrantable cavils and speculations impair confidence in the Divine averments, and produce the very echoings of disbelief which they adduce to prove the inefficacy of the motive referred to. Impenitent men feel encouraged thus to disregard that motive, and it fails to influence them. The plea that this effect is produced through a perception of the incompatibility of connecting endless punishment with the sins of this probationary state, is false in the statement and disproved by fact. When did ever a truly awakened sinner, burdened with a sense of his guilt, utter a syllable about such disproportion? And is the thoughtless, impenitent soul, "who loves darkness rather than light"—is "the natural man that receiveth not the things of the Spirit of God because they are foolishness unto him," to be taken as a better judge in such things than the soul awakened by the Holy Spirit to see and feel the true nature and desert of sin? But the same plea, only varied in form, has always been urged

* Boswell's Tour to the Hebrides, p. 28.

in the effort to get rid of all the leading doctrines of revelation which are unsatisfactory and distasteful to the carnal heart. Read the exceptions of Socinus to the doctrine of Christ's vicarious satisfaction, or of the Unitarians to his Divine nature, or of Swedenborg to the doctrine of the Trinity, or of Professor Bush to the doctrine of the resurrection, or of the Rationalists to the doctrine respecting demoniacs, and you find this principle applied just as Mr. Dobney and his coadjutors apply it in relation to future punishment. (See sect. 64, above.) And the argument is as conclusive in the one case as in the other. And then further, the question is one simply of exegesis; and *as an exegetical question*, (as every thorough scholar has ever admitted,) there is not room even for a rational doubt respecting it. As speculative *theologians*, some such have doubted it; but as *exegetes*, they confess that they must admit it; so that our opponents cannot even plead in their defense that they bring philosophy into the account in order to settle a doubtful matter in revelation; and the aim of the objection is, therefore, to prove, not so much that God has not thus spoken, as that he could not thus speak. And, contemplated in either point of view, it is an impertinent assumption of knowing infinitely more of the inscrutable counsels and ways of God than ever was vouchsafed to mortals. How can such men, professing as they do to read their Bible, forget the apostolic declaration: "How unsearchable are his judgments, and his ways past finding out." Rom. xi, 33. See also Isa. lv, 8, 9. It is always more rational to believe God (though fools may call it "a blind faith") than to follow any human fancy whatever. (Prov. xiv, 12; xii, 15; Rom. i, 22.)

The Gospel comes to sinful man in this form: "You have entered upon an existence from which there is no escape; you have sinned, and thus severed yourself from God, and are in a ruined and helpless condition, and if you pass out of probation with this guilt upon you there will be no opportunity of retrieving your loss through all the eternal ages. God has provided a full and free deliverance from sin and its curse, and now entreats you to accept of that deliverance and be forever happy. He takes no pleasure in your destruction, but would rather pardon and save you. But you are a moral agent, and he must treat you as such. As you have no other probation, so if you now reject eternal happiness you choose eternal misery and alienation from Him who is now ready and willing to save you. Then hear his voice to-day, and harden not your heart." In this manner does the Gospel present this motive; and how inexpressibly iniquitous is it to tell the impenitent and perishing that such a motive is calculated only to promote unbelief and harden the heart! See the shameless perversions of Mr. Dobney, D. 253–262.

Now let this motive be clothed with any degree of uncertainty in the minds of careless and impenitent men, and who can fail to trace the effect? Let them be assured that God did not mean what his words declare, and that there is no hell; or that sinners shall be saved if even they do not accept of the Gospel offer; or that if existence become too great a burden to them they shall be annihilated; let the mind in love with sin get possession of either of these impressions, and the whole force of the aforesaid motive, and of all the appeals of the Gospel, is at once neutralized. The soul in love with sensuality, and absorbed by selfishness, labors to exclude from the mind all thoughts of the future; such thoughts are always most unwelcome intruders in every such case; and let such a spirit obtain but the idea that God does not mean what his words seem to indicate respecting future punishment, and that man is not to live forever in misery, and how gross an insult to common sense would it be to say that his mind would not be thereby relieved, and that he would not be thereby encouraged to persist in impenitence and sin. Yet such is precisely the message which our opponents convey to souls that are in love with their own ungodliness.

The statement that fear as a motive is not so efficacious

as love, is, in this connection, an absurdity. Is it true or false that the carnal mind is enmity against God, and is not in subjection to him, neither indeed can be? (Rom. viii, 7.) and that the imagination of man's heart is evil, only evil, continually? (Gen. vi, 3;) and that those who are the friends of the world are the enemies of God? (James iv, 4.) If this is true, then what can exceed the folly of such a representation as the aforesaid? The statement is, moreover, false, from the fact that it implies that the Gospel offer, as presented above, is one of *fear*, when the great point of its appeal is the wonderful love of God in providing, at such a cost, the way for the depraved and perishing to flee from eternal burnings. But to speak to them of love, and not at the same time remind them of the awful consequences of sin, would be a great absurdity. We cannot now, however, dwell upon these points. Let it suffice to remark that for Destructionists and Restorationists to object to *fear* as a motive, and to talk about substituting love, is rather ludicrous, and has already been, in a preceding section, proved to be absurd.

It is obvious, however, that the whole of these antagonistic speculations proceed from a sympathy with the wicked and rebellious creature, rather than with the claims of a holy, just, and good Creator. It is certainly right and proper to feel tender compassion for the wicked and depraved, and perishing, and to evince it by our best efforts to save them. But when this compassion degenerates into sympathy with their wickedness, and into attempts to extenuate their rebellion, it alters the case greatly; and the effect is, moreover, the same, whether it is through inadvertence or design. The soul is hopelessly ruined, nor can it be rescued on the plea that there was no intention to destroy it.

I presume that no one who denies not the existence or personality of God will deny that, as we receive life and breath, and all things from him, his right to us is perfect and entire. Among men it is freely conceded that there is no right so perfect, no title so complete and inalienable, as that which is obtained by creation or by manufacture. The title of the artist to his productions, and that of the inventor to his inventions, and their right to dispose of them, are all unquestioned; and even in regard to the original creations of the mind and imagination, this right is by common consent so fully recognized, that it is regarded as literary robbery to appropriate them to ourselves without a proper acknowledgment of our obligations. We moreover recognize the application of the same principle in cases where, by specific arrangement or contract, we acquire a right to the time or services of another; he is under obligation to respect our right, and cannot, without manifest sin and dishonesty, appropriate to his own pleasure or emolument that time and those energies which by specific arrangement belong to us.

It is perfectly obvious, therefore, that if we are creatures, and consequently have a Creator, we have an owner; and that Creator and owner, as Paul before the Areopagus so beautifully illustrated, (Acts xvii, 28, 29,) must possess the same moral, intellectual, and spiritual nature which he imparted to his offspring. And hence we have an owner and proprietor who is infinitely intelligent, and wise, and good. But these points need hardly be here insisted on, since they are admitted freely by all our opponents. The practical application of them is what concerns us now.

If then I am a creature, I have a Creator and an owner, and of course a ruler too; one whose unquestioned prerogative it is to prescribe to me, to give me laws, and to appoint to me what I am to do, and what I am not to do, through the whole course of my being; for he who is the original and author of my being must be the end of it. He that is the first to me must be the last also;* for it is obviously a matter of common sense that what could not be of itself must not be for itself, and that it is wholly inconsistent with the state of a creature to be its own end. And this being undoubtedly so, it clearly follows that all intelli-

* See Howe's Works, p. 759.

gent creatures are bound to recognize the truth, that as it is right and proper for God to order all things for himself, his will and pleasure should be regarded by us in preference to our own, and though contrary to the will and pleasure of all other beings. True holiness is the practical recognition of this truth, and sin is the practical rejection of it.

The illustration of this whole subject furnished by the case of our first parents, is directly in point. With Adam, in his primal state of rectitude, there was not only a manifest conformity to the will of God, (or a practical recognition of the aforesaid principle,) but his desire was to have it so, and not otherwise. He felt that he should obey God, and be entirely at his disposal, and could form no idea of happiness unless in such a course of obedience. And it is equally clear that he fell from this state of rectitude the moment that he yielded to the temptation to do his own will, or to seek his own pleasure, as distinct from that of God. Thus he severed himself from God, lost his holiness and primal rectitude, and brought sin and death into the world.

It is therefore obvious that God is infinitely better qualified than his creatures are to make a righteous and benevolent disposal of them; that it is right and proper for him to do with us what he pleases, and that we are in every way bound to do with ourselves only what he would have us to do. And on this subject we have a full revelation of his will.

These things being so, the inquiry becomes deeply important in this connection, What is the present state or condition of man, as developed by his life and actions? Is this great principle, which commends itself to every man's conscience in the sight of God, ever practically recognized by him in his numerous pursuits and vocations? or is it not utterly, perpetually, and practically ignored? What man in an unregenerate state ever makes the glory of God his design or end? Men talk and write much of virtue, and extol it to the skies; but true virtue is a proper regard for the glory of Him who gave us being. And where do we ever find it exemplified by the unrenewed heart? In no instance whatever.

Now that this disposition to live for ourselves, and to make ourselves our great end, is contrary to right reason, to the law of God, and is exceedingly sinful, cannot be intelligently denied by any but an atheist; for, that while we love ourselves supremely, and live to ourselves ultimately, we do really in our hearts, and by our practice, prefer ourselves above God, and so cast contempt upon his right to rule over us, and his claim to us is undeniable. And as no one will venture to deny that men naturally love themselves above all, and that the native bent or bias of their hearts is to make their ease, comfort, and happiness their last end and their all, and to seek their all from the creature, or from that which is not God,* (and this is apparent in all things and in all circumstances,) so it is plain that mankind are in a state of utter alienation from God, and rebels against the Divine government. And as this alienation and rebellion are voluntary, it is obviously ridiculous to pretend that God can consistently treat us as rational and accountable creatures, otherwise than in accordance with the character which we sustain toward him.

Now it is to man in this fallen and ruined condition that the Gospel brings the offer of relief. It is a free and full offer, and effectual to all who truly receive it. But it is just here that the Universalists, and such writers as Whately, and "Thorndale," and Dobney, and Ham, and Hudson come in, and, instead of evincing any sympathy with God in his claims upon the creature, throw their whole sympathy about the creature in his selfishness, rebellion, and iniquity, and labor to convince him that God has no such claims upon him, and that he does not mean what his words seem to indicate respecting the nature of sin and its punishment in the world to come. And the result of such inculcations, and of such iniquitous tampering with divine things, ever has been and ever must be the rejection of the Gospel offer of salvation in the case of all who are thus influenced, and their hopeless ruin to all eternity.

* See this point presented with great ability in Bellamy's True Religion Delineated, Discourse I, sect. v.

And now, reader, let me say to you, that while the renewed investigation of the stupendous themes treated upon in this volume has only deepened my full conviction of the entire accuracy of the teaching of the Church of Christ in relation to them, and that while my spirit has thus been frequently brought into delightful association, as it were, with the lovely and the good of all ages who are gathered before the eternal throne, and with whom, through the infinite mercy of delivering love, I expect one day to be, I arrogate to myself no claim of superiority, on the score of any personal merit or desert, to the humblest partaker of our common nature. The Gospel offer has been made to me, and I humbly hope that through infinite mercy I have been led to accept of it. My soul rests with delight ineffable upon the expiatory power of my Saviour's blood, and there alone rest all my hopes for eternity. I own from my inmost soul the perfect justice of the sentence which would consign me as a sinner to an eternal severance from God and salvation, and I neither know, nor can I imagine any way by which to escape that sentence, except the mercy proffered through our Lord Jesus Christ, to whom be praise and glory and dominion forever and ever.

This same deliverance is freely proffered to you, and, whoever you may be, you are as much in need of it as I am. You too have entered upon an existence from which there is no escape, and your probationary state will soon be past forever. If you die in a state of sin and alienation from God, there is no hope for you. If, therefore, you have not accepted of the overture of salvation which is now made to you, through the infinite love and mercy of Him who is not willing that any should perish, I entreat you to consider that you have no time to lose. There is no other way by which to escape from the curse and consequences of sin. But that way is still open to you, and you can now escape if, without delay, you will truly accept the mercy offered through the redemption that is in Christ Jesus. He is waiting to be gracious to you; hear then his voice, and harden not your heart.

# INDEX OF TEXTS

## ILLUSTRATED OR EXPLAINED.

# INDEX.

FOR THE FULL TITLES OF THE WORKS INDICATED BY LETTERS ONLY, SEE "NOTE TO THE READER," AT THE END OF THE PREFACE.

## A.



## B.

**P.**



**Q.**



**R.**



**S.**

**X.**



**Z.**

# NEW BOOKS,

## PUBLISHED BY CARLTON AND PORTER,

### 200 Mulberry-street, New-York.

FOR SALE ALSO BY J. P. MAGEE, 5 CORNHILL, BOSTON, AND H. H. OTIS, SENECA-STREET, BUFFALO.

## Systematic Beneficence.

*THREE PRIZE ESSAYS.*

The Great Reform, by ABEL STEVENS.
The Great Question, by LORENZO WHITE.
Property Consecrated, by BENJAMIN ST. JAMES FRY. Price, in one volume, 40 cents.

This long-expected work is at length published. It comprises three essays. THE GREAT REFORM, by Abel Stevens, covers 126 pages. It is invincible in argument, stirring and eloquent in expression. THE GREAT QUESTION, by Rev. Lorenzo White, of the New-England Conference, covers 234 pages. It lacks the directness of the former, but is scarcely less powerful in argument or stirring in appeal. The elucidation of Scriptural rules of beneficence should be carefully studied. We commend chapter tenth to the consideration of those in the ministry who have excused themselves from giving, because they had given themselves to the ministry. PROPERTY CONSECRATED, by Rev. Benjamin St. James Fry, of the Ohio Conference, covers 124 pages. It is full of strong thoughts, clearly and forcibly expressed, and is well worthy of the honor awarded to it. Its title is strikingly expressive as well as its arguments.—*Ladies' Repository.*

## Selections from the British Poets.

By ELIZA WOODWORTH. With *twelve* Illustrations. Large 12mo., pp. 365. Price $1.

The plan of this book of Selections is well conceived. It takes in the whole range of British poets, from Chaucer down to Tennyson, and gives brief biographical and critical notices of each, with some of their best and most striking passages as specimens.—*Methodist Quarterly Review.*

## Natural Goodness.

By Rev. T. F. RANDOLPH MERCEIN, M. A. Price 65 cents.

Its full title-page will sufficiently declare its object. It is set forth as containing "suggestions toward an appreciative view of moral men, the philosophy of the present system of morality, and the relation of natural virtue to religion." Without agreeing with the author fully in his view of the natural virtues, we have found his discussion one of the most interesting and able which has ever fallen 'er our notice, and we earnestly commend it to the attention of that large of intelligent and amiable men who are resting upon their morality. For sale by Ide & Dutton.—*Christian Witness.*

## Daniel verified in History and Chronology.

Showing the complete Fulfillment of all his Prophecies relating to Civil Affairs, before the close of the Fifth Century. By A. M. OSBON, D. D. With an Introduction, by D. D. WHEDON, D. D. 12mo., pp. 202. Price 60 cents.

As the result of much patient study, Dr. Osbon has here given us new and striking views of that portion of Holy Writ to which his attention has been pecially directed. His positions are antagonistic to those of all previous expositors with which we are acquainted. He states them clearly and forcibly, yet with becoming modesty, and meets the objections to his theory with arguments not easily refuted.—*Christian Advocate and Journal.*

BOOKS PUBLISHED BY CARLTON & PORTER,
200 Mulberry-street, New York.

---

## Ministering Children.

A Story showing how even a Child may be as a Ministering Angel of Love to the Poor and Sorrowful.

| Large 16mo., pp. 542. | Price | $0 90 |
|---|---|---|
| ——— | Illustrated edition, gilt edges | 1 25 |
| ——— | Morocco, gilt | 2 00 |

This is one of the most moving narrations in the whole list of our publications. Its sale in England has reached FORTY THOUSAND copies. The illustrated edition contains more than a dozen superb cuts on plate paper.

## Life in the Itinerancy;

In its Relation to the Circuit and Station, and to the Minister's Home and Family.

12mo., pp. 335. Price ........ $1 00

## Life in the Laity;

Or, the History of a Station. By Rev. L. D. DAVIS, Author of "Life in the Itinerancy."

16mo., pp. 200 Price ........ $0 50

## Chart of Life.

By Rev. JAMES PORTER, D.D.

12mo., pp. 259. Price ........ $0 60

The design of this book is to indicate the dangers and securities connected with the voyage of life, all which are accurately and admirably described.

## Heroines of Methodism;

Or, Pen and Ink Sketches of the Mothers and Daughters of the Church. By Rev. GEORGE COLES.

12mo., pp. 336. Price ........ $0 90

## Heroes of Methodism.

Containing Sketches of Eminent Methodist Ministers, and Characteristic Anecdotes of their Personal History. By Rev. J. B. WAKELEY. With Portraits of Bishops Asbury, Coke, and M'Kendree.

| 12mo., pp. 470. | Price | $1 00 |
|---|---|---|
| ——— | Morocco | 2 00 |

Life-like and interesting sketches of early Methodist preachers, their toils, hardships, and achievements, interspersed with anecdotes lively and entertaining.

## Harmony of Divine Dispensations.

Harmony of the Divine Dispensations. Being a Series of Discourses on Select Portions of Holy Scripture, designed to show the Spirituality, Efficacy, and Harmony of the Divine Revelations made to Mankind from the Beginning. With Notes, Critical, Historical, and Explanatory. By GEORGE SMITH, F. A. S., Member of the Royal Asiatic Society, of the Royal Society of Literature, Fellow of the Genealogical and Historical Society, etc., etc.

8vo., pp. 319. Sheep........................................ $1 50
———— Half calf........................................ 2 00

This is a new work, being reprinted from the London edition to correspond with the "Patriarchal Age," "Hebrew People," and "Gentile Nations," by the same distinguished author. It will be sold in connection with the others, or separately. It is a profound work, and will have a large sale.

## Lady Huntingdon Portrayed.

Including Brief Sketches of some of her Friends and Co-laborers. By the Author of "The Missionary Teacher," "Sketches of Mission Life," etc.

Large 16mo., pp. 319. Muslin........................................ $0 75
———— Morocco........................................ 1 75

## Hibbard on the Psalms.

The Psalms Chronologically Arranged, with Historical Introductions, and a General Introduction to the whole Book. By F. G. HIBBARD.

8vo., pp. 589. Muslin........................................ $2 00
———— Half Morocco........................................ 2 50
———— Morocco........................................ 5 00

This book occupies an important place in Biblical interpretation, and is a valuable contributio i to Biblical literature.

## The Object of Life:

A Narrative Illustrating the Insufficiency of the World, and the Sufficiency of Christ. With four Illustrations.

Large 16mo., pp. 357. Price........................................ $0 75
———— Morocco........................................ 1 75

## The Living Way;

Or, Suggestions and Counsels concerning some of the Privileges and Duties of the Christian Life. By Rev. JOHN ATKINSON.

16mo., pp. 139. Price........................................ $0 40

## Reasons for becoming a Methodist.

By Rev. I. SMITH, for some Years a Member of the Close-Communion Calvinist Baptist Church. Including a brief Account of the Author's Religious Experience up to the Time of his becoming a Methodist.

18mo., pp. 160. Price........................................ $0 30

This work was written by Rev. I. Smith, now a member of the New England Conference. It was printed in Boston a few years ago, and seventeen thousand copies have been sold. Knowing the work from its first issue, and believing it to be calculated to do great good, we have recently bought the plates, and shall soon bring out the nineteenth edition, with some improvements. Brother Smith was formerly a Calvinistic Close-Communion Baptist, but being placed in circumstances obliging him to consider the principles he professed to believe, he was led to renounce them. He subsequently joined the Methodists, and became a preacher. This book develops the reasons which influenced his action in the premises, and they are well stated. Preachers who are molested by Baptist influences, will find this work just the thing to circulate. We have put it upon our list to extend its usefulness, more than to make money out of it.

## The Pioneers of the West;

Or, Life in the Woods. By W. P. STRICKLAND.

12mo., pp. 403. Price........................................ $1 00

This decidedly popular book, which sketches to the life the Pioneer Explorers, Settlers, Preachers, Hunters, Lawyers, Doctors, School Teachers, and Institutions of the West, is meeting with an extensive sale.

## The True Woman;

Or, Life and Happiness at Home and Abroad. By JESSE T. PECK, D.D., Author of "The Central Idea of Christianity."

12mo., pp. 400. Price........................................ $1 00
———— Gilt edges........................................ 1 25
———— Gilt edges, beveled........................................ 1 50
———— Morocco........................................ 2 00

In this volume the author has illustrated his ideal of female character by a series of didactic precepts and familiar examples. His standard is not taken from the prevailing customs and opinions of society, but from the highest teachings of Christian ethics. In his remarks on the intellectual cultivation of woman, he condemns novel-reading in decided terms, regarding it as a "crime, murderous to the heart, the intellect, and the body;" while he as warmly recommends the perusal of literary periodicals, and insists on having access to at least one daily or weekly newspaper. The work is written with great earnestness and feeling, with an occasional exuberance of expression.—*N. Y. Tribune.*

# BOOKS AND PERIODICALS.

# CARLTON & PORTER,

Agents of the Methodist Book Concern, 200 Mulberry-street, New-York, would call attention to a few of their numerous publications.

## THE SUNDAY SCHOOL ADVOCATE

Is a beautifully illustrated child's paper, edited by the distinguished friend of children, the veritable FRANCIS FORRESTER, and is issued semi-monthly. The seventeenth volume will commence in October, 1857. The circulation is some 160,000 copies. Price 25 cents single, and 20 cents per copy when ten or more copies are ordered to one address.

## SABBATH-SCHOOL BOOKS.

Of these we have about 1,100 bound volumes, besides multitudes of Question Books, Hymn Books, Picture Books, Catechisms, Cards, and Tracts, adapted to children of all ranks and ages, and we are adding to the number monthly. They are being ordered and prized by schools of all denominations.

Then we have a large list of other works, beautifully illustrated for gift-books for children and youth, which are equal to any in the land, such as,

| | | | |
|---|---|---|---|
| **Harry Budd** | **Price $0 50** | **Poor Nelly** | **Price $0 32** |
| **Illustrated Olio** | **0 70** | **Pictorial Gatherings** | **0 65** |
| **Six Steps to Honor** | **0 65** | **Here and There** | **0 15** |
| **Uncle Toby's Library, 12 vols.** | **2 00** | **Historical Series, 10 vols.** | **2 50** |
| **Pictorial Catechism** | **0 70** | **Henry's Birthday** | **0 35** |
| **Child's Sabbath-Day Book** | **0 25** | **Bird-Book** | **0 70** |

To these we may add the popular volumes, entitled,

| | | | |
|---|---|---|---|
| **Pilgrim's Progress** | **Price $1 50** | **Young Man's Counselor** | **Price $0 55** |
| **Path of Life** | **0 50** | **Young Lady's Counselor** | **0 55** |
| **Manly Character** | **0 40** | **Young Man Advised** | **0 75** |
| **Bridal Greetings** | **0 30** | **Frank Harley** | **0 20** |
| **Chart of Life** | **0 60** | **Ministering Children** | **0 90** |
| **The Successful Merchant** | **0 40** | **Object of Life** | **0 75** |

## HIBBARD ON THE PSALMS,

Giving the time when, and the circumstances under which each Psalm was written, is a new and splendid work for preachers, teachers, and for reading in family worship. Price, $2 00.

We have BIBLES also, Royal Octavo and Imperial Quarto, in different styles of binding, ranging in prices from $3 to $50 per copy. Besides, we have a large list of Miscellaneous Works of various sizes and costs, on moral and religious subjects, which only need to be known to be appreciated.

Catalogues will be sent, gratuitously, to all who order, and on receiving the retail price of any of our books, we will forward said books free of charge. Orders sent to us as above, or to J. P. MAGEE, No. 5 Cornhill, Boston; or J. L. READ, Pittsburgh, Pa.; or to H. H. MATTESON, Seneca-street, Buffalo, N. Y.; or SWORMSTEDT & POE, Cincinnati, or any other Methodist Booksellers, will receive prompt attention.

# NEW BOOKS,

## PUBLISHED BY CARLTON AND PORTER,

**200 Mulberry-street, New-York.**

FOR SALE ALSO BY J. P. MAGEE, 5 CORNHILL, BOSTON, AND H. H. OTIS, SENECA-STREET, BUFFALO.

## A Model for Men of Business.

A Model for Men of Business: or, the Christian Layman contemplated among his Secular Occupations. Revised and Modified from the Lectures of Rev. HUGH STOWELL, M. A., Incumbent of Christ's Church, Salford. With an Introduction, by Rev. D. CURRY. 16mo., pp. 322. Price, 35 cents.

An excellent little volume, indicating its character in its title-page, and forcibly presenting the morality of the Gospel to the acceptance of men of business. There is so much in every day life to call our thoughts away from God—so much to blunt our sensibilities to the moral principles which should govern and direct every Christian man in all his intercourse with the world, that a book like this cannot but be a most profitable companion for all who desire to be at last accepted in Christ Jesus. We welcome its appearance. For sale at the Methodist bookstores generally.—*Meth. Protestant.*

This is a work much wanted to carry the sanctity of the Sabbath into the business of the week—to make religion, with business men, an ever-present and all-pervading principle. It is well written, and highly edifying. Let it be widely circulated.—*Pittsburgh Christian Advocate.*

## The Life and Times of Bishop Hedding.

Life and Times of Rev. Elijah Hedding, D. D., late Senior Bishop of the Methodist Episcopal Church. By Rev. D. W. CLARK, D. D. With an Introduction, by Rev. Bishop E. S. JANES. Pp. 686. Price, large 12mo., $1 50; 8vo., $2 00.

## The Temporal Power of the Pope.

The Temporal Power of the Pope: containing the Speech of the Hon. Joseph R. Chandler, delivered in the House of Representatives of the United States, January 11, 1855. With Nine Letters, stating the prevailing Roman Catholic Theory in the Language of Papal Writers. By JOHN M'CLINTOCK, D. D. 12mo., pp. 154. Price, 45 cents.

Last winter Hon. Joseph R. Chandler, a Catholic, and Representative in Congress from Pennsylvania, being hard pressed by anti-Romanist influences, made a speech, in which he denied the political supremacy of the pope. In doing this, he showed himself possessed of the cunning of a Jesuit, or the weakness of a neophyte. Dr. M'Clintock, in a series of nine letters, has thoroughly exposed the weakness and sophistry of Mr. Chandler's speech. It is a volume for intelligent readers—none others will relish the learning and the nice discrimination which pervade the work.—*Northern Christian Advocate, Auburn, N. Y.*

A series of letters to the Hon. J. R. Chandler, stating the prevailing Roman Catholic theory in the language of papal writers, forms the substance of this volume. They were prepared in reference to the speech of Mr. Chandler, delivered at the last session of Congress, and from the position and character of the writer, as well as from his mode of treating the subject, are eminently deserving of public attention.—*N. Y. Tribune.*

Carlton & Phillips, No. 200 Mulberry-street, New-York, have just issued a neat duodecimo volume of one hundred and fifty-four pages, with the foregoing title. It needs not that we say the work is a most timely and masterly production.—*Western Christian Advocate.*